5 STEPS TO A 5™

AP U.S. Government & Politics

2023

ELITE STUDENT EDITION

5 STEPS TO A 5

AP U.S. Government & Politics

2023

Pamela K. Lamb

McGraw Hill

New York   Chicago   San Francisco   Athens   London   Madrid
Mexico City   Milan   New Delhi   Singapore   Sydney   Toronto

1 2 3 4 5 6 7 8 9   LHS   27 26 25 24 23 22 (Cross-Platform Prep Course only)
1 2 3 4 5 6 7 8 9   LHS   27 26 25 24 23 22 (Elite Student Edition)

ISBN   978-1-264-46900-0   (Cross-Platform Prep Course only)
MHID   1-264-46900-4

e-ISBN   978-1-264-47070-9   (e-book Cross-Platform Prep Course only)
e-MHID   1-264-47070-3

ISBN   978-1-264-47291-8   (Elite Student Edition)
MHID   1-264-47291-9

e-ISBN   978-1-264-47328-1   (e-book Elite Student Edition)
e-MHID   1-264-47328-1

McGraw Hill, the McGraw Hill logo, 5 Steps to a 5, and related trade dress are trademarks or registered trademarks of McGraw Hill and/or its affiliates in the United States and other countries and may not be used without written permission. All other trademarks are the property of their respective owners. McGraw Hill is not associated with any product or vendor mentioned in this book.

AP, Advanced Placement Program, and College Board are registered trademarks of the College Board, which was not involved in the production of, and does not endorse, this product.

The series editor was Grace Freedson, and the project editor was Del Franz.
Series design by Jane Tenenbaum.

McGraw Hill products are available at special quantity discounts to use as premiums and sales or for use in corporate training programs. To contact a representative, please visit the Contact Us pages at www.mhprofessional.com.

McGraw Hill is committed to making our products accessible to all learners. To learn more about the available support and accommodations we offer, please contact us at accessibility@mheducation.com. We also participate in the Access Text Network (www.accesstext.org), and ATN members may submit requests through ATN.

CONTENTS

UNIT 6 Pulling It All Together: Public Policy

STEP 5 Build Your Test-Taking Confidence

ELITE STUDENT EDITION

5 Minutes to a 5

PREFACE

Welcome to AP U.S. Government and Politics. I am, first and foremost, a teacher who has taught Advanced Placement courses to many students who have successfully taken the AP exam. I am also a table leader and reader—one of those crazy teachers who spends a week in the summer reading thousands of student free-response questions. With this guide I hope to share with you what I know, including what I have learned from students and other AP teachers, to help you be successful on the exam.

My philosophy is not to teach *only* for the AP exam. Instead, my goal is to help students develop skills and abilities that lead to advanced levels of aptitude in government and politics. These are the same skills that will enable you to do well on the AP U.S. Government and Politics exam. My aim is to remove your nervousness and to improve your comfort level with the test. I believe that you are already motivated to succeed; otherwise, you would not have come this far. And obviously, you would not have purchased this prep book.

Since you have taken or are already taking a government and politics class, this book is going to supplement your course readings, writing, and analysis. I am going to give you the opportunity to practice the skills and techniques that I know from experience *really work*! I am confident that if you apply the techniques and processes presented in this book, you can succeed.

Let's begin.

PAMELA K. LAMB

ACKNOWLEDGMENTS

My love and appreciation to Mark H. Lamb for his constant support, encouragement, and belief in my abilities and in me. Without his collaboration, this book would never have been completed. Special thanks to Frances New for her suggestions and encouragement. To Derek James (DJ) New: May this book someday help you in your studies. To Wallace Good: may your love of political science continue to grow. To my AP Government and Politics colleagues and friends: Thanks for all the ideas you have shared over the years— I'll see you at the reading. To my students, past, present, and future: Thank you for the inspiration you give to all teachers.

I would also like to thank my editors, Grace Freedson and Del Franz for their support and patience in this rewrite.

ABOUT THE AUTHOR

Pamela K. Lamb teaches Advanced Placement and Dual Credit U.S. Government and Politics and Macroeconomics at Del Rio High School in Del Rio, Texas. She also teaches U.S. Government and Economics-Free Enterprise. She holds a B.A. in history and a M.A. in both history and political science. She has been teaching for thirty-four years, twenty-nine in AP. Ms. Lamb also teaches history and political science classes at Southwest Texas Junior College and Sul Ross State University, Rio Grande College. Ms. Lamb has served as a reader, table leader and question leader at the U.S. Government and Politics AP reading. Ms. Lamb has been a workshop consultant for the Southwest Regional Office of the College Board since 1994 and received the Special Recognition Award for Excellence in Teaching from the Southwest Region in 2000. She has been recognized by *Who's Who Among America's Teachers* numerous times, received the Harvard Book Club Award and was a HEB Excellence in Teaching semi-finalist in 2008. Ms. Lamb lives with her husband, three dogs and three cats in Del Rio, Texas.

INTRODUCTION: THE FIVE-STEP PROGRAM

The Basics

Not too long ago, you decided to enroll in AP U.S. Government and Politics. Maybe you have always been interested in political affairs, or maybe a respected teacher encouraged you and you accepted the challenge. Either way, you find yourself here, flipping through a book that promises to help you culminate your efforts with the highest of honors, a 5 in AP U.S. Government and Politics. Can it be done without this book? Sure, there are some students out there every year who achieve a 5 on the strength of classwork alone. But I am here to tell you that, for the majority of students in your shoes, using this book is a smart way to make sure you're ready for this difficult exam.

Introducing the Five-Step Preparation Program

This book is organized as a five-step program to prepare you for success on the exam. These steps are designed to provide you with the skills and strategies vital to the exam and the practice that can lead you to that perfect 5. Each of the five steps will provide you with the opportunity to get closer and closer to that prize trophy 5. Here are the five steps.

Step 1: Set Up Your Study Program

In this step you'll read a brief overview of the AP U.S. Government and Politics exam, including an outline of topics and the approximate percentage of the exam that will test knowledge of each topic. You will also follow a process to help determine which of the following preparation programs is right for you:

- Full school year: September through May
- One semester: January through May
- Six weeks: Basic training for the exam

Step 2: Determine Your Test Readiness

In this step you'll take a diagnostic exam in AP U.S. Government and Politics. This pretest should give you an idea of how prepared you are to take the real exam before beginning to study for it.

- Go through the diagnostic exam step by step and question by question to build your confidence level.
- Review the correct answers and explanations so that you see what you do and do not yet fully understand.

Step 3: Develop Strategies for Success

In this step you will learn strategies that will help you do your best on the exam. These strategies cover both the multiple-choice and free-response sections of the exam. Some of these tips are based upon my understanding of how the questions are designed, and others have been gleaned from my years of experience reading (grading) the AP U.S. Government and Politics exam.

- Learn to read multiple-choice questions.
- Learn how to answer multiple-choice questions, including whether or not to guess.
- Learn how to plan and write the free-response questions.

Step 4: Review the Knowledge You Need to Score High

In this step you will learn or review the material you need to know for the test. This review takes up the bulk of this book. It contains:

- A comprehensive review of the themes and concepts of AP U.S. Government and Politics
- Key terms
- Rapid reviews of the main ideas of each chapter

Step 5: Build Your Test-Taking Confidence

In this step you will complete your preparation by testing yourself on practice exams. This book provides you with three complete exams, answers, explanations, and rubrics. Be aware that these practice exams are *not* reproduced questions from actual AP U.S. Government and Politics exams, but they mirror both the material tested by AP and the way in which it is tested.

Finally, at the back of this book you will find additional resources to aid your participation. These include:

- A list of websites related to the AP U.S. Government and Politics exam
- A glossary of terms related to the AP U.S. Government and Politics exam

Introduction to the Graphics Used in This Book

To emphasize particular skills and strategies, we use several icons throughout this book. An icon in the margin will alert you that you should pay particular attention to the accompanying text. We use three icons:

This icon points out a very important concept or fact that you should not pass over.

This icon calls your attention to a strategy that you may want to try.

This icon indicates a tip that you might find useful.

Boldfaced words indicate terms that are included in the glossary at the end of this book.

5 STEPS TO A 5™

AP U.S. Government & Politics

2023

Set Up Your Study Program

CHAPTER 1

What You Need to Know About the AP U.S. Government and Politics Exam

IN THIS CHAPTER

Summary: Learn how the test is structured, what topics are tested, how the test is scored, and basic test-taking information.

Key Ideas

✪ A score of 3 or above on the AP exam may allow you to get college credit for your AP course; each college sets its own AP credit policy.

✪ Multiple-choice questions count as one-half of your total score.

✪ Free-response questions count for one-half of your total score.

✪ Your composite score on the two test sections is converted to a score on the 1-to-5 scale.

Background of the Advanced Placement Program

The Advanced Placement program was begun by the College Board in 1955 to construct standard achievement exams that would allow highly motivated high school students the opportunity to be awarded advanced placement as first-year students in colleges and universities in the United States. Today, there are 38 courses and exams with more than two million students from every state in the nation, and from foreign countries, taking the annual exams in May.

The AP programs are designed for high school students who wish to take college-level courses. In our case, the AP U.S. Government and Politics course is designed to be the equivalent of a one-semester introductory college course in U.S. government.

The New AP U.S. Government and Politics Exam

A new AP U.S. Government and Politics Exam was administered beginning in May 2019. This exam is different in a number of ways from the previous AP exam. Here's what you need to know about the new exam:

The Format of the New Exam

The following table summarizes the format of the AP U.S. Government and Politics exam.

AP U.S. Government and Politics

SECTION	NUMBER OF QUESTIONS	TIME LIMIT
I. Multiple-Choice Questions	55	Total Time: 80 minutes
II. Free-Response Questions	4	Total Time: 100 minutes

The multiple-choice questions and the free-response questions each count as 50% of your final AP score.

The New Multiple-Choice Questions

While the number of questions is being reduced from 60 to 55, and the time you are given is increasing from 45 minutes to 80 minutes, don't expect this section to be easy. Most of the new multiple-choice questions are more complicated and involved than the ones on the previous test. Rather than simply testing whether you remember a fact, the questions often involve interpreting, analyzing, comparing, and applying information.

Many of the questions are based on a "stimulus"—that is, a table, a graph, a political cartoon, a map, a reading passage, or something similar. Each stimulus may be followed by one to four questions based on that stimulus. These questions test your ability to understand and interpret the information presented, and then to analyze, compare, and apply the information using your knowledge of the U.S. government and politics. On your test, you can expect to see at least one of each of the following: a line graph, a bar graph, a pie chart, a table, a political cartoon, and a map. You should also expect at least a couple quotations from political figures or philosophers as stimuli for questions that follow.

One other change: The new multiple-choice questions have only four answer choices, rather than five.

The New Free-Response Questions

Like on the previous AP U.S. Government and Politics exams, you will have 100 minutes to answer four free-response questions. But the types of questions on the new test are different. The new test contains one of each of the following types of questions:

- **Concept application question**—You will need to write an essay to respond to a political situation presented in the question, explaining how it relates to some key concept, which could be a political principle, an institution, a political process, a policy, or a behavior.

- **Quantitative analysis question**—You will be presented with a graph or chart that presents quantitative data. You will need to write an essay identifying a trend or pattern and explaining how the data relates to political process, institution, policy, or behavior.
- **SCOTUS (Supreme Court of the United States) comparison question**—A (nonrequired) Supreme Court case will be presented and you will need to write an essay comparing it to a required Supreme Court case (see below).
- **Argument essay**—You will need to take a position and write an argument (in the form of an essay) supporting your position. You will need to back up your argument with evidence, including evidence from at least one of the required foundational documents (see below).

Each of the four questions will be given equal weight, with each question accounting for 12.5% of your total score. The College Board recommends that you allot 20 minutes for each of the first three questions and 40 minutes to the argument essay.

The Required Supreme Court Cases

The new exam requires you to interpret, compare, and analyze Supreme Court decisions. Fifteen Supreme Court cases have been identified as required. You should be able to state the facts of these cases, the issue involved, the holdings (the decision and dissenting opinions), and the reasoning behind the decision. Here are the required cases:

- *McCulloch v. Maryland* (1819)—established the supremacy of the United States Constitution and federal laws over state laws
- *United States v. Lopez* (1995)—the use of the commerce clause by Congress to make possession of a gun in a school zone a federal crime unconstitutional
- *Engel v. Vitale* (1962)—school sponsorship of religious activities is a violation of the establishment clause of the First Amendment
- *Wisconsin v. Yoder* (1972)—requiring Amish students to attend school past the eighth grade is a violation of the free exercise clause of the First Amendment
- *Tinker v. Des Moines Independent Community School District* (1969)—students do not lose their rights of free speech in schools
- *New York Times Co. v. United States* (1971)—reinforced freedom of the press with protections against prior restraint, even in cases involving national security
- *Schenck v. United States* (1919)—the First Amendment does not protect speech which creates a "clear and present danger"
- *Gideon v. Wainwright* (1963)—guaranteed a right to an attorney for the poor, even in state trials
- *Roe v. Wade* (1973)—extended the right to privacy to include a woman's decision to have an abortion
- *McDonald v. Chicago* (2010)—incorporated the Second Amendment's right to keep and bear arms to the states
- *Brown v. Board of Education* (1954)—school segregation is a violation of the equal protection clause of the Fourteenth Amendment and is therefore unconstitutional
- *Citizens United v. Federal Election Commission* (2010)—political spending by corporations and labor unions is a form of protected speech under the First Amendment
- *Baker v. Carr* (1961)—established equal protection challenges to redistricting and the "one-person-one-vote" principle
- *Shaw v. Reno* (1993)—legislative redistricting must take into account race and comply with the Voting Rights Act of 1965
- *Marbury v. Madison* (1803)—established the principle of judicial review, which allows the Supreme Court to determine the constitutionality of acts of Congress and the executive branch.

Your knowledge of the required cases will be specifically tested in the SCOTUS comparison question. You should also expect other questions about these cases in both the multiple-choice and free-response sections of the test.

The Required Documents

The AP U.S. Government and Politics exam requires you to be familiar with these nine foundational documents that are important to understanding the philosophies of the founders of our government and their critics.

- Declaration of Independence
- Articles of Confederation
- Constitution of the United States, including the Bill of Rights and subsequent amendments
- Federalist No. 10
- Federalist No. 51
- Federalist No. 70
- Federalist No. 78
- Brutus No. 1
- Letter from a Birmingham Jail (Martin Luther King, Jr.)

Your knowledge of the required documents will be specifically tested in the argument essay free-response question. You should also expect other questions about these documents in both the multiple-choice and free-response sections of the exam.

The Composition of the New Test

The new AP U.S. Government and Politics course is divided into five units. The chart below shows these units and the number of multiple-choice questions you can expect on each unit.

Unit 1	Foundations of American Democracy	8–12 questions
Unit 2	Interaction Among Branches of Government	14–20 questions
Unit 3	Civil Liberties and Civil Rights	7–10 questions
Unit 4	American Political Ideologies and Beliefs	5–8 questions
Unit 5	Political Participation	11–15 questions

Frequently Asked Questions About the AP U.S. Government and Politics Exam

Why Take the AP U.S. Government and Politics Exam?

Most students take the exam because they are seeking college credit. The majority of colleges and universities will consider a 4 or 5 as acceptable credit for their introductory U.S. Government and Politics course. Some schools will accept a 3 on the exam. This means you might be one course closer to graduation before you even attend your first college class or possibly be exempt from an introductory government course. Even if you do not score high enough to earn college credit, the fact that you elected to enroll in AP courses tells admission committees that you are a high achiever and serious about your education.

What Is the Distribution of Grades on the AP U.S. Government and Politics Exam?

Currently nearly 350,000 students take the AP U.S. Government and Politics exam every year. The score breakdown on the test is typically similar to the ranges shown below:

SCORE	INTERPRETATION	PERCENT OF TEST TAKERS
5	Extremely well qualified for college credit	12.0%
4	Well qualified	13.0%
3	Qualified	25.0%
2	Possibly qualified	25.0%
1	Not qualified	25.0%

Obviously this is in no way a "pushover" test; you must prepare to do well on it.

Who Writes the AP U.S. Government and Politics Exam?

Development of each AP exam is a multi-year effort that involves many education and testing professionals and students. At the heart of the effort is the AP U.S. Government and Politics Test Development Committee, a group of college and high school government teachers who are typically asked to serve for three years. The committee creates a large pool of multiple-choice questions. With the help of the testing experts at Educational Testing Service (ETS), these questions are then pretested with college students enrolled in introductory U.S. Government and Politics classes for accuracy, appropriateness, clarity, and assurance that there is only one possible answer. The results of this pretesting allow these questions to be categorized as easy, average, or difficult. After more months of development and refinement, Section I of the exam is ready to be administered.

The free-response essay questions that make up Section II go through a similar process of creation, modification, pretesting, and final refinement so that the questions cover the necessary areas of material and are at an appropriate level of difficulty and clarity. The committee also makes a great effort to construct a free-response exam that will allow for clear and equitable grading by the AP readers.

At the conclusion of each AP reading and scoring of exams, the exam itself and the results are thoroughly evaluated by the committee and by ETS. In this way, the College Board can use the results to make suggestions for course development in high schools and to plan future exams.

Who Grades My AP U.S. Government and Politics Exam?

Every June a group of government teachers gathers for a week to assign grades to your hard work. Each of these "faculty consultants" spends a day or so getting trained on one question. Because each reader becomes an expert on that question, and because each exam book is anonymous, this process provides a very consistent and unbiased scoring of that question. During a typical day of grading, a random sample of each reader's scores is selected and cross-checked by other experienced "table leaders" to ensure that the consistency is maintained throughout the day and the week. Each reader's scores on a given question are also analyzed statistically to make sure that they are not giving scores that are significantly higher or lower than the mean scores given by other readers of that question. All measures are taken to maintain consistency and fairness for your benefit.

Will My Exam Remain Anonymous?

Absolutely. Even if your high school teacher happens to randomly read your booklet, there is virtually no way he or she will know it is you. To the reader, each student is a number, and to the computer, each student is a bar code.

What About That Permission Box on the Back?

The College Board uses some exams to help train high school teachers so that they can help the next generation of government students to avoid common mistakes. If you check this box, you simply give permission to use your exam in this way. Even if you give permission, your anonymity is still maintained.

How Is My Multiple-Choice Exam Scored?

The multiple-choice section of each U.S. Government and Politics exam is 55 questions and is worth one-half of your final score. Your sheet of little bubbles is run through the computer, which adds up your correct responses. No points are deducted for incorrect answers. Your score is based solely on the number of questions answered correctly. No points are awarded (or deducted) for unanswered questions or for questions answered incorrectly. You should fill in a bubble for each question even if you have to guess; don't leave any questions blank.

How Is My Free-Response Exam Scored?

Your performance on the free-response section is worth one-half of your final score. The free-response section consists of four questions. All four questions are weighed equally in determining your score on this section of the test. Each essay is scored on a scale based on the rubric for that essay. Free-response question 1 will be scored between 0–3. Questions 2 and 3 will be scored between 0–4. Question 4 will be scored between 0–6. These scores are then weighted so that each of the four questions consitutes 12.5% of your score.

How Do I Register and How Much Does It Cost?

If you are enrolled in AP U.S. Government and Politics in your high school, your teacher is going to provide all of these details, but a quick summary will not hurt. After all, you do not have to enroll in the AP course to register for and complete the AP exam. When in doubt, the best source of information is the College Board's website: www.collegeboard.com.

The fee for taking the 2021 AP U.S. Government and Politics exam is $94. Students who demonstrate a financial need may receive a refund to help offset the cost of testing. There are also several optional fees that must be paid if you want your scores rushed to you or if you wish to receive multiple grade reports.

The coordinator of the AP program at your school will inform you where and when you will take the exam. If you live in a small community, your exam may not be administered at your school, so be sure to get this information.

What Should I Bring to the Exam?

On exam day, you should bring the following items:
- Several pencils and an eraser that does not leave smudges.
- Black or blue colored pens for the free-response section.

- A watch so that you can monitor your time. You never know if the exam room will, or will not, have a clock on the wall. Make sure you turn off the beep that goes off on the hour.
- Your school code.
- Your photo identification and social security number.
- Tissues.
- Your quiet confidence that you are prepared and ready.

What Should I NOT Bring to the Exam?

Leave the following items at home:

- A cell phone, beeper, PDA, walkie-talkie, or calculator.
- Books, a dictionary, study notes, flash cards, highlighting pens, correction fluid, a ruler, or any other office supplies.
- Portable music of any kind. No CD players, MP3 players, or iPods are allowed.
- Panic or fear. It is natural to be nervous, but you can comfort yourself that you have used this book and that there is no room for fear on your exam. Let this test be an opportunity to show what you have learned this year!

CHAPTER 2

How to Plan Your Time

IN THIS CHAPTER

Summary: The right preparation plan for you depends on your study habits, your strengths and weaknesses, and the amount of time you have to prepare for the test. This chapter recommends some study plans to get you started.

KEY IDEA

Key Ideas

✪ Preparing for the exam is important. It helps to have a plan—and stick with it!

✪ Create a study plan that best suits your situation and prioritize your review based on your strengths and weaknesses.

✪ The first step in creating your study plan is to take the diagnostic test in the next chapter. This will tell you what the test is actually like and identify your priorities for practice.

Three Approaches to Preparing for the AP U.S. Government and Politics Exam

It's up to you to decide how you want to use this book to study for the AP U.S. Government and Politics exam. This book is designed for flexibility; you can work through it in order, or skip around however you want. In fact, no two students who purchase this book will probably use it in exactly the same way. Chapters 4 and 5 focus on strategies for taking the test and Chapters 6 through 15 review the content you need to know, including the required documents and Supreme Court cases.

The first step in developing your plan is to take the diagnostic test in the next chapter. This practice exam closely mirrors the actual exam. By taking the diagnostic test, you'll find out exactly what the exam is like. You should also learn what you are reasonably good at and what things you need to practice. Identify your weaknesses and focus on these first.

The Full School-Year Plan

Choose this plan if you like taking your time going through the material. Following this plan will allow you to practice your skills and develop your confidence gradually as you go through the AP course. This book is filled with practice exercises. Beginning to work through them at the beginning of the school year will allow you to get to all the practice exercises and tests in the book and maximize your preparation for the exam.

If you choose this option of beginning early, you should still start by taking the diagnostic test in the next chapter. This will show you exactly what the exam is like, so you know what you are up against. You can take Practice Exam 1 in February or March to see what progress you are making. Take the final practice exam shortly before you take the actual exam in May. Since you've practiced the whole year, you'll be in peak condition to perform your best on the exam.

The One-Semester Plan

Starting in the middle of the school year should give you ample time to review and prepare for the test. Of course, if you also need to prepare for other AP exams, or if you are super-busy with extracurricular activities, your time will be more limited.

Regardless of how much time you are able to devote to prepping for the AP U.S. Government and Politics Exam, start by taking the diagnostic test in the next chapter. This will give you an accurate idea of what the test is like. You'll get a sense of how hard the test will be for you, how much time you need to devote to practice, and which types of questions and areas of content you most need to work on. Skip around in this book, focusing on the chapters that deal with the content you find most difficult. Find time to take both practice exams at the end of this book. Take the final practice test a few days before you take the actual test.

The Six-Week Plan

OK, maybe you procrastinated a bit too long. But this might not be a problem if you are doing well in your AP U.S. Government and Politics class and just need to review areas where you are relatively weak, and practice with the types of questions on the exam. In fact, practice with testlike questions is included in most AP U.S. Government and Politics classes. So you may be readier for the exam than you realize.

If you find the diagnostic test in the next chapter difficult, devote as much time as possible to the practice questions in the chapters you most need to review. Skip around in this book, focusing first on the content areas where you are weakest. Save time to take the two practice tests at the end of this book. Even if you do well on the diagnostic test, take these tests to practice pacing yourself within the time limits of the exam.

When to Take the Practice Exams

KEY IDEA

Take the diagnostic test in Chapter 3 when you begin your test preparation. It will show you what the exam is like and, based on your performance, you can identify your strong points as well as the weakness you'll need to focus on. Take the first practice test at the end of this book midway through your test preparation to measure your progress and see if your priorities should change. Take the final practice test a week or so before the actual test. The practice tests are perhaps the most important part of this book. Taking them will help you do all of the following:

- Give you practice with all the different types of questions and tasks on the AP U.S. Government and Politics Exam.
- Allow you to measure progress and identify areas you need to focus on in your test preparation.
- Allow you to practice pacing yourself within the time limits imposed on the test.

Below are some things to remember as you plan your test-prep effort, regardless of when you start and how long you plan to practice:

- Establish a calendar of review and start as early as you can.
- Use your mobile phone to time yourself on every timed test you take.
- Be sure that you know your AP U.S. Government and Politics concepts, along with the required Supreme Court cases and required documents.
- Take advantage of the practice tests in this book. They are your friends.
- Don't stay up the night before the test doing last-minute cramming; this may be counterproductive.

Good Luck!

STEP 2

Determine Your Test Readiness

CHAPTER 3   Take a Diagnostic Exam

CHAPTER 3

Take a Diagnostic Exam

IN THIS CHAPTER

Summary: In the following pages you will find a diagnostic exam that is modeled on the actual AP exam. It is intended to give you an idea of your level of preparation in AP U.S. Government and Politics. After you have completed both the multiple-choice and the free-response questions, use the answer key to check your answers to the multiple-choice questions and read over the sample rubrics for the free-response questions.

Key Ideas

✪ Practice the kind of multiple-choice and free-response questions you will be given on the real exam.
✪ Answer questions that approximate the coverage of topics on the actual exam.
✪ Check your work against the given answers and the free-response rubrics.
✪ Determine your strengths and weaknesses.
✪ Earmark the concepts that you must give special attention.

AP U.S. Government and Politics
Diagnostic Exam

SECTION I

ANSWER SHEET

Tear out this page and use it to mark your answers as you take Section I of the diagnostic test.

1 Ⓐ Ⓑ Ⓒ Ⓓ	21 Ⓐ Ⓑ Ⓒ Ⓓ	41 Ⓐ Ⓑ Ⓒ Ⓓ
2 Ⓐ Ⓑ Ⓒ Ⓓ	22 Ⓐ Ⓑ Ⓒ Ⓓ	42 Ⓐ Ⓑ Ⓒ Ⓓ
3 Ⓐ Ⓑ Ⓒ Ⓓ	23 Ⓐ Ⓑ Ⓒ Ⓓ	43 Ⓐ Ⓑ Ⓒ Ⓓ
4 Ⓐ Ⓑ Ⓒ Ⓓ	24 Ⓐ Ⓑ Ⓒ Ⓓ	44 Ⓐ Ⓑ Ⓒ Ⓓ
5 Ⓐ Ⓑ Ⓒ Ⓓ	25 Ⓐ Ⓑ Ⓒ Ⓓ	45 Ⓐ Ⓑ Ⓒ Ⓓ
6 Ⓐ Ⓑ Ⓒ Ⓓ	26 Ⓐ Ⓑ Ⓒ Ⓓ	46 Ⓐ Ⓑ Ⓒ Ⓓ
7 Ⓐ Ⓑ Ⓒ Ⓓ	27 Ⓐ Ⓑ Ⓒ Ⓓ	47 Ⓐ Ⓑ Ⓒ Ⓓ
8 Ⓐ Ⓑ Ⓒ Ⓓ	28 Ⓐ Ⓑ Ⓒ Ⓓ	48 Ⓐ Ⓑ Ⓒ Ⓓ
9 Ⓐ Ⓑ Ⓒ Ⓓ	29 Ⓐ Ⓑ Ⓒ Ⓓ	49 Ⓐ Ⓑ Ⓒ Ⓓ
10 Ⓐ Ⓑ Ⓒ Ⓓ	30 Ⓐ Ⓑ Ⓒ Ⓓ	50 Ⓐ Ⓑ Ⓒ Ⓓ
11 Ⓐ Ⓑ Ⓒ Ⓓ	31 Ⓐ Ⓑ Ⓒ Ⓓ	51 Ⓐ Ⓑ Ⓒ Ⓓ
12 Ⓐ Ⓑ Ⓒ Ⓓ	32 Ⓐ Ⓑ Ⓒ Ⓓ	52 Ⓐ Ⓑ Ⓒ Ⓓ
13 Ⓐ Ⓑ Ⓒ Ⓓ	33 Ⓐ Ⓑ Ⓒ Ⓓ	53 Ⓐ Ⓑ Ⓒ Ⓓ
14 Ⓐ Ⓑ Ⓒ Ⓓ	34 Ⓐ Ⓑ Ⓒ Ⓓ	54 Ⓐ Ⓑ Ⓒ Ⓓ
15 Ⓐ Ⓑ Ⓒ Ⓓ	35 Ⓐ Ⓑ Ⓒ Ⓓ	55 Ⓐ Ⓑ Ⓒ Ⓓ
16 Ⓐ Ⓑ Ⓒ Ⓓ	36 Ⓐ Ⓑ Ⓒ Ⓓ	
17 Ⓐ Ⓑ Ⓒ Ⓓ	37 Ⓐ Ⓑ Ⓒ Ⓓ	
18 Ⓐ Ⓑ Ⓒ Ⓓ	38 Ⓐ Ⓑ Ⓒ Ⓓ	
19 Ⓐ Ⓑ Ⓒ Ⓓ	39 Ⓐ Ⓑ Ⓒ Ⓓ	
20 Ⓐ Ⓑ Ⓒ Ⓓ	40 Ⓐ Ⓑ Ⓒ Ⓓ	

AP U.S. Government and Politics
Diagnostic Exam

Section I: Multiple-Choice Questions
Total Time—80 minutes
55 Questions

Directions: Each question or incomplete sentence below is followed by four suggested answers or completions. Select the one that is best, and then fill in the corresponding oval on the answer sheet.

Questions 1 and 2 refer to the graph below.

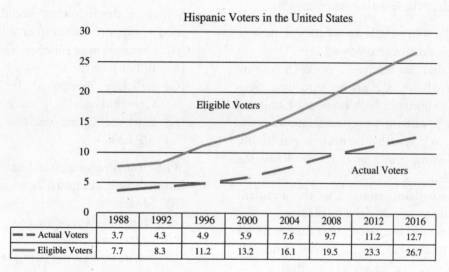

Hispanic Voters in the United States

	1988	1992	1996	2000	2004	2008	2012	2016
Actual Voters	3.7	4.3	4.9	5.9	7.6	9.7	11.2	12.7
Eligible Voters	7.7	8.3	11.2	13.2	16.1	19.5	23.3	26.7

Source: Pew Research Center

1. Which of the following best describes a trend in the line graph above?
   (A) Hispanic voters are less likely to vote than white voters.
   (B) Although the number of Hispanics becoming eligible to vote is increasing, the number of Hispanics who are voting is decreasing.
   (C) Hispanics are more likely to vote Democratic.
   (D) Since 1988, the number of Hispanic eligible voters and actual voters have increased.

2. Which of the following is an accurate conclusion based on the information in the graph and your knowledge of voter behavior?
   (A) Significant growth in the number of Hispanic eligible voters has helped make the U.S. electorate more racially and ethnically diverse.
   (B) Hispanic voters tend to vote Republican more often then they vote Democratic.
   (C) The debate over immigration will probably not encourage Hispanics to vote in larger numbers.
   (D) The Hispanic vote is not an important bloc of voters for either political party.

GO ON TO THE NEXT PAGE

3. Which of the following most accurately describes voter behavior in the United States?
   - (A) The voting population added by the passage of the Twenty-Sixth Amendment shows the highest percentage of participation in U.S. elections.
   - (B) Voters who are not active participants in a religious group are more likely to vote than active members.
   - (C) Single people are more likely to participate in elections than those who are married.
   - (D) Persons with white-collar jobs show a higher percentage of participation in elections than those with blue-collar jobs.

4. Which of the following is an accurate statement about the president's veto power?
   - (A) A bill that has received a pocket veto may be passed over the pocket veto by a two-thirds majority of both houses of Congress.
   - (B) Congress often shows consideration for the president's veto by revising a vetoed bill and passing it in a form acceptable to the president.
   - (C) The veto demonstrates that the president has little power over the legislature.
   - (D) Presidents whose party is not the dominant party in the House and Senate frequently have a veto overridden by Congress.

5. Which of the following statements best describes a concurring opinion of a Supreme Court decision?
   - (A) It is written by a justice who agrees with the majority opinion but disagrees with the reasoning behind the majority opinion.
   - (B) It must be written by the Chief Justice of the Supreme Court.
   - (C) It is an informal poll of the justices to determine their opinion during the discussions of the case, but it is not binding on the justices.
   - (D) It is an opinion of a justice or justices who disagree with the majority opinion.

6. Which of the following would most likely be used to support American civil liberties?
   - (A) Declaration of Independence
   - (B) Bill of Rights
   - (C) Judiciary Article of the United States Constitution
   - (D) Supreme Court decision in *Marbury v. Madison*

7. When the President has been impeached, the impeachment case must be tried in the
   - (A) Senate
   - (B) House of Representatives
   - (C) Senate and House
   - (D) Senate and House with the Supreme Court presiding

8. Which of the following is an accurate comparison of the Federalist and Anti-Federalist views on government?

	FEDERALIST	ANTI-FEDERALIST
(A)	Favored a strong central government to protect the nation and solve domestic problems	Favored strong state overnments
(B)	Protection of property rights	Checks and balances would protect the people against abuses by government
(C)	Wanted a bill of rights to protect citizens against government	Stressed the weaknesses of the Articles of Confederation; a strong national government was needed to protect the nation
(D)	Wanted strong state governments	Protection of property rights

GO ON TO THE NEXT PAGE

Questions 9–10 refer to the graph bellow.

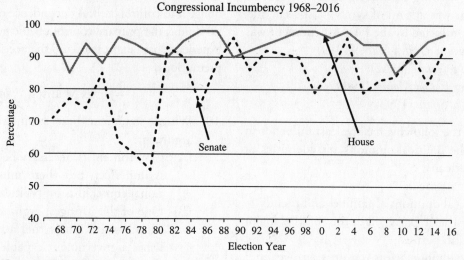

Congressional Incumbency 1968–2016

Source: Open Secrets

9. Which of the following best describes a trend in the line graph above?
   (A) There is a lower percentage of incumbency in the House than in the Senate.
   (B) There is a higher percentage of incumbency in the Senate than in the House.
   (C) There is a higher percentage of incumbency in the House than in the Senate.
   (D) Incumbency rates in the Senate are more stable than incumbency rate in the House.

10. Which of the following conclusions may be drawn about incumbency based on the data in the graph above?
    (A) Incumbency rates in the Senate are almost always higher than incumbency rates in the House.
    (B) Senate incumbency rates were at their lowest in 1982.
    (C) House incumbency rates were at their highest in 1990.
    (D) In the past 30 years, more than half of incumbents have won reelection.

11. Which of the following is an advantage to an incumbent when running for reelection?
    (A) name recognition
    (B) the incumbent may be perceived as stale
    (C) possible scandal or corruption
    (D) voter fatigue at the ballot

12. Which of the following best describe the purpose of primary elections?
    (A) They narrow down the field of candidates within a political party.
    (B) They are used to expand the field of candidates within a political party.
    (C) They give the voters more choice in the general election.
    (D) They lead to increased participation of third-party candidates.

13. The primary purpose of major U.S. political parties is to control government by
    (A) affecting public policy
    (B) defining party principles
    (C) winning elections through peaceful legal actions
    (D) pushing legislation through Congress

14. Senatorial elections
    (A) occur within single-member districts
    (B) attract less media attention than elections of representatives
    (C) promote frequent personal contact with senatorial constituencies
    (D) provide for a continuous body in the Senate

GO ON TO THE NEXT PAGE

15. The pivotal Supreme Court decision which ruled that wearing black armbands in school to protest war was a form of symbolic speech, and therefore protected by the First Amendment was
    (A) *Schenck v. United States* (1919)
    (B) *Engel v. Vitale* (1962)
    (C) *Tinker v. Des Moines* (1969)
    (D) *Reno v. Shaw* (1993)

16. Which of the following has the least influence in creating the political opinions and identities of most Americans?
    (A) the mass media
    (B) political opinions of families and friends
    (C) the official party platforms of the major political parties
    (D) demographic factors (occupation, age, etc.)

17. Which of the following best describe the average person's political participation in the United States?
    (A) voting in local elections
    (B) voting in presidential elections
    (C) a basic understanding of government
    (D) ignoring government altogether

18. The membership of the House of Representatives
    (A) is a continuous body
    (B) is dependent on the national census
    (C) is permanently restricted to 435 members
    (D) is elected in 50 statewide at-large elections

Questions 19–21 refer to the passage below.

But the great security against a gradual concentration of the several powers in the same department, consists in giving to those who administer each department the necessary constitutional means and personal motives to resist encroachments of the others. The provision for defense must in this, as in all other cases, be made commensurate to the danger of attack. Ambition must be made to counteract ambition. The interest of the man must be connected with the constitutional rights of the place. It may be a reflection on human nature, that such devices should be necessary to control the abuses of government. But what is government itself, but the greatest of all reflections on human nature? If men were angels, no government would be necessary. If angels were to govern men, neither external nor internal controls on government would be necessary. In framing a government which is to be administered by men over men, the great difficulty lies in this: you must first enable the government to control the governed; and in the next place oblige it to control itself. A dependence on the people is, no doubt, the primary control on the government; but experience has taught mankind the necessity of auxiliary precautions.

—James Madison, *The Federalist* #51

19. Which statement best summarizes Madison's argument?
    (A) Government is necessary because mankind is imperfect, but there must be constitutional constraints on political authority.
    (B) One of the strongest arguments in favor of the Constitution is the fact that it establishes a government capable of controlling the violence and damage caused by factions.
    (C) An independent judicial branch with federal judges holding their office for life, subject to good behavior, is necessary to the future of the nation.
    (D) The Constitution and laws of Congress would be invalidated if they were inconsistent with the states.

20. Which of the following constitutional principles limits the power of the national government in Madison's argument?
    (A) federalism and minority rule
    (B) popular sovereignty and state's rights
    (C) conservativism and majority rule
    (D) separation of powers and checks and balances

21. Based on the quote, with which of the following statements would the author most agree?
    (A) Each branch of government should be responsible for the appointment of members of the other branches.
    (B) In a government of diverse powers, it is essential that each branch have a degree of control over the others.
    (C) Each branch of government should be totally independent from the other branches of government and they should have no authority over each other.
    (D) Government should be based on the protection of states' rights by creating a separation of powers based on legislative, executive, and judicial branches.

GO ON TO THE NEXT PAGE

22. Which of the following best describes a major defect of the electoral college?
    (A) The Senate, not the people, decides elections for president.
    (B) Electors are not legally pledged to their candidate.
    (C) The candidate winning the popular vote always wins.
    (D) Federal law apportions an equal number of electors to each state.

23. Which of the following best describes the voting process in America?
    (A) The federal government regulates voter registration in all states.
    (B) State governments regulate voter registration within their respective state.
    (C) All individuals over the age of 18 are required to register to vote.
    (D) Anyone may vote regardless of registration status.

24. Which of the following most accurately describes the Senate?
    (A) The Senate is the larger, more powerful house of Congress.
    (B) Membership in the Senate is determined by the population of the respective states.
    (C) The most influential member of the Senate is the majority leader.
    (D) Revenue bills must originate in the Senate.

25. The Supreme Court case that established the implied powers of Congress and upheld the supremacy of the federal government over state governments was
    (A) *United States v. Lopez* (1995)
    (B) *Baker v. Carr* (1962)
    (C) *Marbury v. Madison* (1803)
    (D) *McCulloch v. Maryland* (1819)

26. Which of the following is a specific power of the House of Representatives?
    (A) ratification of treaties
    (B) election of the vice president if the electoral college fails
    (C) initiation of revenue bills
    (D) trial of presidential impeachment cases

27. Members of the federal executive bureaucracy tend to represent the interests of
    (A) the president
    (B) the departments in which they work
    (C) the special interests to which they belong
    (D) the political party to which they belong

Questions 28–29 refer to the passage below.

The President of the United States has an extraordinary range of formal powers, of authority in statute law and in the Constitution. Here is testimony that despite his "powers" he does not obtain results by giving orders—or not, at any rate, merely by giving orders. He also has extraordinary status, ex officio, according to the customs of our government and politics. Here is testimony that despite his status he does not get action without argument. Presidential power is the power to persuade . . . .

—Richard Neustadt, *Presidential Power and the Modern President*, 1991

28. Which of the following best summarizes Neustadt's argument?
    (A) Persuasion and bargaining are major means that presidents use to influence policy.
    (B) Presidents do not need to bargain to influence other branches of government.
    (C) Presidents can accomplish more by commanding others in government to act.
    (D) The American presidency is defined primarily by the strength in their formal powers while their informal powers are not only unnecessary, but also unconstitutional.

29. Based on the text from the quote, with which of the following statements would the author most agree?
    (A) Presidential power comes from the president's power to command others in government.
    (B) Presidents face many challenges in office and therefore must use informal resources to maximize their power and accomplish their goals.
    (C) The modern presidency has increased in both size and power in recent years.
    (D) Presidents use their office to enhance the powers of the president to carry out unconstitutional actions.

GO ON TO THE NEXT PAGE

30. Which of the following is an accurate comparison of the advantages and disadvantages of federalism?

	ADVANTAGE OF FEDERALISM	DISADVANTAGE OF FEDERALISM
(A)	Complex, with many governments to deal with	Keeps government close to the people
(B)	Duplication of offices and functions of government	Accommodates already existing state governments
(C)	Avoids concentration of political power	Conflicts of authority may arise
(D)	States serve as training grounds for national leaders	Ideally suited for smaller geographic areas because it discourages diversity

31. In the United States, the powers of government are divided between a national government, state governments, and several regional and local governments. This system is called
    (A) Delegated government
    (B) Federalism
    (C) Democracy
    (D) Checks and balances

32. In the United States, the Congress has created two types of federal courts. What are these?
    (A) Special and legislative courts
    (B) District and constitutional courts
    (C) Constitutional and appellate courts
    (D) Constitutional and legislative courts

33. Which of the following best describes political parties in the United States?
    (A) Political parties are addressed in the Constitution.
    (B) Membership is voluntary and represents a good cross section of the country's population.
    (C) Membership is voluntary, but only a small portion of the voting public belongs.
    (D) Party membership is strengthening.

34. In developing the United States Constitution, which of the following plans called for a strong national government with three separate branches?
    (A) Virginia plan
    (B) New Jersey plan
    (C) Connecticut plan
    (D) Philadelphia plan

35. An interest group, a bureaucratic government agency, and a committee of Congress working together would be an example of
    (A) an iron triangle
    (B) a government corporation
    (C) an independent regulatory agency
    (D) an independent executive agency

36. The president's cabinet is designed to
    (A) issue executive orders
    (B) negotiate executive agreements
    (C) set the Supreme Court's agenda before the Congress
    (D) advise the president and administer the departments of government

37. What criticism is most often heard from critics of the news media in the United States?
    (A) the tendency of the media to lean to the liberal side when covering the news
    (B) the tendency of the media to only cover the president and not give as much coverage to Congress
    (C) the tendency of the media to lean to the conservative side when covering the news
    (D) the tendency of the media to only cover American politics

GO ON TO THE NEXT PAGE

Questions 38–39 refer to the map below.

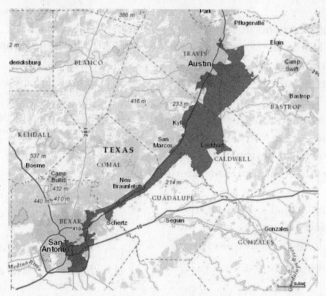

Source: Texas Congressional Districts—Texas Observer
https://www.texasobserver.org/lloyd-doggett-back-in-
primary-race-with-san-antonio-challengers/

38. The map shows the outline of the 35th Congressional District of Texas. Which statement best explains the drawing?
    (A) Members of Congress are chosen from the entire state at-large.
    (B) State legislatures draw congressional districts by manipulating the size and shape of the district to favor one political party or group over another.
    (C) The drawing of congressional districts by state legislatures occurs every four years.
    (D) Congressional districts are often drawn to make them more competitive.

39. Which Supreme Court decision supports declaring this redistricting unconstitutional?
    (A) *Citizens United v. Federal Election Committee* (2010)
    (B) *United States v. Lopez* (1995)
    (C) *Shaw v. Reno* (1993)
    (D) *McDonald v. Chicago* (2010)

Questions 40–42 refer to the quote below.

Segregation of white and colored children in public schools has a detrimental effect upon the colored children. The impact is greater when it has the sanction of the law, for the policy of separating the races is usually interpreted as denoting the inferiority of the Negro group …. Any language in contrary to this finding is rejected. We conclude that in the field of public education the doctrine of "separate but equal" has no place. Separate educational facilities are inherently unequal.

—Earl Warren, *Chief Justice of the
U.S. Supreme Court*

GO ON TO THE NEXT PAGE

40. Which of the following best summarizes Warren's opinion?
    (A) Segregation of public schools does not violate the "separate but equal" doctrine.
    (B) Local governments must act "with all deliberate speed" to carry out the "separate but equal" doctrine.
    (C) Segregation of public education based on race taught a sense of inferiority that had a hugely detrimental effect on the education and personal growth of African American children.
    (D) The "separate but equal" doctrine that stated separate facilities for the races was constitutional as long as the facilities were "substantially equal."

41. Which of the following constitutional provisions limits the power of the state governments in Warren's opinion?
    (A) Equal Protection Clause of the Fourteenth Amendment
    (B) Establishment Clause of the First Amendment
    (C) Necessary and Proper Clause in Article I
    (D) Due Process Clause of the Fourteenth Amendment

42. The quote above is from which of the following Supreme Court cases?
    (A) *Baker v. Carr* (1961)
    (B) *McDonald v. Chicago* (2010)
    (C) *Shaw v. Reno* (1993)
    (D) *Brown v. Board of Education* (1954)

43. Which of the following is an accurate comparison of political parties and interest groups?

	POLITICAL PARTIES	INTEREST GROUPS
(A)	Were created under the Necessary and Proper Clause of the Constitution	Are often required to use different strategies depending on which branch of government is being influenced and by which group
(B)	Require voters to join and pay dues for membership	Membership is often used to determine political appointments
(C)	Goal is to win elections and gain control of government	Goal is to influence public policy
(D)	Play an important role in the nomination of candidates	Used as a method of government organization

44. As a result of recent events on school campuses and wanting to create safer schools for students, some citizens have advocated repealing the Second Amendment's right to bear arms. Which of the following is necessary for that amendment to be repealed?
    (A) proposal by the United States House of Representatives and ratification by the Senate
    (B) proposal by the United States Senate and ratification by the House of Representatives
    (C) proposal and ratification by both houses of Congress
    (D) proposal by the United States Congress and ratification by the states

Questions 45–46 refer to the political cartoon below.

Clay Bennett Editorial Cartoon is used with the permission of Clay Bennett, the Washington Post Writers Group and the Cartoonist Group. All rights reserved.

GO ON TO THE NEXT PAGE

45. Which of the following best describes the main idea or message of the political cartoon?
    (A) Lobbyists pursue relationships with lawmakers to shape legislation so that it benefits clients who would be affected by new laws or regulations.
    (B) Lawmakers frequently target lobbyists to make donations as sources of campaign money.
    (C) Lawmakers are sometimes wary of monetary donations because the public may interpret them as evidence of corruption.
    (D) The number of lobbyists is decreasing because of the increased amount of government regulation.

46. Which of the following has been used to control the negative effects of interest groups?
    (A) Political action committees have been outlawed, giving more power to special interest groups and their lobbyists.
    (B) Lobbyists are required to provide campaign contributions to candidates for political office.
    (C) Lobbyists are required to register with the clerk of the House and the secretary of the Senate and indicate what group they are representing.
    (D) Congress has created a "revolving door" for members of government who leave government service and join a lobbyist group, making it easier to become a lobbyist after leaving government service.

47. Which of the following is an executive power of the Senate?
    (A) Reviewing presidential vetoes
    (B) Approving appointments and treaties
    (C) Trying impeachment cases
    (D) Proposing constitutional amendments

48. Which of the following is an accurate comparison of the two court cases?

	ENGEL V. VITALE (1962)	WISCONSIN V. YODER (1972)
(A)	A prayer's nondenominational or voluntary character prevent it from being unconstitutional	Nondenominational, school-sponsored prayer forces religion on impressionable children
(B)	Became the basis for subsequent decisions concerning freedom of speech	Local laws, which were not neutral or generally applied, were not narrowly tailored to a compelling governmental interest
(C)	A state's interest in universal education must be balanced against parents' interest in the religious upbringing of their children.	The First Amendment was only meant to prohibit the establishment of a state-sponsored church, not prohibit all types of government involvement with religion
(D)	School sponsorship of religious activities violates the establishment clause	Compelling Amish students to attend school past the eighth grade violates the free exercise clause

49. Which Supreme Court case established the principle of judicial review in the American court system?
    (A) *McCulloch v. Maryland* (1819)
    (B) *McDonald v. Chicago* (2010)
    (C) *Marbury v. Madison* (1803)
    (D) *Wisconsin v. Yoder* (1972)

GO ON TO THE NEXT PAGE

50. Which of the following is an accurate comparison of pluralist and elite theory?

	PLURALIST THEORY	ELITE THEORY
(A)	A majority of people determine policy on a particular issue.	Many groups are strong and have influence over government at the same time.
(B)	There is a hierarchical structure, impersonality, standardized procedures, and specialized division of labor.	The wealthiest people influence government.
(C)	No one group dominates on every issue, but groups compete for power.	The civil liberties and civil rights of minorities are protected by the majority.
(D)	Certain groups have power on certain topics but not all groups are equally powerful.	There is a powerful group of corporate leaders, top military officers and government officials who strongly influence governmental decisions.

Questions 51–52 refer to the graph below.

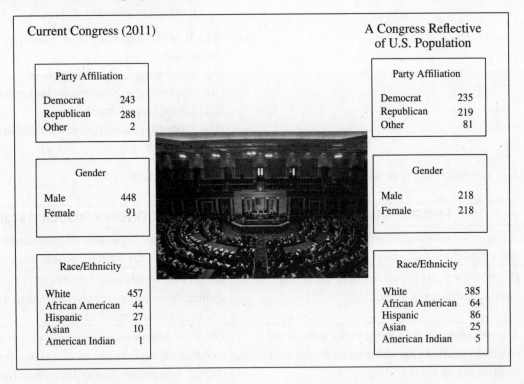

Current Congress (2011)

Party Affiliation

Democrat 243
Republican 288
Other 2

Gender

Male 448
Female 91

Race/Ethnicity

White 457
African American 44
Hispanic 27
Asian 10
American Indian 1

A Congress Reflective of U.S. Population

Party Affiliation

Democrat 235
Republican 219
Other 81

Gender

Male 218
Female 218

Race/Ethnicity

White 385
African American 64
Hispanic 86
Asian 25
American Indian 5

51. While America is getting more diverse, the demographics of Congress are not a true reflection of American society. Based on the infographic, which of the following best illustrates the lack of diversity in Congress?
    (A) There should be more whites in Congress.
    (B) There should be fewer African Americans in Congress.
    (C) There should be more women in Congress.
    (D) There should be more Democrats in Congress.

52. Based on the infographic, which of the following would best create diversity in Congress?
    (A) Constitutional limits on the number of terms which one person can serve
    (B) Increased salaries for members of Congress
    (C) Adjustment of congressional committee assignments
    (D) Stricter voter identification laws in the states

GO ON TO THE NEXT PAGE

Questions 53–54 refer to the graph below.

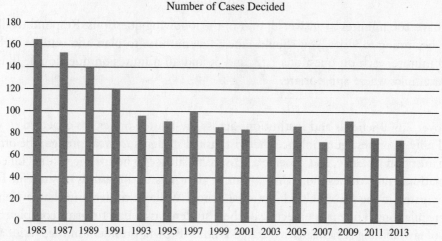

Number of Cases Decided

Source: Supreme Court Database

53. Which of the following trends is reflected in the data in the graph?
   (A) There has been a steady increase in the number of cases heard by the Supreme Court.
   (B) The Supreme Court decides its caseload based on the rule of four.
   (C) There has been a decrease in the number of cases being appealed to the Supreme Court.
   (D) There has been a decrease in the number of cases being decided each term by the Supreme Court.

54. Which of the following is a potential explanation for the trend illustrated in the bar graph?
   (A) Fewer cases are being appealed to the Supreme Court because the lower courts are making better decisions.
   (B) The Supreme Court is only composed of nine justices and they don't have the time to hear more cases.
   (C) Justices are less likely to take on an issue in which they believe precedent has already been established or that they might not be able to provide a clear answer.
   (D) Congress has mandated a decrease in the number of cases that the Supreme Court may hear.

55. Which of the following best describes the use of scientific polling methods for measuring public opinion?
   (A) A pollster uses data collected from telephone interviews of 500 people.
   (B) A pollster uses internet polling of anyone who wishes to participate.
   (C) A pollster surveys the first person to answer the phone and does not call back if no one answers.
   (D) A pollster generates a random sample of individuals who fit the various demographics needed.

STOP. END OF SECTION I

Section II: Free-Response Questions
Time—100 minutes

Directions: You have 100 minutes to answer all four of the following questions. Respond to all parts of all four questions. Before beginning to write, you should take a few minutes to plan and outline each answer. Spend approximately 20 minutes each on questions 1, 2, and 3, and 40 minutes on question 4. Illustrate your essay with substantive examples where appropriate.

1. Students at over 2,600 schools and institutions across the United States are expected to walk out of class in a national rally to protest gun violence. Activists asked students to wear orange, the official color of the campaign against gun violence, and observe a 13-second silence to honor the victims killed at Columbine. "The latest national rally comes more than a month after tens of thousands of students from some 3,000 schools participated in the #ENOUGH National School Walkout to demand that lawmakers seek tighter gun control regulations. The main objective of these students is to ban firearms completely, and confiscate the firearms of law-abiding Americans…," stated Dudley Brown, president of the National Association for Gun Rights.

   —*Politics, April 18, 2018*

   After reading the scenario, respond to the following:
   (A) Describe a power that Congress might use to address the issue outlined in the scenario.
   (B) In the context of the scenario, explain how the Supreme Court has ruled on the issue of gun control.
   (C) In the context of the scenario, explain how the interaction between Congress and the Supreme Court might be affected by interest groups.

Presidential Vetoes and Congressional Overrides, 1961–2021

PRESIDENT (YEARS)	COINCIDING CONGRESS	VETOES			VETOES OVERRIDDEN
		REGULAR VETOES	POCKET VETOES	TOTAL VETOES	
Trump (2017-2021	115–116	10	—	10	1
Obama (2009–2017)	111–114	12	0	12	1
GW Bush (2001–2009)	107–110	12	0	12	4
Clinton (1993–2001)	103–106	36	1	37	2
GHW Bush (1989–1993)	101–102	29	15	44	1
Reagan (1981–1989)	97–100	39	39	78	9
Carter (1977–1981)	95–96	13	18	31	2
Ford (1974–1977)	93–94	48	18	66	12
Nixon (1969–1974)	91–92	26	17	43	7
Johnson (1963–1969)	88–90	16	14	30	—
Kennedy (1961–1963)	87–88	12	9	21	—

2. Use the chart above to answer the questions.
   (A) Identify the administration with the largest number of vetoes.
   (B) Describe a pattern in presidential vetoes and congressional overrides as illustrated in the graphic and draw a conclusion about that pattern.
   (C) Explain how presidential vetoes and congressional overrides as shown in the quantitative graphic demonstrates the constitutional principles of separation of powers and checks and balances.

GO ON TO THE NEXT PAGE

3. In 1927, Jay Near and Howard Guilford began publishing *The Saturday Press* in Minneapolis. The paper strongly criticized elected officials, accusing them of dishonesty and corruption, and charging that they were operating with gangsters. As a result, one official filed a complaint against the paper.

Minnesota had a law subjecting newspapers to official approval before publication. Publishers had to show "good motives and justifiable ends" for what they were about to print. If they could not, the paper could be censored in advance. Additionally, it was a crime to publish "obscene, lewd, and lascivious" or "malicious, scandalous, and defamatory" materials. Near eventually stopped publishing his newspaper on the basis of the Minnesota law.

The Supreme Court used the Fourteenth Amendment's requirement of due process to apply the First Amendment's protection of freedom of the press to state governments in *Near v. Minnesota* (1931).

The Court held that prior restraint on publication in Minnesota was "the essence of censorship" and the heart of what the First Amendment was designed to prevent. Justice Hughes stated: "… the fact that liberty of press may be abused does not make any less necessary the immunity of the press from prior restraint … a more serious evil would result if officials could determine which stories can be published … ."

(A) Identify the free press issue that is common to both *Near v. Minnesota* (1931) and *New York Times Co. v. United States* (1971).

(B) Based on information in the passage above and your knowledge of government and politics, describe the facts and explain how the facts of *New York Times Co. v. United States* strengthened freedom of the press, even in cases involving national security.

(C) Describe an action that the legislative branch can take to limit the impact of the ruling in *Near v. Minnesota*.

4. There has been considerable debate over the years on what the role of the Supreme Court should be. Some courts have practiced judicial activism, while others have practiced judicial restraint. Develop an argument that explains the proper role of the Supreme Court in American democracy.

In your essay, you must:
- Articulate a defensible claim or thesis that responds to the prompt and establishes a line of reasoning
- Support your claim or thesis with at least TWO pieces of accurate and relevant information:
  — At least ONE piece of evidence must be from one of the following foundational documents:
    — Brutus No. 1
    — Federalist No. 78
    — U.S. Constitution
  — Use a second piece of evidence from another foundational document from the list or from your study of the electoral process
- Use reasoning to explain why your evidence supports your claim or theses
- Respond to an opposing or alternative perspective using refutation, concession, or rebuttal

STOP. END OF SECTION II

Answer Key for Multiple-Choice Questions

1. D	15. C	29. B	43. C
2. A	16. C	30. C	44. D
3. D	17. B	31. B	45. A
4. B	18. B	32. D	46. C
5. A	19. A	33. B	47. B
6. B	20. D	34. A	48. D
7. A	21. B	35. A	49. C
8. A	22. B	36. D	50. D
9. C	23. B	37. A	51. C
10. D	24. C	38. B	52. A
11. A	25. D	39. C	53. D
12. A	26. C	40. C	54. C
13. C	27. B	41. A	55. D
14. D	28. A	42. D	

› Answers and Explanations for the Multiple-Choice Questions

1. **D.** The graph indicates that the number of both Hispanic eligible voters and actual voters have increased (B). The graph does not provide information about Hispanics being more or less likely to vote than whites (A) or the likelihood that Hispanics will vote Democratic (C).

2. **A.** Because there is significant growth in the number of Hispanic eligible voters, it is an accurate conclusion that the U.S. electorate is becoming more racially and ethnically diverse. Hispanic voters are more likely to vote Democratic than Republican (B). Immigration is an issue that will probably encourage more Hispanics to vote (C). Both political parties view the Hispanic vote as an important bloc (D).

3. **D.** Persons with white-collar jobs and higher income levels are more likely to vote than those with blue-collar jobs and lower income levels. The Twenty-Sixth Amendment lowered the voting age from 21 to 18 years. Voters between the ages of 18 and 21 show a low level of participation in elections (A). Active members of religious groups are more likely to vote than those who rarely attend religious services (B). Married people are more likely to vote than those who are single (C).

4. **B.** Congress may alter a bill after it has been vetoed by the president so that the new form is suitable to the president. A bill that has received a pocket veto dies (A). Very few vetoes have been overridden (D). The fact that few vetoed bills have been overridden demonstrates the considerable veto power of the president (C).

5. **A.** A justice writing a concurring opinion differs with the majority only because of the reasoning substantiating the majority opinion. The concurring opinion does not have to be written by the chief justice (B). A poll to determine how each justice is leaning in his or her opinion takes place during the conference phase of the Court's deliberations and is not made public (C). A dissenting opinion is written by a justice who disagrees with the majority and votes with the minority (D).

6. **B.** The Bill of Rights established basic rights, including freedom of speech, petition, assembly, religion, and the press; the right to bear arms; freedom from unreasonable search and seizure; the right to a speedy and public jury trial; and freedom from cruel and unusual punishment. Although the Declaration of Independence (A) was a statement of the ideals of the new United States, it did not have the force of law, and therefore, did not establish civil liberties. The Judiciary Article (C) grants only the right of trial by jury in federal cases. *Marbury v. Madison* (D) established the principle of judicial review.

7. **A.** According to the Constitution, the House of Representatives brings charges of impeachment, whereas the Senate tries, or sits in judgment of, impeachment cases.

8. **A.** The Federalists favored a strong central government, while the Anti-Federalists favored strong state governments. Federalists supported the protection of property rights and the concept of checks and balances to protect the people against abuses by the government (B). The Anti-Federalists wanted a Bill of Rights to protect citizens against the government, while the Federalists stressed the weaknesses of the Articles of Confederation and called for a stronger national government (C). Anti-Federalists wanted strong state governments, while Federalists supported the protection of property rights (D).

9. **C.** There is a higher percentage of incumbency in the House than in the Senate.

10. **D.** Incumbency rates are generally higher in the House than in the Senate (A). Senate incumbency rates were at their lowest in 1980 (B). House incumbency rates were at their highest in 2004 (C).

11. **A.** Advantages of incumbency include name recognition, credit claiming, casework for constituents, visibility, ease of fundraising, experience in

campaigning, and running based on a proven voting record. If the incumbent is perceived as stale (B) or is involved in a scandal or corruption (C), or if voters experience ballot fatigue, are not advantageous to incumbents.

12. **A.** Primary elections are "first elections" held to nominate candidates from within a political party. Primary elections narrow the field of party candidates to one (B), giving voters the choice of only one candidate per party in the general election (C). Primary elections are among the factors that limit the influence and participation of third-party candidates(D).

13. **C.** The primary goal of political parties is to seek to control government through the winning of elections. Choice (D) reflects only one aspect of the role of political parties at the national level. The goals of affecting public policy (A) and defining party principles (B), are secondary goals for major U.S. political parties, which are election oriented.

14. **D.** Although senators are elected for six-year terms, senatorial elections are staggered so that only one-third of the Senate is elected every two years, providing for a continuous body. The prestige of the Senate leads to more media interest (B). Because senators are elected from the entire state (A), their constituencies are generally more diverse than those of representatives (C).

15. **C.** *Schenck v. United States* was a 1919 case in which the Court ruled speech creating a "clear and present danger" was not protected by the First Amendment (A). In *Engel v. Vitale* (1962), the Court ruled school sponsorship of religious activities violates the establishment clause of the First Amendment (B). *Reno v. Shaw* (1993) stated that redistricting based on race violated the Voting Rights Act of 1965 and was therefore unconstitutional (D).

16. **C.** The official political party platform has little influence on anyone, including candidates running for office from that political party; there are many cases of candidates repudiating or ignoring parts of the platform of their own party during the campaign. The other answer choices all list factors that often influence the political opinions and identities of Americans.

17. **B.** Voting in presidential elections is the method of participation used by the largest number of Americans. Most Americans do not vote in local elections (A). Choice (C) refers to knowledge rather than participation, while choice (D) involves a lack of political participation.

18. **B.** The number of representatives apportioned to each state depends on the findings of the most recent census. The members of the House of Representatives are elected every two years, preventing a continuous body as in the Senate (A). Congress may vote to alter the "permanent" size of the House (C). Only those states whose population is small enough to allow for only one representative elect representatives in at-large elections; most states elect representatives from single-member districts (D).

19. **A.** Federalist #51 relates the reasoning behind the creation of a separation of powers and checks and balances under the Constitution. Federalist #10 discusses the role of government in controlling factions (B). Federalist #78 discusses the judiciary (C). The Constitution and laws of Congress cannot be invalidated by the states (D).

20. **D.** Constitutional principles include limited government, popular sovereignty, separation of powers, checks and balances, and federalism. Minority rule (A), state's rights (B), and majority rule (C) are not constitutional principles about which Madison wrote in Federalist #51.

21. **B.** Madison stated that each branch of government should not be responsible for the appointment of members to the other branches (A). While each branch of government should be independent from the other branches, there should be a system of checks and balances (C) which would give power over the other branches. Separation of powers would be provided to prevent one branch of government from becoming too powerful over other branches of government (D).

22. **B.** An electoral college was created under the Constitution to elect the president. If no candidate wins a majority of electoral votes, the House of Representatives, not the Senate, decides the election (A). The candidate winning the popular vote sometimes loses the election, as occurred in 2000 and 2016 (C). Each state is apportioned

electors according to its number of representatives plus senators (D) in Congress.

23. **B.** Voter registration is regulated by state governments (A). Registration to vote is not required of anyone in the United States (C); most states, however, require those wanting to vote to register prior to the election (D).

24. **C.** The majority leader is the most influential member of the Senate. The Senate is smaller than the House of Representatives (A). Membership in the Senate is determined through the Constitution creating an equal number of seats (two) per state (B). Revenue bills must originate in the House of Representatives (D).

25. **D.** The 1819 ruling in *McCulloch v. Maryland* established the implied powers of the national government; the authority of the federal government to act, the Court ruled, could come from the Necessary and Proper Clause of the Constitution. *United States v. Lopez* was a 1995 Court decision forbidding Congress from using the commerce clause to make possession of a gun in a school zone a federal crime (A). *Baker v. Carr* was a 1962 decision challenging redistricting and providing the "one person, one vote" doctrine (B). *Marbury v. Madison* was the 1803 decision that established judicial review (C).

26. **C.** The Senate ratifies treaties (A), chooses the vice-president if the electoral college fails (B), and tries the president on impeachment charges (D).

27. **B.** A bureaucracy is an organization composed of several levels of authority. It often uses specialization to carry out the tasks of its departments and agencies. Members of the federal bureaucracy tend to represent the departments in which they work rather than the president (A), special interest groups (C), or political parties (D).

28. **A.** Neustadt suggests that the power of the president is based on the power to persuade and bargain (A), rather than the power to command (B, C). While presidents have many formal powers, the informal powers of the executive are important and necessary (D).

29. **B.** Presidents do not gain power from only the power to command others (A). While the mod-

ern presidency has increased in both size and power in recent years, Neustadt did not address this issue in the passage (C). The president cannot use his office to carry out unconstitutional actions (D).

30. **C.** Complexity of government is a disadvantage of federalism (A). Duplication of offices and functions of government is a disadvantage of federalism (B). An advantage of federalism is that it is ideally suited for some larger geographic areas because it encourages diversity in local government (D).

31. **B.** U.S. federalism is the division of governmental powers between national, state, and several regional and local governments. Delegated government (A) receives its powers through a constitution. Democracy (C) is rule by the people Checks and balances (D) are the limits placed by one branch of the federal government over another.

32. **D.** Constitutional courts are the federal courts created by Congress under Article III of the Constitution. Legislative courts are special courts that hear cases arising from the powers given to Congress under Article I (A). District courts, a type of constitutional court, serve as federal trial courts (B). Appellate courts (C), which decide appeals from district courts, are constitutional courts.

33. **B.** Membership in U.S. political parties is voluntary and represents voters from a variety of geographical regions, ethnic and racial groups, income and educational levels, religions, and ideologies. Political parties are not mentioned in the Constitution, and George Washington was elected to the presidency without membership in a party (A). A substantial portion of the voting public claims party membership (C). More and more U.S. voters are classifying themselves as independents (D).

34. **A.** The Virginia Plan provided for a strong central government with three branches. The New Jersey Plan (B) called for a weak national government with three separate branches. The Great (Connecticut) Compromise (not a proposed plan) created a strong national government with

three separate branches (C). There was no Philadelphia Plan (D).

35. **A.** An iron triangle is an alliance that develops between bureaucratic agencies, interest groups, and congressional committees or subcommittees in pursuit of a common goal. A government corporation is created by Congress to carry out businesslike activities (B). An independent regulatory agency (C) is a portion of the executive branch created to impose and enforce regulations free of political influence. An independent executive agency (D) is similar to a department, but has no cabinet status.

36. **D.** The president's cabinet advises the president; each secretary administers a department of the government. Only the president has the power to issue executive orders (A) or negotiate executive agreements (B); the Supreme Court does not set an agenda before Congress (C).

37. **A.** The media is often criticized as having a liberal bias when covering the news (B). Although the media does cover the president more than Congress (C), this has not been a criticism. The media covers both American and international news (D).

38. **B.** Members of Congress are chosen from districts within each state (A). The drawing of congressional districts by state legislatures takes place every 10 years, after the census (C). Congressional districts are often drawn to favor one political party or group over another, making them less competitive (D).

39. **C.** *Citizens United v. FEC* specified that political spending by corporations, associations, and labor unions is a form of protected speech under the First Amendment (A). *United States v. Lopez* specified that Congress may not use the commerce clause to make the possession of a gun in a school zone a federal crime (B). *McDonald v. Chicago* specified that the Fourteenth Amendment extends the Second Amendment's right to keep and bear arms to the states (D).

40. **C.** Warren ruled in *Brown v. Board* of Education that the doctrine of "separate but equal" was unconstitutional under the Equal Protection Clause of the Fourteenth Amendment. Segregation of public schools under this doctrine is also unconstitutional (A). Warren states that separate educational facilities are inherently unequal and therefore unconstitutional (D). In a subsequent opinion, *Brown v. Board II*, Warren encouraged states and local governments to act "with all deliberate speed" to end segregation (B).

41. **A.** The Establishment Clause of the First Amendment provides that Congress cannot establish a national religion for the United States (B). The Necessary and Proper Clause in Article I gives Congress the powers to pass all laws necessary to carry out their constitutional duties (C). The Due Process Clause of the Fourteenth Amendment forbids government from taking life, liberty, or property without due process (D).

42. **D.** In *Brown v. Board* of Education, Warren ruled that school segregation violates the equal protection clause of the Fourteenth Amendment (D). *Baker v. Carr* established the court's power to review redistricting issues by ruling that challenges to redistricting did not raise "political questions" that would keep federal courts from reviewing such challenges, leading to the development of "one person, one vote" (A). *McDonald v. Chicago* specified that the Fourteenth Amendment extends the Second Amendment's protections of the right to keep and bear arms to the states (B). *Shaw v. Reno* established that legislative redistricting must be mindful of race and ensure compliance with the Voting Rights Act of 1965 (C).

43. **C.** The goal of political parties is to win elections to control government, while the goal of interest groups is to influence public policy (C). Political parties are not provided for in the Constitution (A). Political parties do not require voters to join, nor do they charge dues if voters choose to join (B). Political parties, not interest groups, are used as a method of government organization (D).

44. **D.** Amending the Constitution requires Congress to propose amendments by a two-thirds vote in both houses. The proposed amendment must then be ratified by the state legislatures of three-fourths of the states or by conventions held

in three-fourths of the states. Another method of amendment allows Congress to call a national convention when requested by three-fourths of the state legislatures. This convention then initiates the process by proposing the amendment. To date, no national convention has been called to propose an amendment.

45. **A.** Lawmakers frequently target lobbyists to make donations as sources of campaign money. The political cartoon makes no mention of money for campaign contributions (B) or lawmakers being wary of monetary donations (C). The number of lobbyists is increasing (D).

46. **C.** Political action committees have not been abolished (A). Lobbyists are regulated by law and are not required to donate to candidates (B). Congress has established regulations for the "revolving door" of government officials who leave government service and go to work as lobbyists (D).

47. **B.** Approving appointments and treaties are executive powers of the Senate because they are used in conjunction with a power of the president. Reviewing presidential vetoes (A) and proposing constitutional amendments (D) are two of the Senate's legislative powers. Trying impeachment cases (C) is a nonlegislative power of the Senate.

48. **D.** *Engel v. Vitale* dealt with school sponsorship of religious activities. *Wisconsin v. Yoder* was about forcing Amish students to attend school past the eighth grade, not school-sponsored prayer (A). *Engel v. Vitale* was about nondenominational, school-sponsored prayer, not freedom of speech (B) or universal education (C).

49. **C.** *Marbury v. Madison* (1803) established the principle of judicial review. *McCulloch v. Maryland* (1819) upheld the power of the national government by denying the right of a state to tax the Bank of the United States (A). *McDonald v. Chicago* addressed issues with the Second Amendment (B). *Wisconsin v. Yoder* dealt with how Amish students being compelled to attend school past the eighth grade violated the free exercise clause of the First Amendment.

50. **D.** The pluralist theory provides that certain groups have power on certain topics, while the elite theory states that there is a powerful group of elites (corporate leaders, top military officers, and government officials) who strongly influence governmental decisions (D). Traditional democratic theory proposes that majority rule determines policy, while pluralist theory proposes that groups control policymaking (A). Bureaucratic theory describes a hierarchical structure (B). Traditional theory states that civil liberties and civil rights of minorities are protected by the majority (C).

51. **C.** The American population is almost 50% women, which is not reflected in the current Congress. There should be fewer whites (A), more African Americans (B), and fewer Democrats in Congress.

52. **A.** Term limits would offer greater opportunity for more people, including women and minorities, to run for Congress. None of the other answer choices would encourage turnover in Congress.

53. **D.** There has been a decrease in the number of cases heard by the Supreme Court (A). The graph provides no information about the rule of four (B) or the number of cases appealed to the Supreme Court (C).

54. **C.** Justices are less likely to take on an issue in which they believe precedent has already been established, or that they might not be able to provide a clear answer. Technological changes have made court rulings and the establishment of precedents easier to find resulting in less decisions from the lower courts that conflict with each other. More cases are being appealed to the Supreme Court (B). The Supreme Court uses the rule of four to determine which cases they will consider (C). Congress does not mandate the number of cases heard by the Supreme Court (D).

55. **D.** Scientific polling involves the use of a random sample of 1,000–2,000 people (A), whereby any member of the population has an equal chance of being selected (B). People most likely to answer the phone are often older and include more men than women, which would bias the sample selected (C).

Scoring the Free-Response Questions

1. **Scoring the Concept Application Question: Total Value–3 points**
   (A) **1 point:** Describe a political institution, process, or behavior that links to the scenario. (Must link content from the scenario and provide a description to receive credit.)
   (B) **1 point:** Explain how a required Supreme Court case applies to the scenario. (Must reference a required Supreme Court decision, and how the court has ruled based on that decision.)
   (C) **1 point:** Explain how the scenario relates to a political institutions, behaviors, or processes. (Must demonstrate how interest groups provide opportunities for participation and how citizens relate to government and policymakers.)

2. **Scoring the Quantitative Analysis Question: Total Value–4 points**
   (A) **1 point:** Describe the data presented in the quantitative graphic.
   (B) **2 points:** Describe a pattern, and draw a conclusion for that pattern. (Must describe a pattern for 1 point, and draw a conclusion about the pattern for the second point.)
   (C) **1 point:** Explain how specific data in the quantitative graphic demonstrates the constitutional principles referenced in the prompt. (Must address both constitutional principles.)

3. **Scoring the SCOTUS Comparison Question: Total Value–4 points**
   (A) **1 point:** Identify the free-press issue that is common to both Supreme Court cases. (Must go beyond freedom of the press and address the issue of prior restraint.)
   (B) **2 points:** Provide factual information from the required Supreme Court case (1 point) and explain how the reasoning and decisions of the required Supreme Court case apply to scenarios involving freedom of the press (1 point).
   (C) **1 point:** Describe an interaction between the holding in the nonrequired Supreme Court case (*Near v. Minnesota*) and a relevant political institution (legislative branch) that can limit the impact of prior restraint being unconstitutional.

4. **Scoring the Argument Essay: Total Value–6 points**
   - **1 point:** Articulate a defensible claim or thesis that responds to the question and establishes a line of reasoning.
   - **2 points:** Describe one piece of evidence from one of the listed foundational documents (1 point) that is accurately linked to the proper role of the Supreme Court and indicate how that evidence supports the argument (1 point). (Must show how evidence supports argument to earn second point.)
   - **1 point:** Use a second piece of specific and relevant evidence to support the argument. (Must indicate how evidence supports argument.)
   - **1 point:** Explain how or why the evidence supports the claim or thesis.
   - **1 point:** Respond to an opposing or alternate perspective using refutation, concession, or rebuttal.

Score Conversion Worksheet

Using this worksheet, you can get a rough approximation of what your score would be on the AP U.S. Government and Politics Exam. Use the answer key to check the multiple-choice questions and the scoring rubrics to award yourself points on the free-response questions. Then compute your raw score on the exam using the worksheet below. Finally, refer to the table below to translate your raw score to an AP score of 1 to 5.

Section I: Multiple Choice

Number of questions answered correctly (55 possible) _____ × 1.09 = _____

Section I: Free-Response

Question 1 (3 points possible): _____ × 5 = _____

Question 2 (4 points possible): _____ × 3.75 = _____

Question 3 (4 points possible): _____ × 3.75 = _____

Question 4 (6 points possible): _____ × 2.5 = _____

RAW SCORE: Add your points in the column above (120 possible): _____

Conversion Table

RAW SCORE	APPROXIMATE AP SCORE
Mid 80s to 120	5
Mid 70s to low-mid 80s	4
High 40s to mid 70s	3
High 20s to high 40s	2
0 to high 20s	1

Note: This score conversion worksheet is based on the assumption that the ranges for each grade (1–5) will remain similar from year to year.

STEP 3

Develop Strategies for Success

CHAPTER 4

Section I of the Exam: How to Approach the Multiple-Choice Questions

IN THIS CHAPTER

Summary: Use these question-answering strategies to raise your score on the multiple-choice section of the exam.

Key Ideas

✪ Familiarize yourself with the format of multiple-choice questions on the AP exam.
✪ Review strategies for answering multiple-choice questions.
✪ Learn the skill of eliminating incorrect answer choices.
✪ Learn.

Introduction to the Multiple-Choice Section of the Exam

What Should I Expect in Section I?

For this first section of the U.S. Government and Politics exam, you are allotted 80 minutes to answer 55 objective questions. These are questions that any student in any introductory government and politics class might know. It is not expected that everyone will know the answer to every question; however, you should try to answer as many questions as you can.

The AP U.S. Government and Politics questions always have four answer choices. Points are given for every correct answer. No points are given or deducted for incorrect or blank answers.

How Does the Scoring of the Multiple-Choice Section Work?

The multiple-choice section of the exam is taken on a scan sheet. The sheet is run through a computer that calculates the number of correct answers. This score would then be added to the free-response score for a composite score on the exam. The composite score would be equated to an AP score of 5, 4, 3, 2, or 1.

If I Don't Know the Answer, Should I Guess?

On the multiple-choice section of the test, no points are deducted for incorrect answers. Therefore, it is to your advantage to guess on every question when you are not sure of the correct answer.

Types of Multiple-Choice Questions

Multiple-choice questions are not written randomly. There are certain general formats you will encounter.

- **Quantitative Analysis Questions**
  This type of question involves the analysis and application of data. Included on the test will be questions that involve the following:
  o A bar graph
  o A line graph
  o A pie graph
  o A table

- **Qualitative Analysis Questions**
  This type of question involves the analysis and application of primary and secondary sources. Expect to encounter questions that involve the following:
  o Quotes from foundational documents and Supreme Court cases
  o Quotes from primary and secondary sources
  o A map
  o A political cartoon

- **Visual Analysis Questions**
  Many of the questions require visual analysis. As mentioned above these questions will be based on visuals like graphs, maps, cartoons, and infographics.

- **Concept Application Questions**
  These questions require you to apply political concepts through scenarios you are given.

- **Comparison Questions**
  These questions ask you to explain similarities and differences regarding political concepts or situations.

- **Knowledge-Based Questions**
  These questions require you to identify or define political principles, institutions, processes, policies, and behaviors.

There will be at least five sets of quantitative-analysis questions, with each set involving two or three questions based on a graph or table. There will also be at least five sets of qualitative-analysis questions, with each set containing two through four questions based on a quote, map, political cartoon, or the like. You can expect five comparison questions and several concept-application scenarios. In addition, there will be direct questions about the required foundational documents and Supreme Court cases.

Strategies for Answering the Multiple-Choice Questions

You probably have been answering multiple-choice questions most of your academic life, and you've probably figured out ways to deal with them. However, there may be some points you have not considered that will be helpful for this particular exam.

Starting Out

- **Take a quick look at the entire multiple-choice section.** This brief preview will show you what's ahead and help put your mind at ease—you needn't fear the unknown. Don't spend too much time previewing. Remember, this is a timed test.
- **Work in order.** This is a good approach: It's clear, and you won't lose your place on the scan sheet. Also, there may be a logic to working sequentially that will help you answer previous questions. But this is your call. If you are more comfortable skipping around the exam, you can do so. But don't be misled by the length or appearance of a question. There is no correlation between length or appearance and the difficulty of the question. If you are skipping around, be extra careful that you are marking your answers in the correct row.
- **Write in the exam booklet.** Mark it up; make it yours. Mark questions you want to come back to if you have time. Cross out answer choices you know are wrong when using the process of elimination. Interact with the test.

Attacking the Questions

- **Read the question carefully.** Don't try to guess at the question—read the *entire* question. Pay special attention and key terms.
- **Read *all* the answer choices.** Don't jump at the first answer choice. Slow down and really consider all the choices. You may find that your first choice is not the best or most appropriate answer choice. Also remember that all parts of an answer must be correct for it to be the correct choice.

Pacing Yourself

- **Maintain an awareness of time.** Wear a watch or put it directly in front of you on the desk. Always be aware of how much time you have left. If you are almost out of time and haven't finished the questions, mark in answer choices for all the remaining questions. There is no penalty for guessing, and you have a one-in-four chance of getting a question correct.
- **Work at a pace that is comfortable.** Keep moving ahead at a comfortable pace. You'll need to move quickly, but not so fast that you start missing answers that you know. Don't rush; there are no bonus points for finishing early.

- **Don't get bogged down on a question.** Every question is worth the same number of points, so don't spend too much time on one or two questions that bother you. Don't panic if you don't know the answer to a question; you can miss questions and still score a 5. Just do your best. If you are hung up on a question, take an educated guess and move on.
- **Practice pacing yourself before you take the test.** Test day should not be your first time taking the multiple-choice exam. You've probably been practicing timed exams in class. In addition, this book provides you with three opportunities to take timed practice tests. Use the practice exams to practice pacing yourself.

Using the Process of Elimination

The process of elimination is your primary tool if you don't know the answer to a question. Remember, the correct answer is right there in front of you. If you don't know which of the four choices it is, then you can work from the other direction, eliminating answer choices that you know are incorrect.

You're probably familiar with this strategy from previous multiple-choice tests you've taken. Here's how it specifically works on the AP U.S. Government and Politics exam:

1. Read the four choices.

2. If no choice immediately strikes you as correct, you can
   — eliminate those that are obviously wrong
   — eliminate those choices that are too narrow or too broad
   — eliminate illogical choices
   — eliminate answers that are synonymous (identical)

3. If two answers are close, do one *or* the other of the following:
   — Find the one that is general enough to cover all aspects of the question.
   — Find the one that is limited enough to be the detail the question is looking for.

4. If you still have two or more choices you cannot eliminate, make an educted guess. You have a wealth of skills and knowledge. A question or choice may trigger your memory. This may form the basis of your educated guess. Have confidence to use the educated guess as a valid technique.

Section II of the Exam: How to Approach the Free-Response Questions

IN THIS CHAPTER

Summary: Use these question-answering strategies to raise your score on the free-response questions.

Key Ideas

✪ Become familiar with the four types of questions in the free-response section of the exam.
✪ Get help tips that can improve your score on the free-response section of the test.
✪ Acquire strategies for responding to the free-response questions.
✪ Lean how the free-response answers are scored.

Introduction to the Free-Response Questions

The free-response section of the U.S. Government and Politics exam contains four questions. Each of the four questions is a specific type of question; these are described below:

- **Question 1: Concept Application Question**

  This question requires you to respond to a real-world, contemporary, political scenario. Here are the skills you can expect to use:
  - Analyze how the course content applies to the scenario.
  - Identify how the Constitution applies to the scenario and identify the part of the Constitution that applies.
  - Make connections and apply your knowledge from the course.

- **Question 2: Quantitative Analysis Question**

  This question will require you to interpret a graph, table, or chart. You will need to be able to:
  - Read and describe the data.
  - Identify a trend or pattern.
  - Compare and contrast the data; analyze the data.
  - Explain how the data relates to a political principle, institution, process, policy, or behavior.

- **Question 3: SCOTUS Comparison**

  For this question, you will need to compare a nonrequired Supreme Court case with a required Supreme Court case. You will need to be able to do the following:
  - Explain how information from the nonrequired case is relevant to the information from the required case.
  - Explain the constitutional applications of the cases.
  - Explain how the cases relate to a political principle, institution, process, or behavior.

- **Question 4: Argument Essay**

  This question requires the development of an argument in essay form, using evidence from one or more of the required foundational documents. In your essay you must do the following:
  - State a thesis or claim.
  - Develop a strong and consistent argument to support the thesis.
  - Provide evidence to support the argument from required documents.
  - Provide a second piece of evidence from another source to support the argument.
  - Explain how or why the evidence supports the thesis or claim.
  - Respond to an opposing/alternate perspective using refutation, concession, or rebuttal.

How Do I Prepare for the Free-Response Questions?

"You must be prepared to read with comprehension and write with consistency."
—JW, AP teacher

"Pay close attention to examples: You can use them in your essays."
—DC, AP student

You need to begin preparing for the free-response questions as soon as the course begins. Focus on your writing skills, and practice as if you were writing for the AP exam every time you are assigned an essay in your government and politics class. Determine your strengths and weaknesses, and work to correct areas of weakness. Don't worry, your teacher will probably give you plenty of opportunities to complete these types of questions.

- Broaden your knowledge base by reading your textbook and supplemental texts. They will give you basic information to draw from when writing the free-response answers. Do not skim the text—READ—paying attention to details and focusing on people, events, examples, and linkages between different political institutions and processes (for example, interactions between the branches of government or how the media influence lawmakers).
- Watch the news, and pay attention to current events relating to government and politics.
- Pay attention in class to lectures and discussions. Take notes and study them.

- Take advantage of practice writing whenever possible. Make sure your thoughts are well organized and coherent. Watch and correct grammar, spelling, and punctuation in classroom essays.
- Check out the free-response questions, rubrics, and sample scored student essays on the College Board website, www.apcentral.collegeboard.com. You will have to register to access the specific course sites, but it is worth your time.

Types of Free-Response Question Prompts

Free-response questions are generally straightforward and ask you to perform certain tasks. Understanding what the prompt is asking you to do will help you perform the task correctly.

Prompt Vocabulary

- analyze—examine each part of the whole in a systematic way; evaluate
- define—briefly tell what something is or means
- describe—create a mental picture by using details or examples
- discuss—give details about; illustrate with examples
- explain—make something clear by giving reasons or examples; tell how and why
- argue/defend/justify/support—give evidence to show why an idea or view is right or good
- categorize/classify—sort into groups according to a given set of traits or features
- compare and contrast—point out similarities (compare) and differences (contrast)
- determine cause and effect—decide what leads to an event or circumstance (cause) and what results from an event or circumstance (effect)
- evaluate/judge—determine the worth or wisdom of an opinion, belief, or idea

> *"Pay attention to vocabulary terms."*
> —AL, AP student

Responding to the Prompt

- Recognize the subject matter of the question. When you see "Congress," don't just start writing about Congress. Analyze what the question is asking about Congress.
- Recognize what task you are being asked to perform in relation to the question. Are you being asked to list, explain, describe, identify and explain, or explain and give examples? Often you will be asked to perform more than one task.
- Remember that there is a general order to the tasks within the question. Organize your response to answer the question or address the tasks in their order of appearance.

Developing the Free-Response Answers

STRATEGY

Strategies for Writing the Free-Response Answers

- Read the question carefully, in its entirety, and determine what you are being asked to write about. Analyze the question and identify the topics, issues, and key terms that define your task (define, discuss, explain). Underline key terms to focus your attention.
- Brainstorm ideas.
- Organize ideas and outline your response before you begin to write. Use the blank space in your test booklet to plan. (Brainstorming and outlining should take about five to eight minutes per question.)
- Write the essay. Include an introduction that restates the question, the factual information, evidence and examples, and a conclusion. Answer each part of the question in the

> *"Knowing how to evaluate provided me with confidence in my free-response answers."*
> —DK, AP student

order it was presented. Stick to your outline and keep sentences simple. If time is short, forget the introduction and conclusion and jump into the essay, using bulleted lists with explanations or an outline.

- Reread the question and your essay to determine if you answered the question or questions. NOTE: Many of the free-response questions will have several parts; make sure you answer them all.
- Proofread for grammar, spelling, and punctuation errors. Even though these errors will not count against you, they can make your essay harder to read and can make your answer less understandable.

Helpful Tips for Answering the Free-Response Questions

- **Don't** use words that you are uncomfortable using or not familiar with. Readers are not impressed if you use "big words" but don't understand what they mean or use them incorrectly.
- **Don't** try to "fake out" the reader. They are government professors and teachers. Trying to do this will *always* hurt you more than help you.
- **Don't** preach, moralize, editorialize, or use "cute" comments. Remember, you want the reader to think positively about your response.
- **Don't** "data dump" or create "laundry lists." Do not provide information (names, court cases, laws) without explanation or relevant link.
- **Do** write neatly and legibly. Write or print in blue or black ink (not pencil; it's harder to read) as clearly as you can.
- **Do** use correct grammar, spelling, and punctuation. They make your response much easier to score.
- **Do** answer all questions and all parts of each question. You may answer the questions in any order. Answer the questions you feel you know best, first. That way, if you run out of time and don't finish, no harm is done. Even though the questions are graded on different scales, they are weighted equally and together count for half your total score. (Each question is 12.5 percent of your total score.)
- **Do** support your response with specific evidence and examples. If the question asks for examples, supply not only the example but also a discussion of how that example illustrates the concept. Provide however many examples the question asks for; hypothetical examples may sometimes be used, if they are backed up with facts.
- **Do** pay attention to dates and terms like "modern." When time frames are used, keep your evidence and examples within that time frame (modern presidency would not include Jefferson, Jackson, Lincoln).
- **Do** stop when you finish your responses. If you ramble on after you have answered the question completely, you might contradict yourself, causing the reader to question your answer.
- **Do** proofread.

What Are the Pitfalls of the Free-Response Questions?

The free-response questions can be a double-edged sword. They can cause some students to experience test anxiety (what's "free" in the free-response?). At the same time, they can cause other students to suffer from overconfidence because of the open nature of these questions.

"The free-response essays often involve the student choosing between options—look at all options before you begin writing."
—LA, AP teacher

"Be sure your free-response essay is brief and gets directly to the point."
—JB, AP student

*"Remember, on free-response questions, AP means answer **all parts** of the question."*
—MN, AP teacher

The greatest pitfall is *the failure to plan.* Remember to pace yourself; no one question is more important than another. *Plan your strategy for answering each question, and stick to it.* Don't ramble in vague and unsupported generalities. Rambling may cause you to contradict yourself or make mistakes. Even though your time is limited, creating a general outline may help you in this section.

Scoring the Free-Response Answers

Readers look for responses that answer the questions asked. They assign points of the basis of specific criteria called rubrics.

What Is a Rubric?

Rubrics are scoring guidelines used to evaluate your performance on each of the free-response questions. They are based on the sum of points earned by meeting the preestablished criteria.

How Are Rubrics Developed and Applied?

The number of points students may earn for each free-response question is assigned by members of the Test Development Committee. The chief faculty consultant, exam leaders, and question leaders develop preliminary rubrics for each question based on these points. These rubrics are sampled against actual student responses and revised if necessary. Table leaders are then trained using these standards. When the reading begins, table leaders train the AP readers at their table (usually five to seven readers) in the use of the rubric for that particular question. Once the reading begins, the rubrics are not changed.

Common Characteristics of Rubrics

Since each free-response question is different, each scoring rubric will differ. There are, however, several characteristics common to all U.S. Government and Politics rubrics. Each rubric:

- Addresses all aspects and tasks of the question. Points are awarded for each task or response requested—one point for a correct identification and two points for the discussion.
- Contains evaluative criteria. These distinguish what is acceptable from what is not acceptable in the answer; for example, accept AARP as an interest group but do not accept the Democratic Party.
- Has a scoring strategy, a scale of points to be awarded for successfully completing a task. For example, identification of an interest group is worth one point.
- Awards points for correct responses; points are not deducted.
- Can be applied clearly and consistently by different scorers. If more than one reader were to score a particular response, it would receive the same score, based on the same standards.

STEP 4

Review the Knowledge You Need to Score High

Foundations of
American Democracy

CHAPTER 6

Constitutional Foundations

IN THIS CHAPTER

Summary: Government is the institution that creates public policy. The democratic government of the United States traces its roots from the Greco-Roman era to the Enlightenment. The key founding documents of U.S. government, the Declaration of Independence and the Constitution, set forth the principles that define the character of American democracy. The U.S. Constitution is a flexible document that provides for its own changes, or amendments. Among the key principles of U.S. government inherent in the Constitution are federalism, separation of powers, and a system of checks and balances. The power of the Supreme Court broadened with the establishment of judicial review in *Marbury v. Madison* (1803).

Key Terms and Concepts

government
politics
public policy
democracy
direct democracy
representative democracy
participatory democracy
pluralist theory
elite theory
bureaucratic theory
hyperpluralism
social contract
natural rights
Declaration of
  Independence

limited government
popular sovereignty
republicanism
Articles of Confederation
Shay's Rebellion
federal system
Virginia Plan
New Jersey Plan
Grand Committee
Great (Connecticut)
  Compromise
Three-Fifths Compromise
Commerce and Slave
  Trade Compromise
electoral college

ratification
Federalists
Federalist Papers
Federalist No. 10
Anti-Federalists
Bill of Rights
Brutus No. 1
constitution
separation of powers
checks and balances
federalism
Federalsit No. 51
amendments
judicial review
Marbury v. Madison

Principles of Government

What Is Government? What is Politics?

In any nation a **government** is composed of the formal and informal institutions, people, and processes used to create and conduct public policy. Political scientist Harold Laswell defined **politics** as "who gets what, when, and how." Think of government as the formal rules of a game, and politics as the informal ways in which the game might be played. Government and politics are methods by which a country develops public policy. **Public policy** is the exercise of government power in doing those things necessary to maintain legitimate authority and control over society.

Purposes of Government

Every nation must decide for itself what goals will be translated into public policy and the methods by which those goals will be translated. The Preamble of the United States Constitution addresses the goals of public policy for the United States:

- forming a more perfect union: creation of a strong union of the states, while also maintaining state sovereignty
- establishing justice: reasonable, fair, and impartial law
- insuring domestic tranquility: preservation of public order
- providing for the common defense: protection and maintenance of national defense
- promoting the general welfare: providing public services and economic health of the nation
- securing the blessings of liberty: promoting individual freedoms

Forms of Government

Greek philosopher Aristotle attempted to classify governments based on the number of individuals who participated in making political decisions: rule by one, rule by the few, or rule by the many. His early classification system is still useful in describing governments today:

- *anarchy*—Lack of government.
- *autocracy*—Rule by one.
  - absolute monarchy—Ruler gains power through inheritance; there are no restrictions on the ruler's power.
  - constitutional monarchy—Ruler gains power through inheritance; formal restrictions limit power, often restricting the monarch to ceremonial status.
  - dictatorship—Ruler seizes power, keeps power by force, and restricts opposition to regime; no restrictions on dictator's power.
- *oligarchy*—Rule by a few.
  - aristocracy: Rule by the elite, usually determined by social status or wealth.
  - theocracy: Rule by religious leaders.
- *democracy*—Rule by the people.
  - **direct democracy**—Citizens meet and make decisions about public policy issues.
  - **representative democracy**—Citizens choose officials (representatives) who make decisions about public policy. This is the system in place in most "democratic" nations.

Theories of Democratic Government

Theories of democratic government are theories about who has power and influence over public policy and decision making at the local, state, and national levels of government.

- ***participatory democratic theory***—Government depends on the consent of the governed, which may be given directly or through representatives often referred to as traditional government because it emphasizes citizen participation.

- *pluralist theory*—Interest groups compete in the political arena, with each promoting its policy preferences through organized efforts. Conflict among groups may result, requiring bargaining and compromise (Robert Dahl).
- *elite theory*—A small number of powerful elites (corporate leaders, top military officers, government leaders) form an upper class, which rules in its own self-interest (C. Wright Mills).
- *bureaucratic theory*—The hierarchical structure and standardized procedures of modern governments allow bureaucrats, who carry out the day-to-day workings of government, to hold the real power over public policy (Max Weber).
- *hyperpluralism*—Democracy is a system of many groups having so much strength that government is often "pulled" in numerous directions at the same time, causing gridlock and ineffectiveness.

Origins of American Government

Influences on American Government

In 1607 the British established a permanent colony at Jamestown, Virginia. Early colonists brought ideas and traditions that would form the basis of American government as a part of the British colonial empire, and as an independent United States. Two of the early traditions were limited government and representative government.

During the Enlightenment Era, philosophers such as John Locke supported the concept of a social contract. Locke viewed the **social contract** as a voluntary agreement between the government and the governed. In *Two Treatises on Civil Government* (1689), Locke argued that people are born with **natural rights** to life, liberty, and property (natural law). Locke also believed that governments are created to support those rights, but that if the government fails to do so, the people may choose to change their government. Thomas Jefferson adopted these ideas in the **Declaration of Independence**. Another Enlightenment thinker, Montesquieu, wrote about the need for branches of government.

The United States government today is based on ideas of:

- **limited government**—Government's power is limited by the rule of law, which includes the Constitution and the laws, which are passed in implementation of that Constitution; this means that government is not all-powerful.
- **natural rights**—Basic rights that are guaranteed to all people and which cannot be denied or restricted by any government or individual.
- **popular sovereignty**—People are the source of all governmental power; ultimate power and final authority rest with "we the people" or all the citizens.
- **republicanism**—A system in which the people give authority to government and exercise their power by delegating it to representatives chosen by them through the election process.
- **social contract**—A voluntary agreement among the members of society and the government which defines and limits the rights and duties between the government and the governed.

Colonial Experiences

From 1607 to 1776, the American colonies were in a continuous state of political self-development. This was due to several factors, such as the long distance from England, indifference of the colonists to the king's authority, and the disputed political authority in England. As the colonies developed, they made the most of their English heritage but made changes to create a new and unique style of government. This new government was founded on the principles of equality, liberty, and limited government.

- *Difficulties with Britain*—As the colonies grew, so did problems with Britain. Prior to 1750, the British provided defense and manufactured goods for the colonies. The colonies in return provided raw materials and markets for manufactured goods. Britain allowed the colonies to control their own internal affairs. After the French and Indian War (1756–1763), however, the British government expected the colonies to help pay the cost of the war and pay for their own future defense. The British government began enforcing taxes already levied and passed new taxes to replenish the king's treasury. These new taxes included the Sugar Act (1764), the Stamp Act (1765), and the Townshend Acts (1767). As the colonists began protesting, violence and conflict began to break out between the colonies and Britain. After the Boston Massacre (1770) and Boston Tea Party (1772), the British government passed a series of punishing acts collectively known as the Coercive or Intolerable Acts. In response the colonies began to unite in an effort to influence the British government and to express dissatisfaction with British policies.
- *Continental Congresses*—The First Continental Congress included delegates from 12 colonies (all except Georgia) who met in Philadelphia in 1774. This Continental Congress resolved to send a Declaration of Rights to the king in protest of Britain's policies. They also agreed to meet again the following year. The Second Continental Congress began meeting in May 1775, more than one month after the battles of Lexington and Concord. The Second Continental Congress became America's first national government. Delegates from all 13 colonies were present, among them John Hancock, George Washington, Ben Franklin, Thomas Jefferson, John Adams, and Patrick Henry. The Second Continental Congress created the Continental Army and appointed George Washington as its commander-in-chief, borrowed money from France and the Netherlands, created a monetary system, made treaties with foreign governments, and commissioned the writing of the Declaration of Independence and the **Articles of Confederation**.

Declaration of Independence

The Declaration of Independence is mainly the work of Thomas Jefferson with the help of John Adams and Benjamin Franklin. The principles are largely based on the works of Enlightenment philosopher John Locke.

- "All men are created equal."
- People are born with inalienable rights given by God, not the king. Among those rights are "life, liberty, and the pursuit of happiness." This statement by Jefferson is based on John Locke's "life, liberty and property."
- Governments are created by men, so Jefferson supported the notion of "consent of the governed."
- If a government did not act on behalf of the people, the people have not only a right, but a duty, to "alter or abolish" the government.

The Declaration of Independence can be divided into three parts: a theory of government based on social contract and natural rights, a list of grievances against the king and "others" (Parliament), and a statement of colonial unity and separation from Britain based on a resolution proposed by Richard Henry Lee of Virginia that "these United Colonies are, and of right ought to be Free and Independent States." The Declaration of Independence supports and provides the foundation for popular sovereignty, the idea that the people are the ultimate source of government's power. The Declaration of Independence was approved by the Second Continental Congress on July 4, 1776, proclaiming the separation of the thirteen British colonies in North America from the British government, therefore, creating the United States.

The impact of the Declaration of Independence can be seen and felt within the United States and around the world. Several portions of the United States Constitution and its amendments address grievances Jefferson levied against the king.

Articles of Confederation

The Articles of Confederation (1781–1789), written by the Second Continental Congress in November 1777, became the first national constitution for governing the American states. The Articles created a confederation or "league of friendship" among the states. The Confederation would be composed of a relatively weak national government with a unicameral legislature. Writers of the Articles did not want to replicate the strong national government of Great Britain. Congress would have limited powers such as borrowing money, creating a national army and navy, declaring war, creating post offices, and signing treaties with foreign governments. Congress was not given the power to tax, draft soldiers for military service, or regulate commerce. There was no national executive or judicial branch under the Articles of Confederation. Each state was equal, with one vote, regardless of population or size. The votes of 9 of the 13 states were required for legislation to pass the Confederation Congress; amending the Articles of Confederation required a unanimous vote.

The weaknesses evident in the Articles of Confederation allowed the states to focus on their own powers. With no central government to control them, the states taxed each other, printed their own money, made treaties with foreign governments, and often refused to uphold the laws of the Confederation government. The government's inability to tax, its lack of enforcement powers over the states, and the lack of a centralized military led to economic chaos and violence, resulting in conferences at Mt. Vernon and Annapolis. These meetings proved to be unsuccessful, and eventually a rebellion of farmers in Massachusetts **(Shays' Rebellion)** led to the calling of a Constitutional Convention.

Constitutional Convention

The Constitutional Convention was convened in Philadelphia in May of 1787, for the purpose of revising the Articles of Confederation. (See Figure 6-1.) Delegates representing all the states except Rhode Island attended. While waiting for the delegates to arrive and the convention to officially begin, James Madison sketched out his Virginia Plan, based on the idea of a strong national government. Once the convention began, George Washington was chosen to preside over the convention.

- Very early in the convention, the delegates decided that they would write a new constitution instead of revising the Articles of Confederation.
- The delegates agreed that the new government would be a republic, a **federal system**, and would be composed of three branches (executive, legislative, judicial).
- Several plans, including the **Virginia Plan** and the **New Jersey Plan**, were presented to the delegates. (See Figure 6-2.)

Compromises

- The Constitutional Convention debated for weeks over how representatives to a national legislature should be chosen. The report of the Grand Committee was an effort to find a compromise between the positions of the large and small states. The convention adopted the **Great (Connecticut) Compromise** based on this report. Congress would be a bicameral legislature, with representation in the lower house based on the population of the state and equal representation of the states in the upper house.

Weaknesses of the Articles of Confederation and Constitutional Remedies

Weaknesses of the Articles of Confederation	How the Constitution Remedied Weaknesses
Articles created a "league of friendship" between the states	The Constitution created a federal system of government between the national and state levels
Congress could not tax; it could only request contributions from the states	National government was given the power to tax
Congress could not regulate interstate trade or foreign commerce	Congress was given the power to regulate commerce between the states and with foreign nations
No separate executive to enforce the acts of Congress	Article II created a separate executive department whose job is to enforce the laws of Congress
No national judiciary to handle state disputes	Article III created a national judiciary with a Supreme Court and lower courts as established by Congress
States and the national government had the authority to coin money	Only the national government has the authority to coin money
Each state had one vote, regardless of size or population	States are represented based on population in the House of Representatives and equality in the Senate
Nine of thirteen states required to pass legislation	Bills need a simple majority in both houses of Congress
Unanimous consent required to amend the Articles of Confederation	Two-thirds of Congress and three-fourths of the states are necessary to amend the Constitution

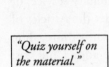
KEY IDEA

"Quiz yourself on the material."
—JS, AP student

Figure 6-1

Comparison of the Virginia and New Jersey Plans

Virginia Plan	New Jersey Plan
Bicameral legislature —lower house elected by the people —upper house chosen by lower house from nominees submitted by state legislatures	Unicameral legislature —representatives chosen by state legislatures —each state receives one vote
Representation in each house based on population and/or monetary contributions to the national government by the state	Representation in House would be equal among the states
Single executive chosen by legislative branch, limited to one term only, could veto legislative acts, removed by Congress	Plural executives chosen by legislative branch, no veto powers, removal by the states
Judges chosen by legislative branch	Judges appointed for life by the executive

Figure 6-2

- A second compromise concerned the counting of slaves for the purpose of determining population for representation in Congress and for taxation. Southern states wanted slaves to be counted for representation but not taxation. Northern states wanted slaves counted for taxation but not for representation. The **Three-Fifths Compromise** resolved this issue: Each state would count three-fifths of its slave population for purposes of determining both representation and taxation.

- The **Commerce and Slave Trade Compromise** resolved other differences between southern and northern states. Congress was prohibited from taxing exports from the states and from banning the slave trade for a period of 20 years.

- Numerous other compromises were made at the Constitutional Convention concerning the executive and judicial branches as well as the electoral process for choosing a chief executive. The founding fathers established the concept of the **electoral college** in the Constitution as a compromise between election of the President by a vote in Congress and election of the President by a popular vote of qualified citizens.

Ratification of the Constitution

Although the delegates at the convention signed the Constitution on September 17, 1787, it still had to be ratified by 9 of the 13 states before it could go into effect. In each state, special ratifying conventions would be held over the next two years. Debate over **ratification** divided citizens into Federalist and Anti-Federalist positions (Figure 6-3).

- The **Federalists** stressed the weaknesses of the Articles of Confederation and the government it created. They supported a stronger central government with expanded legislative powers. The Federalist cause was helped by James Madison, Alexander Hamilton, and John Jay in a collection of 85 essays published in the New York newspapers under the name "Publius." (Hamilton wrote 51, Madison wrote 26, Jay wrote 5, and Hamilton and Madison coauthored 3 of these essays.) These *Federalist Papers* defended the new government created under the Constitution and even today provide insight into the framers' original intent.

Federalists Versus Anti-Federalists

KEY IDEA

Federalists	Anti-Federalists
Favored Constitution	Opposed Constitution
Led by James Madison, Alexander Hamilton, John Jay	Led by Patrick Henry, Richard Henry Lee, George Mason, Samuel Adams
Stressed weaknesses of Articles; strong government needed to protect nation and solve domestic problems	Wanted strong state governments; feared a strong national government
Checks and balances would protect against abuses	Created a strong executive similar to monarchy
Protection of property rights	Wanted fewer limits on popular participation
Constitution is a bill of rights with limitations and reserved powers for the states; state constitutions already had protections in bill of rights	Wanted a bill of rights to protect citizens against government

Figure 6-3

- **Federalist No. 10,** written by James Madison, argues that the union under the new constitution is a safeguard against domestic faction and insurrection. Madison begins by defining factions as groups of people who gather together to protect and promote their special economic interests and political opinions. He then argues that there are only two ways to deal with factions: either eliminate factions by removing their causes, or limit their impact by controlling their effects. Madison believed that any damage caused by factions could be controlled by the government under the new constitution.
- The **Anti-Federalists** believed that the new Constitution gave too much power to the national government at the expense of the state governments. Another objection was the lack of a **Bill of Rights,** ensuring fundamental liberties.
- **Brutus No. 1** was written by Anti-Federalist Robert Yates of New York in 1787, in an attempt to convince the people of New York to not ratify the Constitution. Like other opponents of the proposed Constitution, Brutus believed that republics had to be small and homogeneous—not large and diverse—in order to be successful. Allowing the government too much power would result in the people losing their liberties. Along with many other Anti-Federalists, Brutus argued that a Bill of Rights was a critical part in the protection of the people's liberties.

The United States Constitution

A **constitution** details the structure of a government. The Constitution of the United States is the oldest national constitution in use today. Although the Constitution is relatively short, it describes the structure and powers of the national government as well as the relationship between the national and state governments.

Basic Principles Within the Constitution

Embodied within the Constitution are the basic principles of:

KEY IDEA

- *limited government*—belief that government is not all-powerful; government has only those powers given to it
- *popular sovereignty*—the people are the source of government's authority
- *separation of powers*—power is separated among three branches of government; each has its own powers and duties and is independent of and equal to the other branches
- *checks and balances*—each branch is subject to restraints by the other two branches (see Figure 6-4)
- *federalism*—a division of governmental powers between the national government and the states

Checks and Balances

The constitutional system of checks and balances prevents one branch of the federal government from becoming more powerful than the other two.

- **Federalist No. 51,** written by James Madison, argues that the government under the new Constitution will not become too powerful because the separation of powers will keep each branch in check.
- Madison claims that the legislative branch in a republic is naturally the most powerful and that the executive is weaker.

- Madison sees it as human nature to increase one's power, therefore there must be safeguards to protect against a person or group from seizing too much power.
- Concentration of power in a single person or group is a threat to the liberty of the people. Madison accepts that men cannot be trusted with unchecked power.

The Constitution may be divided into three major parts: the Preamble, articles, and **amendments**.

Preamble

The opening paragraph of the Constitution is called the Preamble. It lists the six goals for American government and explains why the Constitution was written.

> *We the People of the United States, in Order to form a more perfect Union, establish Justice, insure domestic Tranquility, provide for the common defense, promote the general Welfare, and secure the Blessings of Liberty to ourselves and our Posterity, do ordain and establish this Constitution for the United States of America.*

Articles

The Constitution is divided into seven articles. Each of the articles covers a specific topic. Article I is the longest, devoted to the legislative branch of government.

- Article I—Legislative Branch
- Article II—Executive Branch
- Article III—Judicial Branch
- Article IV—Intergovernmental Relationships
- Article V—Amendment Process
- Article VI—Supremacy of the Constitution
- Article VII—Ratification Process

Formal Amendment Process

One major weakness of the Articles of Confederation was the amendment process, which required unanimous approval for amendments to become effective. The framers of the Constitution anticipated the need to change the Constitution and provided a process to amend the Constitution (Article V) that required both state and national action. Amending the Constitution requires proposal, a national function, and ratification, a state function. Amendments may be proposed in Congress by two methods and ratified by two methods, creating four possible methods for formally amending the Constitution:

- proposed by two-thirds vote of each house of Congress and ratified by three-quarters of the state legislatures (used 26 times)
- proposed by two-thirds vote of each house of Congress and ratified by special conventions in at least three-quarters of the states (used once, to ratify the Twenty-First Amendment)
- proposed by a national convention called by Congress at the request of two-thirds of the state legislatures and ratified by three-quarters of the state legislatures (never used)
- proposed by a national convention called by Congress at the request of two-thirds of the state legislatures and ratified by special conventions in at least three-quarters of the states (never used)

Formal Amendments

Formal amendments are written changes to the Constitution. They add to, change the wording of, or delete language from the Constitution. Only 27 formal amendments have been

Separation of Powers and Checks and Balances

Legislative Branch (Passes Laws)

Over Executive:
May override president's veto by two-thirds vote of both houses
May impeach and remove president from office
Senate may refuse to confirm presidential appointments or ratify treaties
Creates executive agencies and programs
Appropriates funds

Over Judiciary:
Creates lower federal courts
Sets salaries of federal judges
May refuse to confirm judicial appointments
May propose constitutional amendments which overrule court decisions
May impeach and remove federal judges

Executive Branch (Enforces Laws)

Over Legislature:
President may veto acts of Congress
President may call special sessions of Congress
President may recommend legislation

Over Judiciary:
President appoints federal judges
President may grant reprieves and pardons to federal offenders
May refuse to enforce court decisions

Judicial Branch (Interprets Laws)

Over Legislature:
May rule legislative acts unconstitutional
Chief justice presides over impeachment of president

Over Executive:
May rule executive actions unconstitutional

Figure 6-4

added to the Constitution since its adoption. (See Figure 6-5.) The first 10 amendments, the Bill of Rights, were added in 1791.

Informal Amendment Process

Although the United States Constitution has been formally changed only 27 times, there have been many changes in the way in which the American government operates. Most of those changes have come about through the informal amendment process and do not involve

Constitutional Amendments

- Amendment 1—guarantees freedom of religion, speech, press, assembly, and petition
- Amendment 2—ensures the right to keep and bear arms
- Amendment 3—sets conditions for quartering of troops in private homes
- Amendment 4—regulates search, seizure, and warrants
- Amendment 5—addresses protections against self-incrimination, guarantees of due process, eminent domain, and grand jury indictment for capital crimes
- Amendment 6—guarantees rights to a speedy, public trial and an impartial jury; to confront witnesses; and to have an attorney
- Amendment 7—preserves the right to a jury trial in civil cases
- Amendment 8—ensures no excessive bails or fines, nor cruel and unusual punishment
- Amendment 9—cites unenumerated rights of the people
- Amendment 10—reserves powers of the states and the people
- Amendment 11—restricts lawsuits against states
- Amendment 12—provides for election of president and vice-president by separate ballot in electoral college
- Amendment 13—abolishes slavery
- Amendment 14—guarantees rights of citizenship, due process, and equal protection
- Amendment 15—guarantees citizens' right to vote regardless of race, color, or previous condition of servitude
- Amendment 16—authorizes income tax
- Amendment 17—establishes direct election of senators by popular vote
- Amendment 18—prohibits intoxicating liquors
- Amendment 19—establishes women's suffrage
- Amendment 20—sets terms and sessions of executive and legislative branches; "lame duck"
- Amendment 21—repeals prohibition (18th amendment)
- Amendment 22—limits presidential terms of office
- Amendment 23—allows for voting rights in District of Columbia in presidential elections
- Amendment 24—abolishes poll taxes
- Amendment 25—addresses presidential succession, disability, and vice-presidential vacancies
- Amendment 26—gives 18-year-olds the right to vote
- Amendment 27—addresses congressional pay

Figure 6-5

actually changing the wording of the Constitution. Informal changes in the Constitution may occur in the following ways:

- *legislative actions*—Congress has passed various acts that have altered or made clear the meaning of the Constitution. For example, under Article III Congress is given the authority to create lower courts, which they did through the Judiciary Act of 1789.
- *executive actions*—The manner in which presidents use their powers can create informal amendments and expand presidential authority. The use of executive agreements rather than treaties allows the president to bypass the Senate.
- *judicial interpretation/**judicial review***—The people who serve as judges and the times in which they serve affect how courts interpret laws. The concept of judicial review resulted from ***Marbury v. Madison*** (1803); it is not mentioned in the Constitution.
- *custom and usage*—Traditions that have been incorporated into the political system and which have lasted over time have changed the meaning of the Constitution. Senatorial courtesy in the Senate and the "no-third-term" tradition in the presidency (until the Twenty-Second Amendment made it part of the Constitution) are examples.

Marbury v. Madison (1803)

In the election of 1800 political parties played an active role. Federalists supported John Adams, and Democratic-Republicans supported Thomas Jefferson. At the conclusion of the election, Adams and the Federalists had lost control of the presidency and Congress. In an effort to retain some control in the government, the "lame duck" Federalist Congress created numerous new judicial positions, which outgoing President Adams attempted to fill. Late into the night prior to Jefferson's inauguration, Adams was still signing the commissions of the "midnight appointments" which the secretary of state was to deliver. Not all the commissions were delivered, and when Jefferson took office, he ordered the commissions withheld, intending to make his own appointments. William Marbury expected to receive a commission as a justice of the peace for the District of Columbia. He petitioned the Supreme Court to issue a writ of mandamus (allowed under the Judiciary Act of 1791) ordering Secretary of State James Madison to deliver the commission to Marbury and several others. The Supreme Court under Chief Justice John Marshall ruled that although Marbury was entitled to the commission, the Supreme Court would not order Madison to give it to him because the Court did not have authority under the Constitution to decide this type of case, and that the portion of the Judiciary Act of 1791 that allowed the Court to hear these cases was unconstitutional. This case established the principle of **judicial review** and was the first time the Court declared an act of Congress unconstitutional.

› Review Questions

Multiple-Choice Questions

1. Which of the following is the best example of checks and balances as it functions today?
   (A) The congressional veto
   (B) A declaration of war by Congress
   (C) The appointment of the Speaker of the House
   (D) The ratification of treaties by the Senate

2. Which of the following documents best describes a government based on unity, natural rights, and the social contract theory?
   (A) Articles of Confederation
   (B) Declaration of Independence
   (C) Mayflower Compact
   (D) U.S. Constitution

3. The original purpose of the Constitutional Convention was to
   (A) write a new constitution
   (B) review the problems of the state governments
   (C) revise the Articles of Confederation
   (D) deal with the issue of slavery

4. Compared to government under the Articles of Confederation, the Constitution
   (A) is harder to amend
   (B) created a league of friendship among the states
   (C) created a unitary system of government
   (D) called for separation of powers among the three branches of government

5. Which of the following was NOT a weakness of government under the Articles of Confederation?
   (A) The national judiciary resolved arguments between the states.
   (B) Congress lacked the power to tax.
   (C) It lacked a national judiciary.
   (D) It was unable to control commercial interests.

6. Slavery and the taxation of exports were important topics to the Founding Fathers. Which compromise describes how the Founding Fathers resolved both of these issues?
   (A) Great Compromise
   (B) Commerce and Slave Trade Compromise
   (C) Electoral Compromise
   (D) Three-Fifths Compromise

7. Those who support the pluralist theory of democracy believe that
   (A) government depends on the "consent of the governed"
   (B) interest groups compete to promote their preferences
   (C) democracy is based on choosing officials to run the government
   (D) a small number of powerful corporate and military leaders rule in their own self-interest

8. The Supreme Court's decision in *Marbury v. Madison* (1803)
   (A) supported the concept of national supremacy
   (B) established the principle of judicial review
   (C) allowed Congress to amend the Constitution
   (D) strengthened the powers of the states

9. The Bill of Rights includes
   (A) the Preamble
   (B) the Articles of Confederation
   (C) the articles of the Constitution
   (D) the first 10 amendments

10. Amending the Constitution is a multi-step process. Which of the following steps are required to amend the Constitution?
    (A) proposal at the national level
    (B) proposal at the state level
    (C) presidential signature
    (D) congressional ratification

Use the infographic below to answer the question 11.

Federalists	Anti-Federalists
Favored Constitution	Opposed Constitution
Led by James Madison, Alexander Hamilton, John Jay	Led by Patrick Henry, Richard Henry Lee, George Mason, Samuel Adams
Stressed weaknesses of Articles; strong government needed to protect nation and solve domestic problems	Wanted strong state governments; feared a strong national government
Checks and balances would protect against abuses	Created a strong executive similar to monarchy
Protection of property rights	Wanted fewer limits on popular participation
Constitution is a bill of rights with limitations and reserved powers for the states; state constitutions already had protections in bill of rights	Wanted a bill of rights to protect citizens against government

11. Which of the following best describes the positions of the Federalists and Anti-Federalists regarding the powers given to the national government under the proposed U.S. Constitution?
    (A) The Federalists wanted a Bill of Rights to protect the states and the people, while the Anti-Federalists wanted the national government to be stronger than the state governments.
    (B) The Federalists wanted a stronger national government and weaker state governments, while the Anti-Federalists wanted a weaker national government and stronger state governments.
    (C) The Anti-Federalists wanted a stronger national government and weaker state governments, while the Federalists wanted a weaker national government and stronger state governments.
    (D) The Anti-Federalists wanted checks and balances to counter the stronger state governments, while the Federalists wanted the protection of property rights through a Bill of Rights.

Free-Response Question

12. One major weakness of the Articles of Confederation was the amendment process, which required unanimous approval for amendments to become effective. The Founding Fathers anticipated the need to change the Constitution and provided a process to amend the Constitution.
    (A) Identify the two steps involved in the formal amendment process.
    (B) Describe two informal methods that have been used to change the meaning of the Constitution.
    (C) Explain why the informal amendment process has been used more often than the formal amendment process.

› Answers and Explanations

1. **D.** A congressional (legislative) veto (A) is unconstitutional and therefore not a check. The power to declare war (B) is a congressional power under Article I, Section 8. While some may consider the Congress's power to declare war a check on the president, it is no longer considered an effective check on the president's powers since all military engagements since World War II have been conducted without a declaration of war. The Speaker of the House is elected by members of the House (C).

2. **B.** The Declaration of Independence was based on the writings of John Locke and his theory of a social contract between government and the governed. The document unified the colonies to fight for independence by advancing the ideas of natural law, which states that there are certain rights that government cannot take away from the people. The Mayflower Compact (C) was based on the consent of the governed, but it did not enumerate natural rights. The U.S. Constitution (D) reflects the ideals of unity and the consent of the governed, but does not specifically define the concepts of natural rights and the social contract theory as the Declaration does. The Articles of Confederation (A) did not specifically address the concepts of natural rights and the social contract.

3. **C.** Because of the problems among the states under the Articles of Confederation, the Constitutional Convention was convened to revise the Articles and to strengthen the power of the government. This convention dealt with the problems of the national government and not those of the states (B). Neither was the convention called to deal with the slavery issue (D) nor to write an entirely new plan of government (A).

4. **D.** The Constitution created a federal system of government, allowed for an easier amendment process. The Articles created a unitary government (C) and a league of friendship among the states (B).

5. **A.** Under the Articles of Confederation, there was no national judiciary. State courts resolved differences among the states. The remaining answer choices are correct.

6. **B.** Differences between northern and southern interests at the Constitutional Convention led to a compromise concerning the slave trade and the taxation of exports from the states. The Commerce and Slave Trade Compromise prohibited Congress from ending the slave trade for a period of 20 years and prohibited the taxation of exports from the states. The Great (Connecticut) Compromise (A) resolved the question of representation in Congress. The Three-Fifths Compromise (D) counted slaves as three-fifths of a person for purposes of taxation and representation in Congress. Another compromise created the electoral college (C).

7. **B.** Robert Dahl's pluralist theory is based upon the idea of competing interest groups vying for power. Choices (A) and (C) describe traditional democratic theory. Choice (D) represents the elite theory.

8. **B.** *Marbury v. Madison* established the principle of judicial review, allowing the courts to determine the constitutionality of acts of Congress.

9. **D.** The Bill of Rights, adopted in 1791, includes the first 10 amendments to the Constitution. The Preamble sets forth the purposes of the Constitution (A). The articles are the sections of the Constitution (C). The Articles of Confederation (B) predated the Constitution.

10. **A.** Article V of the Constitution outlines the formal amendment process, which includes congressional proposal of amendments at the national level and state ratification of amendments.

11. **B.** The Federalists wanted a stronger national government and weaker state governments, while the Anti-Federalists wanted a weaker national government and stronger state governments. The Anti-Federalists wanted a Bill of Rights (A). Answer C is the opposite of answer A. The Federalists believed that the Constitution itself was a Bill of Rights, and therefore a separate document was not needed (D).

12. **A.** The two steps in the formal amendment process are proposal and ratification. Proposal occurs at the national level, with a proposal by two-thirds of each house of Congress or the calling for a national convention by Congress at the request of two-thirds of the states. Ratification is by three-fourths of the state legislatures or three-fourths of the states in special conventions.

B. Informal methods of amending the Constitution include legislative actions, executive actions, judicial interpretation/review, and custom or usage. Legislative action includes acts passed by Congress. Executive actions are ways in which the president use his powers. Judicial interpretation/review is the way in which the courts interpret the laws and the Constitution. Custom and usage are traditions incorporated into the political system.

C. The informal amendment process has been used more often than the formal amendment process because the supermajorities that are required to propose and ratify an amendment are difficult to obtain. This is demonstrated by the fact that the Constitution has been formally amended only 27 times in more than 200 years. Informal methods such as court decisions and legislation do not require supermajorities and are therefore far easier to accomplish.

〉 Rapid Review

- Political scientist Harold Laswell defined government as "who gets what, when, and how."
- Every nation has defined public policy goals. The United States defines its goals in the Preamble of the Constitution.
- Aristotle's methods of classifying governments can still be used today.
- Modern theories about democratic government include traditional democratic theory, pluralist theory, elitist theory, bureaucratic theory, and hyperpluralism.
- The ancient Greeks and Romans, Enlightenment philosophers such as John Locke, British documents, and colonial experiences influenced the establishment of American government.
- The Declaration of Independence was a statement of colonial unity and a justification for separation from Britain.
- The Articles of Confederation, the first national constitution, created a "league of friendship" among the states. This weak national government failed to solve the postwar problems of the United States, and its weaknesses led to the writing of the U.S. Constitution.
- The Constitutional Convention, called to revise the Articles of Confederation, realized the need to create a new form of government with broader powers. The resulting Constitution created a federal system of three branches of government, with checks and balances.
- Various plans for the new government resulted in a series of compromises, including the Great (Connecticut) Compromise, Three-Fifths Compromise, Commerce and Slave Trade Compromise, and a compromise creating an electoral college to elect the President and Vice President.
- Debates over ratification of the Constitution led to the creation of the Federalists and Anti-Federalists.
- The Constitution is composed of the Preamble, seven articles, and the 27 formal amendments.
- The Constitution is a plan of government based on several basic principles: limited government, popular sovereignty, separation of powers, checks and balances, and federalism.
- Formal amendments are added to the Constitution through the process outlined in Article V. The proposal stage is accomplished at the national level, while ratification takes place within the states.
- The Constitution may be informally amended through legislative actions, executive actions, judicial interpretations, and custom and usage.
- *Marbury v. Madison* established the principle of judicial review.

CHAPTER 7

Federalism

IN THIS CHAPTER

Summary: One of the basic principles embodied in the United States Constitution is federalism. Federalism arose from the framers' desire to create a stronger national government than under the Articles of Confederation but preserve the existing states and state governments. **Federalism** is a political system where the powers of government are divided between a national government and regional (state and local) governments. Each level of government has certain authority over the same territory and people. A constitution outlines each level of government's authority, powers, and prohibitions.

Key Terms

federalism
delegated powers
enumerated (expressed)
 powers
implied powers
Necessary and Proper
 (Elastic) Clause
inherent powers
concurrent powers
reserved powers

10th Amendment
Commerce Clause
Full Faith and Credit
 Clause
Privileges and Immunities
 Clause
extradition
interstate compacts
Supremacy Clause
McCulloch v. Maryland

U.S. v. Lopez
dual federalism
cooperative federalism
devolution
fiscal federalism
fiscal policy
grants-in-aid
categorical grants
block grants
revenue sharing

The Constitutional Basis of Federalism

Why Federalism?
- States wanted to retain some powers independent of the national government to prevent tyranny of the national government
- Keep government closer to the people (local control)
- It was necessary to get the states to agree to the constitution

Although the term federalism is not found in the United States Constitution, it is clearly defined in the delegated, concurrent, and reserved powers of the national and state governments (see Figure 7-1):

- *delegated powers*—Expressed, or **enumerated**, powers given specifically to the national government (Articles I–V).
- *implied powers*—Although not expressed, powers that may be reasonably inferred from the Constitution (Article I, Section 8, Clause 18—the **Necessary and Proper Clause**, or **Elastic Clause**).
- *inherent powers*—Powers that exist for the national government because the government is sovereign.
- *concurrent powers*—Powers that belong to both the national and state governments.
- *reserved powers*—Powers belonging specifically to the states because they were neither delegated to the national government nor denied to the states (Article IV; Amendment 10).
- *prohibited powers*—Powers that are denied to the national government, state governments, or both (Article I, Sections 9 and 10; Amendments); for example, neither the national government nor state governments may pass an ex post facto law or a bill of attainder.

Powers of Government Under Federalism

National Powers (Expressed, Implied, Inherent)	National and State Powers (Concurrent)	State Powers (Reserved)
Regulate foreign and interstate commerce	Levy taxes	Regulate intrastate commerce
Coin and print money	Borrow money	Establish local governments
Provide an army and navy	Spend for general welfare	Establish public school systems
Declare war	Establish courts	Administer elections
Establish federal courts below the Supreme Court	Enact and enforce laws	Protect the public's health, welfare, and morals
Conduct foreign relations	Charter banks	Regulate corporations
Make all laws "necessary and proper"		Establish licensing requirements for certain regulated professions
Acquire and govern U.S. territories and admit new states		
Regulate immigration and naturalization		

Figure 7-1

- **10th Amendment**—"The powers not delegated to the United States by the Constitution, nor prohibited by it to the States, are reserved to the States respectively, or to the people."
- **14th Amendment**—"No State shall make or enforce any law which shall abridge the privileges or immunities of citizens of the United States; nor shall any State deprive any person of life, liberty, or property, without due process of law; nor deny to any person within its jurisdiction the equal protection of the laws."
- **Commerce Clause**—Article 1, Section 8, Clause 3 of the U.S. Constitution, which gives Congress the power "to regulate commerce with foreign nations, and among the several states, and with the Indian tribes."
- **Necessary and Proper Clause**—Congress has the power "To make all Laws which shall be necessary and proper for carrying into Execution the foregoing Powers, and all other Powers vested by this Constitution in the Government of the United States, or in any Department or Officer thereof."

Federalism in Practice

Interstate Relations

Article IV of the Constitution addresses the issue of relationships between the states. It offers several provisions:

- *Full Faith and Credit Clause*—States are required to recognize the laws and legal documents of other states, such as birth certificates, marriage licenses, driver's licenses, wills.
- *Privileges and Immunities Clause*—States are prohibited from unreasonably discriminating against residents of other states. Nonresidents may travel through other states; buy, sell, and hold property; and enter into contracts (does not extend to political rights such as the right to vote or run for political office, or to the right to practice certain regulated professions such as teaching).
- *Extradition*—States may return fugitives to a state from which they have fled to avoid criminal prosecution at the request of the governor of the state.
- *Interstate compacts*—States may make agreements, sometimes requiring congressional approval, to work together to solve regional problems. Some examples are "hot-pursuit agreements," parole and probation agreements, the Port Authority of New York and New Jersey, and regulating the common use of shared natural resources.

Guarantees to the States

Article IV of the Constitution provides national guarantees to the states:

- republican form of government
- protections against foreign invasion
- protections against domestic violence
- respect for the geographic integrity of states

Some of the advantages and disadvantages of federalism are shown in Figure 7-2.

Establishing National Supremacy

Article VI of the United States Constitution contains the **Supremacy Clause**, which helps to resolve conflicts between national and state laws. Because two levels of government are operating within the same territory and over the same people, conflicts are bound to arise.

Advantages and Disadvantages of Federalism

Advantages of Federalism	Disadvantages of Federalism
Ideally suited to large geographic area because it encourages diversity in local government	Inflexibility inherent in a written constitution
Avoids concentration of political power	Complex, with many governments to deal with
Accommodated already existing state governments	Duplication of offices and functions
States serve as training grounds for national leaders	Conflicts of authority may arise
Keeps government close to the people	

Figure 7-2

The Supremacy Clause states that the Constitution, its laws and treaties shall be the "supreme law of the land." The Supreme Court upheld this supremacy in ***McCulloch v. Maryland*** (1819). The Supreme Court continued to expand the powers of Congress over interstate commerce in *Gibbons v. Ogden* (1824).

McCulloch v. Maryland (1819)

The Supreme Court dealt with the issues of the Necessary and Proper Clause and the Supremacy Clause when Maryland imposed a tax on the Baltimore branch of the Second National Bank of the United States. Chief cashier James McCulloch refused to pay the tax, Maryland state courts ruled in the state's favor, and the United States government appealed to the Supreme Court. The Marshall Court ruled that although no provision of the Constitution grants the national government the expressed power to create a national bank, the authority to do so can be implied by the Necessary and Proper Clause (Article I, Section 8, Clause 18). This ruling established the implied powers of the national government and national supremacy, the basis used to strengthen the power of the national government.

Gibbons v. Ogden (1824)

At issue was the definition of commerce and whether the national government had exclusive power to regulate interstate commerce. The New York legislature gave Robert Livingston and Robert Fulton exclusive rights to operate steamboats in New York waters and Aaron Ogden the right to operate a ferry between New York and New Jersey. Thomas Gibbons had received a national government license to operate boats in interstate waters. Ogden sued Gibbons and won in the New York courts; Gibbons appealed to the Supreme Court. The Marshall court defined commerce as including all business dealings, and the power to regulate interstate commerce belongs exclusively to the national government. Today, the national government uses the Commerce Clause to justify the regulation of numerous areas of economic activity.

United States v. Lopez (1995)

U.S. v. Lopez, which declared the Gun Free School Zones Act an unconstitutional over-reach, was seen by some experts as signaling a shift in the Court's interpretation of the Commerce Clause after nearly 50 years of rulings that resulted in an expansion of Congress's power. Alfonso Lopez carried a concealed weapon into his San Antonio high school. He was originally charged with violating a Texas law that banned firearms in schools, but the state charges were dismissed after he was charged with violating a federal law: the Gun Free School Zones Act of 1990. This Act made it a federal offense "for any individual knowingly to possess a firearm [in] a school zone." Lopez was tried and convicted for carrying a weapon on school grounds. Lopez challenged his conviction, arguing that the Gun Free School Zones Act was an unconstitutional exercise of Congress's power. Schools were controlled by state and local governments and were not under the authority of the federal government. The federal government claimed that it had the authority to ban guns in schools under its commerce power because guns in school led to gun violence. A violent crime ultimately affects the condition of the school and the well-being of the population. In a 5-4 decision supporting Lopez, the Supreme Court found that the 1990 Gun Free School Zones Act did violate the Constitution, claiming Congress was overreaching its powers granted under the Commerce Clause.

Federalism Today

KEY IDEA

Since the founding of the United States, society has changed, and federalism has evolved to meet the changes and challenges.

Dual Federalism

The earliest (1789–1932) interpretation of federalism is the concept of **dual federalism**, which views the national and state governments each remaining supreme within their own sphere of influence. This form of federalism is often referred to as "layer cake federalism," because each level of government is seen as separate from the other, with the national government having authority over national matters and state governments having authority over state matters. The early beliefs that states had the sole responsibility for educating their citizens and the national government had the sole responsibility for foreign policy issues are examples of dual federalism.

Cooperative Federalism

In the 1930s the interpretation of federalism shifted to that of the national and state governments sharing policymaking and cooperating in solving problems. **Cooperative federalism** or "marble cake federalism" as it came to be known, grew from the policies of the New Deal era and the need for the national government to increase government spending and public assistance programs during the Great Depression. The cooperation of the national and state governments to build the national interstate highway system beginning in the 1950s is an example of cooperative federalism. The expansion of cooperative federalism during (President Lyndon B. Johnson's) Great Society required even greater cooperation from the states in return for federal grants.

New Federalism

During the administrations of Richard Nixon, Ronald Reagan, and George H. W. Bush the national government attempted to implement a reversal of cooperative federalism and place more responsibility on the states about how grant money would be spent. The term **devolution**—a transfer of power to political subunits—has been used to describe the goals of new federalism. An example of new federalism is welfare reform legislation, which has returned more authority over welfare programs to the states. The national government directed where much of the money should be spent in the stimulus-spending bills during the first year of the Obama administration.

Fiscal Federalism

The national government's patterns of spending, taxation, and providing grants to influence state and local governments is known today as **fiscal federalism**. The national government uses **fiscal policy** to influence the states through granting or withholding money to pay for programs:

- *grants-in-aid* programs—Money and resources provided by the federal government to the state and local governments to be used for specific projects or programs. The earliest grants often covered public works projects such as building canals, roads, and railroads, and land grants for state colleges.

- *categorical grants*—Grants that have a specific purpose defined by law, such as sewage treatment facilities or school lunch programs; may even require "matching funds" from the state or local governments; categorical grants may be in the form of project grants (awarded on the basis of a competitive application, such as university research grants) or formula grants (awarded on the basis of an established formula, such as Medicaid).

- *block grants*—General grants that can be used for a variety of purposes within a broad category, such as education, health care, or public services; fewer strings attached so state and local governments have greater freedom in how the money is spent; preferred by states over categorical grants.

- *revenue sharing*—Proposed under the Johnson administration and popular under the Nixon administration, a "no strings attached" form of aid to state and local governments; could be used for virtually any project but never exceeded more than 2 percent of revenues; eliminated during the Reagan administration.

- *mandates*—Requirements that are imposed by the national government on the state and local governments; for example, the Americans with Disabilities Act (1990) mandates that all public buildings be accessible to persons with disabilities. Mandates often require state or local governments to meet the requirement at their own expense (**unfunded mandates**). After the mid-term elections of 1994, the Republican-controlled Congress passed the Unfunded Mandate Reform Act, which imposed limitations on Congress's ability to pass unfunded mandate legislation.

› Review Questions

Multiple-Choice Questions

1. A major strength of federalism lies in the fact that it promotes both national and state activities in which of the following manners?
   (A) provides for complex government activities
   (B) avoids concentration of political power
   (C) guarantees the inherent inflexibility of a written constitution
   (D) allows for the duplication of government offices and functions

2. *McCulloch v. Maryland* (1819) was an important Supreme Court case involving federalism because
   (A) it called for a republican form of government
   (B) it provided for a national law protecting against domestic violence
   (C) following this case, the Supreme Court became the third powerful branch of the national government
   (D) the Supremacy Clause of the Constitution was upheld

3. Article IV of the United States Constitution guarantees which of the following to the states?
   (A) extradition privileges
   (B) reserved powers of the states
   (C) grants-in-aid
   (D) a republican form of government

4. Which of the following is NOT a concurrent power of national and state governments?
   (A) protecting the public's health, welfare, and morals
   (B) borrowing money
   (C) chartering banks
   (D) establishing courts

5. Cooperative federalism can best be described as
   (A) the national government's ability to help the states through the spending of tax dollars and the providing of project grants
   (B) placing more responsibility on the states as to how grant money is to be spent
   (C) "marble-cake federalism"
   (D) "layer-cake federalism"

6. The president most responsible for the implementation of new federalism was:
   (A) George H. W. Bush
   (B) Richard Nixon
   (C) Ronald Reagan
   (D) Bill Clinton

7. Which of the following is true about federalism?
   (A) Cooperative federalism implies agreement between national and state governments on major social issues.
   (B) Interstate highway projects are an example of dual federalism.
   (C) Fiscal federalism involves limited control of the national government over the states.
   (D) Nixon's revenue-sharing plan is an example of fiscal federalism.

8. Which of the following has the fewest "strings" attached when it comes to spending government monies?
   (A) mandates
   (B) categorical grants
   (C) block grants
   (D) grants-in-aid

9. Federalism as a form of government has many disadvantages. A major disadvantage of federalism is
   (A) conflicts may arise over authority of government
   (B) there is concentration of political power
   (C) government is not close to the people
   (D) existing state governments are not accommodated

10. Prohibited powers are powers that are denied to both the national and state governments. These denied powers are found in
    (A) Article I, Section 8
    (B) Article I, Sections 9 and 10
    (C) Article IV, Section 4
    (D) Article I, Section 8, Clause 18

Free-Response Questions

Use the line graph below to answer question 11.

Government Employment 1940–2015

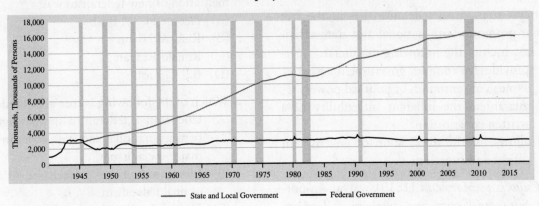

Source: St. Louis Fed

11. Using the data in the graph above, and your knowledge of U.S. government and politics, perform the following tasks:
    (A) Identify a trend shown in the graph.
    (B) Explain how each of the following supports the trend identified in Part A.
    - Block grants
    - Revenue sharing

12. One basic principle embodied in the Constitution is federalism, which developed from the Founding Fathers' desire to create a stronger national government than under the Articles of Confederation. That national government, however, is limited by the provisions of the U.S. Constitution.
    (A) Define federalism.
    (B) Describe two advantages of federalism.
    (C) Explain how each of these Supreme Court decisions either expands or limits the power of the national government:
    - *McCulloch v. Maryland* (1819)
    - *U.S. v. Lopez* (1995)

› Answers and Explanations

1. **B.** Governmental power is divided between the national and state governments, each operating within the same geographic territory with power over a single population. Providing for complex governmental activities (A) and allowing for the duplication of government offices and functions (D) are not usually considered major strengths of federalism. The Constitution is a very flexible document (C).

2. **D.** *McCulloch v. Maryland* upheld Article VI of the Constitution, which declares the Constitution the "supreme law of the land." The Supreme Court (C) was established by Article III of the Constitution as the highest court of the judicial branch. Answer choices (A) and (B) were not provisions of the decision in *McCulloch v. Maryland*.

3. **D.** The United States Constitution guarantees a republican form of government to each state. Extradition occurs between states when one state requests an accused person be returned to the state where the crime occurred (A). The reserved powers of the states is found in the Tenth Amendment, not Article IV (B). There is no guaranteed that the federal government will provide grants-in aid to the states (C).

4. **A.** Protecting the public health, welfare, and morals is a reserved power of the states. The other answer choices represent concurrent powers, or those shared by both the national and state governments.

5. **C.** Cooperative federalism involves the national government and state governments working together to solve problems, often with a blending (similar to that of a marble cake) of responsibilities. Choices (A) and (B) are not the best descriptions of cooperative federalism, because neither reflects mutual sharing and planning between the national and state governments. "Layer-cake federalism" (D) describes dual federalism.

6. **B.** Richard Nixon began the program of new federalism to place responsibility on the states for the spending of grant money. New federalism continued under succeeding presidents, particu-larly Ronald Reagan (C) and George H. W. Bush (A).

7. **D.** Revenue sharing is an example of fiscal federalism, in which the federal government uses grants to influence the states. Cooperative federalism may involve differences between two levels of government. For example, interstate highways were constructed in the South during the Civil Rights Movement, even though the southern states clashed with federal civil rights policies (A). The interstate highway system is an example of cooperative federalism, which involves sharing between two levels of government (B). Fiscal federalism involves some control over the states by the national government's granting or withholding money for programs (C).

8. **C.** Block grants (C) have fewer strings attached than categorical grants (B), which may require matching funds from state or local governments. Some mandates require the use of state or local funds (A). The federal government requires grants-in-aid (D) to be used for specific projects or programs.

9. **A.** Conflicts between national and state authority may arise under the system of federalism. While federalism provides for a strong national government, power is not concentrated in the national government (B). State governments remain close to the people (C), and the needs of state governments are accommodated under federalism (D).

10. **B.** Article I, Section 9, denies certain powers to the national government; Article I, Section 10 denies powers to the state governments. Article I, Section 8 (A) details the powers of Congress. Article IV, Section 4 (C) guarantees each state a republican form of government. Article I, Section 8, Clause 18 (D) is the "necessary and proper clause."

11. **(A)** Any of the following two are acceptable trends:
    - Federal level of employment remains constant
    - State and local level of employment increases

- There is a widening gap between federal and state/local employment

(B) Block grants support the trend because the federal government gives money to the states and local government with few strings attached. The governments receiving the money can use it for a variety of purposes within a broad category, such as education, health care, or transportation. With few strings attached, state and local governments have a great amount of freedom in how to use the money. Revenue sharing is also a plan to give aid to state and local governments with no strings attached, allowing the money to be used for virtually any project. Because the federal government is giving more money and freedom to spend that money to state and local governments, there is a greater need for employees at the state and local level and fewer employees at the federal level.

12. **(A)** Federalism is defined a political system where the powers of government are divided between a national government and regional (state, province, etc.) governments. Each level of government has certain authority over the same territory and people.

(B) Advantages of federalism include:
- being ideally suited to large geographic areas because it encourages diversity in local government
- avoiding the concentration of politial power
- accommodating already existing state governments
- having states serve as training grounds for national leaders
- keeping government close to the people

(C) In *McCulloch v. Maryland*, the Supreme Court expanded the powers of the national government by holding that Congress has implied powers derived from those listed in Article I, Section 8. The Court allowed that the "necessary and proper" Clause gave Congress the power to establish a national bank. In *U.S. v. Lopez*, The Supreme Court limited the powers of Congress by ruling that Congress may not use the commerce clause to make possession of a gun in a school zone a federal crime. The Gun Free School Zones Act passed by Congress in 1990 was unconstitutional because Congress had exceeded its power to legislate under the Commerce Clause.

› Rapid Review

- Federalism is a system of government in which the powers of government are divided between a national government and regional (state and local) governments.
- There are both advantages and disadvantages to federalism as a form of government.
- Federalism can be found in the delegated, reserved, and concurrent powers of the Constitution.
- Article IV of the Constitution provides for interstate relations, including full faith and credit, privileges and immunities, extradition, interstate compacts.
- Article IV of the Constitution provides national guarantees to the states.
- *McCulloch v. Maryland* and *Gibbons v. Ogden* upheld national supremacy and expanded the powers of Congress under the Commerce Clause, respectively.
- As practiced in the United States, federalism has evolved through many phases, including dual federalism, cooperative federalism, new federalism, and fiscal federalism.

UNIT **2**

Interactions Among Branches of Government

CHAPTER 8

The Legislative Branch

IN THIS CHAPTER

Summary: Article I of the United States Constitution creates a **bicameral**, or two-house, legislature consisting of the House of Representatives and the Senate. The current structure of the Congress was the result of the Great (Connecticut) Compromise, reached at the Constitutional Convention. The Founding Fathers based their compromise in part on the belief that each house would serve as a check on the power of the other house. The House of Representatives was to be based on the population in the states, representative of the people, with its members chosen by popular vote. The Senate was to represent the states equally, with each state having the same number of senators, chosen by the state legislatures.

Key Terms

bicameral	president pro tempore	bills
apportionment	floor leaders	discharge petition
reapportionment	seniority system	mark-up
congressional districting	standing committee	filibuster
gerrymandering	select committee	cloture
majority-minority district	joint committee	hold
Baker v. Carr	conference committee	pork barrel legislation
Shaw v. Reno	Committee of the Whole	logrolling
at-large	Rules Committee	riders
incumbency effect	legislative caucus	amendments
casework	delegate	lobbying
constituents	trustee	legislative veto
constituency service	politico	divided government
Speaker of the House	franking privilege	political polarization
majority leader	oversight powers	

Structure of Congress

Figure 8-1 shows the structure of the two houses of Congress.

Structure of Congress: A Comparison of the House and Senate

	House of Representatives	**Senate**
Membership	435 members (apportioned by population)	100 members (two from each state)
Term of office	2 years; entire House elected every 2 years	6 years; staggered terms with one-third of the Senate elected every 2 years
Qualifications	At least 25 years of age; citizen for 7 years; must live in state where district is located	At least 30 years of age; citizen for 9 years; must live in state
Constituencies	Smaller, by districts	Larger, entire state
Prestige	Less prestige	More prestige

Figure 8-1

Organization of Congress

- Two houses meet for terms of two years beginning on January 3 of odd-numbered years; each term is divided into two one-year sessions
- The president may call special sessions in cases of national emergency
- Each house of Congress chooses its own leadership and determines its own rules

Election to Congress

Getting Elected to the House of Representatives

The Constitution guarantees each state at least one representative. Members are chosen from districts within each state. Some practices related to determining congressional representation are:

- *apportionment*—Distribution among the states based on the population of each of the states.
- *reapportionment*—The redistribution of congressional seats after the census determines changes in population distribution among the states.
- *congressional districting*—The drawing by state legislatures of congressional districts for those states with more than one representative.
- *gerrymandering*—Drawing congressional districts to favor one political party or group over another.

Gerrymandering and the Supreme Court

Gerrymandering can be based on partisanship, with districts being drawn to benefit candidates of one party and hurt the candidates of the other party. Sometimes district lines are drawn to benefit incumbents, or certain individuals such as state officials who run for the House of Representatives. Redistricting may also be based on helping or hurting the chances of minority candidates. Racial gerrymandering occurs when district lines are drawn to prevent racial minorities from electing their chosen candidate. This has led to the creation of

majority-minority district, districts in which a racial minority group or groups comprise a majority of the district's total population. Federal law allows majority-minority districts to be created to prevent the weakening of minorities' voting strength in compliance with the Voting Rights Act of 1965 and its amendments.

The Supreme Court has ruled on several cases involving the fairness of reapportionment and redistricting:

- *Baker v. Carr* (1962)—The Supreme Court ruled that reapportionment challenges are not political questions if brought under the Equal Protection Clause of the Fourteenth Amendment.
- *Wesberry v. Sanders* (1964)—The Supreme Court ruled that districts must be drawn to approximately the same population size as other districts. This opened the door to challenges to redistricting and the development of the "one-man, one-vote principle."
- *Shaw v. Reno* (1993)—The Supreme Court ruled that legislative redistricting must be mindful of race and compliance with the Voting Rights Act of 1965 and its amendments.

Getting Elected to the Senate

The Constitution guarantees that "no state, without its consent, shall be deprived of its equal suffrage in the Senate" (Article V).

- Members were originally chosen by the state legislatures in each state.
- Since 1913, the Seventeenth Amendment allows for the direct election of senators by the people of the state.
- Election of senators is by the people **at-large**. All voters of the state elect the senators from the state.

Incumbency Effect

The **incumbency effect** is the tendency of those already holding office to win reelection. The effect tends to be stronger for members of the House of Representatives and weaker for the Senate. Advantages may include:

- *name recognition*—Voters are more likely to recognize the office holder than the challenger.
- *credit claiming*—The office holder may have brought government projects and money into the state or district.
- **casework** *for* **constituents**—Office holders may have helped constituents solve problems (**constituency service**) involving government and the bureaucracy.
- *more visible to constituents*—Members can use the "perks" of the office to communicate with constituents. Franking, the privilege of sending official mail using the incumbent's signature as postage, provides communication with constituents.
- *media exposure*—Incumbents are more likely to gain "free" publicity during a campaign through the media.
- *fundraising abilities*—It is generally greater for incumbents.
- *experience in campaigning*—Incumbents have already experienced the campaign process.
- *voting record*—Voters can evaluate their performance based on their record.

Term Limits

Although several states have passed legislation establishing term limits for members of Congress, the Supreme Court has ruled that neither the states nor Congress may impose term limits without a constitutional amendment. Therefore, today, there are no limitations on the number of terms a member of Congress may serve.

Leadership of Congress

The majority political party in each house controls the leadership positions of Congress.

House of Representatives

- The **Speaker of the House** is the presiding officer and most powerful member of the House. Major duties include assigning bills to committee, controlling floor debate, and appointing party members to committees. The speaker is elected by members of his or her political party within the House.
- Majority and minority leaders
  — The **majority leader** serves as the major assistant to the speaker, helps plan the party's legislative program, and directs floor debate.
  — The minority floor leader is the major spokesperson for the minority party and organizes opposition to the majority party.
- Whips help floor leaders by directing party members in voting, informing members of impending voting, keeping track of vote counts, and pressuring members to vote with the party.

Senate

- The U.S. vice president, although not a Senate member, is the presiding officer of the Senate, according to the Constitution. The vice president may not debate and only votes to break a tie.
- The **president** *pro tempore* is a senior member of the majority party chosen to preside in the absence of the Senate president. This is a mostly ceremonial position lacking real power.
- Majority and minority **floor leaders**
  —The majority floor leader is the most influential member of the Senate and often the majority party spokesperson.
  —The minority floor leader performs the same role as the House minority leader.
- Whips serve the same role as whips in the House of Representatives.

The Committee System

Most of the work of Congress is accomplished through committees. Committees permit Congress to divide the work among members, thus allowing for the study of legislation by specialists and helping speed up the passage of legislation.

Leadership of Committees

Committee chairpersons are members of the majority party in each house chosen by party caucus. They set agendas, assign members to subcommittees, and decide whether the committee will hold public hearings and which witnesses to call. They manage floor debate of the bill when it is presented to the full House or Senate. Traditionally chairpersons were chosen based on the **seniority system**, with the majority party member having the longest length of committee service chosen as chairperson. Today, reforms allow for the selection of chairpersons who are not the most senior majority-party member on the committee. However, most are long-standing members of the committee.

Membership on Committees

The percentage of each committee's membership reflects the overall percentage of Democrats and Republicans in each house. Members try to serve on committees where they can influence public policy relating to their district or state (for example, a Kansas senator on the agriculture committee) or influence important national public policy.

Types of Committees

- A **standing committee** is a permanent committee that deals with specific policy matters (agriculture, energy and natural resources, veterans' affairs).
- A **select committee** is a temporary committee appointed for a specific purpose. Most are formed to investigate a particular issue, such as the Senate Watergate Committee.
- A **joint committee** is made up of members of both houses of Congress. It may be a select committee (Iran-Contra Committee) or perform routine duties (Joint Committee on the Library of Congress).
- A **conference committee** is a temporary committee of members from both houses of Congress, created to resolve the differences in House and Senate versions of a bill. It is a compromise committee.

Important Committees

HOUSE OF REPRESENTATIVES	SENATE
Committee of the Whole—a committee on which all representatives serve, and which meets in the House Chamber for the consideration of measures	Appropriations—responsible for all spending of the federal budget
Rules Committee—responsible for determining under what rules other committees' bills will come to the floor; the committee decides for how long and under what rules the full body will debate bills	Foreign Relations—oversees the foreign policy agencies of the U.S. government such as funding foreign aid programs and arms sales; reviews and considers all diplomatic nominations and international treaties and legislation relating to U.S. foreign policy
Ways and Means Committee—a committee that, along with the Senate Finance Committee, writes the tax codes, subject to the approval of Congress as a whole; jurisdiction over all taxation, tariffs, and other revenue raising measures	Judiciary—conducts hearings prior to the Senate vote on whether to confirm prospective federal judge nominations by the president; provides oversight of the Department of Justice and all the agencies under the Department of Justice

Caucuses

A **legislative caucus** is an informal group formed by members of Congress who share a common purpose or set of goals (Congressional Black Caucus, Women's Caucus, Democratic or Republican Caucus).

Congressional Staff and Support

- Personal staff work directly for members of Congress in Washington, D.C., and their district offices in their home states.
- Committee staff work for committees and subcommittees in Congress, researching problems and analyzing information.
- Support agencies provide services to members of Congress (Library of Congress, Government Printing Office).

Roles of Members of Congress

Members of Congress have several roles:

- *policymaker*—Make public policy through the passage of legislation.
- *representative*—Represent constituents.
  - **delegate**—Members vote based on the wishes of constituents, regardless of their own opinions.
  - **trustee**—After listening to constituents, members vote based on their own opinions.
  - **politico**—Members vote based on party loyalty.
- *constituent servant*—Help constituents with problems.
- *committee member*—Serve on committees.
- *politician/party member*—Work to support their political party platform and get reelected.

Privileges of Members of Congress

Members of Congress enjoy several privileges, including:

- allowances for offices in their district or home state
- travel allowances
- the **franking privilege** allows members of Congress to send mailings to constituents postage free
- immunity from arrest while conducting congressional business
- immunity from libel or slander suits for their speech or debate in Congress

Powers of Congress

Congress has legislative and nonlegislative powers.

1. Legislative powers—Power to make laws.

KEY IDEA

- *expressed (enumerated) powers*—Powers specifically granted to Congress, mostly found in Article I, Section 8 of the Constitution (enacting legislation, coining money, passing the federal budget, raising revenue, declaring war, raising and maintaining an armed forces).
- *implied powers*—Powers that may be reasonably suggested to carry out the expressed powers; found in Article I, Section 8, Clause 18, "necessary and proper" or elastic clause; allows for the expansion of Congress's powers (expressed power to raise armies and navy implies the power to draft men into the military).
- *limitations on powers*—Powers denied Congress by Article I, Section 9 and the Tenth Amendment.

2. Nonlegislative powers—Duties other than lawmaking.

- *electoral powers*—Selection of the president by the House of Representatives and/or vice president by the Senate upon the failure of the electoral college to achieve a majority vote.
- *amendment powers*—Congress may propose amendments by a two-thirds vote of each house or by calling a national convention to propose amendments if requested by two-thirds of the state legislatures.
- *impeachment*—The House may bring charges, or impeach, the president, vice president, or any civil officer; case is tried in the Senate with the Senate acting as the jury (Andrew Johnson and Bill Clinton were both impeached by the House but not convicted by the Senate).
- *executive powers of Senate*—The Senate shares the appointment and treaty-making powers with the executive branch; the Senate must approve appointments by majority vote and treaties by two-thirds vote.
- *investigative/**oversight** powers*—Investigate matters falling within the range of its legislative authority; often involves the review of policies and programs of the executive branch.

The Lawmaking Process

Figure 8-2 shows the steps involved for a bill to become a law.

How a Bill Becomes a Law

> **Bills,** or proposed laws, may begin in either house, except revenue bills, which must begin in the House of Representatives.

HOUSE OF REPRESENTATIVES	SENATE
A bill is introduced, numbered, and assigned to a committee.	A bill is introduced, numbered, and assigned to a committee.
The bill may be assigned to a subcommittee for further study.	The bill may be assigned to a subcommittee for further study.
The bill is returned to committee, where it is approved or rejected.	The bill is returned to committee, where it is approved or rejected.
The **rules committee** sets terms of debate for the bill.	No rules committee!
The bill is debated by the House.	The bill is debated by the Senate.
A vote is taken, where the bill is passed or defeated. Bills that pass the House are sent to the Senate.	A vote is taken, where the bill is passed or defeated. Bills that pass the Senate are sent to the House.

> Conference committee resolves differences between House and Senate versions of a bill. Compromise versions may not contain any new material.

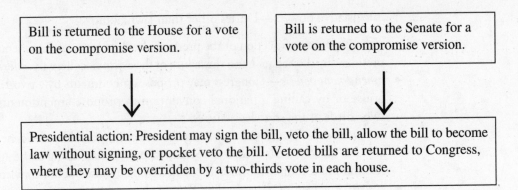

Bill is returned to the House for a vote on the compromise version.	Bill is returned to the Senate for a vote on the compromise version.

Presidential action: President may sign the bill, veto the bill, allow the bill to become law without signing, or pocket veto the bill. Vetoed bills are returned to Congress, where they may be overridden by a two-thirds vote in each house.

Figure 8-2

Legislative Tactics

Legislative tactics are the strategies and devices used by Congress and others in an attempt to block legislation or to get legislation passed.

- *caucuses*—May form voting blocs.
- the *committee system*—Plays a major role in the passage of legislation; bills may die if committees fail to act upon them or reject them.
- *discharge petition*—A discharge petition is a method of bringing a bill out of committee and to the floor for consideration without a report from the committee. It becomes necessary when a committee chair refuses to place the bill or on the committee's agenda: by never reporting a bill, the bill will never leave the committee, and the full House will not be able to consider it. The discharge petition, or the threat of one, gives more power to individual members of the House and takes a small amount of power from the leadership and committee chairs.
- *mark-up*—rewrite a bill into its final form after hearings have been held on it.
- *filibuster and cloture*—Filibuster is unlimited debate in an attempt to stall action on a bill. It occurs in the Senate only, and is possible because the Senate's rules for debate are almost unrestricted. Cloture is the method by which the Senate limits a filibuster. It involves a petition to end debate and requires the vote of at least 60 senators.
- *hold*—informal practice by which a senator informs his or her floor leader that he or she does not wish a particular bill or other measure to reach the floor for consideration; the majority leader need not follow the senator's wishes, but is on notice that the opposing senator may filibuster any motion to proceed to consider the bill.
- *pork barrel legislation*—An attempt to provide funds and projects for a member's home district or state. When the funds are directed to a specific purpose or project, they are known as *earmarks*.
- *logrolling*—An attempt by members to gain the support of other members in return for their support on the member's legislation; "I'll support your bill, if you will support mine."
- *riders*—Additions to legislation which generally have no connection to the legislation; generally legislation that would not pass on its own merit; when a bill has lots of riders it becomes a "Christmas tree bill."
- *amendments*—Additions or changes to legislation that deal specifically with the legislation.
- *lobbying*—Trying to influence members of Congress to support or reject legislation.
- *conference committees*—May affect the wording and therefore the final intent of the legislation.

- *legislative veto*—The rejection of a presidential or executive branch action by a vote of one or both houses of Congress, used mostly between 1932 and 1980 but declared unconstitutional by the Supreme Court in 1983 (*Immigration and Naturalization Service v. Chadha*) stating that Congress cannot take any actions having the force of law unless the president agrees.

Influences on Congress

Various individuals and groups influence Congress members.

- *constituents*—Members, especially those who hope to win reelection, often take into consideration the opinions of their constituents and voters back home in their district or state.
- *other lawmakers and staff*—More senior members often influence newer members; committee members who worked on legislation often influence other members; and staff often research issues and advise members.
- *party influences*—Each party's platform takes a stand on major issues, and loyal members often adhere to the "party line." Members in the House are more likely to support the party position than are Senators.
- *president*—Presidents often lobby members to support legislation through phone calls, invitations to the White House, or even appeals to the public to gain support from voters to bring pressure on members.
- *lobbyists and interest groups*—Often provide members with information on topics relating to their group's interest or possible financial support in future campaigns.

Divided Government

Divided government occurs when one party controls the executive branch (White House) and another party controls one or both houses of the legislative branch (Congress). Two factors increase the chances of divided government: an increasing number of independent voters, and an increase in split-ticket voting. One major disadvantage of divided government is partisanship and gridlock.

Political Polarization and Gridlock

In recent years, members of the House and Senate have gained a reputation for their ability to create partisan gridlock. Divided by issues like health care, immigration, and gun control, they have been ineffective in reaching compromises, hindering the political process. **Political polarization**—one factor leading to this gridlock—has become very noticeable. Increasing ideological differences between the parties has created a distance where members of political parties vote along party line; therefore, they are less likely to cross party lines to vote with the other party. This can lead to gridlock, a political stalemate making it difficult to pass legislation.

› Review Questions

Multiple-Choice Questions

1. After a national census has been taken, changes in population distribution cause the changing of congressional seats among the states. This effect is commonly called
   (A) congressional districting
   (B) apportionment
   (C) gerrymandering
   (D) reapportionment

2. Which of the following is NOT true of the Congress?
   (A) Each house determines its own leadership and rules.
   (B) Terms of Congress last for two years.
   (C) Congress is unicameral in nature.
   (D) Only the president may call special sessions of Congress.

3. Which of the following is true about the officers of the House of Representatives?
   (A) It is the responsibility of the party whip to keep track of vote counts and pressure members to vote with the party.
   (B) The presiding officer is the majority leader.
   (C) Minority leaders direct floor debates.
   (D) The major duty of the majority leader is to assign bills to committee.

4. Temporary committees appointed for the specific purpose of investigating a particular issue are called
   (A) joint committees
   (B) select committees
   (C) standing committees
   (D) investigating committees

5. Which of the following is NOT true of members of Congress?
   (A) Members of Congress act as policymakers and make public policy through the passage of legislation.
   (B) Members of Congress are constituent servants.
   (C) Members of Congress work to support their political party platform.
   (D) After listening to constituents, members vote based on the opinions of those constituents; that is, they become the trustee of the constituent.

6. Which of the following best describes a nonlegislative power of Congress?
   (A) power to declare war
   (B) power to tax
   (C) impeachment power
   (D) power to regulate commerce

7. Which of the following is NOT a step that a proposed bill would encounter on its journey through Congress?
   (A) The bill is debated.
   (B) The bill is voted on, at which time it may pass or be defeated.
   (C) The bill may be assigned to a subcommittee.
   (D) The bill is introduced by a president or by a member of the executive branch.

8. After a presidential veto of a bill, Congress may
   (A) sign the bill, and it becomes law
   (B) override the bill if one house of Congress approves it
   (C) override the president's veto with a two-thirds vote of both houses of Congress
   (D) pocket veto the bill, thereby allowing it to become law without the president's signature.

9. Which legislative tactic is most effectively used only in the Senate?
   (A) filibustering
   (B) logrolling
   (C) caucusing
   (D) riders

10. Which of the following is NOT considered to be a contributing factor to the incumbency effect?
    (A) name recognition
    (B) voting record
    (C) educational background
    (D) experience in campaigning

11. Which of the following is an accurate comparison of the House of Representatives and the Senate?

	HOUSE OF REPRESENTATIVES	SENATE
(A)	The Speaker of the House may only vote to break a tie in the House	The president of the Senate may vote on any legislation before the Senate
(B)	Members can delay the vote on legislation by filibustering	Members must send all legislation through the Rules Committee
(C)	Members represent the entire state	Members represent districts within the state
(D)	The Speaker of the House is the most powerful position in the House	The majority leader is the most powerful position in the Senate

Free-Response Question

12. (A) Describe the primary role of Congress.
    (B) Describe the role of each of the following in the lawmaking process:
    • Hold
    • Discharge petition
    (C) Define divided government and explain how divided government impacts the lawmaking process.

› Answers and Explanations

1. **D.** Reapportionment is the change in the number of congressional seats per state based on state population changes. Gerrymandering (C) is the drawing of congressional electoral districts in order to give an advantage to a group or party.

2. **C.** Congress is a bicameral legislature composed of the House of Representatives and the Senate. The other responses are correct descriptions of Congress.

3. **A.** The minority and majority whips are responsible for keeping track of vote counts and pressuring members to support the party vote. The presiding officer is the Speaker of the House (B). The speaker directs floor debates (C) and largely controls the assignment of bills to committee (D).

4. **B.** Select committees are temporary committees responsible for investigating specific issues. Some select committees investigate issues (D). Joint committees (A) are made up of members of both houses of Congress. Standing committees (C) are permanent committees that deal with specific policy matters.

5. **D.** Members of Congress who vote according to constituent wishes are delegates of the constituents. The remaining answer choices accurately reflect the duties of members of Congress.

6. **C.** The impeachment power of Congress is a nonlegislative power, having nothing to do with the passage of legislation. The powers to declare war (A), to tax (B), and to regulate commerce (D), deal with the passage of legislation. They are, therefore, among the legislative powers of Congress.

7. **D.** Although bills may be suggested by members of the executive branch, they may be introduced only by members of Congress. The remaining answer choices are correct and occur in the following order: (C), (A), (B).

8. **C.** Congress may override a presidential veto with a two-thirds vote of both houses of Congress. Congress cannot sign a bill into law (A) and neither house may override a veto by itself (B). Only the president may pocket veto a bill; therefore it does not become law (D)

9. **A.** Filibustering is a stalling tactic used only in the Senate. Logrolling (B), caucuses (C), and riders (D), are used in both houses of Congress.

10. **C.** The incumbency effect is the tendency of those already holding office to win reelection because of advantages of holding that office. A candidate's educational background does not contribute to the incumbency effect. Name recognition (A), voting record (B), and campaign experience (D), are factors that contribute to the incumbency effect.

11. **D.** The Speaker of the House may vote at any time, and the president of the Senate (the vice-president of US) may only vote to break a tie (A). Members of the House send legislation through the Rules Committee, and members of the Senate may delay a vote by filibustering (B). Members of the House represent districts within a state, and members of the Senate represent the entire state (C).

12. **A.** The primary role of Congress is to make laws or pass legislation.

B. A hold is an informal practice that allows a senator to inform his or her floor leader that he or she does not wish a particular bill to reach the floor for debate and vote. This practice allows senators to block or threaten to block legislation and can slow the legislative process. A discharge petition is a method of bringing a bill out of committee and to the floor for consideration without a report from the committee. It becomes necessary when a committee chair refuses to place the bill or on the committee's agenda: By never reporting it, a bill will never leave the committee, and the full House will not be able to consider it. The discharge petition, or the threat of one, gives more power to individual members of the House and takes a small amount of power from the leadership and committee chairs.

C. Divided government exists when one party controls the executive branch (White House) and another party controls one or both houses of the legislative branch (Congress). Divided government impacts the lawmaking system by creating a heightened sense of partisanship, which can lead to gridlock and a slowdown of government. It can increase voters' sense of frustration with government if they believe that nothing is being accomplished. Divided government can also lead to more extremes in government and less willingness to compromise.

› Rapid Review

- Congress is bicameral in nature.
- Members of the House of Representatives are chosen from districts within a state. The number of representatives per state is based on state population.
- Members of the Senate are elected from the state. States are equally represented, with two senators from each state.
- Reelection to Congress is often a consequence of the incumbency effect. Several factors may contribute to the incumbency effect.
- There are no term limits in Congress.
- Leaders of the House of Representatives include the Speaker of the House, the floor leaders, and the whips. Leaders of the Senate include the president of the Senate (vice president), the president *pro tempore*, the floor leaders, and the whips.
- Most of the legislative work of Congress is accomplished through committees. Membership on committees is based on party strength. Types of committees include standing, joint, select, and conference committees.
- Personal staff, committee staff, and support agencies aid members of Congress and the committees.
- Congresspeople serve in many roles.
- Congress has both legislative and nonlegislative powers. Legislative powers include expressed, implied, and denied powers. Nonlegislative powers include electoral powers, amendment powers, impeachment powers, executive powers of the Senate, and oversight powers.
- Congress has a specific process for how a bill becomes a law.
- Legislative tactics are used in the process of passing, stopping, or slowing legislation.
- Constituents, other lawmakers, party influences, the president, lobbyists, and interest groups influence members of Congress.

CHAPTER 9

The Executive Branch and the Bureaucracy

IN THIS CHAPTER

Summary: The office of the president is the most important single position in the government of the United States. The president of the United States has many responsibilities and functions originating in Article II of the Constitution. From the time of George Washington to the present, holders of the office of the president have striven to be more than just a ceremonial head of state. The American president is not just a figurehead but also a personality who commands power and respect.

Key Terms

Federalist No. 70
Twenty-Second
    Amendment
Twenty-Fifth Amendment
impeachment
electoral college
line-item veto
executive agreements
pardons
veto
pocket veto
executive orders

executive privilege
Watergate
signing statements
War Powers Act
legislative vetoes
White House staff
bureaucracy
Civil Service
merit system
Hatch Act
cabinet
iron triangles

issue networks
White House Office
Department of
    Transportation
Department of Education
Department of Veterans'
    Affairs
Department of Homeland
    Security

Constitutional Origins of the Presidency

The Debate Over a Strong Versus a Weak Executive

Delegates to the constitutional convention studied the writings of philosophers Montesquieu and Locke, analyzed the powers of the British monarchs, and studied the role of governors in the American colonial governments. The delegates decided they did not want a king; they wanted power to rest with the people. Debate arose over a single versus a plural executive, and a weak executive appointed by Congress versus a strong executive independent of the legislature. The final compromise created a single executive with powers limited by the checks and balances of the legislative and judicial branches.

- **Federalist No. 70**

In **Federalist No. 70**, Alexander Hamilton argues the need for a strong executive leader. He states, "energy in the executive is the leading character in the definition of good government. It is essential to the protection of the community against foreign attacks ... to the steady administration of the laws, to the protection of property ... to justice; [and] to the security of liberty ...".

While some delegates to the Constitutional Convention had called for an executive council, Hamilton defended a single executive as "far more safe." A council of two or more persons leads to the dangers of "difference of opinion" and "bitter dissensions." This would weaken the executive because it would "lessen the respectability, weaken the authority" of the office. Hamilton also argued that a single executive would be watched "more narrowly" than would be a group of people. The president should bear sole responsibility for his acts. There was no need for a "council to the executive."

Qualifications

Article II of the Constitution establishes the formal qualifications of the president:

- natural-born citizen
- at least 35 years of age
- resident of United States for 14 years prior to election

Historically, many candidates who have run for the office of the president have also shared several characteristics:

- political or military experience
- political acceptability
- married
- white male
- Protestant
- northern European ancestry

In the 2008 presidential election, Barack Obama presented himself as a new type of presidential candidate. Obama was the first African-American to receive a major party nomination to the presidency, Obama won election in 2008 and 2012. In 2016, Hillary Clinton became the first woman to win a major party nomination, but Clinton lost in the general election to Donald Trump.

Term and Tenure

The concept of a popularly elected president is an American invention. After much debate and compromise, the Founding Fathers created a single executive, elected indirectly through an electoral college for a four-year term. Until the addition of the **Twenty-Second Amendment** in 1951, the number of terms of the president was unlimited. After Franklin D. Roosevelt won the office an unprecedented four times, the Twenty-Second Amendment was added, limiting the president to two elected terms.

Succession and Disability

The Constitution provides that if the president can no longer serve in office, the vice president will carry out the powers and duties of the office. The Constitution does not state that the vice president shall actually become president; that tradition began with the death of W. H. Harrison. After the assassination of John F. Kennedy, the **Twenty-Fifth Amendment** was added to the Constitution, stating that the vice president becomes president if the office of president becomes vacant. That amendment also provides for the new president to nominate a new vice president, with the approval of a majority of both houses of Congress. The first use of the Twenty-Fifth Amendment occurred when Spiro Agnew resigned the vice presidency and was replaced by Gerald Ford in 1973. The following year it was used again when President Richard Nixon resigned; Vice President Gerald Ford became president; and Ford nominated, and Congress confirmed, Nelson Rockefeller as his new vice president.

The Twenty-Fifth Amendment also provides for presidential disability. If the president is unable to perform the duties of his office, the vice president may become "acting president" under one of the following conditions:

- The president informs Congress of the inability to perform the duties of president.
- The vice president and a majority of the cabinet inform Congress, in writing, that the president is disabled and unable to perform those duties.

The president may resume the duties of office upon informing Congress that no disability exists. If the vice president and a majority of the cabinet disagree, Congress has 21 days to decide the issue of presidential disability by a two-thirds vote of both houses.

Impeachment and Removal

The Constitution allows for the removal of a president from office through the impeachment process. **Impeachment** involves bringing charges of wrongdoing against a government official. The United States Constitution gives the House of Representatives the authority to impeach the president or vice president for "Treason, Bribery or other High Crimes and Misdemeanors." Once charges of impeachment have been levied against the president or vice president, the Senate then sits in judgment of the charges. The chief justice of the Supreme Court presides over the trial. If found guilty of the charges, the official may be removed from office. Conviction requires a two-thirds vote of the Senate.

The Road to the White House

There are two basic methods of becoming president: succeed to the office or win election to the office. Most presidents have been elected to the office. Many nominees seeking the office have gained political experience through elected or appointed offices—in Congress (mostly the Senate), as state governors, as vice president, or as a cabinet member. Several nominees gained recognition as military leaders.

The Electoral College System

According to the Constitution and the Twelfth Amendment, an **electoral college** elects the president and vice president. Each state chooses a number of electors equal to its number of members in the House of Representatives and Senate in a method set by the state legislatures. In the general election, voters go to the polls and vote for the candidates of their choice. In December, the electors of the respective candidates meet in each state capital to cast ballots for president and vice president. The electoral college then sends the ballots to the president of the Senate, where they are opened before a joint session of Congress and counted. To win the election, a candidate must receive a majority of electoral votes (270). If no candidate for president receives a majority of electoral votes, the House of Representatives chooses the president from among the top three candidates. If no candidate for vice president receives a majority of electoral votes, the Senate chooses the vice president from the top two candidates.

Contested Elections

The electoral college is a distinctive American institution and no stranger to controversy. Although contested presidential elections are not the pattern, contested elections have occurred. The elections of 1876, 2000, and 2020 have been among the most contentious in American history. In each case, the losing candidate and party dealt with the disputed results differently.

- 1876—After election day in 1876, three states, South Carolina, Florida, and Louisiana, sent two different slates of electors to Congress to be counted. As a result of the disputed electors, Congress established a special bipartisan commission composed of five members of the Senate, five members of the House of Representatives and five members of the Supreme Court to decide the election. The commission awarded all 20 disputed electoral votes to Republican Rutherford B. Hayes just one day before the inauguration.
- 2000—In 2000, several states, including Florida, were using a punch card ballot system, which had proven to cause counting machine malfunctions and missed votes. Some Florida counties were using a "butterfly ballot" form of the punch card, which created confusion for voters. Voters who thought they were voting for Democrat Al Gore, unknowingly voted for other candidates. By the end of election day, Florida, a pivotal state in the election, was too close to call. After initially conceding the election, Gore withdrew his concession and sent a legal team to Florida to pursue a manual recount in some counties. The state engaged in a month-long process to determine the winner of the election. The biggest issue was that of the "hanging chads." Little pieces of paper that get punched when a voter votes (chads) were hanging from the ballot, causing over 60,000 ballots not to be counted when scanned by the counting machines. Gore sued in court to have those ballots counted by hand, winning in the Florida Supreme Court. Bush challenged the ruling in the United States Supreme Court to stop the recount since it did not involve a recount of the entire state. In *Bush v. Gore* (2000), the United States Supreme Court ruled 7–2 that recounting ballots in different ways violated the Equal Protection Clause of the Constitution. The Supreme Court ruled 5–4 that no constitutional recount could be held within the time left before the electoral college was scheduled to meet. Gore conceded the next day, losing Florida's electoral votes to Bush by 537 votes.
- 2020—Due to the coronavirus pandemic, unprecedented changes in voting procedures were authorized for this election. States made changes to election dates, procedures, and election administration, including:
  - Voter registration deadlines extended
  - Early voting periods extended
  - Consolidation of polling places
  - Absentee/mail-in voting eligibility extended or suspended
  - Mail-in ballot applications sent to all voters

- Mail-in ballots sent to all voters
- Prepaid return postage for mail-in ballots
- Drop boxes for mail-in ballots
- Receipt deadlines for mail-in ballots extended

On election night, Joe Biden led in the projected electoral vote count with several states either too close to call or large numbers of ballots remaining to be counted. By the next afternoon, the Trump campaign began filing lawsuits and requesting recounts in several states. President Trump indicated he would contest the election results—stating he believed the election would ultimately be decided by the Supreme Court. As states concluded their counts and recounts, Biden was ultimately declared president-elect.

After the electoral college met in December, the results were sent to Congress for the formal counting of the states' electoral votes. Several Republican representatives and senators challenged the votes from some states, thus delaying final certification of the votes. As the debate and vote count were occurring, protestors marched on the United States Capitol, entered the building, attacking the Capitol police and vandalizing the building, causing the final vote count to be delayed. Once the protesters were removed, the debate and final count continued with Joe Biden being declared the next president.

The Vice Presidency

During much of American history, the office of the vice president has been seen as one to be avoided by ambitious politicians. Constitutionally, the vice president has two duties:

- preside over the Senate, casting tie-breaking votes if necessary
- help determine presidential disability under the Twenty-Fifth Amendment and take over the presidency if necessary

Because the vice president may some day become president, the formal qualifications for vice president are the same as those for the president. The vice president serves a four-year term; however, the number of terms a vice president may serve is not limited. The selection of the nominee for vice president occurs at the national convention when the presidential nominee selects a "running mate." Often the choice of nominee is influenced by the party's desire to balance the ticket; that is, to improve a candidate's chances of winning the election by choosing someone from a different faction of the party or from a different geographic section of the country. With the assassination of Kennedy and attempts on the lives of Ford and Reagan, more attention has focused on the vice president. Today, the vice president is often given a larger role in government, taking part in cabinet meetings, serving on the National Security Council, and acting as the president's representative on diplomatic missions. More consideration is also given to the background, health, and other qualifications of vice presidents.

Presidential Powers

Article II of the Constitution outlines the powers of the president. The checks and balances of the other branches of government limit them. The power of the modern presidency comes from the men who have held the office and have shaped the use of these powers. Historians have often rated presidents as strong or weak. After the 1960s and 1970s, Arthur Schlesinger, Jr., argued that the presidency had become so powerful that an "imperial presidency" existed, applying the term to Richard Nixon and his administration in particular. Richard Neustadt contended that the president's powers lie in the ability to persuade others through negotiation, influence, and compromise. From 2002 to 2008 President George W. Bush and Vice President Dick Cheney argued for greatly expanded powers for the presidency in both domestic and foreign affairs.

Some of these powers are formal, meaning they are provided for by the U.S. Constitution, while others are considered informal, can be categorized as executive, legislative, diplomatic, military, judicial, and party powers.

Executive Powers

- "Faithfully execute" the laws—enforces laws, treaties, and court decisions.
- Presides over the cabinet and executive departments.
- Grants pardons for federal offenses except in cases of impeachment.
- Nominates judges of the Supreme Court and all other officers of the United States (with the consent of the Senate).

Legislative Powers

- Gives annual State of the Union message (constitutionally required) identifying problems, recommending policies, and submitting specific proposals (president's legislative agenda). Expectations are that the president will propose a comprehensive legislative program to deal with national problems (the Budget and Accounting Act of 1921 requires the president to prepare and propose a federal budget).
- Issues annual budget and economic reports.
- Signs or vetoes bills. Presidents must sign or reject the bill in its entirety. The Line Item Veto Act of 1996 granted the President the power to **line-item veto** (partial veto) budget bills passed by Congress. The act was ruled unconstitutional by the Supreme Court in *Clinton v. City of New York*.
- Proposes legislation and uses influence to get it passed.
- Calls for special sessions of Congress.

Diplomatic Powers

- Appoints ambassadors and other diplomats.
- Negotiates treaties and **executive agreements**.
- Meets with foreign leaders in international conferences.
- Accords diplomatic recognition to foreign governments.
- Receives foreign dignitaries.

Military Powers

- Serves as commander-in-chief of the armed forces.
- Has final decision-making authority in matters of national and foreign defense.
- Provides for domestic order.

Judicial Powers

- Appoints members of the federal judiciary.
- Grants reprieves, **pardons**, and amnesty.

Party Powers

- Is the recognized leader of the party.
- Chooses vice-presidential nominee.
- Strengthens the party by helping members get elected (coattails).
- Appoints party members to government positions (patronage).
- Influences policies and platform of the party.

Summary of Presidential Powers

FORMAL POWERS	INFORMAL POWERS
Faithfully execute the laws	**Executive orders**: Orders issued by the president that carry the force of law (i.e., FDR's internment of Japanese-Americans during World War II)
Sign or **veto** legislation, including **pocket veto** when the president refuses to sign a bill at the end of a legislative session and the bill dies	**Executive agreements**: International agreements made by a president that have the force of treaty but do not require Senate approval (i.e., Jefferson's purchase of Louisiana from France in 1803)
Commander-in-chief of Army and Navy and of the militia of the several states	**Executive privilege**: Claim by presidents that they have the discretion to decide that the national interest will be better served if certain information is withheld from the public, including the courts and Congress (For example, Nixon's refusal to turn over the **Watergate** tapes. In *United States v. Nixon*, the Supreme Court ruled that executive privilege did not apply and Nixon must turn over the tapes. They did not strike down executive privilege.)
Make treaties, with the advice and consent of the Senate	**Signing statements**: written comment issued by a president at the time legislation is signed. Signing statements may make comments about the bill signed, or indicate the president's attitude towards the bill and how he intends to ignore it or to implement it
Appoint ambassadors, other public ministers and consuls, judges of the Supreme Court, and all other officers of the United States (with Senate approval)	Persuader (bully pulpit): Teddy Roosevelt's referred to the White House as a "bully pulpit," a platform to communicate with the American people and promote his agenda through the media coverage of presidential events.
Receive ambassadors and other public Ministers	Crisis manager: President is a key player in domestic and foreign crisis management.
Power to grant reprieves and pardons, except in cases of impeachment	Leader of the free world: Meets with world leaders in international conferences.
Provide Congress with information on the state of the union	Party leader: Head of his own political party.
Fill vacancies that may happen during the recess of the Senate	
Convene in special session or adjourn Congress when it cannot agree on adjournment	
Commission all officers of the United States.	

Limitations on Presidential Powers

In order to avoid the possibility of abuses by the executive, the Founding Fathers provided for checks upon the powers of the executive.

- Congressional checks
  — Override presidential vetoes; requires a two-thirds vote of both houses of Congress.
  — Power of the purse; agency budgets must be authorized and appropriated by Congress. In 1974 Congress passed the Congressional Budget and **Impoundment** Control Act, which denied the president the right to refuse to spend money appropriated by Congress and gave Congress a greater role in the budget process.
  — Power of impeachment.
  — Approval powers over appointments.
  — Legislation that limits the president's powers (for example, the **War Powers Act** limited the president's ability to use military force).
  — **Legislative vetoes** to reject the actions of the president or executive agency by a vote of one or both houses of Congress without the consent of the president; declared unconstitutional by the Supreme Court in 1983.
- Judicial checks—Judicial review of executive actions.
- Political checks
  — public opinion
  — media attention
  — popularity

Presidential Character

Political scientist James David Barber examined the importance of a president's personality and character, classifying presidents into four distinct types based on their childhood and other experiences. Barber measured each president's assertiveness in office as active or passive, and how positive or negative his feelings were about the office itself. His classifications were:

- *active-positive*—Takes pleasure in the work of the office, easily adjusts to new situations, and is confident in himself (FDR, Truman, Kennedy, Ford, Carter, Bush).
- *active-negative*—Hard worker but doesn't enjoy the work, insecure in the position, may be obsessive or antagonistic (Wilson, Hoover, LBJ, Nixon).
- *passive-positive*—Easygoing, wanting agreement from others with no dissent, may be overly confident (Taft, Harding, Reagan).
- *passive-negative*—Dislikes politics and tends to withdraw from close relationships (Coolidge, Eisenhower).

The President and Congress

As James Madison states in Federalist No. 51, the Founding Fathers wanted "ambition to counteract ambition" as a way to prevent tyranny. The Founders deliberately created a rivalry between the executive and legislative branches by assigning important constitutional powers to each. By granting institutional rivals independent bases of political power, the Constitution also ensured that each would be capable of protecting and advancing its interests.

The relationship between the president and Congress is often combative. Although both branches work closely together to address critically important problems, they are most likely to agree in first year of president's term or when one party controls both branches. They are most likely to fight late in president's first term and off and on throughout the president's entire second term, often unable to reach agreement on difficult issues. Several reasons account for this conflict:

- Different electoral constituencies—While the president represents entire nation, senators represent states, and congressmen (H.R.) represent individual geographical districts. The president tends to see issues from a national/international (as commander-in-chief and diplomatic duties) perspective, while Congress is concerned with how law will affect their home state or district constituency first.
- Internal design (structure) of institutions—The presidency is highly centralized with all or most decisions and orders coming from a centralized source, usually the members from the top levels of the organizational structure; Congress is highly decentralized with decision-making distributed throughout a larger group, often with different people in charge on different issues.
- Information and expertise—The number-one resource in government is information, which is necessary for policy decisions. The president has the ability to have more information than anyone on the planet. His White House staff mirrors the bureaucracy and acquires information for the president immediately. Congress relies on interest groups, executive departments and agencies, personal staff and committee staff, and their own research to gain information, taking more time to gather the necessary information to make decisions.
- Differing timetables—The president and Congress serve different terms. The president has a maximum of 8 years (must get things done quickly before time runs out), while senators and representatives may serve for decades (so they can wait). Time affects decision-making and policymaking strategy. Legislation moves faster through the House than the Senate. The Senate is willing to take more time—to be the "deliberative body" that the Founding Fathers wanted.
- Competing campaigns—The president must campaign on national issues, while Congress makes elections about local issues.

Congress and the president also are cooperative at times:

- Party loyalty and public expectations—Party provides a common ground to start from (theoretically). The president and Congress may have a "We are all in this together" attitude. Constituents who voted along party lines expect party loyalty from their elected officials. Exceptions to these expectations may occur when presidential approval starts to fall.
- Bargaining and compromise—The president and congress need each other, creating an interdependence between the two. Both have things to bargain with, such as the budget, policies, and access.
- Informal links and associations which draws them together—Members of government know each other. Many went to school together or their families associate with each other socially.

The Bureaucracy

A **bureaucracy** is a systematic way of organizing a complex and large administrative structure. The bureaucracy is responsible for carrying out the day-to-day tasks of the organization. The bureaucracy of the federal government is the single largest in the United States, with 2.8 million employees. Bureaucracies generally follow three basic principles:

- *hierarchical authority*—Similar to a pyramid, with those at the top having authority over those below.
- *job specialization*—Each worker has defined duties and responsibilities, a division of labor among workers.
- *formal rules*—Established regulations and procedures that must be followed.

History and Growth

- *beginnings*—Standards for office included qualifications and political acceptability.
- *spoils system*—Practice of giving offices and government favors to political supporters and friends.
- *reform movement*—Competitive exams were tried but failed due to inadequate funding from Congress.
- *Pendleton Act*—**Civil Service** Act of 1883, passed after the assassination of Garfield by a disappointed office-seeker; replaced the spoils system with a **merit system** as the basis for hiring and promotion.
- *Hatch Act of 1939, amended in 1993*—Prohibits government employees from engaging in political activities while on duty or running for office or seeking political funding while off duty; if in sensitive positions, may not be involved with political activities on or off duty.
- *Civil Service Reform Act of 1978*—Created the Office of Personnel Management (replaced the Civil Service Commission) to recruit, train, and establish classifications and salaries for federal employees.

Organization

The federal bureaucracy is generally divided into four basic types:

- *cabinet departments*—Fifteen executive departments created to advise the president and operate a specific policy area of governmental activity (Department of State, Department of Labor, Department of the Interior); each department is headed by a secretary, except the Department of Justice, which is headed by the attorney general.
- *independent executive agencies*—Similar to departments but without cabinet status (NASA, Small Business Administration, **Environmental Protection Agency**).
- *independent regulatory agencies*—Independent from the executive; created to regulate or police (**Securities and Exchange Commission**, **Federal Election Commission**, Nuclear Regulatory Commission, Federal Reserve Board).
- *government corporations*—Created by Congress to carry out business-like activities; generally charge for services (Tennessee Valley Authority, National Railroad Passenger Corporation [AMTRAK], United States Postal Service).

Influences on the Federal Bureaucracy

- *executive influences*—Appointing the right people, issuing executive orders, affecting the agency's budget, reorganization of the agency.
- *Congressional influences*—Influencing appointments, affecting the agency's budget, holding hearings, rewriting legislation or making legislation more detailed.
- *iron triangles (subgovernments)*—Alliances that develop between bureaucratic agencies, interest groups, and congressional committees or subcommittees. Because of a common goal, these alliances may work to help each other achieve their goals, with Congress and the president often deferring to their influence.
- *issue networks*—Individuals in Washington—located within interest groups, congressional staff, think tanks, universities, and the media—who regularly discuss and advocate public policies. Unlike iron triangles, issue networks continually form and disband according to the policy issues.

The Executive Office of the President (EOP)

The Executive Office of the President includes the closest advisors to the president. Although it was established in 1939, every president has reorganized the EOP according to his style of leadership. Within the executive office are several separate agencies.

- *White House Office*—Personal and political staff members who help with the day-to-day management of the executive branch; includes the chief of staff, counsel to the president, press secretary.
- *National Security Council*—Established by the National Security Act of 1947; advises the president on matters of domestic and foreign national security.
- *Office of Management and Budget*—Helps the president prepare the annual federal budget.
- *Office of Faith-Based and Community Initiatives*—Created by George W. Bush to encourage and expand private efforts to deal with social problems.
- *Office of National Drug Control Policy*—Advisory and planning agency to combat the nation's drug problems.
- *Office of Policy Development*—Gives the president domestic policy advice.
- *Council of Economic Advisers*—Informs the president about economic developments and problems.
- *Office of U.S. Trade Representative*—Advises the president about foreign trade and helps negotiate foreign trade agreements.
- *Office of Administration*—Provides administrative services to personnel of the EOC and gives direct support services to the president.
- *Council on Environmental Quality*—Coordinates federal environmental efforts and analyzes environmental policies and initiatives.
- *Office of Science and Technology Policy*—Advises the president on the effects of science and technology on domestic and international affairs; it also works with the private sector and state and local governments to implement effective science and technology policies.
- *Office of the Vice President*—Consists of the vice president's staff.

Executive Departments

- *State (1789)*—Advises the president on foreign policy, negotiates treaties, represents the United States in international organizations.
- *Treasury (1789)*—Collects federal revenues; pays federal bills; mints coins and prints paper money; enforces alcohol, tobacco, and firearm laws.
- *Defense (1789)*—Formed from the Department of War and the Department of the Navy (1789) but changed to the Department of Defense in 1947; manages the armed forces, operates military bases.
- *Interior (1849)*—Manages federal lands, refuges, and parks; operates hydroelectric facilities; manages Native American affairs.
- *Justice (1870)*—Provides legal advice to the president, enforces federal laws, represents the United States in court, operates federal prisons.
- *Agriculture (1889)*—Provides agricultural assistance to farmers and ranchers, inspects food, manages national forests.
- *Commerce (1903)*—Grants patents and trademarks; conducts the national census; promotes international trade.
- *Labor (1913)*—Enforces federal labor laws (child labor, minimum wage, safe working conditions); administers unemployment and job training programs.

- *Health and Human Services (1953)*—Administers Social Security and Medicare/Medicaid programs; promotes health care research; enforces pure food and drug laws.
- *Housing and Urban Development (1965)*—Provides home financing and public housing programs, enforces fair housing laws.
- **Transportation** *(1967)*—Promotes mass transit programs and programs for highways, railroads, and air traffic; enforces maritime law.
- *Energy (1977)*—Promotes development and conservation of fossil fuels, nuclear energy, research programs.
- **Education** *(1979)*—Administers federal aid programs to schools; engages in educational research.
- **Veterans' Affairs** *(1989)*—Promotes the welfare of veterans of the armed forces.
- **Homeland Security** *(2002)*—Prevents terrorist attacks within the United States, reduces America's susceptibility to terrorism, and minimizes damage and helps recovery from attacks that do occur; includes Coast Guard, Secret Service, Border Patrol, Immigration and Visa Services, and Federal Emergency Management Agency (FEMA).

The Bureaucracy and Policymaking

The bureaucracy engages in writing and enforcing legislation, issuing fines, and testifying before Congress, but its primary role is the implementation of public policy. Because bureaucrats put policy into action, they have a significant impact on public policymaking. When Congress passes legislation, it does not establish all the details on how the policy will be implemented. The bureaucracy has been delegated authority because the president and Congress cannot handle every detail of every piece of legislation. This discretionary authority allows the bureaucracy to interpret legislation and "fill in the gaps" where Congress has left the legislation vague. The bureaucratic agency can therefore write specific regulations that determine the implementation of public policy (rule-making). Bureaucratic discretion and rule-making allow agencies to work out the specifics of the legislation. Although the agency is bound by the legislation, the interpretation of that legislation allows a great deal of latitude in determining how to carry it out. Controlling the actions of bureaucracy can be difficult because:

- The size of the bureaucracy makes it difficult to monitor.
- Bureaucrats have expertise—often more than the president or members of Congress on issues related to their department or agency.
- Civil service laws make firing bureaucrats very difficult.
- Independent agencies are politically independent.

The president, Congress, and the courts have checks over the bureaucracy. The president suggests an annual budget that can increase or decrease an agency's funding. The Office of Management and Budget (OMB) oversees agency budgets. The president also appoints top-level officials to run the bureaucratic agencies. These officials will most likely be supportive of the president's agenda. Congress sets appropriations for agencies and can increase or decrease funding. Congress can also pass legislation that affects how the agency operates, and can approve or reject appointments to the agency. Congress can check the bureaucracy with its oversight function. It can hold hearings and conduct investigations. The courts can check the bureaucracy with rulings that support or oppose the agency's actions.

Interest groups can influence the bureaucracy. They seek to influence bureaucracies through lobbying relevant congressional committees. An "iron triangle" may emerge between a bureaucratic agency, interest group, and congressional committee. Bureaucratic capture refers to a situation when regulatory agencies are more obligated to the interest groups they regulate than the elected officials for whom they work. For example, if lobbyists can get the bureaucratic agency to enforce policies in a way that are beneficial to the special interest rather than the general public.

〉 Review Questions

Multiple-Choice Questions

1. The office of the president of the United States can best be described as an office
   (A) of great responsibility and function
   (B) created as a mere ceremonial head of state
   (C) full of conflict and by nature difficult to understand
   (D) untouched by the power and experience of the person holding it

2. Which of the following amendments provides for presidential succession and disability?
   (A) Twenty-Second
   (B) Twentieth
   (C) Twenty-Fifth
   (D) Twenty-Third

3. When the Founding Fathers finally decided on the length of the presidential term of office, they established a term
   (A) of 8 years
   (B) of 4 years
   (C) not to exceed 10 years
   (D) that could not be renewed after 4 years

4. The president decides to send American troops into Syria to help in the fight against ISIS. This is an example of which of the president's powers?
   (A) powers as party leader
   (B) power as commander-in-chief
   (C) power of appointment
   (D) power to "faithfully execute the law"

5. If the president becomes disabled and cannot perform his duties, how may the vice president take over the office of the president?
   (A) The president may write a letter to the chief justice of the Supreme Court stating his inability to perform the duties of office.
   (B) Congress removes the president.
   (C) The Speaker of the House and president *pro tempore* of the Senate may remove the president.
   (D) The vice president and a majority of the cabinet may inform Congress of the president's disability.

6. Which of the following is NOT considered to be a part of the Executive Office of the President?
   (A) National Security Council
   (B) White House Office
   (C) Office of Management and Budget
   (D) Office of Personnel Management

7. Members of the president's cabinet are usually individuals of great ability but little or no political power. Which of the following best describes this statement?
   (A) The Senate must approve all appointments made by the president.
   (B) The primary functions of cabinet members are to effectively run a department of government and advise the president.
   (C) Cabinet members serve as long as the president remains in office.
   (D) Cabinet members serve as an informal advisory body.

8. Which of the following was NOT an original cabinet position?
   (A) secretary of state
   (B) secretary of war
   (C) attorney general
   (D) secretary of the interior

9. Which power is used by the president for enforcing federal law?
   (A) general executive power
   (B) veto power
   (C) executive agreements
   (D) patronage

10. The partisan power of the president is most recognizable in the fact that the president
    (A) is an elected leader
    (B) checks the power of the party controlling Congress
    (C) is the head of a political party
    (D) alone must write the party platform

Use the following passage to answer question 11.

"The president and the executive branch are always going to have greater latitude and greater authority when it comes to protecting America because sometimes you just have to respond quickly and not everything that is a danger can be publicized and be subject to open debate, but there have to be some guardrails."

—Barak Obama

11. Which of the following statements best depicts the role of the president referred to in the quote?
(A) The president serves as commander-in-chief of the armed forces.
(B) The president must "faithfully execute" the laws of the United States.
(C) The president serves as a crisis manager and although he may have expanded powers during times of crisis, he can also be restrained by the other branches.
(D) The president can check or restrain the other two branches of government.

Free-Response Question

12. The modern presidency exercises powers far beyond those envisioned by the Founding Fathers.
(A) Describe two formal powers that allow the executive branch to influence public policymaking.
(B) Describe two informal powers that allow the executive branch to influence public policymaking.
(C) Explain how the president interacts with the bureaucracy.

› Answers and Explanations

1. **A.** The presidency is the most important single office in the United States, and the powers of the president extend beyond just ceremonial duties (B). The roles and powers of the presidency are clearly defined by Article II of the Constitution (C). The power and experience of the president contribute to the prestige of the office (D).

2. **C.** The Twenty-Fifth Amendment provides for succession and disability. The Twenty-Second Amendment (A) deals with presidential tenure. The Twentieth Amendment (B) sets the beginning dates of the terms for the president, vice president, and members of Congress. The Twenty-Third Amendment (D) provides presidential electors for the District of Columbia.

3. **B.** The term of office for the president is four years.

4. **B.** Sending troops to combat is the role as commander-in-chief of the armed forces. When the president acts as party leader (A), uses his powers of appointment (C), or "faithfully executes" the law (D), he is not fulfilling the commander-in-chief function.

5. **D.** Either the president may inform Congress, not the chief justice (A), of his or her inability to perform the duties of office, or the vice president and a majority of the cabinet may inform Congress of the president's inability to perform his or her duties. Congress may not remove a president from office unless the president is impeached and found guilty (B). The Speaker of the House and president *pro tempore* of the Senate do not have the ability to remove the president (C).

6. **D.** The Office of Personnel Management is an independent agency that is not a part of the EOC. The other answer choices are offices in the EOC.

7. **B.** Cabinet members must possess the administrative skills necessary to run a cabinet-level department, as well as to advise the president. At the same time, they serve largely at the request of the president (C, D) and by approval of the Senate (A).

8. **D.** The secretary of the interior was not added to the cabinet until 1849. Washington's cabinet was composed of secretaries of state (A), war (B), and the attorney general (C).

9. **A.** The president uses administrative powers as chief executive to enforce federal laws. The president's veto power (B) is a legislative power; executive agreements (C) are included in the president's diplomatic powers. Patronage (D) is the practice of offering political positions or jobs to friends and supporters.

10. **C.** Partisan power refers to the president serving as the elected leader of his or her political party.

11. **C.** President Obama's statement refers to the president serving as a crisis manager. Even though the president may have expanded powers during crisis times, Obama states that there must also be checks/restraints on those powers by the other branches of government. Obama is not referring to the president as commander-in-chief (A), chief executive "faithfully executing" the law (B), or imposing checks and balances over the other branches of government.

12. **A.** Formal powers that allow the executive branch to influence public policymaking include:
    - Role as chief executive to "faithfully execute"
    - Legislative powers to sign/veto/pocket veto
    - Role as commander-in-chief/power to commit troops
    - Negotiate treaties
    - Appointment powers
    - State of the Union Address
    - Calling special sessions of Congress
    - Preparing/proposing the federal budget

    B. Describe two informal powers that allow the executive branch to influence public policymaking.
    - Executive orders
    - Executive agreements
    - Signing statements
    - Bully pulpit
    - Crisis manager
    - Global leader
    - Party leader

C. The primary function of bureaucratic agencies is policy implementation; they carry out the decisions of Congress, the president, and the courts. The president has the ability and responsibility of choosing the leaders of bureaucratic agencies, which allows him to choose someone who will guide the bureaucratic agency in a direction the president wants. The president has the power to issue executive orders and signing statements which can influence policy by directing an agency to enforce the legislation in a certain direction. The president also has the ability to influence the budgets of the bureaucratic agencies which can impact how those agencies can operate and how they might enforce legislation.

> Rapid Review

- Article II of the Constitution establishes the office of the president and outlines the powers and duties of the office.
- The presidency was a compromise creating a single executive with limited powers.
- There are both formal and informal qualifications for the president.
- The Twenty-Fifth Amendment provides for the succession and disability of the president.
- The House of Representatives impeaches and the Senate tries cases of impeachment of the president. Only two presidents have been impeached, and none has been removed from office.
- To become president one must succeed to the office or win election to the office.
- The electoral college is an indirect method of electing the president.
- The constitutional duties of the vice president include presiding over the Senate and determining presidential disability.
- Presidents have numerous powers: executive, legislative, diplomatic, military, judicial, and party.
- The powers of the president may be limited by congressional, judicial, and political checks.
- James David Barber described presidential personality and character by classifying presidents as one of four distinct types: active-positive, passive-positive, active-negative, and passive-negative.
- The bureaucracy is a systematic way of organizing government.
- The development of the current bureaucracy has undergone several changes and reforms.
- The organization of the bureaucracy may be divided into four major types: cabinet departments, independent executive agencies, independent regulatory agencies, and government corporations.
- The executive, Congress, iron triangles, and issue networks may influence the federal bureaucracy.
- There are currently 15 executive departments in the executive branch of government.

CHAPTER 10

The National Judiciary

IN THIS CHAPTER

Summary: The United States has a dual system of courts—a federal court system and the court systems of each of the 50 states. Under the Articles of Confederation, there was no national court system. State courts had the sole power to interpret and apply laws. This weakness led to Article III of the Constitution, which states that there shall be one Supreme Court and that Congress may establish a system of inferior courts.

Key Terms

Article III	legislative courts	concurring opinion
Federalist No. 78	Supreme Court	dissenting opinion
Marbury v. Madison	senatorial courtesy	precedents
jurisdiction	rule of four	*stare decisis*
original jurisdiction	brief orders	executive privilege
appellate jurisdiction	writ of certiorari	judicial activism
concurrent jurisdiction	certificate	judicial restraint
constitutional courts	brief	loose constructionist
district courts	*amicus curiae* briefs	strict constructionist
Courts of Appeals	majority opinion	

The Federal Court System

Foundation for Powers

- **Article III**—establishes the Supreme Court and gives Congress the power to establish the lower (inferior) courts, provides that judicial compensation cannot be lowered during tenure, provides **jurisdiction** of the courts, and addresses treason and its punishment.

- **Federalist No. 78**—deals specifically with the judicial branch and addresses the scope of power of the judicial branch; Hamilton proclaims that the judicial branch is the weakest of the three branches because they will have no influence over the purse (funding) or the sword (military). Judges shall have life tenure to assure the judiciary is truly independent and not swayed by outside forces. Judges don't have to worry about reelection or pleasing the other branches to retain their positions. Hamilton states that the judicial branch is created to protect the Constitution and maintain separation of powers and checks and balances. Hamilton even hints at the power of judicial review.
- *Marbury v. Madison* (1803)—Supreme Court case that established the principle of judicial review, which gave the courts the ability to declare acts of the legislature or executive unconstitutional. This case greatly expanded the power of the Supreme Court and established the judicial branch as equal to the other two branches.

Jurisdiction

Jurisdiction is the authority of the courts to hear certain cases. Under the Constitution, federal courts have jurisdiction in cases involving federal law, treaties, and the interpretation of the Constitution.

- *original jurisdiction*—Lower courts have the authority to hear cases for the first time; in the federal system district courts and the Supreme Court (in a limited number of cases) have original jurisdiction where trials are conducted, evidence is presented, and juries determine the outcome of the case.
- *appellate jurisdiction*—Courts that hear reviews or appeals of decisions from the lower courts; Courts of Appeals and the Supreme Court have appellate jurisdiction.
- *concurrent jurisdiction*—Allows certain types of cases to be tried in either the federal or state courts.

Structure of the Judicial System

The federal judicial system consists of constitutional courts and legislative courts. **Constitutional courts** are the federal courts created by Congress under Article III of the Constitution and the Supreme Court. Also included are the **district courts**, **Courts of Appeals**, Court of Appeals for the Federal Circuit, and the U.S. Court of International Trade. Congress has created special or **legislative courts** (Territorial Courts, U.S. Tax Court, U.S. Court of Appeals for the Armed Forces) to hear cases arising from the powers given to Congress under Article I. These legislative courts have a narrower range of authority than the constitutional courts.

District Courts

Congress, under the Judiciary Act of 1789, created the district courts to serve as trial courts at the federal level. Every state has at least one district court; larger states may have several, with Washington D.C., and Puerto Rico each having one court. There are currently 94 districts. The district courts have original jurisdiction; they do not hear appeals. District courts decide civil and criminal cases arising under the Constitution and federal laws or treaties. More than 80% of all federal cases are heard in the district courts.

Courts of Appeals

Congress created the Courts of Appeals in 1891 to help lessen the work load of the Supreme Court. The Courts of Appeals decide appeals from U.S. district courts and review decisions of federal administrative agencies. There are 13 U.S. Courts of Appeals. The states are divided into circuits, or geographic judicial districts. There is also a circuit for Washington, D.C., and a Federal Circuit, which hears cases involving federal agencies. The Courts of Appeals have appellate jurisdiction only; they may only review cases already decided by a lower court. A panel of judges decides cases in the Courts of Appeals.

Supreme Court

The only court actually created directly by the Constitution is the **Supreme Court**. It is the highest court in the federal judicial system. It is the final authority in dealing with all questions arising from the Constitution, federal laws, and treaties. The Supreme Court has both original and appellate jurisdiction. Most of the cases heard in the Supreme Court are on appeal from the district and appellate courts of the federal judicial system; however, cases may come to the Supreme Court from state Supreme Courts, if a federal law or the Constitution is involved. The U.S. Supreme Court may also hear cases of original jurisdiction if the cases involve representatives of a foreign government, or certain types of cases where a state is a party.

The decisions of the Supreme Court may have a strong impact on social, economic, and political forces in our society. Congress establishes the size of the Supreme Court, having the power to change the number of justices. The current size of the Supreme Court was set in 1869. Today, the Supreme Court consists of nine judges—eight associate justices and one chief justice. They are all nominated by the president and confirmed by the Senate.

Judicial Selection

The president appoints federal judges, with confirmation by the Senate. Under the Constitution, there are no formal qualifications for federal judges. Federal judges serve "during good behavior," which generally means for life. The notion of the life term was to allow judges to be free from political pressures when deciding cases. Federal judges may be removed from office through impeachment and conviction.

Lower Courts

Because of the large number of appointments made to the lower courts, the Department of Justice and White House staff handle most of these nominations. **Senatorial courtesy**, the practice of allowing individual senators who represent the state where the district is located to approve or disapprove potential nominees, has traditionally been used to make appointments to the district courts. Because the circuits for the Courts of Appeals cover several states, individual senators have less influence and senatorial courtesy does not play a role in the nomination process. The Senate tends to scrutinize appeals court judges more closely, since they are more likely to interpret the law and set precedent.

Supreme Court

The higher visibility and importance of the Supreme Court demands that the president give greater attention to the nomination of Supreme Court justices. Presidents only make appointments to the Supreme Court if a vacancy occurs during their term of office. When making appointments, presidents often consider:

- *party affiliation*—Choosing judges from their own political party.
- *judicial philosophy*—Appointing judges who share their political ideology.

- *race, gender, religion, region*—Considering these criteria may help bring balance to the court or satisfy certain segments of society.
- *judicial experience*—Previous judicial experience as judges in district courts, Courts of Appeals, state courts.
- *"litmus test"*—A test of ideological purity toward a liberal or conservative stand on certain issues such as abortion.
- *acceptability*—Noncontroversial and therefore acceptable to members of the Senate Judiciary Committee and the Senate.
  — American Bar Association—The largest national organization of attorneys; often consulted by presidents; rates nominees' qualifications.
  — interest groups—May support or oppose a nominee based on his or her position on issues of importance to the interest group; use lobbyists to pressure senators.
  — justices—Endorsements from members of the Supreme Court may help a nominee.

Background of Judges

Almost all federal judges have had some form of legal training, have held positions in government, or have served as lawyers for leading law firms, as federal district attorneys, or as law school professors. Some federal judges have served as state court judges. Until recently, few African Americans, Hispanics, or women were appointed as judges to the lower federal courts. Lyndon Johnson appointed the first African American, Thurgood Marshall, to the Supreme Court; Ronald Reagan appointed the first woman, Sandra Day O'Connor.

The Court at Work

The term of the Supreme Court begins on the first Monday in October and generally lasts until June or July of the following year.

Accepting Cases

Thousands of cases are appealed to the Supreme Court every year; only a few hundred cases are actually heard. Most of the cases are denied because the justices either agree with the lower court decision or believe that the case does not involve a significant point of law. Cases that are accepted for review must pass the **rule of four**—four of the nine justices must agree to hear the case. Many of the cases accepted may be disposed of in **brief orders**—returned to the lower court for reconsideration because of a related case that was recently decided. Those cases presented to the Supreme Court for possible review may be appealed through:

- *writ of certiorari*—An order by the Court (when petitioned) directing a lower court to send up the records of a case for review; usually requires the need to interpret law or decide a constitutional question.
- *certificate*—A lower court may ask the Supreme Court about a rule of law or procedures in specific cases.

Briefs and Oral Arguments

Once a case reaches the Supreme Court, lawyers for each party to the case file a written **brief**. A brief is a detailed statement of the facts of the case supporting a particular position by presenting arguments based on relevant facts and citations from previous cases. Interested parties may also be invited to submit *amicus curiae* ("friends of the court") **briefs**, supporting or rejecting arguments of the case.

Oral arguments allow both sides to present their positions to the justices during a 30-minute period. Justices may interrupt the lawyers during this time, raising questions or challenging points of law.

Research and Conferences

Justices use law clerks to research the information presented in oral arguments and briefs. Throughout the term, the justices meet in private conferences to consider cases heard in oral argument, with the chief justice presiding over the conferences. Each justice may speak about the cases under discussion. An informal poll determines how each justice is leaning in the case.

Writing Opinions

Once the Supreme Court has made a decision in a case, the decision is explained in a written statement called an opinion. If voting with the majority, the chief justice selects who will write the opinion; if voting with the minority, the most senior associate justice of the majority selects who will write the opinion.

- *majority opinion*—A majority of the justices agree on the decision and its reasons.
- *concurring opinion*—A justice who agrees with the majority opinion but not with the reasoning behind the decision.
- *dissenting opinion*—A justice or justices who disagree with the majority opinion.

Opinions of the Supreme Court are as important as the decisions they explain. Majority opinions become **precedents**, standards or guides to be followed in deciding similar cases in the future. *Stare decisis* is the doctrine or policy of following rules or principles laid down in previous judicial decisions (precedents).

Courts as Policymakers

New Deal Era

Controversy surrounded the Supreme Court during the New Deal era, as Congress passed numerous laws designed to end the Depression and the conservative Court ruled these laws unconstitutional. In response, Franklin Roosevelt proposed what opponents termed a "court-packing plan" to increase the number of justices, allowing Roosevelt to appoint justices supportive of New Deal legislation. Although Congress did not pass Roosevelt's plan to expand the Court, two justices, Chief Justice Charles Evans Hughes and Associate Justice Owen Roberts, began voting in favor of New Deal legislation (sometimes referred to as "the switch in time to save nine").

The Warren Court (1953–1969)

Often termed "the most liberal court ever," the Warren Court under Chief Justice Earl Warren was especially active in the area of civil rights and civil liberties. This Court heard *Brown v. Board of Education* (1954), declaring segregation in public schools unconstitutional.

The Warren Court also expanded the rights of criminal defendants in *Gideon v. Wainwright* (1963) and *Miranda v. Arizona* (1966).

The Burger Court (1969–1986)

Richard Nixon's appointment of Warren Burger as chief justice returned the Supreme Court to a more conservative ideology with regard to narrowing the rights of defendants. The Burger Court permitted abortions in *Roe v. Wade* (1973) and ruled that Nixon did not have **executive privilege** over information in a criminal proceeding in *U.S. v. Nixon* (1974). In *Regents of the University of California v. Bakke* (1978), the Court ruled against the use of quotas in the admissions process. At the same time, the Court upheld the legality of affirmative action.

The Rehnquist and Roberts Courts (1986–present)

The conservative Court under Chief Justice William Rehnquist continued to limit, but not reverse, decisions of the earlier more liberal courts in the areas of defendants' rights, abortion (*Planned Parenthood v. Casey,* 1992), and affirmative action. The court of Chief Justice John Roberts (2005–present) continued the conservative ideology of the Rehnquist Court. In 2007 the Roberts Court upheld the federal Partial-Birth Abortion Act of 2003. New justices Sonia Sotomayor and Elena Kagan were sworn in during the Obama administration and Neil Gorsuch was sworn in during early days of the Trump administration. The impact of these appointments on the complexion and outlook of the Supreme Court is still to be determined.

Judicial Philosophy

Judicial philosophy of activism or restraint is not the same as political philosophy such as liberal or conservative. Although some recent justices who supported an activist philosophy (Warren and T. Marshall) were also more liberal, this has not always been the case. The Marshall Court was activist in establishing judicial review but conservative in protecting property rights.

Judicial Activism

The philosophy of **judicial activism**, or judicial intervention, holds that the Court should play an active role in determining national policies. The philosophy advocates applying the Constitution to social and political questions, especially where constitutional rights have been violated or unacceptable conditions exist (**loose constructionist**).

Judicial activism can take at least three forms. These include:

- The act of overturning laws as unconstitutional
- Overruling judicial precedent
- Ruling contrary to a previously issued constitutional interpretation

An example of judicial activism is the 1954 case of *Brown v. Board of Education*. A lawsuit in 1951 requested that the school district reverse its policy of racial segregation, in which the district operated separate schools for black and white children. The plaintiffs in the case claimed that racial segregation resulted in inferior facilities, accommodations, and treatment of their children.

The lower courts ruled in favor of the Board of Education, based on the prior ruling of *Plessy v. Ferguson*, a case that upheld state laws requiring segregated transportation on trains. When the case was appealed to the U.S. Supreme Court, the Court ruled that segregation of whites and blacks in school was indeed unconstitutional, as it was harmful to black students.

This ruling ignored the legal doctrine of stare decisis, which requires judges to uphold prior rulings of higher courts. Instead of relying on the ruling in *Plessy v. Ferguson*, which was a similar case, the Supreme Court overruled it.

Judicial Restraint

The philosophy of **judicial restraint** holds that the Court should avoid taking the initiative on social and political questions, operating strictly within the limits of the Constitution (**strict constructionist**) and upholding acts of Congress unless the acts clearly violate specific provisions of the Constitution. Judicial restraint involves only a limited use of judicial powers and advocates the belief that the Court should be more passive, allowing the executive and legislative branches to lead the way in policymaking.

Examples of judicial restraint include *Dred Scott v. Sandford* (1857), which declared that slaves were not protected by the Constitution and could never become citizens, and *Plessy v. Ferguson* (1896), which upheld the constitutionality of "separate but equal," preserving segregation.

Checks on the Supreme Court

The Supreme Court plays a very important role in our government. It is the highest court in the land, the court of last resort. Through the power of judicial review, it plays a vital role in providing for limited government. It protects civil rights and liberties by striking down laws that violate the Constitution.

The Supreme Court is also subject to limitations under the system of checks and balances:

- The president nominates and the Senate can approve or reject Supreme Court justices, which impacts the ideological makeup of the court and affects its rulings
- The Supreme Court lacks the ability to enforce its rulings. The president or the states can ignore the ruling.
- Congress has the power to write new legislation which can clarify a law and modify the impact of the Court's decision
- Congress has the power to propose constitutional amendments which, if approved by the states, can undo Supreme Court decisions
- Congress has the authority to create courts inferior to the Supreme Court
- Congress has the authority to establish jurisdiction of courts which can affect the Court's ability to hear certain types of cases
- Congress may alter the size of the Supreme Court, changing the balance of power within the Court
- The House of Representatives can impeach federal judges and the Senate, after conducting a trial of impeachment, can remove a judge from a federal court
- The Supreme Court cannot initiate judicial review of legislation. The Court is required to wait until a party who has been directly and significantly injured by the legislation challenges its constitutionality.

› Review Questions

Multiple-Choice Questions

1. Under the guidelines of the Constitution, which of the following is NOT within the jurisdiction of the federal courts?
   (A) cases involving federal law
   (B) cases involving interpretation of state constitutions
   (C) cases involving interpretation of the federal Constitution
   (D) treaties

2. Federal courts created by Congress under Article III of the Constitution include the Supreme Court, district courts, the Courts of Appeals, Court of Appeals for the Federal Circuit, and the U.S. Court of International Trade. These courts can best be described as
   (A) legislative courts
   (B) territorial courts
   (C) constitutional courts
   (D) original courts

3. When making an appointment to the Supreme Court, presidents
   (A) remain impartial by refusing candidate endorsements from members of the Supreme Court
   (B) often select a candidate who is neither decidedly liberal or conservative
   (C) tend to ignore race as a consideration for selecting a judge
   (D) tend to choose judges from their own political party

4. Which of the following best describes the formal qualifications for a federal judge?
   (A) They serve "during good behavior."
   (B) The president appoints them with the approval of the House of Representatives.
   (C) They serve at the discretion of the president.
   (D) They serve at the discretion of the Congress.

5. Which of the following has little bearing when the president makes an appointment to the Supreme Court?
   (A) party affiliation
   (B) judicial philosophy
   (C) likability
   (D) "litmus test"

6. Who was the first president to appoint an African American to the Supreme Court?
   (A) Richard Nixon
   (B) Lyndon Johnson
   (C) Ronald Reagan
   (D) John Kennedy

7. Which term best describes the Supreme Court's issuance of an order directing a lower court to send up its record for review?
   (A) certificate
   (B) rule of four
   (C) amicus curiae
   (D) writ of certiorari

8. The majority opinion, issued by the Supreme Court as the final decision of a case, becomes the standard or guide that will be followed in deciding similar cases in the future. This standard or guide is known as a
   (A) precedent
   (B) brief
   (C) argument
   (D) decision

9. Which court was first known for narrowing the rights of defendants?
   (A) Warren Court
   (B) Rehnquist Court
   (C) Burger Court
   (D) New Deal Court

10. The judicial philosophy that advocates the courts' active role in policymaking is called
    (A) strict constructionist
    (B) judicial activism
    (C) loose constructionist
    (D) judicial restraint

Question 11 refers to the quotation below.

"It is emphatically the province and duty of the judicial department to say what the law is. Those who apply the rule to particular cases, must of necessity expound and interpret that rule. If two laws conflict with each other, the courts must decide on the operation of each."

— Chief Justice John Marshall

11. Which of the following principles is most accurately reflected in the quote from John Marshall?
    (A) republicanism
    (B) constitutionalism
    (C) judicial review
    (D) checks and balances

Free-Response Question

12. There has been considerable debate over the years on what the role of the Supreme Court should be. Some courts have practiced judicial activism, while others have not.
    (A) Describe the principle of judicial activism.
    (B) Discuss one argument in favor of a Supreme Court that practices judicial activism.
    (C) Discuss one argument against a Supreme Court that practices judicial activism.

› Answers and Explanations

1. **B.** Cases involving state constitutions are heard in state courts, not federal courts. The other answer choices are within the jurisdiction of the federal courts.

2. **C.** Constitutional courts include the Supreme Court, district courts, the Courts of Appeals, the Court of Appeals for the Federal Circuit, and the U.S. Court of International Trade. Legislative courts (A) hear cases arising from the powers given to Congress under Article I. Territorial courts (B) are a type of legislative court. There are courts with original jurisdiction, but there are no courts termed "original courts" (D).

3. **D.** The Supreme Court has both original and appellate jurisdiction.

4. **A.** Federal judges are appointed by the president with confirmation by the Senate (B) and serve during "good behavior" (C, D).

5. **C.** The nominee's personality is not a primary consideration in the nomination process. The president may consider party affiliation (A) and judicial philosophy (B) when appointing justices to the Supreme Court. A "litmus test" may also serve as a gauge of the nominee's purity toward a liberal or conservative stand on certain issues (D).

6. **B.** In 1967, Lyndon Johnson appointed Thurgood Marshall, the first African American on the Supreme Court.

7. **D.** A writ of certiorari is a court order directing a lower court to send up the records of a case for review. A certificate (A) is an appeal in which a lower court asks the Supreme Court about a rule. The rule of four is used to determine which cases the justices will consider (B). An *amicus curiae* brief is a "friend of the court" brief submitted by nonlitigants who have an interest in the outcome of the case (C).

8. **A.** A precedent is a standard used by the courts to decide similar cases. A brief (B) is a detailed statement of the facts of a case supporting a particular position. An argument (C) is the presentation of a case before a court. A decision (D) is the final ruling of a court.

9. **C.** The Supreme Court under Chief Justice Warren Burger was the first to narrow the rights of defendants after those rights were broadened under the Warren Court (A). The Rehnquist Court (B) continued to narrow the rights of defendants. The New Deal Court (D) focused on consideration of laws designed to end the Great Depression.

10. **B.** The philosophy of judicial activism advocates policymaking by the courts. A strict constructionist (A) view holds that justices should base decisions on a narrow interpretation of the Constitution. A loose constructionist view (C) believes that judges should have freedom in interpreting the Constitution. Judicial restraint (D) is a philosophy that holds that the court should avoid taking the initiative on social and political questions (D).

11. **C.** John Marshall's quote, from the opinion in *Marbury v. Madison*, describes the power of judicial review. Republicanism occurs when the people exercise their power by delegating it to representatives chosen by them through the election process (A). Constitutionalism is when government is based upon constitutional principles (B). Checks and balances occurs when each branch of the national government has certain controls (checks) over the other two branches.

12. **A.** Judicial activism is the belief that the courts should play an active role in determining national policies. This philosophy advocates applying the Constitution to social and political questions.

    B. Supporters of judicial activism argue that it is necessary to correct injustices and promote needed social changes. Justices can use their powers to correct justices and shape social policy on such issues as civil rights and protections of civil liberties.

    C. Opponents of judicial activism believe that activist judges are making laws, not just interpreting them. The courts are assuming responsibilities that belong exclusively to the legislative and executive branches of government. Critics point out that federal judges are not elected, they are appointed for life terms. As a result, when judges begin making policy decisions about social or political changes society should make, they become "unelected legislators." Consequently, the people lose control of the right to govern themselves.

› Rapid Review

- Article III of the Constitution establishes the Supreme Court and a system of inferior courts.
- Jurisdiction is the authority of the federal courts to hear certain cases. Jurisdiction may be original, appellate, or concurrent.
- The Supreme Court, the Courts of Appeals, and district courts are constitutional courts.
- The Supreme Court was created directly by the Constitution. It is the highest court in the United States, having both original and appellate jurisdiction.
- Federal judges are appointed by the president and confirmed by a majority of the Senate.
- Presidents make appointments to the Supreme Court only when a vacancy occurs during a president's term of office.
- Almost all federal judges have some form of legal training.
- The Supreme Court hears only a few hundred cases each year from the several thousand cases submitted.
- Cases may be presented to the Supreme Court for possible review by writ of certiorari, certificate, or the submission of an *amicus curiae* brief.
- Oral arguments allow both sides time to present their arguments to the justices.
- Law clerks research information presented in oral arguments and briefs.
- Supreme Court decisions are explained in written statements known as opinions. Opinions may be majority, concurring, or dissenting.
- Courts are often termed liberal or conservative, depending on the decisions of the court and the guidance of the chief justice.
- Judicial philosophy may follow the lines of judicial activism or judicial restraint.

UNIT

3

Civil Liberties and Civil Rights

CHAPTER 11

Civil Liberties and Civil Rights

IN THIS CHAPTER

Summary: In the Declaration of Independence, Thomas Jefferson wrote that all people "are endowed by their creator with certain unalienable rights." **Civil liberties** are those rights that belong to everyone; they are protections against government and are guaranteed by the Constitution, legislation, and judicial decisions. **Civil rights** are the positive acts of government, designed to prevent discrimination and provide equality before the law.

Key Terms

civil liberties	Establishment Clause	exclusionary rule
civil rights	Free Exercise Clause	*Miranda v. Arizona*
writ of habeas corpus	Lemon Test	*Plessy v. Ferguson*
bills of attainder	pure speech	*Brown v. Board of*
ex post facto laws	speech plus	*Education*
self-incrimination	prior restraint	Equal Protection Clause
double jeopardy	substantive due process	affirmative action
incorporation	procedural due process	
symbolic speech	eminent domain	

Civil Liberties

- *Constitution*—The original Constitution mentions specific rights considered to be fundamental freedoms by the Founding Fathers:
  - **writ of habeas corpus**—You must be brought before the court and informed of charges against you.
  - no **bills of attainder**—You cannot be punished without a trial.

— no **ex post facto laws**—Laws applied to acts committed before the laws' passage are unconstitutional.
— trial by jury

- *Bill of Rights*—Added in 1791 to the original Constitution to provide specific guarantees by the national government:
  — freedom of religion, speech, press, petition, and assembly
  — no unreasonable searches and seizure
  — protections against **self-incrimination** and **double jeopardy**
  — protections in criminal procedures

- *The Fourteenth Amendment provided for the expansion of individual rights*—The Supreme Court in *Gitlow v. New York* (1925) and subsequent cases has interpreted the Due Process Clause of the Fourteenth Amendment to apply the guarantees of the Bill of Rights to state and local governments (**incorporation**). Today, most guarantees of the Bill of Rights have been incorporated to apply to the state and local governments.
- *Legislative actions are laws that set limits or boundaries on one person's rights over another's or bring balance between the rights of individuals and the interests of society*—For example, false advertising is not protected under the First Amendment guarantee of freedom of speech.
- *Court decisions protect rights through the use of judicial review*—Flag burning (*Texas v. Johnson*, 1989) is protected, but burning a draft card (*United States v. O'Brien*, 1968) is not protected **symbolic speech.**

Freedom of Religion

Two protections for freedom of religion exist: the **Establishment Clause** and the **Free Exercise Clause.**

> *Congress shall make no law respecting an establishment of religion, or prohibiting the free exercise thereof.*—Amendment 1

The Establishment Clause

According to Thomas Jefferson, the Constitution creates a "wall of separation between Church and State." Because the church and government are separate in the United States, Congress cannot establish any religion as the national religion, nor favor one religion over another, nor tax American citizens to support any one religion. Controversy concerning the exact meaning and extent of the Establishment Clause has led to actions by the Supreme Court in defining the parameters of the clause, including:

- *Everson v. Board of Education (1947)*—The Court upheld a New Jersey policy of reimbursing parents of Catholic school students for the costs of busing their children to school.
- ***Engel v. Vitale (1962)***—The Court ruled school-sanctioned prayer in public schools is unconstitutional.
- *Abington School District v. Schempp (1963)*—The Court struck down a Pennsylvania law requiring the reading of a Bible passage at the beginning of each day.
- *Lemon v. Kurtzman (1971)*—The Court struck down a Pennsylvania law reimbursing parochial schools for textbooks and teacher salaries and established the **Lemon Test**. To pass the test (1) a law must have a primarily secular purpose; (2) its principal effect must neither aid nor inhibit religion; and (3) it must not create excessive entanglement between government and religion.

- *Lynch v. Donnelly (1984)*—The Court upheld the right of governmental entities to celebrate the Christmas holiday with Christmas displays that might include nativity scenes, if secular displays are also sufficiently included.
- *Wallace v. Jaffree (1985)*—The Court overturned a state law setting aside time for "voluntary prayer" in public schools.
- *Edwards v. Aguillard (1987)*—The Court ruled that Louisiana could not force public schools that taught evolution to also teach creationism.
- *Board of Education of Westside Community Schools v. Mergens (1990)*—The Court upheld the Equal Access Act of 1984, which required public secondary schools to provide religious groups the same access to facilities that other extracurricular groups had.
- *Lee v. Weisman (1992)*—The Court ruled against clergy-led prayer at high school graduation ceremonies.
- *Santa Fe Independent School District v. Doe (2002)*—The Court overturned a Texas law allowing high school students to read a prayer at athletic events such as football games.

The Free Exercise Clause

The Free Exercise Clause guarantees the right to practice any religion or no religion at all. In its interpretations of the Free Exercise Clause, the Supreme Court has made distinctions between belief and practice. The Court has ruled that while religious belief is absolute, the practice of those beliefs may be restricted, especially if those practices conflict with criminal laws. For example:

- *Reynolds v. United States (1879)*—The Court upheld the federal law that prohibited polygamy even though Reynolds, a Mormon from Utah, claimed that the law limited his religious freedom.
- **Wisconsin v. Yoder** *(1972)*—The Court ruled that Wisconsin could not require Amish parents to send their children to public school beyond the eighth grade because it would violate long-held religious beliefs.
- *Employment Division of Oregon v. Smith (1990)*—The Court ruled that Oregon could deny unemployment benefits to workers fired for using drugs (peyote) as part of a religious ceremony.
- *Church of the Lukumi Babalu Aye v. City of Hialeah (1993)*—The Court ruled that laws banning animal sacrifice were unconstitutional because they targeted the Santeria religion.

In 1993 Congress passed the Religious Freedom Restoration Act, giving people the right to practice religious activities unless prohibited by laws that are narrowly tailored and the government can show a "compelling interest." In 1997 the Supreme Court ruled this law unconstitutional in *City of Boerne, Texas v. Flores.*

Freedom of Speech

Types of Speech

There are several different classifications of speech:

- *pure speech*—The most common form of speech, verbal speech; given the most protection by the courts.
- *speech plus*—Verbal and symbolic speech used together, such as a rally and then picketing; may also be limited.

- *symbolic speech*—Using actions and symbols to convey an idea rather than words (burning a draft card or flag, wearing an armband in protest); may be subject to government restrictions if it endangers public safety.

Regulating Speech

Limitations on free speech have generally existed in the area of providing for national security. In 1798 Congress passed the Alien and Sedition Acts, making it illegal to say anything "false, scandalous and malicious against the government or its officials." Although these acts were aimed at the opponents of President John Adams and his Federalist supporters, others were convicted under these laws. The Alien and Sedition Acts were never challenged in court, and they expired in 1801.

After the assassination of President McKinley by an anarchist in 1901 and the entrance of the United States into World War I, Congress again passed sedition laws forbidding verbal attacks on the government, and the states began following suit. These and subsequent laws were challenged in the courts.

- ***Schenck v. United States (1919)***—Schenck mailed fliers to draftees during World War I urging them to protest the draft peacefully; he was convicted of violating a federal law against encouraging the disobedience of military orders. Oliver Wendell Holmes wrote in the opinion that such speech was not protected during wartime because it would create a clear and present danger, establishing a standard for measuring what would and would not be protected speech.
- *Gitlow v. New York (1925)*—The Court applied the protections of free speech to the states under the Due Process Clause of the Fourteenth Amendment.
- *Cox v. New Hampshire (1941)*—The Court ruled that, although the government cannot regulate the contents of speech, it can place reasonable time, place, and manner restrictions on speech for the public safety.
- *Chaplinsky v. New Hampshire (1942)*—The Court ruled that the First Amendment did not protect "fighting words."
- ***Tinker v. Des Moines (1969)***—The Court ruled that wearing black armbands in protest of the Vietnam War was symbolic speech, protected by the First Amendment.
- *Brandenburg v. Ohio (1969)*—The Court made the "clear and present" danger test less restrictive by ruling that using inflammatory speech would be punished only if there was imminent danger that this speech would incite an illegal act.
- *Miller v. California (1973)*—The Court established the Miller test, which sets standards for measuring obscenity: (1) major theme appeals to indecent sexual desires applying contemporary community standards; (2) shows in clearly offensive way sexual behavior outlawed by state law; and (3) "lacks serious literary, artistic, political, or scientific value."
- *Texas v. Johnson (1989)*—The Court ruled that flag burning is a protected form of symbolic speech.
- *Reno v. ACLU (1997)*—The Court ruled the Communications Decency Act unconstitutional because it was "overly broad and vague" in regulating Internet speech.

Since the 1940s the Court has supported the preferred position doctrine: First Amendment freedoms are more fundamental than other freedoms because they provide a basis for other liberties; therefore, they hold a preferred position and laws regulating these freedoms must be shown to be absolutely necessary to be declared constitutional.

Freedom of the Press

Freedom of the press is often protected because it is closely related to freedom of speech; the press is used as a form of expression. Today the press includes newspapers, magazines, radio, television, and the Internet.

- *Near v. Minnesota (1931)*—The Court applied the protections of free press to the states under the Due Process Clause of the Fourteenth Amendment and prohibited **prior restraint**.
- *New York Times v. Sullivan (1964)*—The Court protected statements about public officials.
- ***New York Times v. United States** (1971)*—The Court reaffirmed its position of prior restraint, refusing to stop the publication of the Pentagon Papers and strengthening freedom of the press.
- *Hazelwood School District v. Kuhlmeier (1988)*—The Court ruled in favor of school district censorship of student newspapers as long as censorship is related to legitimate concerns.

Freedom of Assembly and Petition

The First Amendment guarantees the "right of the people peacefully to assemble, and to petition the Government for a redress of grievances." Freedom of assembly and petition applies to both private and public places, allowing citizens to make their views known to government officials through petitions, letters, picketing, demonstrations, parades, and marches. The courts have protected these rights while allowing the government to set limits to protect the rights and safety of others.

- *Dejonge v. Oregon (1937)*—The Court established that the right of association (assembly) was as important as other First Amendment rights and used the Due Process Clause of the Fourteenth Amendment to apply freedom of assembly to the states.

The courts have generally ruled that:

- To protect public order, government may require groups wanting to parade or demonstrate to first obtain a permit.
- Certain public facilities (schools, airports, jails) not generally open to the public may be restricted from demonstrations.
- Restrictions on assembly must be worded precisely and must apply to all groups equally.
- The right to assemble does not allow groups to use private property for its own uses (creates buffer zones around abortion clinics).
- Police may disperse demonstrations in order to keep the peace or protect the public's safety (if demonstrations become violent or dangerous to public safety).

Second Amendment

Until recently, challenges involving the Second Amendment have been rare. In 2008, however, the Supreme Court ruled in *District of Columbia v. Heller* that a federal law that forbidding civilians from possessing handguns in the nation's capital was unconstitutional. A 5–4 majority ruled that the Second Amendment protects a private right of individuals to have arms for their own defense, not a right of the states to maintain a militia. In ***McDonald v. City of Chicago** (2010)*, the Court struck down a similar handgun ban at the state level, using judicial precedents under the Fourteenth Amendment's Due Process Clause. These rulings strengthen citizens' rights to keep and bear arms for self-defense in your own home.

Property Rights

The Due Process Clauses of the Fifth and Fourteenth Amendments provide for the protection of private property by guaranteeing that the government cannot deprive a person of "life, liberty, or property, without due process of law." Although the Supreme Court has not defined the term due process, it has generally accepted the concept of government acting in a fair manner according to established rules. **Substantive due process** involves the policies of government or the subject matter of the laws, determining whether the law is fair or if it violates constitutional protections. **Procedural due process** is the method of government action or how the law is carried out, according to established rules and procedures. Although the Due Process Clause has often been applied to those accused of crimes (the guarantee of a fair trial would be due process), due process has also been used to protect property rights. The Fifth Amendment states that government cannot take private property for public use without paying a fair price for it. This right of **eminent domain** allows government to take property for public use but also requires that government provide just compensation for that property.

Right to Privacy

The Constitution makes no mention of a "right to privacy." The Supreme Court, however, has interpreted several rights that might fall under the category of privacy. The Due Process Clause of the Fourteenth Amendment has been used by the Court to protect the right of privacy from state infringement.

- *Griswold v. Connecticut (1965)*—The Court ruled that the First, Third, Fourth, Ninth, and Fourteenth Amendments created "zones of privacy" and enhanced the concept of enumerated rights.
- ***Roe v. Wade*** *(1973)*—The outcome was a continuation of the recognition of a constitutional right of privacy for a woman to determine whether to terminate a pregnancy while recognizing that the state may have a compelling interest in maternal life and health.

Rights of the Accused

Several amendments of the Bill of Rights address the rights of those accused of crimes. The Fourteenth Amendment extends those protections to apply to the states.

Fourth Amendment: Search and Seizure

- *Wolf v. Colorado (1949)*—The Court applied protections against unreasonable search and seizure to the states under the Due Process Clause of the Fourteenth Amendment.
- *Mapp v. Ohio (1961)*—The Court ruled that evidence obtained without a search warrant was excluded from trial in state courts. *Mapp v. Ohio* involved the application of the **exclusionary rule** to the states. The exclusionary rule is the Court's effort to deter illegal police conduct by barring from court evidence that has been obtained in violation of the Fourth Amendment.
- *Terry v. Ohio (1968)*—The Court ruled that searches of criminal suspects are constitutional and police may search suspects for safety purposes.

- *Nix v. Williams (1984)*—The Court established the inevitable discovery rule, allowing evidence discovered as the result of an illegal search to be introduced if it can be shown that the evidence would have been found anyway.
- *United States v. Leon (1984)*—The Court established the good faith exception to the exclusionary rule.

Fifth Amendment: Self-Incrimination

- *Miranda v. Arizona (1966)*—The Court ruled that suspects in police custody have certain rights and that they must be informed of those rights (right to remain silent; right to an attorney).

Sixth Amendment: Right to an Attorney

- *Powell v. Alabama (1932)*—The Court established that the Due Process Clause of the Fourteenth Amendment guarantees defendants in death penalty cases the right to an attorney.
- *Betts v. Brady (1942)*—The Court ruled that poor defendants in noncapital cases are not entitled to an attorney at government expense.

- **Gideon v. Wainwright (1963)**—The Court ruled that in state trials, those who cannot afford an attorney will have one provided by the state, overturning *Betts v. Brady.*
- *Escobedo v. Illinois (1964)*—The Supreme Court extended the exclusionary rule to illegal confessions in state court cases. The Court also defined the "Escobedo rule," which stated that persons have the right to an attorney when an investigation begins "to focus on a particular suspect." If the suspect has been arrested, has requested an attorney, and has not been warned of his or her right to remain silent, the suspect has been "denied counsel in violation of the Sixth Amendment."

Eighth Amendment: Cruel and Unusual Punishment

- *Furman v. Georgia (1972)*—The Court ruled the death penalty unconstitutional under existing state law because it was imposed arbitrarily.
- *Gregg v. Georgia (1976)*—In this case, the death penalty was constitutional because it was imposed based on the circumstances of the case.

Civil Rights

Civil rights are guaranteed by the Equal Protection Clause of the Fourteenth Amendment, which was added to the Constitution after the Civil War to prevent states from discriminating against former slaves and to protect former slaves' rights. The courts recognize that some forms of discrimination may be valid (preventing those under 21 from consuming alcohol) and have therefore devised the rational basis test to determine if the discrimination has a legitimate purpose. The courts have also developed the strict scrutiny test, a much stricter standard. If the discrimination reflects prejudice, the courts automatically classify it as suspect and require the government to prove a compelling reason for the discrimination. For example, if a city had separate schools for different races, the city would have to prove how this serves a compelling public interest.

The Civil Rights Movement

After the Civil War three amendments were passed to ensure the rights of the former slaves.

- The Thirteenth Amendment abolished slavery.
- The Fourteenth Amendment defined citizenship to include the former slaves and provided for due process and equal protection, which were used by the Supreme Court to apply the Bill of Rights to the state and local governments.
- The Fifteenth Amendment provided that individuals could not be denied the right to vote based on race or the fact that they were once slaves.

Until the 1950s and 1960s states continued to use discriminatory practices to prevent African Americans from participating in the political processes.

- Black codes were state laws passed to keep former slaves in a state of political bondage. The laws included literacy tests, poll taxes, registration laws, and white primaries.
- The Civil Rights Act of 1875 outlawed racial discrimination in public places such as hotels, theaters, and railroads but required African Americans to take their cases to federal court, a time-consuming and costly endeavor. The Act was ruled unconstitutional in 1883.
- Jim Crow laws were laws designed to segregate the races in schools, public transportation, and hotels.
- In **Plessy v. Ferguson** (1896) the Supreme Court upheld the Jim Crow laws by allowing separate facilities for the different races if those facilities were equal. This created the separate but equal doctrine.
- With Executive Order 8802 (1941) Franklin Roosevelt banned racial discrimination in the defense industry and government offices.
- With Executive Order 9981 (1948) Harry Truman ordered the desegregation of the armed forces.
- In **Brown v. Board of Education** (1954) the Supreme Court overturned the *Plessy* decision, ruling that separate but equal is unconstitutional. The Court determined that "separate but equal" was a violation of the Equal Protection Clause of the Fourteenth Amendment.
- In *Brown v. Board of Education II* (1955) the Supreme Court ordered the desegregation of schools "with all deliberate speed."
- The Civil Rights Act of 1957 created the Civil Rights Division within the Justice Department and made it a crime to prevent a person from voting in federal elections.
- The Civil Rights Act of 1964 prohibited discrimination in employment and in places of public accommodation, outlawed bias in federally funded programs, and created the Equal Employment Opportunity Commission (EEOC).
- The Twenty-Fourth Amendment (1964) outlawed poll taxes in federal elections.
- The Voting Rights Act of 1965 allowed federal registrars to register voters and outlawed literacy tests and other discriminatory tests in voter registration.
- **Title IX of the Education Amendments Act of 1972** is a federal law that prohibits sex-based discrimination in any education program or activity that is federally funded. Due to Title IX there have been major advances for women in high school and college athletic and curricular programs.
- The Civil Rights Act of 1991 made it easier for job applicants and employees to bring suit against employers with discriminatory hiring practices.

Letter from a Birmingham Jail

In 1963, at the height of the Civil Rights Movement, Dr. Martin Luther King, Jr. was arrested for leading public demonstrations in Birmingham, Alabama, a violation of a court order forbidding demonstrations. Believing the order unjust, King had decided to demonstrate anyway. King was held for twenty-four hours without being allowed his constitutional right to contact a lawyer.

When Dr. King was finally allowed contact with the outside world, he saw a letter published in a newspaper criticizing the demonstrations and calling them "unwise and untimely." "Letter from a Birmingham Jail" is King's response to that letter in the newspaper. In it, he argues that he and his fellow demonstrations have a duty to fight for justice.

King then goes on to explain the four steps of nonviolent protest: fact finding, negotiation, self-purification, and direct action. After speaking with the officials of Birmingham, King concluded that he needed to take action by leading the public demonstration. He concluded that he doesn't regret his decision, nor should he.

Other Minorities

KEY IDEA

With the successes of the African American Civil Rights Movement, other minorities have also pressed to end discrimination. Hispanics, American Indians, Asian Americans, women, and people with disabilities have all joined in the quest for protections from discriminatory actions.

Hispanic Americans

Hispanic Americans is a term often used to describe people in the United States who have a Spanish-speaking heritage, including Mexican Americans, Cuban Americans, Puerto Ricans, and Central and South Americans. Today, the Hispanic population is the fastest growing minority in America.

Although the number of Hispanics elected to public office has increased since the 1970s, their progress continues to be hampered by unequal educational opportunities and language barriers. Civil rights action on behalf of Hispanics has concentrated on health care for undocumented immigrants, affirmative action, admission of more Hispanic students to state colleges and universities, and redistricting plans that do not discriminate against Hispanic Americans.

Native Americans

More than two million Native Americans live on reservations in the United States. As a result of discrimination, poverty, unemployment, alcoholism, and drug abuse are common problems. Lack of organization has hampered Native American attempts to gain political power. With the formation of militant organizations (National Indian Youth Council and American Indian Movement) and protests (siege at Wounded Knee), Native Americans have brought attention to their concerns. A 1985 Supreme Court ruling upheld treaty rights of Native American tribes. The Indian Gaming Regulatory Act (1988) allowed Native Americans to have gaming operations (casinos) on their reservations, creating an economic boom in many tribes. In 1990 Congress passed the Native American Languages Act, encouraging the continuation of native languages and culture.

Asian Americans

Discrimination against Asians arriving in the United States began almost immediately as Asian workers began competing for jobs. Beginning in 1882, the Chinese Exclusion Act (and other similar acts) limited the number of Asians permitted to enter the United States. After the bombing of Pearl Harbor, people of Japanese descent were forced into relocation camps. The Supreme Court upheld these actions when they declared the internments to be legal in *Korematsu v. United States*. In 1988 Congress appropriated funds to compensate former camp detainees or their survivors.

The Women's Movement

Throughout much of American history, women have not been given the same rights as men.

- The Nineteenth Amendment (1920) gave women the right to vote.
- The Equal Pay Act (1963) made it illegal to base an employee's pay on race, gender, religion, or national origin. This also affected the African American Civil Rights Movement.
- The Civil Rights Act of 1964 banned job discrimination on the basis of gender.
- In *Reed v. Reed* (1971) the Supreme Court ruled against a law that discriminated against women, deciding that the Equal Protection Clause of the Fourteenth Amendment denied unreasonable classifications based on gender.
- The Equal Employment Opportunity Act (1972) prohibited gender discrimination in hiring, firing, promotions, pay, and working conditions.
- The Omnibus Education Act (1972) required schools to give all boys and girls an equal opportunity to participate in sports programs.
- The Equal Credit Opportunity Act (1974) prohibited discrimination against women seeking credit from banks, finance agencies, or the government and made it illegal to ask about a person's gender or marital status on a credit application.
- The Women's Equity in Employment Act (1991) required employers to justify gender discriminations in hiring and job performance.

People with Disabilities

- The Rehabilitation Act (1973) prohibited discrimination against people with disabilities in federal programs.
- The Education for All Handicapped Children Act (1975) guarantees that children with disabilities will receive an "appropriate" education.
- The Americans with Disabilities Act (1990) forbids employers and owners of public accommodations from discriminating against people with disabilities (must make facilities wheelchair accessible, etc.). The Act created the Telecommunications Relay Service, which allows hearing- and speech-impaired people access to telephone communications.

The Gay Rights Movement

Prior to the 1960s and 1970s few people were willing to discuss their sexual preferences in relation to same-sex relationships. After a riot following a police raid of a gay and lesbian bar in 1969, the gay power movement gained momentum. Organizations such as the Gay Activist Alliance and the Gay Liberation Front began exerting pressure and influence on state legislatures to repeal laws prohibiting homosexual conduct. As a result of the growth of the gay rights movement, the Democratic Party has included protection of gay rights as part of its platform, and several states have passed laws prohibiting discrimination against homosexuals in employment, housing, education, and public accommodations. In *Romer v. Evans* (1996) the Supreme Court ruled that a Colorado constitutional amendment invalidating state and local laws that protected gays and lesbians from discrimination was unconstitutional because it violated the **Equal Protection Clause** of the Fourteenth Amendment. Most recently, the Supreme Court ruled in *Obergefell v. Hodges* (2015), that same-sex couples in the United States, no matter where they live, have the same legal right to marry as different-sex couples.

The Elderly

Discrimination has also been an issue with the elderly. Job discrimination made it difficult for older people to find work. As a result, in 1967 Congress passed the Age Discrimination in Employment Act, prohibiting employers from discriminating against individuals over the age of 40 on the basis of age.

Affirmative Action

Affirmative action is a policy designed to correct the effects of past discrimination. Most issues of affirmative action are race or gender based. In 1978 the Supreme Court ruled in *Regents of the University of California v. Bakke* that the affirmative action quotas used by the University of California in their admissions policies were unconstitutional, and that Bakke had been denied equal protection because the university used race as the sole criterion for admissions. In the more recent *Hopwood v. Texas* (1996) the Court struck down the University of Texas Law School's admissions program, stating that race could not be used as a factor in deciding which applicants to admit to achieve student body diversity, to prevent a hostile environment at the law school, to counteract the law school's reputation among minorities, or to end the effects of past discrimination by institutions other than the law school. In 2003 the Supreme Court ruled (*Grutter v. Bollinger*) that universities within the jurisdiction of the Fifth Circuit can use race as a factor in admissions as long as quotas are not used. In recent Court decisions the Court seems to be taking a more conservative view of affirmative action programs and many fear that affirmative action is on the decline.

› Review Questions

Multiple-Choice Questions

1. Which constitutional amendment provides for the expansion of individual rights found in the Bill of Rights?
   (A) Fourteenth Amendment
   (B) Fifteenth Amendment
   (C) Nineteenth Amendment
   (D) Twenty-Second Amendment

2. The Constitution creates a "wall of separation between Church and State" in the words of the
   (A) Elastic Clause
   (B) Establishment Clause
   (C) Exclusionary Clause
   (D) Judiciary Clause

3. The Supreme Court case that reaffirmed the prohibition on prior restraint was
   (A) *McDonald v. Chicago* (2010)
   (B) *Marbury v. Madison* (1803)
   (C) *New York Times Co. v. United States* (1971)
   (D) *Schenck v. United States* (1919)

4. Using actions rather than words to convey an idea would be an example of
   (A) speech plus
   (B) pure speech
   (C) free speech
   (D) symbolic speech

5. Which Supreme Court case ruled that race-based school segregation violates the equal protection clause of the Constitution?
   (A) *Shaw v. Reno* (1993)
   (B) *Gideon v. Wainwright* (1963)
   (C) *Brown v. Board of Education* (1954)
   (D) *Tinker v. Des Moines* (1969)

6. The right of the government to take property for public use as long as the government provides just compensation for the property is called
   (A) substantive due process
   (B) eminent domain
   (C) public domain
   (D) procedural due process

7. The Supreme Court, in *Mapp v. Ohio*, ruled that evidence obtained without a search warrant could be excluded from trial in state courts. This finding upholds the constitutional guarantee of no unreasonable search and seizure found in the
   (A) Fourth Amendment
   (B) Fifth Amendment
   (C) Fourteenth Amendment
   (D) First Amendment

8. What government action brought an end to Jim Crow laws and legal segregation in America?
   (A) the Civil Rights Act of 1875
   (B) Presidential Executive Order 8802
   (C) the Supreme Court ruling in *Plessy v. Ferguson*
   (D) the Supreme Court ruling in *Brown v. Board of Education*

9. Protections of the Bill of Rights have been applied to the states under a process known as
   (A) selective incorporation
   (B) constitutional application
   (C) state application
   (D) the exclusionary rule

10. Which of the following prohibits discrimination in the workplace?
    (A) Equal Pay Act
    (B) Equal Employment Opportunity Act
    (C) Women's Civil Rights Act of 1964
    (D) Nineteenth Amendment

Question 11 refers to the quotation below.

"Injustice anywhere is a threat to justice everywhere."
—Dr. Martin Luther King Jr.,
Letter from Birmingham Jail

11. Which statement is most consistent with the author's argument in this quote?
   (A) We should oppose injustice everywhere we see it.
   (B) It is justifiable that injustice may occur in some places but not others.
   (C) Forcing justice everywhere endangers society.
   (D) Justice cannot occur everywhere.

Free-Response Question

12. Civil rights may be expanded through the passage of new legislation or constitutional amendment.
   (A) Identify and describe two legislative acts which have led to the expansion of civil rights.
   (B) Identify and describe two constitutional amendments which have led to the expansion of civil rights.
   (C) Explain how the Civil Rights Movement has affected a group other than African-Americans.

❯ Answers and Explanations

1. **A.** The Fourteenth Amendment has been used to apply the freedoms listed in the Bill of Rights to the states. The Fifteenth Amendment (B) prevents the states from denying the right to vote to any person on the basis of race, color, or servitude. The Nineteenth Amendment (C) prohibits the denial of suffrage on the basis of sex. The Twenty- Second Amendment (D) addresses presidential tenure

2. **B.** The First Amendment's Establishment Clause creates a wall of separation between church and state.

3. **C.** *New York Times v. United States* (1971) increased the freedom of the press by establishing a "heavy presumption against prior restraint" even in cases involving national security. *McDonald v. Chicago* (2010) held that the Second Amendment right to keep and bear arms for self-defense is applicable tot the states (A). *Marbury v. Madison* (1803) established the principle of judicial review (B). *Schenck v. United States* (1919) held that free speech can be limited if it creates a "clear and present danger" (D).

4. **D.** Symbolic speech is the use of actions and symbols to convey ideas. Speech plus (A) is the use of verbal and symbolic speech together. Pure speech (B) means verbal speech.

5. **C.** *Brown v. Board of Education* (1954) established race-based school segregation violates the equal protection clause of the Fourteenth Amendment. *Shaw v. Reno* (1993) allowed voters to challenge majority-minority districts if race is the only factor used in creating the district (A). *Gideon v. Wainwright* (1963) guaranteed the right to an attorney for the poor or indigent in state felony cases (B). *Tinker v. Des Moines Independent Community School District* (1969) established the right of students to wear black armbands in school to protest the Vietnam War (D).

6. **B.** Eminent domain is the right of the government to take property for public use provided the government compensates for the property. Substantive due process (A) refers to the requirement that the government must create fair laws and policies. Procedural due process (D) refers to the requirement that the government must use fair methods and procedures.

7. **A.** Constitutional guarantees of protections against unreasonable searches and seizures are found in the Fourth Amendment.

8. **D.** The Supreme Court ruling in *Brown v. Board of Education* brought an end to Jim Crow laws and legal segregation in the United States. The Civil Rights Act of 1875 (A) outlawed racial discrimination in public places but required African Americans to take their cases to federal court. Executive Order 8802 (B) banned racial discrimination in the defense industry and government offices. In *Plessy v. Ferguson* (C), the Court upheld Jim Crow laws and created the "separate but equal" doctrine.

9. **C.** *Selective incorporation* is the process of applying the protections of the Bill of Rights to the states under the due process and equal protection clauses of the Fourteenth Amendment.

10. **B.** The Equal Employment Opportunity Act prohibits discrimination in the workplace. The Equal Pay Act (A) made it illegal to base an employee's pay on race, gender, religion, or national origin. The Nineteenth Amendment (D) prohibits the denial of suffrage on the basis of gender. There is no Women's Civil Rights Act (C).

11. **A.** Dr. Martin Luther King connected the struggle for freedom and equality of African Americans to the struggles for the same goals as other people around the world. He believed that if injustice can occur in one place, it can occur in other places, and that if it is allowed to continue, injustice can spread to even more places, endangering all society.

12. **A.** Legislative acts which have led to the expansion of civil rights include:

- The Civil Rights Act of 1865 which outlawed racial discrimination in public places such as hotels, theaters, and railroads
- Executive Order 9981 was given in 1948 by President Truman ordering the desegregation of the armed forces
- The Civil Rights Act of 1957 created the Civil Rights Division within the Justice Department and made it a crime to prevent a person from voting in Federal elections
- The Civil Rights Act of 1964 prohibited discrimination in employment and in places of public accommodation, outlawed bias in federally funded programs, and created the Equal Employment Opportunity Commission (EEOC)
- The Voting Rights Act of 1965 allowed federal registrars to register voters and outlawed literacy tests and other discriminate or eight tests in voter registration
- The Civil Right Act of 1991 made it easier for job applicants and employees to bring a suit against employers with discriminate or a hiring practices

B. Constitutional amendments which have led to the expansion of civil rights include:

- The Thirteenth Amendment abolished slavery
- The Fourteenth Amendment defined citizenship to include former slaves, and provided for due process and equal protection, which were used by the Supreme Court to apply the Bill of Rights to state and local governments
- The Fifteenth Amendment provided that individuals should not be denied the right to vote based on race or the fact that the person was once a slave

C. With the successes of the Civil Rights Movement for African Americans, other minorities have pressed to end discrimination:

- Hispanic Americans benefited by organizing the Mexican-American Legal Defense and Education Fund, the United Farm Workers Union, La Raza Unida, and the League of United Latin American Citizens. These groups have fought for the rights of Hispanic Americans in health care, education, and voting rights. Immigration reform is also a pressing issue, particularly the rights of illegal immigrants and whether they will be able to become American citizens. Hispanic Americans have also benefited directly from the 1975 amendments to the Voting Rights Act requiring that election materials be made available in minority languages such as Spanish where justified by the number of minority voters.
- Native Americans began organizing against discrimination. The Native American Movement and National Indian Youth Council held protests to bring attention to issues that affect Native Americans. The Supreme Court has upheld treaty rights of Native American tribes. Native Americans have also been allowed to open casinos on reservations under the Indian and Gaming Regulatory Act. The Native American Languages Act encourages the continuation of native languages and culture.
- Women have benefited from the Civil Rights Movement with the Equal Pay Act, which made it illegal to base an employee's pay on race, gender, religion, or national origin. The Civil Rights Act of 1964 bans job discrimination on the basis of gender. The Supreme Court has ruled that the equal protection clause of the Fourteenth Amendment protects women from unreasonable classifications. The Equal Employment Opportunity Act prohibits gender discrimination in hiring, firing, promotions, pay, and working conditions. The Omnibus Education Act requires schools to give boys and girls an equal opportunity to participate in sports programs. The Equal Credit Opportunity Act prohibits discrimination against women seeking credit and makes it illegal to ask a person's gender or marital status on credit applications. The Women's Equity in Employment Act requires employers to justify gender discrimination in hiring and job performance.
- The Rehabilitation Act prohibits discrimination against people with disabilities in federal programs. The Education for Handicapped Children Act guarantees that children with disabilities will receive an "appropriate" education. The Americans with Disabilities Act forbids employers and owners of public accommodations from discriminating against

people with disabilities, requiring them to make facilities wheelchair accessible. The Telecommunications Relay Service was created to allow hearing- and speech-impaired people access to telephone communications.

- The LGBT community has been much slower in receiving the benefits of the civil rights movement. In recent years, LGBT members have been elected to higher level of public office, such as Kate Brown being elected governor of Oregon. In 2017, a Court of Appeals for the Seventh Circuit ruled that the Civil Rights Act prohibits workplace discrimination against LGBT employees. The greatest support for LGBT rights came in the 2015 Supreme Court ruling in *Obergefell v. Hodges*. The Supreme Court ruled 5-4 that states cannot ban same-sex marriage.

› Rapid Review

- Civil liberties are those rights that belong to everyone and are guaranteed by the Constitution, Bill of Rights, Fourteenth Amendment, legislative actions, and court decisions.
- The Establishment Clause of the First Amendment has been interpreted to mean that there is a separation between church and state, preventing the government from supporting religion or one religion over another.
- The Lemon Test established standards for measuring separation of church and state.
- The Free Exercise Clause guarantees the right to practice any religion or no religion at all.
- There are three classifications of speech: pure speech, symbolic speech, and speech plus.
- The right to free speech is not absolute. Speech may be regulated if national security is at stake; fighting words and obscenity are not protected forms of free speech. The Internet has not been regulated.
- Freedom of the press is often protected because it is closely related to free speech. Press includes newspapers, magazines, radio, television, and the Internet.
- The First Amendment also guarantees freedom of assembly and petition.
- The Due Process Clauses of the Fifth and Fourteenth Amendments provide for the protection of private property.
- The Constitution makes no mention of the right to privacy; however, the Supreme Court ruled that such a right exists under the Constitution.
- Several amendments of the Bill of Rights address the rights of those accused of crimes, including the Fourth, Fifth, Sixth, and Eighth Amendments. The Fourteenth Amendment extends those protections to apply to the states.
- Civil rights are the positive acts of government designed to prevent discrimination and provide equality before the law.
- The Civil Rights Movement began after the Civil War, with African Americans striving to gain political, social, and economic equality.
- Discriminatory practices were used by the states to prevent political participation by African Americans. These practices included black codes and Jim Crow laws.
- A positive step for African Americans came with the *Brown v. Board of Education* ruling in which the Supreme Court overturned the *Plessy* "separate but equal" ruling.
- The successes of the African American Civil Rights Movement have encouraged other minorities, such as Hispanics, Native Americans, and Asian Americans, to call for an end to discrimination.
- Women have also worked to end discrimination. Their successes include gaining the right to vote and protections against employment discrimination.
- The Americans with Disabilities Act of 1990 forbids discrimination against people with disabilities.
- Affirmative action is a controversial policy designed to correct the effects of past discrimination.

UNIT 4

American Political Ideologies and Beliefs

CHAPTER **12**   Political Socialization, Ideology, and Public Opinion

CHAPTER 12

Political Socialization, Ideology, and Public Opinion

IN THIS CHAPTER

Summary: A **political culture** is a set of basic values and beliefs about a country or government that is shared by most citizens (freedom is precious, for example) and that influences political opinions and behaviors. The U.S. political culture gives citizens a sense of community, creates support for the democratic processes (majority rule, free elections), helps shape attitudes toward public officials, and teaches civic responsibility. The political culture provides a setting for a political system to function.

Key Terms

political culture	public opinion	ideology
individualism	opinion poll	political ideology
equality of opportunity	benchmark	radical
free enterprise	tracking polls	liberal
rule of law	entrance/exit polls	moderate
limited government	straw polls	conservative
political socialization	sampling	reactionary
opinion leaders	sampling errors	

Core Political Values

Although the United States is a diverse society, it is united under a common political culture, or common set of beliefs and attitudes about government and politics. This political culture translates into a consensus of basic concepts that support democracy. Democracy is not guaranteed; therefore, the American people must continue to practice these concepts:

- *Individualism*—Individuals possess the freedom to make choices as they wish.
- *Equality of opportunity*—All people should have the same opportunities to compete and achieve.

- *Free enterprise*—Private businesses operate in competition and free of government control; capitalism.
- *Rule of law*—All people and institutions are subject to and accountable to law that is fairly applied and enforced.
- *Limited government*—Powers of government are restricted in a democracy by the will of the people and the law.

It is vital to note that the importance of each of the above changes over time. During the presidency of George W. Bush (2001–2009), some believed that, because of the "War on Terror," the power of the government should be greatly expanded. During the first two years of the Obama presidency, members of the "Tea Party" and others claimed that the powers of the federal government had gotten too big.

Political Socialization

Political socialization is the process by which citizens acquire a sense of political identity. Socialization is a complex process that begins early in childhood and continues throughout a person's life. It allows citizens to become aware of politics, learn political facts, and form political values and opinions. Lower trade barriers and advances in communications technology have created an interconnected world economy and culture. Globalization has influenced American politics by increasing the degree to which the United States influences, and is influenced by, the ideals and values of other nations. Although the paths to political awareness, knowledge, and values differ, people are exposed to a combination of influences that shape their political identities and opinions:

KEY IDEA

- Family and home influences often help shape political party identification. It is strongest when both parents identify with the same political party.
- Schools teach patriotism, basic governmental functions and structure, and encourage political participation.
- Group affiliations (interest groups, labor unions, professional organizations) provide common bonds between people which may be expressed through the group or its activities.
- Demographic factors (occupation, race, gender, age, religion, region of country, income, education, and ethnicity).
- Mass media inform the public about issues and help set the political and public agendas.
- **Opinion leaders**, those individuals held in great respect because of their position, expertise, or personality, may informally and unintentionally exercise influence.
- Events may instill positive or negative attitudes. For example, the Watergate scandal created a mistrust of government. In the immediate aftermath of the attacks on the World Trade Center on September 11, 2001, patriotic spirit increased in many parts of the United States.

Public Opinion

Public opinion is a collection of shared attitudes of many different people in matters relating to politics, public issues, or the making of public policy. It is shaped by people's political culture and political socialization. An **opinion poll** is an assessment of public opinion by the questioning of a representative sample of the population. **Benchmark** or **tracking polls** are taken as a way to determine who is ahead or behind in an election. **Entrance and exit polls** are often taken at polling places before or after voters cast their ballots. Public opinion can be analyzed according to distribution (physical shape of responses when graphed), intensity (how strongly the opinions are held), and stability (how much the opinion changes over time). A consensus occurs when there is general agreement on an issue. Public opinion that is strongly divided between two very different views is a divisive opinion.

Measuring Public Opinion

The measurement of public opinion is a complex process often conveying unreliable results. Sampling error is an unavoidable error in statistical analysis of the data caused by choosing a sample that does not reflect the entire population (random sampling does not guarantee a perfect sample). Elections, interest groups, the media, and personal contacts may signal public opinion on certain issues; however, the most reliable measure of public opinion is the public opinion poll. Businesses, governments, political candidates, and interest groups use polls. Some polls are mass survey polls, which will survey a large group of people, while other polls are based on a focus group, a small group from the larger population that is questioned together about issues.

Early polling in the United States involved the use of **straw polls**, asking the same question of a large number of people. They were unreliable because they did not necessarily include a cross-section of the general population of the United States. The most famous mishap occurred in 1936 when the *Literary Digest* mailed postcards to more than 10 million people concerning the outcome of the 1936 presidential election. With over 2 million responses, the magazine incorrectly predicted the defeat of Franklin Roosevelt and the victory of challenger Alf Landon. The magazine had used automobile registrations and telephone directories to develop its sample, not realizing that during the Depression many people did not have cars or telephones. Many voters who supported Roosevelt had not been polled. The mailings had also been done early, and some voters changed their minds between answering the poll and actually voting.

Modern polling began in the 1930s when George Gallup helped develop the use of a scientific polling process that includes:

- *sampling*—Those chosen to participate in the poll must be representative of the general population and chosen at random.
- *preparing valid questions*—Directions should be clear and questions should be phrased and ordered in a way that does not lead the respondent to a particular answer (clear, fair, and unbiased).
- *controlling how the poll is taken*—Make sure the respondent has some knowledge of the issues addressed in the poll and that the pollster's appearance and tone do not influence the responses. Survey methods may include telephone, mail, and in-person interviews.
- *analyzing and reporting results*—Reporting the results of polls without providing information about how the poll was conducted, **sampling errors**, or when the poll that was taken can lead to misinformation and error.

In a given election, the reliability of data obtained in a public opinion poll impacts elections and policy debates. Today, the use of statistical analysis through computers has made polling an even more accurate research tool.

Ideology

An **ideology** is a consistent set of beliefs. A **political ideology** is a set of beliefs about politics and public policy that creates the structure for looking at government and public policy. Political ideologies can change over time. Differences in ideology generally occur in the arena of political, economic, and social issues.

Ideology: A Political Spectrum

- **radical**—Favors rapid, fundamental change in existing social, economic, or political order; may be willing to resort to extreme means, even violence or revolution to accomplish such change (extreme change to create an entirely new social system).
- **liberal**—Supports active government in promoting individual welfare and supporting civil rights, and accepts peaceful political and social change within the existing political system. The Democratic Party tends to be more aligned with the liberal ideology.
- **moderate**—Political ideology that falls between liberal and conservative and which may include some of both; usually thought of as tolerant of others' political opinions and not likely to hold extreme views on issues.
- **conservative**—Promotes a limited governmental role in helping individuals economically, supports traditional values and lifestyles, favors a more active role for government in promoting national security, and approaches change cautiously. The Republican Party tends to be more aligned with the conservative ideology.
- **reactionary**—Advocates a return to a previous state of affairs, often a social order or government that existed earlier in history (may be willing to go to extremes to achieve their goals).

› Review Questions

Multiple-Choice Questions

1. Which of the following is NOT a concept found in the political culture of the American democratic society?
   (A) private property
   (B) equality
   (C) majority rule
   (D) minority rule

2. The process by which citizens acquire a sense of their own political identity would best be defined as
   (A) public opinion
   (B) political socialization
   (C) demographics
   (D) political culture

3. Which of the following would be a true statement regarding public opinion?
   (A) Public opinion teaches patriotism.
   (B) Public opinion allows citizens to become aware of politics, learn facts, and form political values.
   (C) Public opinion is shaped by an individual's political culture and political socialization.
   (D) A change in public opinion is always a slow process.

4. Attempting to measure public opinion by asking the same question of a large number of people is
   (A) a straw poll
   (B) a sampling poll
   (C) a controlling poll
   (D) a scientific poll

5. There are many different ideologies within the political spectrum. An ideology that promotes a limited governmental role in helping individuals and supports traditional values and lifestyles would best be defined as a
   (A) liberal ideology
   (B) reactionary ideology
   (C) conservative ideology
   (D) moderate ideology

Use the graph to answer the question 6.

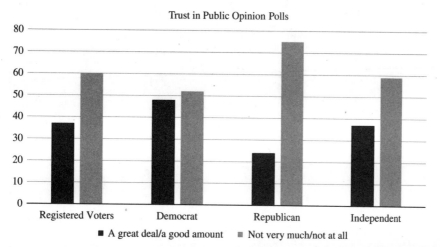

Trust in Public Opinion Polls

■ A great deal/a good amount   ■ Not very much/not at all

6. Which of the following statements is reflected in the data in the graph above?
   (A) Republicans have a greater trust in public opinion polls than Democrats.
   (B) Independents have less trust in public opinion polls than Republicans.
   (C) Democrats have less trust in public opinion polls than Republicans.
   (D) Republicans have more trust in public opinion polls than registered voters.

Free-Response Question

7. Political culture is a set of basic values and beliefs about a country or government shared by most citizens. This political culture translates into a consensus about democracy.
   (A) Define political socialization.
   (B) Describe two factors that shape political socialization.
   (C) Explain how each factor identified in Part B affects political socialization.

› Answers and Explanations

1. **D**. Majority rule/minority rights is a concept found in U.S. political culture. The other answer choices reflect ideals of U.S. democratic society.

2. **B**. Political socialization is the process of acquiring a political identity. Public opinion (A) is a collection of shared attitudes of many different people. Demographics (C) is a factor that shapes political socialization. Political culture (D) is a set of basic values and beliefs about a country or government that is shared by most citizens.

3. **C**. Public opinion is shaped by an individual's political culture and political socialization. Institutions such as the family and schools teach patriotism (A). Public opinion is shaped by facts and political values (B). Change may be slow or sudden and may be analyzed (D).

4. **A**. A straw poll is an attempt to measure public opinion by asking the same question of a large number of people. Sampling (B) and controlling (C) are features of scientific polling (D).

5. **C**. A conservative ideology promotes a limited governmental role in helping individuals and supports traditional values and lifestyles. Liberal ideology (A) supports active government involvement. Reactionary ideology (B) desires a return to an earlier social order or government. Moderate ideology (D) falls between liberal and conservative on the political spectrum.

6. **C**. Republicans have less trust in public opinion polls than do Democrats (A). Independents have more trust in public opinion polls than do Republicans (B). Republicans have less trust in public opinion polls than do registered voters.

7. **(A)** Political socialization is the process by which citizens acquire a sense of political identity. It allows citizens to become aware of politics, learn political facts, and form political values and opinions.

(B) Factors that shape political socialization include family and home influences (parents or other relatives that live with you); schools and educational experiences (teachers and school experiences); group affiliations (interest groups, labor unions, professional organizations); demographic factors (occupation, gender, race, age, religion, etc.); and mass media (radio, television, internet, newspapers, magazines, blogs).

(C) Family and home influences occur when parents talk about politics, or there exists a family tradition of political identification. Schools and educational experiences introduce students to elections and voting, ordered society, or students may enroll in a class in civics or government. Group affiliations such as interest groups, labor unions, or professional organizations help people form a common bond and may encourage a certain ideology. Demographic factors (occupation, gender, race, age, religion, etc.) may influence where and how you live, which could influence your political thoughts. Mass media provides political information and influences political ideas.

> Rapid Review

- A political culture is a set of basic values and beliefs about a country or government that are shared by most citizens.
- America is a heterogeneous (diverse) society with many political cultures.
- Democracy is not guaranteed. In order to ensure democracy, political concepts must be practiced.
- Political socialization is the process of citizens acquiring a political identity. Several factors influence the process of political socialization.
- Public opinion is a collection of ideas and attitudes about government that are shared by the general public.
- Public opinion is shaped by an individual's political culture and political socialization.
- Public opinion polls are the most reliable measure of public opinion.
- Modern polling began in the 1930s with George Gallup. Today, polling is more scientific and based on statistical analysis.
- An ideology is a consistent set of beliefs. A political ideology is beliefs based on politics and public policy.
- Ideological placement on a political spectrum may include classification as radical, liberal, moderate, conservative, or reactionary.

Political Participation

Campaigns, Elections, and Voting

IN THIS CHAPTER

Summary: Most people think of political participation in terms of voting; however, there are other forms of political participation, and sometimes they are more effective than voting. Political participation includes all the actions people use in seeking to influence or support government and politics.

Key Terms

suffrage
electorate
Fifteenth Amendment
Seventeenth Amendment
Nineteenth Amendment
Twenty-Fourth
  Amendment
Twenty-Sixth Amendment
direct primary
recall
referendum
initiative
rational-choice voting
retrospective voting
prospective voting
party-line voting

political efficacy
Motor Voter Law
primary elections
closed primary
open primary
blanket primary
runoff primary
general elections
off-year elections
mid-term elections
coattail effect
caucus
presidential preference
  primary
front-loading
Super Tuesday

superdelegates
electoral college
maintaining elections
deviating elections
critical elections
realigning elections
dealigning elections
split-ticket voting
Federal Election
  Commission
freedom of
  expression
soft money
Bipartisan Campaign
  Reform Act (BCRA)
Citizens United v. FEC

Participation and Voting

Forms of Political Participation

- voting in elections
- discussing politics and attending political meetings
- forming interest groups and PACs
- contacting public officials
- campaigning for a candidate or political party
- contributing money to a candidate or political party
- running for office
- protesting government decisions

Most of these behaviors would be considered conventional or routine, within the acceptable channels of representative government. Less conventional behaviors have been used when groups have felt powerless and ineffective. Although Americans are less approving of unconventional behaviors, those tactics are sometimes effective in influencing government decisions. The often-violent protests against the Vietnam conflict discouraged Lyndon Johnson from running for reelection in 1968. In the modern era of the internet and other forms of "instant news," a single verbal gaffe can cause major problems for a candidate; mistakes by candidates are often quickly spread by supporters of the opposing candidate.

The most common form of political participation in the United States is voting. However, Americans are less likely to vote than citizens of other countries.

Participation Through Voting

Democratic government is "government by the people." In the United States, participation through elections is the basis of the democratic process. According to democratic theory, everyone should be allowed to vote. In practice, however, no nation grants universal suffrage; all nations have requirements for voting.

Expansion of Suffrage

Suffrage is the right to vote. It is a political right that belongs to all those who meet certain requirements set by law. The United States was the first nation to provide for general elections of representatives through mass suffrage. The issue of suffrage is left to the states—the only stipulation found in Article I, Section 2 of the Constitution is that individuals who could vote for "the most numerous branch of the state legislature" could also vote for their congressional representatives.

The composition of the American **electorate** has changed throughout history. Two major trends have marked the development of suffrage: the elimination of a number of restrictive requirements and the transfer of more and more authority from the states to the federal government.

Changes in voting requirements have included:

- elimination of religious qualifications, property ownership, and tax payments after 1800
- elimination of race disqualifications with the passage of the **Fifteenth Amendment** in 1870
- allowing for the direct election of Senators under the **Seventeenth Amendment** in 1913
- elimination of gender disqualifications with the passage of the **Nineteenth Amendment** in 1920
- elimination of grandfather clauses, white primaries, and literacy requirements with the passage of federal civil rights legislation and court decisions (Civil Rights Acts, Voting Rights Act of 1965)

- allowing residents of Washington, D.C., to vote in presidential elections with the passage of the Twenty-Third Amendment in 1961
- elimination of poll taxes in federal elections with the passage of the **Twenty-Fourth Amendment** in 1964 (all poll taxes were ruled unconstitutional in *Harper v. Virginia State Board of Elections,* 1966)
- lowering the minimum age for voting in federal elections to 18 with the passage of the **Twenty-Sixth Amendment** in 1971

Issue or Policy Voting

The Progressive Movement of the early 20th century was a philosophy of political reform that fostered the development of mechanisms for increased direct participation. These included:

- A **direct primary** allows citizens to nominate candidates.
- A **recall** is a special election initiated by petition to allow citizens to remove an official from office before a term expires.
- A **referendum** allows citizens to vote directly on issues called propositions (proposed laws or state constitutional amendments).
- An **initiative** allows voters to petition to propose issues to be decided by qualified voters.

Although the recall, referendum, and initiative do not exist at the national level, several states allow voters to approve or disapprove ballot initiatives on specific issues.

Candidate Voting

Voting for candidates is the most common form of political participation. It allows citizens to choose candidates they think will best serve their interests and makes public officials accountable for their actions. In the United States voters only elect two national office holders—the president and vice president. All remaining candidates represent state or local constituencies.

Models of Voting Behavior

- **Rational-choice voting**—voting based on what voters perceive to be in their own best interest
- **Retrospective voting**—voting based on past performance of the candidate
- **Prospective voting**—voting based on how the voter believes the candidate will perform in office
- **Party-line voting**—voting for candidates based upon the party to which they belong, usually voting a straight ticket

Low Voter Turnout

Voting has been studied more closely than any other form of political participation in the United States. Studies have shown that voter turnout in the United States has decreased when compared with other nations and when compared with the United States over time. Voter turnout is higher if the election is seen as important; voter turnout is higher in presidential elections than in off-year elections. Several reasons might account for the low voter turnout:

- *expansion of the electorate*—Increase in the number of potential voters (Twenty-Sixth Amendment).
- *failure of political parties to mobilize voters*—Negative campaigning, numerous elections, frequent elections, lack of party identification.
- *no perceived differences between the candidates or parties*—Both parties and their candidates are seen as virtually the same.

- *mistrust of government*—A belief that all candidates are untrustworthy or unresponsive, due in part to the Watergate and Iran-Contra scandals.
- *apathy*—A lack of interest in politics; a belief that voting is not important.
- *satisfaction with the way things are*—A belief that by not voting, the status quo will remain in effect.
- lack of **political efficacy**—People do not believe their vote out of millions of votes will make a difference.
- *mobility of electorate*—Moving around leads to a lack of social belonging.
- *registration process*—Differences in registration procedures from state to state may create barriers; the National Voter Registration Act of 1995 (**Motor Voter Law**) was designed to make voter registration easier by allowing people to register at driver's license bureaus and some public offices.

Who Votes?

Several factors affect the likelihood of voting:

- *education*—The higher the level of education, the more likely a person is to vote. This is the most important indicator of voting behavior.
- *occupation and income*—These often depend on education level. Those with white-collar jobs and higher levels of income are more likely to vote than those with blue-collar jobs or lower levels of income.
- *age*—Older people are more likely to vote than younger people.

- *race*—Minorities such as African Americans and Hispanics are less likely to vote than whites, unless they have similar socioeconomic status.
- *gender*—At one time, gender was not a major predictor, but today women are more likely to vote than men.
- *religion*—Those who are more active within their religion are more likely to vote than those who do not attend religious services, or rarely attend.
- *marital status*—Married people are more likely to vote than those who are not married.
- *union membership*—Unions encourage participation, and union members tend to vote regularly.
- *community membership*—People who are well integrated into community life are more likely to vote than those who have moved recently.
- *party identification*—Those who have a strong sense of party identification are more likely to vote.
- *geography*—Residents of states with interparty competition and close elections may be more likely to vote than those who live in states with one-party domination.

Factors Influencing Voter Choice

When voters do decide to go to the polls to vote, one or more of these factors may influence how they vote.

- party identification—Is the voter a loyal party member or independent?
- characteristics of candidates—What personal or professional characteristics of the candidate appeal to voters?
- contemporary issues—What issues are important today? What issues are important to the voter?
- demographic factors—Age, race or ethnicity, education, occupation, income, gender, and religious views

Types of Elections

- **Primary elections** are nominating elections in which voters choose the candidates from each party who will run for office in the general election. There are several major types of primaries:
  - **closed primary**—Only voters who are registered in the party may vote to choose the candidate. Separate primaries are held by each political party, and voters must select a primary in advance.
  - **open primary**—Voters may vote to choose the candidates of either party, whether they belong to that party or not. Voters make the decision of which party to support in the voting booth.
  - **blanket primary**—Voters may vote for candidates of either party, choosing a Republican for one office and a Democrat for another; a form of which is used in California, Washington and Louisiana.
  - **runoff primary**—When no candidate from a party receives a majority of the votes, the top two candidates face each other in a runoff.
- **General elections** are elections in which the voters choose from among all the candidates nominated by political parties or running as independents.
- Special elections are held whenever an issue must be decided by voters before a primary or general election is held, for example, to fill a vacancy in the Senate.

When Elections Are Held

Local, state, and federal laws determine when elections are held. Congress has established that congressional and presidential elections will be held on the first Tuesday after the first Monday in November. Congressional elections are held every even-numbered year, and presidential elections are held every fourth year.

Congressional Elections

Since congressional elections are held every even-numbered year, **mid-term elections** occur during the year when no presidential election is held. Voter turnout in off-year elections is generally lower than during presidential election years. During presidential election years, the popularity of a presidential candidate may create a **coattail effect**, allowing lesser-known or weaker candidates from the presidential candidate's party to win by riding the "coattails" of the nominee.

Presidential Elections

The road to the White House and the presidency begins months and even years prior to the election. Some candidates begin the process as soon as the previous election is over. Phases of a candidacy include:

- *exploration*—In deciding whether to run for president, individuals must determine whether they have enough political and financial support to win against other possible candidates. Often a possible nominee will form an exploratory committee to begin lining up support and finances, as well as to attract media coverage and gain widespread recognition.
- *announcement*—Once a candidate has decided to run, an announcement is generally made in a press conference. This announcement is a formal declaration that the candidate is seeking the party's nomination.

- *presidential primaries and caucuses*—In the past, state party officials would meet in a **caucus** to endorse the party candidate prior to presidential primaries. Abuses of the caucus system led to many states abandoning its use. Iowa still uses caucuses to nominate presidential candidates; however, today they are open to all members of the party. Most states today use the **presidential preference primary** to determine whom the state delegates to the national party convention will support. Voters vote in a primary election, and party delegates to the conventions support the winner of the primary election. As more states began using the primaries to choose delegates, states have been **front-loading**, or choosing earlier and earlier dates to hold their primaries. **Super Tuesday** occurs in early March when the greatest number of states hold presidential preference primaries on the same day.

- *nominating conventions*—Each political party holds a national nominating convention in the summer prior to the general election. The convention is composed of delegates from each state, with each party determining its method of selecting delegates. Elected party officials, **superdelegates**, in the Democratic Party attend the national convention as unpledged delegates. They are seated automatically and choose for themselves for whom to vote. The purpose of the nominating convention is to choose the party's presidential and vice-presidential nominees, write the party platform, and bring unity to the party in support of their chosen nominees.

- *campaigning and the general election*—After the conventions are over, each candidate begins campaigning for the general election. Generally, candidates travel to swing states (those in which neither major party has overwhelming support) and often appear more moderate in an effort to win the largest possible number of votes. Since 1960, the candidates have faced each other in televised debates. The general election is then held to determine which candidate wins the electoral college vote for that state.

- *electoral college*—When voters go to the polls on election day they are casting the popular vote. This vote is actually for electors. Each state has a number of electors equal to its senators and representatives in Congress. Also, Washington, D.C., has three electoral votes. The entire group of 538 electors is known as the electoral college. After the general election, the electors meet in their respective state capitals on the first Monday after the second Wednesday in December. The candidate who wins a majority of popular votes in a state in the general election wins all the state's electoral votes in the electoral college (winner-take-all). Although the electors are not required to vote for their party's candidate, only rarely do they cast a vote for someone else. The votes cast in the electoral college are then sent to Congress, where they are opened and counted before a joint session. The candidate who receives a majority (270) of electoral votes is declared the winner. If no candidate for president receives a majority of electoral votes, the House of Representatives chooses the president from the top three candidates. If no candidate for vice president receives a majority of electoral votes, the Senate chooses the vice president from the top two candidates.

Partisanship in Elections

- **Maintaining elections** occur when the traditional majority power maintains power based on the party loyalty of voters.
- **Deviating elections** occur when the minority party is able to win with the support of majority-party members, independents, and new voters; however, the long-term party preferences of voters do not change.
- **Critical elections** indicate sharp changes in existing patterns of party loyalty due to changing social and economic conditions; for example, elections of 1860, 1896, and 1932.

- **Realigning elections** occur when the minority party wins by building a new coalition of voters that continues over successive elections. This is usually associated with a national crisis such as the Great Depression, when Franklin D. Roosevelt was able to create a new coalition of southerners, African Americans, the poor, Catholics and Jews, labor union members, and urban dwellers.
- **Dealigning elections** occur when party loyalty becomes less important to voters, as may be seen with the increase in independents and **split-ticket voting**.

Campaign Finance

Campaigning for political office is expensive. For the 2000 elections the Republican and Democratic parties raised more than $1.1 billion.

Campaign Finance Regulations and Reforms

Prior to the 1970s candidates for public office received donations from businesses, labor organizations, and individuals to finance campaigns.

Congress passed the Federal Election Campaign Act (FECA) in 1971, restricting the amount of campaign funds that can be spent on advertising, requiring disclosure of campaign contributions and expenditures, and limiting the amounts candidates and their families can donate to their own campaigns. It also allowed taxpayers to designate a donation on their tax return to the major political party candidates, beginning in the 1976 presidential election.

In 1974, after the Watergate scandal, Congress amended the Federal Election Campaign Act to establish a Federal Election Commission (FEC) to enforce the Act, and established public financing for presidential candidates in primaries and the general election. The measure also restricted contributions by prohibiting foreign contributions, limiting individual contributions, and restricting the formation of PACs and their contributions. It was further amended in 1976 and 1979.

In 1976 the Supreme Court ruled in *Buckley v. Valeo* that spending limits established by the FECA Amendments of 1974 were unconstitutional, finding that those restrictions were in violation of the First Amendment's guarantees of **freedom of expression**. *Buckley v. Valeo* also declared that the FECA ban on self-financed campaigns was unconstitutional.

In 1996 new questions arose over the use of "**soft money**," donations to political parties that could be used for general purposes. Originally, the money was supposed to be used for voter registration drives, national party conventions, and issue ads. Political parties were allowed to raise unlimited amounts of money because it was not to be used for campaigning. However, soft money has generally been spent in ways that ultimately help individual candidates. By the 2000 election, soft money donations had exceeded $400 million between the two major parties.

Campaign finance reform has been a major issue in Congress. In 2002, Congress passed the **Bipartisan Campaign Reform Act (BCRA)** banning the use of soft money in federal campaigns and increasing the 1974 limits on individual and group contributions to candidates. A result of the BCRA in the campaign of 2004 was the formation of "527" political organizations. A 527 political organization is a largely unregulated interest group that focuses on a single policy and attempts to influence voters. After the 2004 election, new rules governing 527 organizations regulated their use of soft money and allowed the FEC to examine their expenditures. In *Citizens United v. FEC* (2010), the Supreme Court ruled that limiting the ability of businesses, unions, and other groups to fund their own efforts to elect or defeat candidates for office is unconstitutional. As a result, critics of the decision worried that the financial influence of big corporations on campaigns would be able to overpower the influence of the citizenry. In 2014 the Supreme Court ruled in *McCutcheon v. FEC* that the government cannot prevent citizens from giving campaign contributions to as many different candidates and political parties as they want. Previously, they had been limited under the "aggregate limit" rule.

Characteristics of Modern Campaigns

- **Professional Consultants/Managers**

A political campaign is an organized effort that seeks to influence voters. In a modern political campaign, the campaign organization must have a clear structure and staff to carry out campaign operations. Major campaigns in the United States are often long; campaigns may start anywhere from several months to several years before election day, depending on the office being sought. People have made careers out of working full time for campaigns and groups that support them. However, in other campaigns, much of the staff might be unpaid volunteers.

- **Campaign Costs**

Campaigns cost money. In recent years, those costs have been increasing, forcing candidates to engage in more fundraising activities. These high costs can limit opportunities for individuals to run for office and gives an advantage to wealthier candidates. Rising campaign costs have led to reform of campaign finance laws, but have also led to interest groups having a larger influence in campaign through donations to candidates and encouraged the development of PACs and superPACs.

- **Election Cycles**

An election cycle is the time frame in which an election occurs. The duration of an election cycle lasts depends upon the office being sought. The election cycle for members of the House of Representatives is quite short—they run for election every two years—while the election cycle for members of the Senate is much longer.

- **Social Media**

The use of social media in politics has changed the way campaigns are run and how Americans interact with elected officials. It has made elected officials and candidates for public office more accountable and accessible to voters. It provides the means to reach millions of people instantaneously at virtually no cost. Social media provides politicians the ability to speak directly to voters without paying for advertising. Campaigns can produce political commercials and publish them for free. Social media sites allow voters to share political information and campaign events with each other. It allows candidates to adapt and customize their message for the groups who are following them. Social media provides the means for fundraising, raising substantial amounts of money in very short periods of time. Candidates can use social media to gauge public opinion about certain issues or events. Social media is also popular among young people and may be an effective way to engage and interest voters in an election. President Obama did this successfully during both presidential campaigns.

› Review Questions

Multiple-Choice Questions

1. Which of the following would NOT be a form of political participation?
   (A) voting in elections
   (B) contacting public officials
   (C) paying taxes
   (D) forming an interest group

2. What is the most common form of political participation in America?
   (A) voting
   (B) contributing money for candidates
   (C) working for a political party
   (D) running for office

3. Which of the following best defines a recall?
   (A) Recall allows voters to petition proposed issues presented before them.
   (B) Recall is a form of direct primary.
   (C) Recall is a form of indirect primary.
   (D) Recall is a special election allowing the voters to remove public officials from office before the end of their term.

4. Which of the following is a drawback of modern campaigns?
   (A) increased use of social media
   (B) rising campaign costs
   (C) decreased use of social media
   (D) decreasing campaign costs

5. Which of the following primaries is used by the fewest number of states?
   (A) closed primary
   (B) open primary
   (C) blanket primary
   (D) presidential preference primary

6. Which of the following is NOT true concerning the expansion of suffrage in the United States?
   (A) Religious qualifications and property ownership requirements were abolished after the Civil War.
   (B) The Fifteenth Amendment eliminated race disqualifications in voting.
   (C) The Nineteenth Amendment eliminated gender disqualifications.
   (D) The Twenty-Sixth Amendment lowered the voting age in federal elections to 18.

7. Which of the following is a false statement?
   (A) Most candidates running for president of the United States make formal announcements as to the seeking of their party's nomination.
   (B) After the national convention, candidates begin campaigning for the general election.
   (C) The purpose of a national nominating convention is to select a party's presidential candidate and write a party platform.
   (D) Presidential primaries provide little help for the American voter in determining a party's political candidate.

8. The electoral college, along with the popular vote of the people, determines the winner of a presidential election. What majority of the electoral vote is needed in order to be declared the winner?
   (A) 538
   (B) 435
   (C) 100
   (D) 270

9. The Federal Election Campaign Act of 1971
   (A) limited the number of candidates who could run for any one office
   (B) restricted the amount of campaign funds that could be spent on a single election
   (C) restricted the amount of campaign donations to $1 per person
   (D) restricted the amount of campaign contributions to $400 million for the major political parties

10. In 2010, the Supreme Court ruled that political spending by corporations, associations, and labor unions is a form of protected speech under the First Amendment.
    (A) *Baker v. Carr* (1962)
    (B) *Shaw v. Reno* (1993)
    (C) *Citizens United v. Federal Election Commission* (2020)
    (D) *McCulloch v. Maryland* (1819)

Use the graph below to answer question 11.

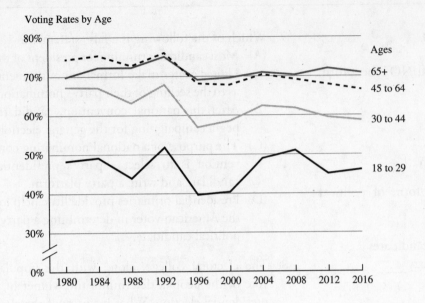

Voting Rates by Age

11. Which of the following is an accurate statement about the information in the line graph?
    (A) Those 65 and older are more likely to vote than those 45 to 64.
    (B) The only age group to see a voter increase since 2012 was the 30 to 44 age group.
    (C) The age group with the lowest voter turnout is those 65 and older.
    (D) Since 2000, all age groups have seen an increase in voter turnout.

Free-Response Question

12. Campaign finance reform has been a major issue in recent years.
    (A) Describe the Supreme Court decision in each of the following cases:
        • *Buckley v. Valeo* (1976)
        • *Citizens United v. Federal Election Commission (FEC)* (2010)
        • *McCutcheon v. Federal Election Commission (FEC)* (2014)
    (B) Explain how the decisions in two of the cases in Part A have affected campaign finance today.

› Answers and Explanations

1. **C.** Paying taxes is not a method of political participation. Voting in elections, contacting public officials, and forming interest groups are methods of political participation.

2. **A.** Voting is the most common form of political participation in the United States. The remaining answer choices are forms of political participation in which fewer party members participate.

3. **D.** A recall is an election that allows voters the opportunity to remove a public official from office prior to the end of a term.

4. **B.** The increased use of social media is a benefit to modern campaigns (A, C). There has been an increase in the costs of campaigns (D).

5. **C.** The blanket primary is used only in California, Washington, and Louisiana. Closed primaries (A), open primaries (B), and presidential preference primaries (D) are used by many states.

6. **A.** Religious qualifications and property ownership requirements were abolished after 1800. The other answer choices are correct.

7. **D.** Presidential primaries are often preference primaries where voters choose which candidate their party should support at the nominating convention. The other answer choices are correct.

8. **D.** Candidates must win at least 270 electoral votes to win a majority and therefore election as president or vice-president.

9. **B.** The Federal Election Campaign Act of 1971 limited the amount of money that could be spent in federal election campaigns. The remaining answer choices were not provisions of the FECA.

10. **C.** *Citizens United v. Federal Election Commission* (2010) provided for free speech protections under the First Amendment for corporations, associations, and labor unions. *Baker v. Shaw* (1962) provided for "one person, one vote" protections in redistricting (A). *Shaw v. Reno* (1993) allows voters to challenge majority-minority districts if race is the only factor used in creating the district (B). *McCulloch v. Maryland* (1819) (D) upheld the Supremacy Clause.

11. **A.** The graph illustrates that those 65 and older are more likely to vote than any other age group. The only age group to see a voter increase since 2012 was the 18 to 29 age group (B). The age group with the lowest voter turnout is those 18 to 29 (C). Since 2000, all age groups except those 18 to 29 have seen a decrease in voter turnout.

12. **A.** In *Buckley v. Valeo* (1976), the Supreme Court ruled that spending limits established by the FECA Amendments of 1974 were unconstitutional because they violated the First Amendment's guarantee of freedom of expression. They also ruled that the FECA ban on self-financed campaigns was unconstitutional. In *Citizens United v. FEC* (2010), the Supreme Court ruled that limiting the ability of businesses, unions, and other groups to fund their own efforts to elect or defeat candidates for office is unconstitutional. In *McCutcheon v. FEC* (2014), the Supreme Court ruled that the government cannot prevent citizens from giving campaign contributions to as many different candidates and political parties as they want.

B. The ruling in *Buckley v. Valeo* (1976) tied campaign finance contributions to the First Amendment's freedom of speech and now allows candidates to fund their own campaigns or citizens to contribute to campaigns as a form of free speech. The ruling in *Citizens United v. FEC* (2010) opened the door for businesses, unions, and other groups to contribute to political campaigns. The ruling in *McCutcheon v. FEC* (2014) allows citizens to participate in the electoral process by donating to as many candidates as they want, even though there are still limits on how much can be donated to any one candidate.

› Rapid Review

- Political participation includes all the actions people use in seeking to influence or support government and politics.
- Voting is the most common form of political participation in the United States.
- According to democratic theory, everyone should be allowed to vote.
- Suffrage is the right to vote. The expansion of suffrage has allowed a larger number of voters.
- In the early 20th century the Progressive Movement helped bring about an increase in direct participation.
- The president and vice president are the only two nationally elected office holders.
- Voter turnout in the United States has been decreasing for numerous reasons.
- Various characteristics have been attributed to those who are more likely to vote.
- Primary elections are intraparty elections held to narrow down the field of candidates.
- General elections are interparty elections where voters choose the office holders.
- Federal, state, and local laws determine the holding of elections.
- Congressional elections that take place in years when no presidential election is occurring are called off-year or mid-term elections.
- The presidential election process includes exploration, announcement, primaries, nominating conventions, campaigning, the general election, and the electoral college vote.
- An electoral college elects the president and vice president.
- Partisanship allows for elections to be maintaining, deviating, critical, realigning, or dealigning in scope.
- The Federal Election Campaign Act and its amendments regulate campaign finances. Reforms of campaign financing include the passage of the Bipartisan Campaign Reform Act that bans the use of "soft money" in federal campaigns. The Supreme Court ruled in *Citizens United v. FEC* (2010) that limiting the ability of businesses, unions, and other groups to fund their own efforts to elect or defeat candidates for office is unconstitutional.

Political Parties

IN THIS CHAPTER

Summary: Political parties are voluntary associations of people who seek to control the government through common principles based upon peaceful and legal actions, such as the winning of elections. Political parties, along with interest groups, the media, and elections serve as a linkage mechanism that brings together the people and the government while holding the government responsible for its actions. Political parties differ from interest groups in that interest groups do not nominate candidates for office.

Key Terms

political parties
party in the electorate
party in government
party in organization
two-party system
single-member districts

New Deal coalition
divided government
gridlock
dealignment
realignment
national chairperson

soft money
straight ticket
candidate centered
  campaigns

Roles of Political Parties

KEY IDEA

- **party in the electorate**—All of the people who associate themselves with one of the political parties.
- **party in government**—All of the appointed and elected officials at the national, state, and local levels who represent the party as members; office holders.
- **party in organization**—All of the people at the various levels of the party organization who work to maintain the strength of the party between elections, help raise money, and organize the conventions and party functions.

Party Systems

One-Party System

In a one-party system only one party exists or has a chance of winning elections. Generally, membership is not voluntary and those who do belong to the party represent a small portion of the population. Party leaders must approve candidates for political office, and voters have no real choice. The result is dictatorial government.

Two-Party System

In a **two-party system** there may be several political parties but only two major political parties compete for power and dominate elections. Minor parties generally have little effect on most elections, especially at the national level. The Electoral College system makes it difficult for third-party candidates to affect presidential elections. It would be difficult for a third-party presidential candidate to actually win a state, which is necessary to capture electoral votes. Systems that operate under the two-party system usually have a general consensus, or agreement, among citizens about the basic principles of government, even though the parties often differ on the means of carrying them out. The use of **single-member districts** promotes the two-party system. Voters are given an "either-or" choice, simplifying decisions and the political process. The two-party system tends to enhance governmental stability; because both parties want to appeal to the largest number of voters, they tend to avoid extremes in ideology.

Multi-Party System

Multi-party systems exist when several major parties and a number of minor parties compete in elections, and any of the parties stands a good chance of winning. This type of system can be composed of from 4 to 20 different parties, based on a particular region, ideology, or class position, and is often found in European nations, as well as in other democratic societies. The multi-party system is usually the result of a proportional representation voting system rather than one with single-member districts. The idea behind multi-party systems is to give voters meaningful choices. This does not always occur because of two major problems: In many elections, no party has a clear majority of the vote, and not receiving a majority forces the sharing of power by several parties (coalitions). The multi-party system tends to promote instability in government, especially when coalition governments are formed.

What Do Political Parties Do?

- *Recruit candidates*—Find candidates interested in running for public office, especially if no incumbent is running.
- *Nominate and support candidates for office*—Help raise money and run candidate campaigns through the party organization.
- *Establish party platforms*—Develop and support the goals of party members through an established platform.
- *Mobilize and educate the electorate*—Inform the voters about the candidates and encourage voters to participate in the election.
- *Organize the government*—The organization of Congress and state legislatures is based on political party controls (majority vs. minority party); political appointments are often made based on political party affiliation.

Party Identification and Membership

Membership in American political parties is voluntary. There are no dues to pay; membership is based on party identification. If you believe you are a member of a particular political party, then you are. Most states require citizens to identify their political party when registering to vote. Most people choose to belong to a political party that shares their views on issues or the role of government. Several factors may influence party identification:

KEY IDEA

- ideology
- education
- income
- occupation
- race or ethnicity
- gender
- religion
- family tradition
- region of the country
- marital status

However, a large number of Americans choose not to join any political party, instead registering as independents.

The Two-Party Tradition in America

The Constitution did not call for political parties, and the Founding Fathers at first did not intend to create them. James Madison, in *Federalist #10*, warned of the divisiveness of "factions." George Washington was elected president without party labels and in his farewell address warned against the "baneful effects of the spirit of the party." During the process for ratification of the Constitution, Federalists and Anti-Federalists conflicted over ideals concerning the proper role of government. This conflict resulted in the development of the first political parties: the Federalists and Jeffersonian Republicans, or Democratic-Republicans as they were later called.

Why a Two-Party Tradition?

Although there have been numerous minor parties throughout its history, why has the United States maintained the two-party tradition?

- *historical roots*—British heritage, Federalist, and Anti-Federalist divisions.
- *electoral system*—Single-member districts mean that only one representative is chosen from each district (one winner per office).
- *election laws*—Vary from state to state, which makes it difficult for minor parties to get on the ballot in many states.

Rise of Political Parties: Party Development (1789–1800)

The earliest political parties began to develop under the administration of George Washington. Alexander Hamilton, secretary of the treasury, supported a strong national government; his followers became known as Federalists. Secretary of State Thomas Jefferson supported states' rights and a less powerful national government. The clash between these two individuals and their supporters led to the development of political parties. In the election of 1796, Jefferson challenged John Adams, the Federalist candidate, for the presidency but lost. By 1800 Jefferson was able to rally his supporters and win the presidency.

Democratic Domination (1800–1860)

The Democratic-Republicans dominated the government from 1800 to 1824, when they split into factions. The faction led by Andrew Jackson, the Jacksonian Democrats or Democrats, won the presidency in 1828. The major opposition to the Democrats during this time was the Whig Party. Although the Whigs were a powerful opposition party in the U.S. Congress, they were able to win the presidency only twice, in 1840 with the victory of William Henry Harrison and in 1848 with that of Zachary Taylor. From that election until the election of 1860, Democrats dominated American politics. The Democratic Party became known as the party of the "common man," encouraging popular participation, and helping to bring about an expansion of suffrage to all adult white males.

Republican Domination (1860–1932)

The Republican Party began as a third party, developed from a split in the Whig Party. The Whigs had been the major opposition to the Democrats. By 1860 the Whig Party had disappeared and the Republican Party had emerged as the second major party. The Republican Party was composed mostly of former members of other political parties, appealing to commercial and antislavery groups. The Republican Party was successful in electing Abraham Lincoln president in 1860, and by the end of the Civil War had become a dominant party. Sometimes called the Grand Old Party or GOP, the Republican Party often controlled both the presidency and Congress.

Return of Democrats (1932–1968)

With the onset of the Depression, new electoral coalitions were formed and the Republicans lost their domination of government. Franklin Delano Roosevelt was able to unite blacks, city dwellers, blue-collar (labor union) workers, Catholics, Jews, and women to create a voting bloc known as the **New Deal coalition**. The election of 1932 brought the Democrats back to power as the dominant party in American politics. Roosevelt was elected to the presidency an unprecedented four times. From 1932 to 1968 only two Republican presidents (Eisenhower and Nixon) were elected. Not until 1994 did the Republicans gain control of both houses of Congress.

Divided Government (1968–Present)

Since 1968 **divided government** has characterized American institutions, a condition in which one political party controls the presidency and the opposing party controls one or both houses of Congress. This division creates a potential **gridlock** when opposing parties and interests often block each other's proposals, creating a political stalemate. In the election of 2000, George W. Bush won the presidency and the Republican Party won control of the House of Representatives and Senate (until Jim Jeffords changed affiliation to Independent). In the mid-term election of 2002, the Republicans again gained control of the executive and legislative branches, creating a unified government. In the 2006 off-year election, the Democrats won control of both houses of Congress, returning divided government to U.S. politics. In the 2008 elections, the Democrats won control of the presidency and both houses of Congress, although few predicted that this would permanently end the era of divided government.

Electoral Dealignment

When significant numbers of voters no longer support a particular political party, **dealignment** has occurred. Often, those voters identify as independents and believe they owe no loyalty to any particular political party.

Electoral Realignment

Historically, as voting patterns have shifted and new coalitions of party supporters have formed, electoral **realignment** has occurred. Several elections can be considered realigning elections (**critical elections**), where the dominant party loses power and a new dominant party takes its place. The elections of 1860 and 1932 are examples. Many consider the 1980 election in this light; the long-term impact of the 2008 and 2010 elections will be studied in the future.

Third or Minor Parties

Although the Republican and Democratic parties have dominated the political scene, there have been minor, or third, parties throughout U.S. history. Minor parties usually have great difficulty in getting candidates elected to office, although they have been more successful at the state and local levels. A few minor party candidates have been elected to Congress, but no minor party candidate has ever been elected president. The limited successes of minor parties is attributed to obstacles that exist within the electoral process.

INSTITUTIONAL BARRIERS	ATTITUDINAL BARRIERS
Single-member districts	"Wasted vote" syndrome
Winner-take-all electoral system	Support by voters for moderate policies
State ballot access laws	
Federal funding guidelines	

Minor parties have been instrumental in providing important reforms that have been adopted by the major parties. Success rather than failure often brings an end to minor parties, as the major parties often adopt popular reforms or ideas, especially if they appeal to the voters.

Types of Third Parties

Some third parties have been permanent, running candidates in every election; however, many third parties disappear after only a few elections. Several types of minor parties have emerged:

- *ideological*—Those based on a particular set of social, political, or economic beliefs (communist, socialist, libertarian).
- *splinter/personality/factional*—Those that have split away from one of the major parties; usually formed around a strong personality who does not win the party nomination; may disappear when that leader steps aside (Theodore Roosevelt's "Bull Moose" Progressive, Strom Thurmond's States' Rights, George Wallace's American Independent).
- *single issue*—Parties that concentrate on a single public policy matter (Free Soil, Right to Life, Prohibition).
- *protest*—Usually rooted in periods of economic discontent; may be sectional in nature (Greenback, Populist); some observers place the "Tea Party," which supported many candidates in the 2010 congressional elections, in this category.

Structure and Organization of Political Parties

A political party must have an effective organization to accomplish its goals. Both of the major parties are organized in much the same manner. Both parties are highly decentralized, or fragmented. The party of the president is normally more solidly united than the opposition. The president is automatically considered the party leader, while the opposition is often without a single strong leader. Usually one or more members of Congress are seen as the opposition leaders.

National Convention

The national convention serves as the party's national voice. Party delegates meet in the summer of every fourth year to select the party's candidates for president and vice president. They are also responsible for writing and adopting the party's platform, which describes the policy beliefs of the party.

National Committee

The national committee manages the political party's business between conventions. They are responsible for selecting the convention site, establishing the rules of the convention, publishing and distributing party literature, and helping the party raise campaign contributions.

National Chairperson

The party's national committee, with the consent of the party's presidential nominee, elects the **national chairperson**. The chairperson is responsible for directing the work of the national committee from their national headquarters in Washington, D.C. The chairperson is involved in fundraising, recruiting new party members, encouraging unity within the party, and helping the party's presidential nominee win election.

Congressional Campaign Committee

Each party has a committee in the House of Representatives and Senate that works to ensure the election or reelection of the party's candidates by raising funds and determining how much money and support each candidate will receive. The committee often works to defeat an opposition party member who appears weak and might be open to defeat.

State and Local Organization

State law largely determines state and local party organization. Differences exist from state to state; however, state and local parties are structured in much the same way as the national party organization. Generally, state parties today are more organized and better funded than in previous years. As a result of **soft money**, money that is distributed from the national political party organization and that does not have to be reported under the Federal Election Campaign Act (1971) or its amendments, state parties have become more dependent on the national party organization and are subject to their influence. In 2002, however, the use of soft money was significantly restricted by the Bipartisan Campaign Reform Act, also known as the McCain-Feingold Act. The Supreme Court, in *Citizens United v. FEC* (2010), ruled that limiting the ability of businesses, unions, and other groups to fund their own efforts to elect or defeat candidates for office is unconstitutional.

Political parties must consider election laws, as well as the political and financial realities under which campaigns function. Campaign finance laws restrict how political parties nominate candidates and raise and spend funds.

Future of Political Parties

The future of political parties in the United States is uncertain. Political parties must modify their policies and present their messages in ways that will appeal to the various demographics of the voters. In recent decades, political parties have been in decline. This decline may be attributed to several factors:

- *third-party challenges*—In recent elections third-party challengers have taken votes from the major candidates, lessening their ability to win a majority of the vote.
- *loss of support by party loyalists*—The number of independent voters has increased.
- *increase in split-ticket voting*—Many voters no longer vote a **straight ticket** (only for candidates of one political party) but rather split their vote among candidates from more than one party.
- *lack of perceived differences between the parties*—Voters often believe there are no major differences in the parties or their candidates.
- *party reforms*—Changes within the parties themselves to create greater diversity and openness have allowed for greater conflict within some parties.
- *methods of campaigning*—New technologies have allowed candidates to become more independent of parties and more directly involved with the voters. The role political parties play in the nomination process is weakened as candidates can appeal directly to voters.
- **candidate-centered campaigns**—election campaigns and other political processes in which candidates, not political parties, have most of the initiative and influence.

❯ Review Questions

Multiple-Choice Questions

1. Which of the following best describes a multi-party system?
   - (A) Membership in the party of choice is not generally voluntary.
   - (B) There is usually a consensus of agreement as to basic principles of government.
   - (C) Multi-party systems usually give the voters meaningful choices.
   - (D) Parties tend to avoid extreme ideologies.

2. Which of the following is NOT a responsibility of a political party?
   - (A) organize the government
   - (B) represent special interests
   - (C) recruit candidates
   - (D) educate voters

3. The Republican and Democratic parties have dominated the political scene throughout American history. Minor parties have often surfaced to fill the void left by the major parties. A splinter party can best be characterized by
   - (A) the fact that it is the result of a revolt within a major party
   - (B) the fact that it is usually built around the working-class American
   - (C) the permanence of its presence on the political scene
   - (D) its presence during times of economic discontent

4. Minor parties seldom win elections at the national level. Which of the following best describes a factor that prevents minor parties from winning elections?
   - (A) gridlock
   - (B) lack of political efficacy
   - (C) proportional member districts
   - (D) winner-take-all electoral system

5. The national convention serves what major purpose for a political party?
   - (A) to allow the people to direct the work of the national committee through a system of national participation
   - (B) to establish the rules of party campaigning
   - (C) to serve as the party's national voice in the selection of the party's candidate
   - (D) to manage the political party's business by the vote of party constituents

6. Which of the following best describes state party organizations?
   - (A) They are independent of the national party.
   - (B) They are subject to their own jurisdiction according to party doctrines.
   - (C) They are determined and organized by the national party in accordance with national law.
   - (D) Their funding has been affected by campaign reform law.

7. Membership in an American political party is voluntary and based on party identification. Which of the following factors influence party identification?
   - (A) education
   - (B) cost of membership
   - (C) history of the party
   - (D) national law

8. Which of the following best describes the structure and organization of a political party?
   - (A) They are close-knit and very organized.
   - (B) They are highly decentralized or fragmented.
   - (C) After election day, they are usually less responsible to the people.
   - (D) The president plays no role in party leadership after his election.

9. The shifting of voting patterns and formation of new coalitions of party supporters is known as
   (A) alignment
   (B) realignment
   (C) divided government
   (D) dealignment

10. The future of political parties in the United States is uncertain due to
    (A) decline of third-party challenges
    (B) perceived differences between the parties
    (C) increase in split-ticket voting
    (D) lack of party reform

Use the graph below to answer question 11.

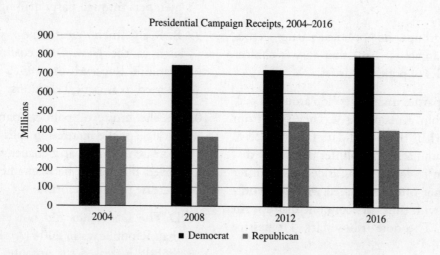

Presidential Campaign Receipts, 2004–2016

■ Democrat ■ Republican

11. Which of the following best describes presidential campaign receipts as shown in the graph?
    (A) Democrats have raised more money in each election cycle than Republicans.
    (B) Republicans have not increased the amount of money raised since 2004.
    (C) The party that raises the largest amount of money wins the election.
    (D) Democrats have more than doubled the amount of money raised since 2004.

Free-Response Question

12. The future of political parties in the United States is uncertain. In recent decades, political parties have been in decline.
    (A) Define each of the following terms:
       • Dealignment
       • Split-ticket voting
    (B) For each of the terms above, explain how they have contributed to the decline of political parties.
    (C) Explain how minor parties contribute to the decline of the major political parties.

› Answers and Explanations

1. **C.** Multi-party systems tend to give voters a greater variety of major and minor party candidate choices. Party membership is voluntary (A). Parties represent a wide variety of ideologies (D). Multi-party systems often result in government by coalition, indicating a general lack of consensus (B).

2. **B.** Interest groups, not political parties, represent special interests. The other answer choices represent roles of political parties.

3. **A.** Splinter parties usually develop around a personality within a major party. They split from that party when their candidate fails to receive the party nomination. A splinter party may disappear when its leader steps aside (C). Splinter parties are not often associated with the working class or with times of economic distress. An example is Theodore Roosevelt's Progressive Party (B, D).

4. **D.** Gridlock occurs when opposing parties and interests block each other's proposals, creating a political stalemate (A). The lack of political efficacy occurs when voters lose faith that they can influence politics and public policymaking (B). A proportional member district gives representation in the legislature in proportion to the popular vote of each party (C).

5. **C.** Two major functions of the national convention are to write the party platform and to nominate the party's candidates for president and vice president. The national committee directs the party (A) and its campaign (B), manages the party's business (D), and promotes party unity and fundraising.

6. **D.** State parties have often received soft money from the national organization. In 2002, the use of soft money was restricted by the Bipartisan Campaign Reform Act.

7. **A.** Education is one of the several factors that influence party identification. Other factors include ideology, income, occupation, race or ethnicity, gender, religion, family tradition, geographical region, and marital status.

8. **B.** Political parties tend to be highly decentralized and fragmented (A), especially at the national level and when no election is immediate. The president is the party leader after his election (D). After election day, political parties continue to communicate with their registered members through party mailings (C).

9. **B.** Realignment creates new voting coalitions such as the New Deal coalition that elected Franklin Roosevelt in 1932. These are often referred to as critical elections.

10. **C.** The future of political parties is uncertain because of the increase in split-ticket voting, an increase in third-party challenges, a lack of perceived differences between the parties, and an increase in party reforms.

11. **D.** The Democrats did not raise more money than Republicans in 2004 (A). Republicans have slightly increased the amount of money raised since 2004 (B). The graph shows no information about who won the elections (C).

12. **(A)** Dealignment, or a dealigning election, occurs when party loyalty become less important to voters, and significant numbers of voters identify with no political party. Split-ticket voting occurs when voters vote for candidates from more than one political party in the same election.

   (B) Dealignment contributes to the decline of political parties because the loss of party voters may mean that party candidates are not going to win elections. Party candidates must appeal to the more moderate voters to attract voters. The party cannot depend on voters automatically supporting their ticket. Split-ticket voting allows voters to vote for members of both political parties, again causing a loss to party candidates in elections and a decline of political parties.

   (C) In recent elections, minor party challengers have taken votes from the major candidates, lessening their ability to win a majority of the vote. This contributes to the decline of political parties, because voters may lose interest in the party or election and either vote independent or not at all.

› Rapid Review

- Political parties are voluntary associations of voters.
- Political parties are different from interest groups.
- Political parties serve the party in the electorate, in government, and in organization.
- One-party, two-party, and multi-party systems exist throughout the world.
- Political parties recruit candidates, nominate and support candidates for office, educate the electorate, and organize the government.
- Party identification may be based on several factors.
- The Constitution does not call for political parties. Two parties developed from factions during the ratification process.
- Historically, there have been periods of one-party domination of the government. More recently, divided control of the branches of government has led to potential gridlock.
- Minor parties have existed throughout American history. There are four major types of minor parties: ideological, splinter/personality, single-issue, and protest parties.
- Political parties must have organization to accomplish their goals. American political parties tend to be decentralized and fragmented.
- The future of political parties in America is uncertain; some maintain that the two-party system is in jeopardy.

CHAPTER 15

Interest Groups and the Mass Media

IN THIS CHAPTER

Summary: People form and join groups to take their concerns before public officials at all levels of government. Interest groups are different from a political party in that they have no legal status in the election process. They do not nominate candidates for public office; however, they may actively support candidates who are sympathetic to their cause. While political parties are interested in controlling government, **interest groups** are concerned with influencing the policies of government, usually focusing on issues that directly affect their membership. Membership in interest groups may be restricted or open to all who are interested. Not all interested people belong to interest groups. Many people belong to various interest groups at the same time.

Key Terms

interest groups
political action
   committees (PACs)
lobbying

grassroots
iron triangle
issue network
mass media

gatekeepers
media events
trial balloon

Interest Groups

Historical Background of Interest Groups

Interest groups have often been viewed with suspicion. In *Federalist #10,* James Madison warned against the dangers of "factions." Although Madison was opposed to the elimination of factions, he believed that the separation of powers under the Constitution would moderate their effect.

Functions of Interest Groups

Interest groups serve several important functions. They:

- raise awareness and stimulate interest in public affairs by educating their members and the public
- represent their membership, serving as a link between members and government
- provide information to government, especially data and testimony useful in making public policy
- provide channels for political participation that enable citizens to work together to achieve a common goal

Types of Interest Groups

Economic Interest Groups

Most interest groups are formed on the basis of economic interests.

- Labor groups promote and protect the interest of organized labor. Examples include the AFL-CIO and the Teamsters Union.
- Business groups promote and protect business interests in general. The Chamber of Commerce of the United States and the National Association of Manufacturers are examples.
- Professional groups maintain standards of the profession, hold professional meetings, and publish journals. Some examples are the National Education Association (NEA), the American Medical Association (AMA), and the American Bar Association (ABA).
- Agricultural groups, such as the National Grange and the National Farmers' Union, promote general agricultural interests.

Groups That Promote Causes

- specific causes
  — American Civil Liberties Union (ACLU)
  — National Rifle Association (NRA)
- welfare of specific groups of individuals
  — American Association of Retired Persons (AARP)
  — National Association for the Advancement of Colored People (NAACP)
  — Veterans of Foreign Wars (VFW)
- religion-related causes
  — National Council of Churches
  — American Jewish Congress

Public Interest Groups

Public interest groups are concerned with issues such as the environment, consumer protection, crime, and civil rights.

- public interests
  — Common Cause
  — League of Women Voters
  — Mothers Against Drunk Driving (MADD)

Strategies of Interest Groups

- *influencing elections*—Encouraging members to vote for candidates who support their views, influencing party platforms and the nomination of candidates, campaigning and contributing money to parties and candidates through **political action committees (PACs)**.

- *lobbying*—Attempting to influence policymakers, often by supplying data to government officials and their staffs to convince these policymakers that their case is more deserving than another's.
  - direct **lobbying**—Using personal contacts between lobbyists and policymakers.
  - **grassroots** lobbying—Interested group members and others outside the organization write letters, send telegrams, e-mails, and faxes, and make telephone calls to influence policymakers.
  - coalition lobbying—Several interest groups with common goals join together to influence policymakers.
- *litigation*—Groups often take an issue to court if they are unsuccessful in gaining the support of Congress; this strategy was used successfully by the NAACP to argue against segregation during the 1950s.
- *going public*—Appealing to the public for support by bringing attention to an issue or using public relations to gain support for the image of the interest group itself.

Political Action Committees

The campaign finance reforms of the 1970s prohibited corporations and labor unions from making direct contributions to candidates running for federal office. Political action committees (PACs) were formed as political arms of interest groups. Federal law regulates PACs; they must register with the federal government, raise money from multiple contributors, donate to several candidates, and follow strict accounting rules.

Regulation of Interest Groups

The first major attempt to regulate lobbying came in 1946 with the passage of the Federal Regulation of Lobbying Act, requiring lobbyists to register with the clerk of the House of Representatives and the secretary of the Senate if their principal purpose was to influence legislation. This law was directed only at those who tried to influence members of Congress. In 1995 Congress passed the Lobbying Disclosure Act, creating much stricter regulations by requiring registration if lobbying was directed at members of Congress, congressional staff, or policymakers within the executive branch. It also required the disclosure of more information concerning the activities and clients of lobbyists.

Interest Group Influence

Not all interest groups exert the same influence over the political system. Interest groups may gain influence because of their access to political and economic resources. Money allows them to hire professional lobbyists or contribute to political campaigns, which can help interest groups gain access to policymakers. Membership size may be another factor that allows some interest groups to be more influential. For example, AARP is composed of millions of members, and policymakers are willing to listen to such a large group.

Interest groups also face certain problems. Members of interest groups share a common cause, but the "free-rider" problem makes it difficult for interest groups to increase their membership when some members just sit back and allow others to do the work to achieve the group's goals.

Interest groups spend millions of dollars each year to lobby members of Congress on various issues. These groups try to influence the legislation passed by Congress, including programs of the government and the budget that supports those programs. For example, AARP lobbies Congress to increase Social Security and Medicare for the elderly.

Many interest groups employ the services of former government officials such as members of Congress or their staff as lobbyists. These former officials can use their personal contacts and knowledge of the policymaking process to help the interests of the group. This phenomenon is called the "revolving door" because so many former government officials end up working for interest groups.

Interest groups can also influence policymaking through their relationships with congressional committees and executive agencies. The **iron triangle** created by this three-way relationship often brings mutual policy outcomes that produce benefits for all members of the "triangle." An **issue network** includes multiple special interests, bureaucratic agencies, mass media, think tanks, and others who work together on policy.

Mass Media

Mass media refers to all forms of communication that transmit information to the general public. Although the mass media are not the only means of communication between citizens and government (political parties, interest groups, and voting are other means), they are the only linkage mechanism that specializes in communication.

Development of the Modern Media

The development of the mass media in the United States reflects the growth of the country, new inventions and technology, and changing attitudes about the role of government.

Newspapers

The earliest American newspapers, operating during colonial times, were expensive, had small circulations, and were often prepared or financed by political organs or those advocating a particular cause. Improvements in printing, the telegraph, and the rotary press led to the growth of newspapers and newspaper circulations. By the 1890s almost every major city in the United States had one or more daily papers. Circulation wars led to "yellow journalism" and political consequences resulted. Since the 1950s newspaper competition has decreased. By 2009, many newspapers in the United States had gone out of business and the very future of the newspaper was being called into question.

Magazines

Magazines tended to have smaller circulations with less frequent publication. The earliest public affairs magazines were published in the mid-1800s. They often exposed political corruption and business exploitation with the writings of muckrakers such as Ida Tarbell, Lincoln Steffens, and Sinclair Lewis. In the 1920s and 1930s, three weekly news magazines, *Time, Newsweek,* and *U.S. News and World Report,* attracted mass readership. Today, they often substitute for daily newspapers. Liberal and conservative magazines have smaller circulations but are read by supporters on both sides.

Radio

The wide use of radio began in the 1920s and made celebrities of news personalities. Franklin Roosevelt successfully used radio to broadcast his "fireside chats" to the American people.

Television

Today, television claims the largest audience of the mass media. After World War II television increased the visibility of broadcast journalists, making them celebrities. Television promoted the careers of politicians such as Joe McCarthy, during hearings of the House Unamerican Activities Committee, and John Kennedy, during his campaign debates against

Richard Nixon. The recent growth of cable TV news and the 24/7 news cycle have greatly changed the coverage of the American political system.

Internet as Media

The rapid growth of Internet usage has led to media organizations using the Internet as a way to convey information. Newspapers, magazines, blogs, and radio and television stations have sites on the World Wide Web. More and more Americans are receiving their news from the Internet. Critics note that Internet news has less "fact-checking" associated with it than does news from the more traditional forms of media; they claim that rumor and unsubstantiated allegations make up a large portion of Internet "news."

Roles of the Media

The media perform several important functions:

- informing the public
- shaping public opinion
- providing a link between citizens and government
- serving as a watchdog that investigates and examines personalities and government policies
- agenda setting by influencing what subjects become national political issues; protests against the Vietnam conflict are an example

Media Ownership and Government Regulation

The mass media are privately owned in the United States, giving them more political freedom than in most other countries, where they are publicly owned, but also making them more dependent on advertising profits. Government regulation of the media affects the broadcast media (radio and television) more than the print media (newspapers and magazines) and the Internet. Government regulation of the broadcast media falls into three categories:

- *technical regulations*—The Federal Communications Act of 1934 created the Federal Communications Commission (FCC) as an independent regulatory agency to regulate interstate and foreign communication by radio, television, telephone, telegraph, cable, and satellite.
- *structural regulations*—These control the organization and ownership of broadcasting companies; in 1996 the Telecommunications Act broadened competition.
- *content regulations*—Although the mass media are protected by the First Amendment, the broadcast media have been subject to regulation of content.

What Is News? Reporting the News

"News" is any important event that has happened within the past 24 hours. The media decide what is news by deciding what to report. News is generally directed through **gatekeepers**—media executives, news editors, and prominent reporters—who decide which events to present and how to present them. Time limitations and the potential impact of the story are major elements in selecting what is news. In political coverage, "horse-race journalism" often focuses on which candidate is winning or losing, rather than the issues of the election.

Media and the President

The major news organizations maintain journalists in major cities and government centers to report political events firsthand. Washington, D.C., has the largest press corps of any city in the United States, with one-third of the press assigned to cover the White House. News events may be staged as **media events**. The White House allows special access to the president, with the press receiving information through the Office of the Press Secretary.

Some ways that journalists receive information are:

- *news releases*—Prepared texts to be used exactly as written.
- *news briefings*—Announcements and daily questioning of the press secretary about news releases.
- *news conferences*—Questioning of high-level officials, often rehearsed.
- *leaks*—Information released by officials who are guaranteed anonymity; may be intentional to interfere with the opposition or to "float" an idea (**trial balloon**) and measure reaction.

Reporters are expected to observe "rules" when talking to officials:

- *on the record*—The official may be quoted by name.
- *off the record*—What the official says cannot be printed.
- *on background*—What the official says can be printed but may not be attributed to the official by name.
- *on deep background*—What the official says can be printed, but it cannot be attributed to anybody.

Media and Congress

Fewer reporters regularly cover Congress, which does not maintain as tight a control over news stories as the White House. Most of the coverage of Congress concerns the House of Representatives, the Senate, or Congress as an organization, rather than individual members. News about Congress may cover confirmation hearings, oversight investigations, or scandals among members.

C-SPAN (Cable-Satellite Public Affairs Network) was created to increase coverage of congressional activities. The floor and some committee proceedings of the House of Representatives and Senate are now broadcast on C-SPAN and C-SPAN II. Members of Congress may also record radio and television messages to their constituents.

Media and Elections

The media plays a crucial role in a democracy. While the media often functions as a "watchdog," it has other roles in the electoral process:

- educating voters
- reporting on campaigns
- providing an avenue for political parties and candidates to communicate their message to voters
- providing an avenue for the public to communicate their concerns, opinions, and needs, to the parties, candidates, and officeholders
- allowing the parties and candidates to debate one another
- reporting and monitoring election results

Media and Public Opinion

While measuring the extent of influence of the media on public opinion is difficult, almost 90% of Americans believe that the media has a strong influence on public opinion. Most people learn about political events through the media; therefore, how events are reported might have a strong impact on public opinion. The media's use of polls, and its coverage of elections, can impact the electoral process. In 2000, the media declared George W. Bush the winner of the presidential election, although the outcome was not certain. This declaration created an impression that the election had already been decided, yet polls were still open in numerous states

Biases in the Media

Critics of the media contend the media are biased in reporting. Reporters are said to have a liberal bias, while media owners, publishers, and editors are said to be more conservative. Studies confirm that reporters have a liberal orientation; however, the bias tends to be against incumbents and frontrunners. There is also a tendency toward "pack journalism," with journalists adopting the viewpoints of other journalists with whom they spend time and exchange information. This bias often extends to viewers, listeners, and readers because individuals often read, watch, or listen to news outlets that support political views that they already have.

> Review Questions

Multiple-Choice Questions

1. How does an interest group differ from a political party?
   - (A) Interest groups often support political candidates for office.
   - (B) Membership in an interest group is nonrestrictive.
   - (C) Interest groups have no legal status in the election process.
   - (D) Interest groups control government.

2. Which of the following is NOT a function of an interest group?
   - (A) represent a broad range of interests
   - (B) raise awareness and stimulate interest in public affairs
   - (C) serve as a link between its members and government
   - (D) provide information to the government

3. An example of an interest group that would promote a specific cause is
   - (A) the National Grange
   - (B) the Teamsters Union
   - (C) the National Rifle Association
   - (D) the American Bar Association

4. An example of a public interest group is
   - (A) the League of Women Voters
   - (B) the American Association of Retired Persons
   - (C) the American Bar Association
   - (D) the National Council of Churches

5. A method of lobbying by which interest group members and others outside the organization write letters, send telegrams, and make telephone calls to influence policymakers is known as
   - (A) litigation lobbying
   - (B) grassroots lobbying
   - (C) direct lobbying
   - (D) coalition lobbying

6. Which of the following is true regarding the regulation of lobbying?
   - (A) The Federal Regulation of Lobbying Act was directed at those who tried to influence members of the executive branch.
   - (B) The first major attempt to regulate lobbying came during the Progressive Era, in the early years of the 20th century.
   - (C) In the second half of the 20th century, laws regulating lobbying became more lenient.
   - (D) Both the Federal Regulation of Lobbying Act and the Lobbying Disclosure Act required lobbyists to register.

7. Which is true of government regulation of the media?
   - (A) Government regulation of the media affects the print media more than the broadcast media.
   - (B) Structural regulations deal with issues affecting the organization of broadcasting companies.
   - (C) The Telecommunications Act (1996) restricted competition among broadcasting companies.
   - (D) The Federal Communications Commission is restricted to the regulation of interstate commerce.

8. In the history of radio as a mode of mass media, which American president was first to make the medium a regular feature of his administration as a method of informing the people?
   - (A) Ronald Reagan
   - (B) Franklin Roosevelt
   - (C) Bill Clinton
   - (D) George H. W. Bush

9. Which of the following has NOT been an important function in the role of the mass media?
    (A) directing government
    (B) agenda setting
    (C) informing the public
    (D) shaping public opinion

10. Those media executives and news editors who decide which events to present and how to present the news are called
    (A) content regulators
    (B) gatekeepers
    (C) technical regulators
    (D) telecommunication regulators

Use the graph below to answer question 11.

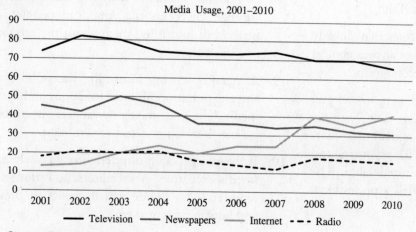

Media Usage, 2001–2010

Television — Newspapers — Internet - - - Radio

Source: Pew Research

11. Which of the following is an accurate statement about the information on the line graph?
    (A) The greatest decrease in media usage was in the use of the radio.
    (B) The greatest increase in media usage was in the use of newspapers.
    (C) The least-used form of media was television.
    (D) The greatest decrease in media usage was in the use of newspapers.

Free-Response Question

12. Interest groups often exert vast influence over public policymaking.
    (A) Identify the primary goal of interest groups.
    (B) Describe two strategies used by interest groups to influence public policymaking.
    (C) Explain how interest groups are limited in achieving their goals by each of the following:
        • the media
        • separation of powers

› Answers and Explanations

1. **C.** Interest groups have no legal status in the election process, whereas political parties fulfill many roles in the election process. Interest groups may support political candidates for office, but only political parties nominate candidates for office (A). Membership in an interest group may be restricted (B). Interest groups influence governmental policies, whereas political parties control government (D).

2. **A.** Interest groups focus on issues that directly affect its membership. The other answer choices reflect the functions of an interest group.

3. **C.** The National Rifle Association promotes gun ownership as a right of citizens. The National Grange (A) promotes general agricultural interests. The Teamsters Union (B) advocates and protects the interests of organized labor. The American Bar Association (D) is a professional group.

4. **A.** The League of Women Voters is a public-interest group created to encourage voter participation. AARP (B) and the National Council of Churches (D) are groups that promote causes. The American Bar Association (C) is a professional group.

5. **B.** Grassroots lobbying attempts to reach the average voter at the local level. Litigation lobbying involves taking an issue to court (A). Direct lobbying (C) uses personal contacts between lobbyists and policymakers. Coalition lobbying (D) brings together several interest groups with common goals.

6. **D.** Both laws require the registration of lobbyists, with the Lobbying Disclosure Act requiring registration under more circumstances than the Federal Regulation of Lobbying Act. The Federal Regulation of Lobbying Act was directed at those trying to influence members of Congress (A). The first major attempt to regulate lobbying came in 1976 (B). Laws regulating lobbying became stricter and more comprehensive (C).

7. **B.** Structural regulations control the organization and ownership of broadcasting companies. Government regulation affects radio and television more than newspapers and magazines (A). The Telecommunications Act broadened competition (C). The FCC regulates interstate and foreign communication (D).

8. **B.** Franklin Roosevelt used the radio to deliver "fireside chats" to the American people as a method of informing them about the economy and the war.

9. **A.** Agenda setting, informing the public, and shaping public opinion are functions of the mass media. The mass media investigate government policies but do not direct government.

10. **B.** News is generally directed through gatekeepers (media executives, news editors, and prominent reporters who decide which events to present and how to present them).

11. **D.** The greatest decrease in media usage was in the use of newspapers, not radio (A). The greatest increase in media usage was in the use of the Internet, not newspapers (B). The least-used form of media was the radio, not television (C).

12. **A.** The primary goal of interest groups is to influence the policies of government, often focusing on issues that affect the interest of their members.

   B. Interest groups can lobby members of government. Lobbying is the activity of trying to persuade someone, such as a government official, to support a group's position on an issue. Interest groups can use electioneering, helping to get a candidate elected who might support a group's position on issues. This may involve contributing to a political campaign or mobilizing voter support for a candidate. Interest groups may use litigation or taking action through the courts. They may file lawsuits against the government, a program or legislation; finance lawsuits filed by others; or file amicus curiae briefs to support a side of an existing court case. Lastly, interest groups may bring the attention of the public to the issue by going public. They could hold strikes, boycotts, rallies, or marches; purchase advertising; or generate news coverage to bring attention to a topic.

C. The media acts as a "watchdog" over the behaviors of interest groups. The media can inform the public about the activities of interest groups. If the media portray the interest group in a negative manner, this can affect the success of the group. The media also acts as a gatekeeper, deciding what news to present and how it will be presented. This can limit the success of interest groups, because their message may not be portrayed the way they want and therefore they lose support for their position on the issue.

› Rapid Review

- Interest groups are different from political parties.
- James Madison warned against the dangers of "factions" in *Federalist #10*.
- Interest groups perform many functions: creating awareness among the public, linking the public and government, providing information, and creating avenues for political participation.
- There are three major types of interest groups: economic, cause-related, and public interest.
- Strategies used by interest groups may include influencing elections, lobbying, litigation, and going public.
- PACs, or political action committees, are political arms of interest groups that raise money for political candidates.
- Federal, state, and local laws regulate interest group activities and fundraising.
- Mass media refers to all the forms of communication that transmit information to the general public. Mass media include newspapers, magazines, radio, television, and the Internet.
- One of the major roles of the media is agenda setting.
- The mass media are privately owned in the United States.
- Government regulation of broadcast media includes technical, structural, and content regulation.
- Gatekeepers are the media executives, news editors, and prominent reporters who decide which events to present and how to present them.
- The Office of the Press Secretary allows the press to have greater access to the president through new releases, briefings, and conferences.
- Media coverage of Congress often centers on the institution rather than individual members.
- Criticism of the media's influence often refers to bias in reporting.
- More and more Americans are receiving their news from the Internet rather than from traditional news outlets; some critics note the potential unreliability of news reported in the Internet age.

UNIT 6

Pulling It All Together: Public Policy

CHAPTER 16   Politics and Public Policymaking

CHAPTER 16

Politics and Public Policymaking

IN THIS CHAPTER

Summary: Public policy is the method by which government attempts to solve the problems of a nation. Governments are constantly making public policy. Even the decision to keep the status quo is a public policy decision. Public policy is made at all levels of government. Policymaking may be a slow process with only small changes (**incrementalism**) or a major shift from previous policies.

Key Terms

incrementalism
agenda setting
political agenda
policy formulation
policy adoption
policy
  implementation
policy evaluation

environmental impact
  statements
fiscal policy
monetary policy
discretionary spending
national debt
federal budget
social welfare programs

entitlement programs
fiscal year
appropriations
North American Free
  Trade Agreement
  (NAFTA)
mandatory spending
constitutional law

The Policymaking Process

The policymaking process involves several steps:

- *agenda setting*—Recognizing an issue as a problem that must be addressed as a part of the political agenda. Problems are often brought to the **political agenda** by citizens, interest groups, the media, or governmental entities.

- *policy formulation*—Finding ways to solve the problem; exploring alternative plans of action and developing proposals to solve the problem.
- *policy adoption*—Adopting a plan of action to solve the problem; may require the passage of legislation.
- *policy implementation*—Executing the plan of action by the appropriate agency or agencies.
- *policy evaluation*—Analysis of policy and its impact upon the problem; judging the effectiveness of the policy and making adjustments if necessary.

Domestic Policy

Domestic policy often refers to the social policies of the United States in the areas of crime prevention, education, energy, the environment, health care, and social welfare.

Crime Prevention

Although crime prevention has traditionally been a state and local matter, as crime and violence have increased, the federal government has become more involved in crime prevention. Lyndon Johnson declared a "war on crime," creating a commission to study the causes of crime and suggest solutions. Today, more crimes are classified as federal crimes, with punishments often more harsh than those for state crimes. Since the shooting of President Ronald Reagan, debate has centered on gun control legislation. President Bill Clinton signed the Brady Bill, requiring a five-day waiting period and background checks before the purchase of a handgun. Clinton also won congressional support of a ban on the sale of some types of semiautomatic assault weapons and legislation authorizing new federal spending on crime initiatives, including the hiring of new police officers and building new prisons and "boot camps" for juvenile offenders. Clinton's crime bill also listed federal crimes punishable by the death penalty and the "three strikes laws," mandating certain sentences if convicted of a third felony. As the federal government has become more involved in crime prevention, federal agencies have played a larger role.

- The Federal Bureau of Investigation (FBI) collects and reports evidence in matters relating to federal law or the crossing of state borders; provides investigative and lab services to local law enforcement agencies.
- The Drug Enforcement Administration (DEA) prohibits the flow of illegal narcotics into the United States and patrols U.S. borders.
- The Bureau of Alcohol, Tobacco, and Firearms (ATF) administers laws dealing with explosives and firearms and regulates the production and distribution of alcohol and tobacco products.

Education

Although public education falls under the authority of the state governments, the federal government has played an increasing role in education. Since the 1950s (*Brown v. Board of Education*, 1954, and the Soviet Union's launch of *Sputnik*) the major goal of education policy has been to ensure equal access to educational opportunities. Under Lyndon Johnson's Great Society, Congress passed the Elementary and Secondary Education Act in 1965, providing federal funding to public school districts with low-income populations. In 1979 Congress created the Department of Education to coordinate education policy. Congress has also provided programs for higher education, including loans and grant programs for college students. Recent proposals in education have concerned the use of school vouchers that would allow parents to choose the schools their children attend at public expense, and the national testing of students.

In 2002 President George W. Bush signed a bill called No Child Left Behind. This Act requires all states to administer proficiency tests in public schools in order to monitor student progress. Though the Act has created some improvement in many of America's public schools, many provisions of the legislation remain controversial. President Barack Obama made education a central part of his domestic agenda.

Energy

Energy policy has traditionally been one of conservation and the study of alternative and renewable sources of fuel. Newer energy policies have addressed issues such as global warming and toxic waste disposal. In 1980 a superfund was established for cleanup of toxic waste sites, and current law provides for the tracking of hazardous chemicals and the disposal of toxic waste. Energy policy often involves highly technical issues about which the average citizen may have limited knowledge. Energy will be an important issue in the coming years.

The Environment

In the late 18th century, the federal government began setting aside public lands as national parks, monuments, and forests. Not until the 1950s, however, did Congress begin passing legislation aimed at protecting the environment and cleaning up polluted air and water. In the 1970s Congress created the Environmental Protection Agency (EPA) to enforce environmental legislation. The Clean Air Acts of 1970 and 1990 were implemented to reduce air pollution. The Water Pollution Control Act of 1972 was designed to clean up the nation's lakes and rivers. Wilderness areas were established, the Endangered Species Act provided government protection of species listed as endangered, and **environmental impact statements** required studies and reports of likely environmental impacts be filed with the Environmental Protection Agency. President Obama repeatedly promised in the 2008 campaign that this would be a key issue for his administration.

Health Care

Unlike Canada or Great Britain, the United States has no national health care system, yet the largest percentage of government spending goes to the Medicare and Medicaid programs. Medicare provides hospitalization insurance for the elderly, and Medicaid provides public assistance in health care for the poor. The government operates several programs aimed at promoting and protecting public health in the United States. The Public Health Service, Centers for Disease Control (CDC), Veterans Affairs (VA), and Food and Drug Administration (FDA) are among the agencies involved in promoting public health. Health care was a major campaign issue in the 1992 presidential election, when Bill Clinton campaigned on a plan to address both the high cost of health care and its limited access. Clinton's proposals to reform health care in the United States died in Congress. A controversial national health care program was passed by Congress late in 2009.

Social Welfare

Social welfare began during the New Deal era. The Great Depression led citizens to want more government help against economic downturns and poverty. The Social Security Act (1935) was a first step in this fight. Lyndon Johnson's Great Society continued the war on poverty by creating new programs (Medicare, school aid, job training) designed to prevent poverty. Housing programs and urban renewal have been implemented with the goal of providing adequate housing for all citizens. In the 1980s Ronald Reagan reduced benefits and removed people from eligibility in an effort to reform the social welfare system amid claims of increasing government. Bill Clinton continued to bring reform to the social welfare system by limiting how long a person could receive benefits and giving money to the states to run their own programs. In 1996, the entitlement program Aid to Families with Dependent Children (AFDC) was replaced by a new program, Temporary Assistance for Needy Families (TANF). Unlike AFDC, TANF is a block grant that limits recipients to no more than five years of assistance. TANF also requires recipients to work, receive vocational training, or participate in community service.

Economic Policy

Economic policy can have a profound effect on national elections. The president and Congress are held responsible for the economic "health" of the nation. Economic policy involves improving the overall economic health of the nation through government spending and taxation policies. While Congress and the President are responsible for **fiscal policy**, the government's taxing and spending policies, the Federal Reserve is responsible for **monetary policy**, controlling the money supply through the banking system.

Raising Revenue

The government raises revenue through the collection of taxes. The federal government collects individual income taxes, corporate income taxes, social insurance taxes, excise taxes, customs duties, and estate and gift taxes. The government also raises revenue through the sale of government securities by the Federal Reserve and through the collection of fees for services provided, such as patents.

Government Spending

Government spending may be discretionary or nondiscretionary (mandatory). **Discretionary spending** is spending about which government planners may make choices, while nondiscretionary spending is required by existing laws for current programs. In recent years the percentage of nondiscretionary spending has grown while the percentage of discretionary spending has decreased. Discretionary spending includes defense spending, education, student loans, scientific research, environmental cleanup, law enforcement, disaster aid, and foreign aid. Nondiscretionary spending includes interest on the **national debt** and **social welfare** and **entitlement programs** such as Social Security, Medicare, Medicaid, veterans' pensions, and unemployment insurance. A large stimulus package was enacted in the first months of the Obama presidency.

The Federal Budget

The **federal budget** indicates the amount of money the federal government expects to receive and authorizes government spending for a fiscal (12-month period) year. The **fiscal year** for the federal government is from October 1 to September 30. The process of preparing the federal budget takes about 18 months and involves several steps:

- *proposals*—Each federal agency submits a detailed estimate of its needs for the coming fiscal year to the Office of Management and Budget (OMB).
- *executive branch*—The OMB holds meetings at which representatives from the various agencies may explain their proposal and try to convince the OMB that their needs are

justified. The OMB works with the president's staff to combine all requests into a single budget package, which the president submits to Congress in January or February.

- *Congress*—Congress debates and often modifies the president's proposal. The Congressional Budget Office (CBO) provides Congress with economic data. Congressional committees hold hearings, analyze the budget proposals, and by September offer budget resolutions to their respective houses (which must be passed by September 15). The Appropriations Committee for each house submits bills to authorize spending.
- *president*—Congress sends **appropriations** bills to the president for approval. If no budget is approved, Congress must pass temporary emergency funding or the government will shut down.

THE BUDGET PROCESS	
President and OMB (Office of Management and Budget)	OMB presents long-range forecasts for the revenues and expenditures to the president. President and OMB develop general guidelines for all federal agencies. Agencies are sent guidelines and forms for their budget proposals.
Executive agencies	Agencies prepare and submit budget requests to OMB.
OMB and agencies	OMB reviews agency requests and holds hearings with agency officials.
OMB and president	OMB presents revised budget to president. President and OMB write budget message for Congress.
President	The president presents budget for the next fiscal year to Congress.
CBO (Congressional Budget Committee) and congressional committees	CBO reviews taxing and spending proposals and reports to House and Senate committees
Congress, House and Senate budget committees	Committees present first concurrent resolutions, which sets overall total for budget outlays in major categories. Full House and Senate vote on resolutions. Committees are instructed to stay within Budget Committee's resolution.
Congress, House and Senate appropriations committees, and budget committees	Appropriations committees and subcommittees draw up detailed appropriations bills and submit them to budget committees for second concurrent resolution. The full House and Senate vote on "reconciliations" and second (firm) concurrent resolution.
Congress and president	House and Senate pass various appropriations bills (nine to sixteen bills, by major functional category, such as "defense"). Each is sent to the president for signature. (If successfully vetoed, a bill is revised and resubmitted to the president.)
	Fiscal year for all federal agencies begins October 1. If no appropriations bill for an agency has been passed by Congress and signed by the president, Congress must pass, and the president must sign a continuing resolution to allow the agency to spend at last year's level until a new appropriations bill is passed. If no continuing resolution is passed, the agency must officially cease spending government funds and must officially shut down.

Foreign and Defense Policy

Foreign policy involves all the strategies and procedures for dealing with other nations. One of the purposes of foreign policy is to maintain peaceful relations with other countries through diplomatic, military, or trade relations. The process of carrying out foreign policy is accomplished through foreign relations. Defense policy is the role that the military establishment plays in providing for the defense of the nation.

The President and Foreign Policy

The president is often considered the leader in the development of foreign policy. Presidential authority for foreign policy originates from the constitutional powers, historical precedent, and institutional advantages of the executive. The president is commander-in-chief of the armed forces, negotiates treaties and executive agreements, and appoints foreign ambassadors, ministers, and consuls. Historically, presidents have often issued foreign policy statements (for example, the Monroe Doctrine and the Truman Doctrine) that have not passed through the legislative process but which set the tone for foreign policy. Executive agreements, or pacts between the president and heads of state of foreign countries, do not require Senate ratification. Also, the president can often respond more quickly than Congress when a national crisis requires quick action (for example, the attack on Pearl Harbor or the events of September 11, 2001).

The Department of State

The Department of State is the major organization for carrying out foreign policy. The secretary of state reports directly to the president with advice about foreign policy matters. The secretary of state also supervises the diplomatic corps of ambassadors, ministers, and consuls. The State Department is organized into bureaus, each specializing in a region of the world.

The Department of Defense

The Department of Defense (DoD) provides military information to the president. The secretary of defense advises the president on troop movements, military installations, and weapons development. Because the secretary of defense is a civilian, the Joint Chiefs of Staff, composed of a chairman and the highest-ranking military officer in the Army, Navy, Air Force, and Marines, also provide advice on military matters.

The National Security Council

The National Security Council (NSC) is part of the Executive Office of the President. Membership includes the president, vice president, the secretaries of state and defense, chairman of the Joint Chiefs of Staff, director of the Central Intelligence Agency, and the president's national security advisor.

The United States Information Agency

The United States Information Agency helps keep the world informed about America, the American way of life, and American views on world problems through information centers around the world. It also sponsors the "Voice of America" radio programs that are broadcast around the world.

The Central Intelligence Agency

The Central Intelligence Agency is responsible for gathering secret information essential to national defense. Although the CIA is an independent agency, it operates within the executive branch to gather information, analyze that information, and brief the president and the National Security Council.

Congress and Foreign Policy

Congress also plays a major role in the development of foreign policy. It is the responsibility of the Senate Foreign Relations Committee and the House Committee on Foreign Affairs to make recommendations to Congress and the president on foreign relations. The Senate must approve all treaties between the United States and foreign nations by a two-thirds vote, and all nominations for ambassadors by majority vote. Congress has the power to declare war and must approve spending for national defense.

Current Issues in Foreign Policy

Current foreign policy issues include:

- *nuclear proliferation*—With only a few nations having nuclear capabilities, how do we prevent possible enemies from gaining access to nuclear technology that might someday be used against the United States or our allies?
- *terrorism*—How does the United States defend itself against possible terrorist attacks? What role will the Department of Homeland Security play in intelligence gathering, border security, immigration, and holding, questioning, and prosecuting suspected terrorists?
- *international trade*—Trade can be used as a tool of foreign policy by providing military or economic aid or by reducing or eliminating tariffs through trade agreements such as the **North American Free Trade Agreement (NAFTA)** and the World Trade Organization (WTO).
- *how to manage conflicts abroad*—During the presidency of George W. Bush many criticized the United States for its "go it alone" policy. Should President Trump and subsequent presidents do more to create alliances and agreements with other nations?

› Review Questions

Multiple-Choice Questions

1. During the policymaking process, when a plan of action is executed by an agency or agencies, what important step has taken place?
   (A) policy formulation
   (B) policy implementation
   (C) policy adoption
   (D) agenda setting

2. What has been the major goal of the government's education policy?
   (A) ensure equal access to educational opportunity
   (B) increase the power of the Department of Education
   (C) provide more money to low-income schools
   (D) provide more programs for higher education

3. Which of the following is NOT associated with U.S. domestic policy?
   (A) The Federal Bureau of Investigation
   (B) The Environmental Protection Agency
   (C) The Drug Enforcement Administration
   (D) The National Security Council

4. In the United States, the largest percentage of government spending goes to
   (A) Medicare and Medicaid programs
   (B) public health services
   (C) the Food and Drug Administration
   (D) Centers for Disease Control

5. Which of the following was the first major government act of economic support?
   (A) the Great Society Act
   (B) the Medicare and Medicaid Act
   (C) the Social Security Act
   (D) the Welfare Act

6. Which of the following is true regarding U.S. economic policy?
   (A) Government planners may make choices about nondiscretionary spending.
   (B) The Department of the Treasury is held responsible for the economic health of the nation.
   (C) The government raises revenue primarily through the collection of taxes.
   (D) Discretionary spending includes interest on the national debt.

7. Which of the following is NOT a part of the federal budget process?
   (A) The Supreme Court reviews budget requests that are outside the realm of constitutional law.
   (B) The executive branch (OMB) holds meetings to review budget proposals.
   (C) Each federal agency submits an estimate of needs to the OMB.
   (D) Congress debates budget proposals.

8. Which of the following is NOT a true statement?
   (A) The purpose of foreign policy is to maintain peaceful relations with foreign nations.
   (B) Foreign policy is the responsibility of the Congress through the secretary of state.
   (C) The process of carrying out foreign policy is accomplished through foreign relations.
   (D) Defense policy is the role that the military establishment plays in providing for the defense of the nation.

9. Which department is most responsible for providing the president with military information that would be useful in dealing with foreign nations?
   (A) the Department of State
   (B) the Department of Defense
   (C) the National Security Council
   (D) the United States Information Agency

10. Current foreign policy issues include all of the following except
    (A) nuclear proliferation
    (B) national defense
    (C) terrorism
    (D) national education

Use the table below to answer question 11.

2017 FEDERAL REVENUE		2017 FEDERAL SPENDING
Individual Income Taxes	49%	Social Security
Payroll Taxes	34%	Defense
Corporate Income Taxes	9%	Medicare, Medicaid, CHIP, Health Insurance
Other	8%	Income Security Programs
		Net Interest
		Other Mandatory

11. Based on the information in the table, which statement is true about the federal budget?
    (A) The largest revenue source of the federal budget is payroll taxes.
    (B) The least spending in the federal budget is on Social Security programs.
    (C) The largest revenue source of the federal budget is individual income taxes.
    (D) The least spending in the federal budget is on income security programs.

Free-Response Question

12. (A) Define federal budget.
    (B) Describe the role of the president and executive branch in the budget process.
    (C) Describe the role of Congress in the budget process.

› Answers and Explanations

1. **B.** Policy implementation is the process of enactment of policy. Policy formulation (A) involves finding ways to solve the problem. Policy adoption (C) is adopting a plan of action. Agenda setting (D) is the recognition of an issue as a problem that must be addressed.

2. **A.** The major educational policy goal of the federal government has been to ensure equal access to educational opportunities. Although choices (B), (C), and (D) are goals of the government's educational policy, these goals are subordinate to the greater goal of equal access to education.

3. **D.** The National Security Council deals with foreign and defense policy and includes the chairman of the Joint Chiefs of Staff, the president's national security advisor, and the director of the CIA. The other answer choices deal with U.S. domestic policy.

4. **A.** Medicare and Medicaid receive the largest percentage of government spending. The other answer choices are programs and agencies that involve somewhat less government spending.

5. **C.** The first major governmental act to aid citizens was the Social Security Act. Answer D is nonexistent. Medicare and Medicaid (B) are programs that began under President Johnson's Great Society (A) in the 1960s.

6. **C.** The primary source of government revenue is taxation. Government planners make choices about discretionary spending (A). The president and the Congress are held responsible for the nation's economic health (B). Interest on the national debt is discretionary spending (D). Mandatory spending is another term for nondiscretionary spending.

7. **A.** The Supreme Court does not participate in the federal budget process. The remaining answer choices are steps in the process of creating the federal budget.

8. **B.** The president, not Congress, works with the secretary of state to develop foreign policy. The other answer choices describe the nature of foreign policy.

9. **B.** The Department of Defense is responsible for providing military information to the president. The Department of State (A) and the National Security Council (C) deal with foreign policy. The United States Information Agency (D) runs radio stations, libraries, and educational programs in foreign countries.

10. **D.** National education is a domestic policy issue. The remaining answer choices deal with foreign-policy issues.

11. **C.** The largest revenue source of the federal budget is individual income taxes at 49%.

12. **A.** The federal budget is an itemized plan for the annual public expenditures or spending of the United States. It is the government's estimate of spending and revenue for each fiscal year.

B. Each federal agency within the executive branch submits a detailed estimate of its funding needs for this coming year to the Office of the Management and Budget (OMB). The OMB holds meetings at which representatives from the various agencies may explain their proposal and try to convince the OMB that their needs are justified. The OMB works with the president's staff to combine requests into a single budget package. The president then submits his budget package to Congress.

C. After the president has submitted his budget proposal to Congress, Congress debates and often modifies the president's proposal. The Congressional Budget Office (CBO) provides Congress with economic data. Congressional committees hold hearings, analyze the budget proposals, and offer budget resolutions to their respective houses. The Appropriations Committee for each house submits bills to authorize spending once the budget has been approved.

❯ Rapid Review

- Public policymaking occurs at all levels of government.
- Policymaking is a slow process involving several steps: agenda setting, policy formulation, policy adoption, policy implementation, and policy evaluation.
- Domestic policies are the social policies of the United States: crime prevention, education, energy, environment, health care, and social welfare.
- Crime prevention at the national level is the responsibility of the Federal Bureau of Investigation, the Drug Enforcement Administration, and the Bureau of Alcohol, Tobacco, and Firearms.
- Education falls under the authority of state governments; however, the federal government has played an increasing role in education.
- The Environmental Protection Agency was created in the 1970s to enforce environmental legislation.
- The government operates several programs aimed at promoting and protecting public health: the Public Health Service, Centers for Disease Control, Veterans Affairs, and the Food and Drug Administration.
- Social welfare programs include Medicare, Medicaid, and Social Security.
- Economic policy can have an impact on national elections.
- Economic policy includes raising revenue, government spending, and formulation of the federal budget.
- The federal budget indicates the amount of money the federal government expects to receive and spend during a fiscal year.
- The Office of Management and Budget (OMB) plays a major role in creating the budget.
- Foreign policy involves all the strategies and procedures for dealing with foreign nations. The president is considered the leader in the development of foreign policy.
- The Department of State, headed by the secretary of state, is responsible for the execution of foreign policy.
- The Department of Defense provides military information to the president.
- Congress plays a role in the development of foreign policy by making recommendations to the president on foreign relations, approving treaties, and approving nominations of ambassadors.
- Current issues in foreign policy include nuclear proliferation, terrorism, international trade, and how to manage conflicts abroad.

STEP 5

Build Your Test-Taking Confidence

AP U.S. Government and Politics Practice Exam 1
AP U.S. Government and Politics Practice Exam 2
AP U.S. Government and Politics Practice Exam 3
AP U.S. Government and Politics Practice Exam 4

AP U.S. Government and Politics
Practice Exam 1

SECTION I
ANSWER SHEET

1 (A) (B) (C) (D)
2 (A) (B) (C) (D)
3 (A) (B) (C) (D)
4 (A) (B) (C) (D)
5 (A) (B) (C) (D)
6 (A) (B) (C) (D)
7 (A) (B) (C) (D)
8 (A) (B) (C) (D)
9 (A) (B) (C) (D)
10 (A) (B) (C) (D)
11 (A) (B) (C) (D)
12 (A) (B) (C) (D)
13 (A) (B) (C) (D)
14 (A) (B) (C) (D)
15 (A) (B) (C) (D)
16 (A) (B) (C) (D)
17 (A) (B) (C) (D)
18 (A) (B) (C) (D)
19 (A) (B) (C) (D)
20 (A) (B) (C) (D)
20 (A) (B) (C) (D)

21 (A) (B) (C) (D)
22 (A) (B) (C) (D)
23 (A) (B) (C) (D)
24 (A) (B) (C) (D)
25 (A) (B) (C) (D)
26 (A) (B) (C) (D)
27 (A) (B) (C) (D)
28 (A) (B) (C) (D)
29 (A) (B) (C) (D)
30 (A) (B) (C) (D)
31 (A) (B) (C) (D)
32 (A) (B) (C) (D)
33 (A) (B) (C) (D)
34 (A) (B) (C) (D)
35 (A) (B) (C) (D)
36 (A) (B) (C) (D)
37 (A) (B) (C) (D)
38 (A) (B) (C) (D)
39 (A) (B) (C) (D)
40 (A) (B) (C) (D)
40 (A) (B) (C) (D)

41 (A) (B) (C) (D)
42 (A) (B) (C) (D)
43 (A) (B) (C) (D)
44 (A) (B) (C) (D)
45 (A) (B) (C) (D)
46 (A) (B) (C) (D)
47 (A) (B) (C) (D)
48 (A) (B) (C) (D)
49 (A) (B) (C) (D)
50 (A) (B) (C) (D)
51 (A) (B) (C) (D)
52 (A) (B) (C) (D)
53 (A) (B) (C) (D)
54 (A) (B) (C) (D)
55 (A) (B) (C) (D)

AP U.S. Government and Politics
Practice Exam 1

Section I: Multiple-Choice Questions
Total Time—80 minutes
55 Questions

Directions: Each question or incomplete sentence below is followed by four suggested answers or completions. Select the one that is best, and then fill in the corresponding oval on the answer sheet.

Questions 1 and 2 refer to the graph below.

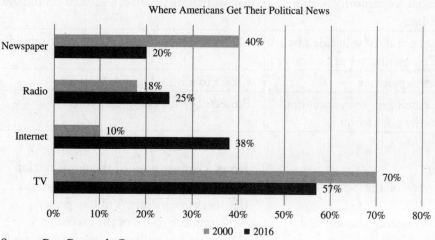

Where Americans Get Their Political News

Source: Pew Research Center

1. Which of the following is an accurate statement about the information in the bar graph?
   (A) Most Americans get their political news from the Internet.
   (B) More Americans are getting their political news from radio in 2016 than they did in 2000.
   (C) More Americans are getting their political news from television in 2016 than they did in 2000.
   (D) Fewer Americans are getting their political news from radio than newspapers in 2016.

2. Based on the information in the bar graph, which of the following is the most likely consequence?
   (A) Television is no longer a major supplier of political news.
   (B) Social network sites provide the largest amount of political news on the Internet.
   (C) Internet news is not as reliable as television or newspapers.
   (D) Newspaper readership is likely to continue to decline.

3. Which of the following would be an accurate statement if a presidential election had to be decided by the House of Representatives?
   (A) Each member of the House is allowed one vote.
   (B) Each state's delegation casts one vote.
   (C) Only the speaker votes.
   (D) The House Rules Committee makes the decision.

GO ON TO THE NEXT PAGE

4. Which of the following is most accurate regarding interest groups?
   - (A) Interest groups always provide accurate and concise information.
   - (B) Some interest groups have influence that is not proportional to their size.
   - (C) Interest groups attempt to control government.
   - (D) Interest groups are well financed.

5. For a case to be heard in the Supreme Court of the United States, a consensus must be reached among the justices. This agreement is known as:
   - (A) A writ of certiorari
   - (B) A precedent
   - (C) *Amicus curiae*
   - (D) "The rule of four"

6. Which of the following is an accurate comparison of popular vote and electoral college vote?

	POPULAR VOTE	ELECTORAL COLLEGE VOTE
(A)	Improves potential for minority parties and their candidates	Favors majority parties and their candidates
(B)	May cause the election to be decided by the House of Representatives or Senate	Most reliable method to choose officeholder
(C)	Reflects indirect democracy	Closer to a true direct democracy
(D)	Outdated and unreliable, with votes not proportional to the population	Protects against "faithless" voters

7. Presidential impeachment
   - (A) requires a majority vote of the Senate for conviction
   - (B) exemplifies the concept of checks and balances
   - (C) is the removal of a president from office
   - (D) is presided over by the vice president

8. Which of the following is an accurate description of the ratification of constitutional amendments?
   - (A) State conventions called by Congress
   - (B) A national convention
   - (C) A two-thirds vote of each house of the Congress
   - (D) Legislatures of three-fourths of the states

9. James Madison applied the term "faction" to
   - (A) political parties and interest groups
   - (B) negative members of Congress
   - (C) splinter groups of the executive
   - (D) states not willing to be a part of the federal union

10. Which of the following would best describe gerrymandering?
   - (A) Drawing electoral districts within a state to favor a political party or candidate
   - (B) The breakdown of a political party within the Congress
   - (C) Dividing the states into regional electoral districts
   - (D) Dividing states along party lines to determine party strategy

GO ON TO THE NEXT PAGE

Questions 11 and 12 refer to the graph below.

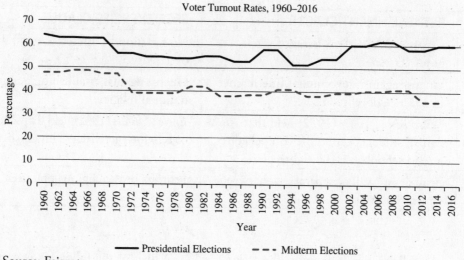

Voter Turnout Rates, 1960–2016

Source: Fairvote

11. Which of the following describes a trend in the line graph above?
    (A) Voter turnout in presidential elections substantially decreased between 2000 and 2016.
    (B) Voter turnout in midterm elections substantially increased between 1992 and 2016.
    (C) Voter turnout in presidential elections substantially increased between 1996 and 2008.
    (D) Voter turnout in midterm elections substantially decreased between 1972 and 1990.

12. Which of the following is an accurate conclusion based on a comparison of the trends in the line graph above and your knowledge of voter behavior?
    (A) More citizens vote in midterm elections, because there is a larger number of candidates running for office in midterm elections than in presidential elections.
    (B) More citizens vote in presidential elections, because presidential elections are perceived to be more important than midterm elections.
    (C) More citizens vote in midterm elections, because political parties are more active in midterm elections than in presidential elections.
    (D) More citizens vote in presidential elections, because presidential elections are held on a voting holiday and midterm elections are not.

13. Which of the following stages generally occurs earliest in the presidential election contest?
    (A) National party conventions
    (B) The popular election
    (C) State primaries and caucuses
    (D) The electoral college election

14. The primary purpose of a conference committee is to:
    (A) provide an investigative step in the passage of a bill
    (B) provide the president with an update on vetoed bills
    (C) compromise proposed bills between the two houses of the Congress
    (D) determine if proposed bills are worthy of continuing the legislative process

GO ON TO THE NEXT PAGE

15. Which of the following is an accurate comparison of the Establishment Clause and the Free Exercise Clause?

	ESTABLISHMENT CLAUSE	FREE EXERCISE CLAUSE
(A)	Offers specialized tax breaks for religious activities	No tax support offered to any religious group or activity
(B)	Guards against government interference in practice of religion	Guards against establishing a mandated national religion
(C)	*Wisconsin v. Yoder* (1972) held that Amish students cannot be compelled to attend school after the eighth grade	*Engle v. Vitale* (1962) held that school sponsorship of religious activities is unconstitutional
(D)	Provides a "wall of separation" between church and state	Protects most religious practices

16. Which of the following best describes the action taken by the Congress when the president vetoes a bill?
    (A) The bill is sent to a conference committee.
    (B) The Speaker of the House is sent to discuss the bill with the president.
    (C) The bill may become a law if both houses override the presidential veto by a two-thirds vote.
    (D) The bill may become a law if both houses override the presidential veto by a simple majority in each house.

17. Which of the following is part of the legislative process in the House of Representatives but NOT in the Senate?
    (A) Debate on the floor
    (B) Filibuster
    (C) Referral to committee
    (D) Assignment of rules

18. An individual has been charged with a federal crime. Which of the following courts would hear the case first?
    (A) Supreme Court
    (B) District court
    (C) appellate court
    (D) Federal circuit court

Questions 19 and 20 refer to the maps below.

1990 Congressional Districts

North Carolina Congressional District 12

Georgia Congressional District 11

Texas Congressional District 30

Florida Congressional District 3

GO ON TO THE NEXT PAGE

19. The maps show several congressional districts. Which statement best explains the motivation behind the way in which these maps were drawn?
    (A) These maps have been drawn by Congress to ensure the winner of the popular vote will win the election.
    (B) These maps have been drawn by the Supreme Court to guarantee fair elections.
    (C) These maps have been drawn by state legislatures to ensure the candidate from the legislature's majority party wins the election.
    (D) These maps have been drawn by the political parties to encourage voters to vote in the next election.

20. Which of the following is a consequence of the way in which the districts are drawn?
    (A) They will likely lead to the office winner representing a minor party.
    (B) They guarantee an increase in voter turnout.
    (C) They have been drawn in a way to encourage more competitive elections.
    (D) They will likely lead to less competition in the election and the protection of "safe districts."

21. Which of the following best describes the role of the Speaker of the House?
    (A) Presiding officer of the House
    (B) Shares power with the president *pro tempore*
    (C) Appointed by the president
    (D) Controls Congress with the help of the president

22. Sometimes litigants that are not part of the formal proceeding of Supreme Court oral arguments wish to have their points of view presented. What may they file?
    (A) A *per curium* decision
    (B) A certificate
    (C) A writ of certiorari
    (D) An *amicus curiae* brief

23. Which of the following is an accurate description of political socialization?
    (A) Individuals playing different political roles in society
    (B) Individuals with diverse beliefs about public policy
    (C) Individuals acquiring their differing beliefs and political orientation
    (D) Individuals defining their political society in relation to their form of government

Questions 24 and 25 refer to the cartoon below.

Cory M. Grenier @ flikr.com. Licensed under Creative Commons.

GO ON TO THE NEXT PAGE

24. Which of the following best describes the author's viewpoint in the political cartoon?
    (A) Only a few corporations play a role in American elections.
    (B) The Supreme Court has made it more difficult for corporations to influence elections.
    (C) Judicial review has allowed the Supreme Court to receive funding from large corporations.
    (D) Corporations and big money have an increased influence on American elections.

25. In *Citizens United v. Federal Election Commission* (2010), the Supreme Court held that
    (A) corporate funding of independent political broadcasts in candidate elections cannot be limited, because doing so would violate the First Amendment
    (B) legislative redistricting must guarantee compliance with the Voting Rights Act of 1965
    (C) corporate funding of elections is prohibited under the First Amendment
    (D) corporation and special interest campaign contributions can be limited

26. Which of the following is a reserved power under the U.S. Constitution?
    (A) Regulation of interstate commerce
    (B) Making all laws that are "necessary and proper"
    (C) Establishment of federal courts below the Supreme Court
    (D) Establishment of public school systems

27. The Full Faith and Credit Clause of the Constitution requiring that each state accept the public acts, records, and judicial proceedings of every other state, is found in the Constitution in
    (A) Article I
    (B) Article VI
    (C) Article IV
    (D) Article III

28. Which of the following is an accurate comparison of the formal and informal powers of the president?

	FORMAL POWERS OF PRESIDENT	INFORMAL POWERS OF PRESIDENT
(A)	Use of the media to shape public opinion	Commander-in-chief of the armed forces
(B)	Power to pardon without condition	Use the "bully pulpit" to promote a particular program or persuasively advocate an agenda
(C)	State of the Union Address to Congress	Veto legislation passed by Congress
(D)	Use signing statements to direct the bureaucracy to implement legislation in a certain way	Negotiate treaties with foreign governments

Questions 29 and 30 refer to the infographic below.

10 States with the Highest Voter Turnout, 2016

74.5%	73%	70.8%	69.8%	69.6%	69.1%	68.3%	68.1%	67.2%	66.7%
Minnesota	Wisconsin	Maine	New Hampshire	Iowa	Oregon	North Dakota	Massachusetts	Mississippi	Louisiana

10 States with the Lowest Voter Turnout, 2016

59.3%	59.2%	58.4%	58.3%	57.7%	55.3%	54.9%	54.3%	52.9%	50%
Georgia	New York	Arizona	Oklahoma	Nevada	Texas	Tennessee	Arkansas	West Virginia	Hawaii

Source: U.S. Census Bureau

GO ON TO THE NEXT PAGE

29. Based on the infographic, which of the following most accurately reflects voter turnout in 2016?
    (A) Voter turnout was highest in presidential elections.
    (B) Voter turnout was greater than 50%.
    (C) Voter turnout decreased in 2016.
    (D) Voter turnout was highest in the most populous states.

30. Based on the infographic, which of the following could be used to increase voter turnout in all states?
    (A) Increase requirements for voter identification to prevent fraud
    (B) Eliminate the Voting Rights Act
    (C) Make election day a holiday
    (D) Allow voters to only vote on election day and vote only in designated polling places

31. Which of the following is a result of the U.S. Supreme Court using the Fourteenth Amendment to bring about change?
    (A) Defend the institution of slavery
    (B) Refuse to apply the Bill of Rights to state and local governments
    (C) Deny Second Amendment rights for gun control
    (D) Reject racial segregation in the public schools

32. Which of the following best describes social welfare spending in the United States?
    (A) Spending decreased in the 1930s because of the Great Depression.
    (B) Social welfare spending was expanded during the Reagan administrations.
    (C) Spending was extended to more recipients during the Clinton administration.
    (D) Spending was expanded to create new programs during the Johnson administration.

33. Which of the following best describes federalism?
    (A) The Founding Fathers interpreted federalism as dual federalism.
    (B) Interstate highway projects are an example of dual federalism.
    (C) Fiscal federalism involves limited control of the national government over the state.
    (D) Nixon's revenue sharing plan is an example of fiscal federalism.

34. Which of the following best describes what the Fifth Amendment and the Fourteenth Amendment have in common?
    (A) Both prevent government from depriving a person of life, liberty, and property without due process of law.
    (B) Both speak of powers reserved to the states.
    (C) Both deal with criminal prosecutions.
    (D) Both prevent the government from denying to any person the equal protection of the law.

35. When making an appointment to the Supreme Court, presidents
    (A) tend to choose judges from their own political party
    (B) often select a candidate who is neither decidedly liberal nor conservative
    (C) tend to ignore race as a consideration for selecting a judge
    (D) remain impartial by refusing candidate endorsements from members of the Supreme Court

36. Which of the following is an accurate comparison of treaties and executive agreements?

	TREATIES	EXECUTIVE AGREEMENTS
(A)	Defined under Article I of the Constitution	Defined under Article II of the Constitution
(B)	Informal agreement not binding on successive officeholders	Formal agreement binding on successive officeholders
(C)	Require the ratification of two-thirds of the Senate	Require the ratification of two-thirds of the House of Representatives
(D)	Number has increased significantly in recent years	Number has decreased significantly in recent years

GO ON TO THE NEXT PAGE

37. Which of the following is an example of informal amendment to the Constitution?
    (A) Creation of the Supreme Court
    (B) Direct election of senators
    (C) Use of executive agreements rather than treaties
    (D) Ratification of treaties by the Senate

38. Which of the following best describes how 21st-century technology has changed political parties?
    (A) Decreasing the frequency of split-ticket voting
    (B) Illuminating the differences between the major parties
    (C) Creating less diversity within major parties
    (D) Allowing candidates to become more directly involved with voters

39. Which of the following best describes gerrymandering?
    (A) It is intended to draw congressional districts of unequal size.
    (B) It is an attempt to give equal representation for all minority groups.
    (C) It is an effort to draw congressional districts to favor one party or group.
    (D) It violates the principle of the single-member district.

Questions 40 and 41 refer to the passage below.

". . . the particular phraseology of the Constitution of the United States confirms and strengthens the principle, supposed to be essential to all written constitutions, that a law repugnant to the Constitution is void; and that courts, as well as other departments, are bound by that instrument."

— John Marshall,
Marbury v. Madison (1803)

40. Which statement is most consistent with the author's argument in the passage?
    (A) The Supreme Court should be the most powerful branch of government.
    (B) The power of the Supreme Court is determined by the Constitution of the United States.
    (C) Government is bound by the Constitution, and laws which are in violation of the Constitution are invalid.
    (D) The status of the Supreme Court as the head of a coequal branch of government should be maintained.

41. Which constitutional principle is most consistent with the passage?
    (A) Separation of powers
    (B) Checks and balances
    (C) Federalism
    (D) Judicial review

42. Which of the following has been used by the Supreme Court to establish a "wall of separation" between church and state?
    (A) Allow prayer in public schools
    (B) Prohibit the teaching of evolution in public schools
    (C) Require the teaching of creationism in public schools
    (D) Prohibit state governments from paying parochial schools' textbooks and teacher salaries

43. Which of the following might an interest group use to influence members of Congress?
    (A) Take an issue to court
    (B) Create multimember districts to win more elections
    (C) Organize the government
    (D) Hold primary elections to narrow down the field of potential candidates

44. Which of the following best describes the vice presidency?
    (A) The vice president presides over cases of presidential impeachment.
    (B) A party's vice-presidential nominee is often chosen to balance the ticket.
    (C) Since the 1960s, the vice president has often been given a smaller role in government.
    (D) The vice president may vote at any time in the Senate.

GO ON TO THE NEXT PAGE

45. Which of the following is an accurate comparison of the House of Representatives and the Senate?

	HOUSE OF REPRESENTATIVES	SENATE
(A)	Simpler rules	More complex rules
(B)	Speech is unlimited	Speech is limited
(C)	Members campaign continuously	Members have longer terms and can pay more attention to legislation
(D)	Members have broader interests and represent statewide constituencies	Members have narrower interests because they represent districts

46. Which of the following best describes the Supreme Court decision in *Gideon v. Wainwright* (1963)?
    (A) Suspects in police custody must be informed of their rights.
    (B) State courts must provide an attorney to poor defendants accused of a felony.
    (C) The death penalty is constitutional when it is imposed based on the circumstances of the case.
    (D) Evidence obtained without a search warrant is excluded from trial in state courts.

Questions 47 and 48 refer to the table below.

Party Control of Congress and the Presidency (1969–2017)

YEAR	PRESIDENT	SENATE	HOUSE
2017	Trump (R)	R	R
2015	D	R	R
2013	D	D	R
2011	D	D	R
2009	Obama (D)	D	D
2007	R	D	D
2005	R	R	R
2003	R	R	R
2001	Bush (R)	D	R
1999	D	R	R
1997	D	R	R
1995	D	R	R
1993	Clinton (D)	D	D
1991	R	D	D
1989	Bush (R)	D	D
1987	R	D	D
1985	R	R	D
1983	R	R	R
1981	Reagan (R)	R	D
1979	D	D	D
1977	Carter (D)	D	D
1975	Ford (R)	D	D
1973	R	D	D
1971	R	D	D
1969	Nixon (R)	D	D

Source: US Congress

GO ON TO THE NEXT PAGE

47. Based on the information in the table, how many times between 1969 and 2017 has the government of the United States been a divided government?
    (A) 10
    (B) 12
    (C) 17
    (D) 19

48. Based on the data shown in the table, which of the following statements is true about divided government?
    (A) All presidents since Richard Nixon have had to deal with divided government.
    (B) Barack Obama is the most recent president who did not have divided government when first elected.
    (C) Jimmy Carter served his entire term without divided government.
    (D) Divided government happens only when both houses are controlled by one party and the presidency is controlled by another party.

49. According to traditional democratic theory, government is dependent upon
    (A) bureaucrats
    (B) a system of several strong groups
    (C) interest groups
    (D) the consent of the governed

50. Which statement is most accurate in describing government spending?
    (A) Expenditures to support troop deployment in the Iraq War are considered nondiscretionary spending.
    (B) In recent years, both discretionary and nondiscretionary spending have increased.
    (C) Entitlements are categorized as nondiscretionary spending.
    (D) Discretionary spending includes interest on the national debt.

51. Which of the following is a function of the media?
    (A) Winning elections to control government
    (B) Agenda setting by influencing what subjects become significant nationally
    (C) Providing a link between political parties and interest groups
    (D) Formulating public policy

Questions 52 and 53 refer to the passage below.

"Many causes contribute to dispersed power in the federal system. One is the simple historical fact that the states existed before the nation. A second is in the form of creed, the traditional opinion of Americans that expresses distrust of centralized power and places great value in the strength and vitality of local units of government. Another is pride in locality and state, nurtured by the nation's size and by variations of regional and state history. Still a fourth cause of decentralization is the sheer wealth of the nation. It allows all groups, including state and local governments, to partake of the central government's largesse, supplies room for experimentation and even waste, and makes unnecessary the tight organization of political power that must follow when the support of one program necessarily means the deprivation of another."

—Morton Grodzins, *The Federal System*

52. Which statement best summarizes the author's argument?
    (A) The purpose of federalism is the distribution of power between central and regional units of government.
    (B) A strict separation of national and state functions needs to exist for federalism to work.
    (C) The federal government should have a dominant role over the states because of economic and political trends.
    (D) Under federalism, it is easy to separate the responsibilities between federal and state governments.

53. Which Supreme Court case supports the supremacy of the national government over the states?
    (A) *Marbury v. Madison* (1803)
    (B) *McCulloch v. Maryland* (1819)
    (C) *Schenck v. United States* (1919)
    (D) *McDonald v. Chicago* (2010)

GO ON TO THE NEXT PAGE

Questions 54 and 55 refer to the pie charts below:

How PACs Allocate Campaign Contributions

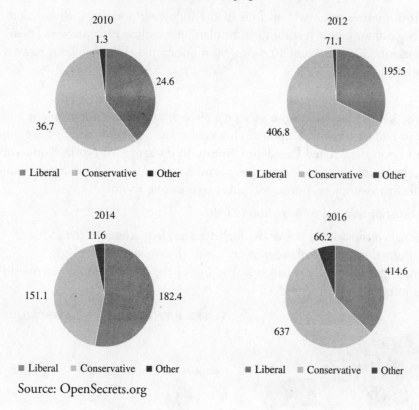

Source: OpenSecrets.org

54. Which of the following accurately describes information presented in the pie charts?
   (A) Political action committees give more campaign contributions to liberals than to conservatives.
   (B) Political action committees provide campaign contributions to both liberal and conservative candidates.
   (C) Political action committees provide almost equal amounts of campaign contributions to liberals and conservatives
   (D) Political action committees gave less in campaign contributions in 2016 than in 2012.

55. Which of the following best explains the differences in campaign contributions over time?
   (A) There has been a rapid increase in the number of PACs in recent years, so it is easier to raise more money for campaigns.
   (B) Supreme Court decisions have made it more difficult for PACs to raise and distribute money.
   (C) PACs do not want to provide contributions to candidates they believe might not win the election.
   (D) PACs have been replaced by superPACs and therefore there is less money available for campaigns.

STOP. END OF SECTION I

Section II: Free-Response Questions
Total Time—100 minutes

Directions: You have 100 minutes to answer all four of the following questions. Respond to all parts of all four questions. Before beginning, take a few minutes to plan and outline each answer. Spend approximately 20 minutes each on questions 1, 2, and 3 and 40 minutes on question 4. Illustrate your essay with substantive examples where appropriate.

1. The president of the United States and the secretary of state negotiate an agreement with North Korea to end their plans to build a nuclear weapon. "This agreement represents the first step on the road to a nuclear-free Korean Peninsula," stated President Clinton. In exchange for North Korea ending its nuclear weapons program, the United States has agreed to normalize relations with the nation—and both nations agreed to pursue "formal assurances" not to use nukes against one another.

   After reading the scenario, respond to A, B, and C below:

   (A) Describe a formal constitutional power the president has that relates to the scenario.
   (B) Describe an informal power the president may use in the situation described.
   (C) In the context of the scenario, explain how the use of the formal power describe in Part A can be affected by its interaction with Congress.

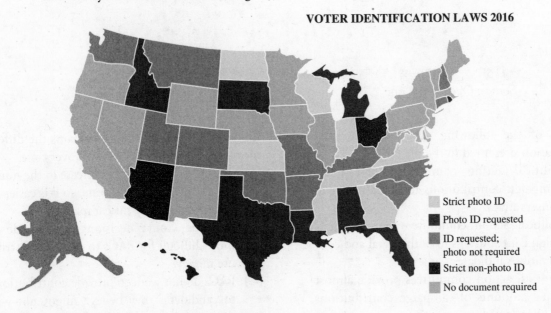

VOTER IDENTIFICATION LAWS 2016

Legend:
- Strict photo ID
- Photo ID requested
- ID requested; photo not required
- Strict non-photo ID
- No document required

Source: National Conference of State Legislatures

2. Use the map to answer the following questions.
   (A) Identify the most common requirement to vote.
   (B) Describe a similarity or difference in voter identification requirements in a region, as illustrated in the information graphic, and draw a conclusion about that similarity or difference.
   (C) Explain why some states may choose to use a stricter requirement of voter identification to vote, and some states may choose a more lenient requirement of voter identification to vote.

3. As a result of the *Texas v. Johnson* decision, Congress passed the Flag Protection Act in 1989, prohibiting abuse of the flag. On the day that the law took effect, protests occurred across the nation. Demonstrators in Seattle and Washington, D.C., were arrested and charged under the new law.

GO ON TO THE NEXT PAGE

In Seattle, flags were burned at a demonstration organized by the Vietnam Veterans Against the War. No one was arrested during the demonstration, but four people identified from photographs were later charged with violating the federal Flag Protection Act of 1989.

In Washington, D.C., Gregory Lee Johnson, the defendant in *Texas v. Johnson*, staged a protest together with three friends, including Shawn Eichmann. They burned flags on the steps of the Capitol in front of reporters and photographers. They released a statement calling for others to express disagreement with "compulsory patriotism" by burning the flag.

In both cases, federal district judges in Seattle and Washington, D.C. dismissed charges against the protesters, citing *Texas v. Johnson*. U.S. attorneys appealed the decisions directly to the Supreme Court. Because the Flag Protection Act called for expedited review, the two cases were consolidated into *United States v. Eichman* (1990), which would serve as a test case for the federal law.

(A) Identify the constitutional provision that is common to both *United States v. Eichman* (1990) and *Texas v. Johnson* (1989).

(B) Based on the constitutional provision identified in Part A, explain how the facts of *Texas v. Johnson* led to a similar decision in *United States v. Eichman*.

(C) Describe an impact the decisions in *Texas v. Johnson* and *United States v. Eichman* have had on the public.

4. Develop an argument that explains how the Civil Rights Movement was a movement for liberty and equality.

In your essay, you must:
- Articulate a defensible claim or thesis that responds to the prompt and establishes a line of reasoning.
- Support your claim or thesis with at least two pieces of accurate and relevant information:
  — At least ONE piece of evidence must be from one of the following foundational documents:
    — Declaration of Independence
    — Letter from a Birmingham Jail
    — U.S. Constitution
  — Use a second piece of evidence from another foundational document from the list or from your study of the electoral process.
- Use reasoning to explain why your evidence supports your claim or thesis.
- Respond to an opposing or alternative perspective using refutation, concession, or rebuttal.

STOP. END OF SECTION II

Answer Key for Multiple-Choice Questions

1. B	16. C	31. D	46. B
2. D	17. D	32. D	47. C
3. B	18. B	33. D	48. C
4. B	19. C	34. A	49. D
5. D	20. D	35. A	50. C
6. A	21. A	36. C	51. B
7. B	22. D	37. C	52. A
8. D	23. C	38. D	53. B
9. A	24. D	39. C	54. B
10. A	25. A	40. C	55. A
11. C	26. D	41. D	
12. B	27. C	42. D	
13. C	28. B	43. A	
14. C	29. B	44. B	
15. D	30. C	45. C	

› Answers and Explanations for the Multiple-Choice Questions

1. **B.** Most Americans get their news from TV (A). Fewer Americans are getting their news from radio in 2016 than in 2000 (C). Fewer Americans are getting their news from newspapers in 2016 than from radio (D).

2. **D.** Television continues to be a major supplier of news (A). No information is provided about social network sites (B) or the reliability of Internet sites (C).

3. **B.** If the House of Representatives were to act upon the failure of the electoral college to elect a president, each state delegation would receive one vote. A majority of 26 votes would be necessary for a candidate to win election.

4. **B.** Some interest groups have influence that is not proportional to the group's number of members. Some interest groups are small in membership and exert considerable influence, while other groups with large memberships may exert very little influence. Interest groups sometimes distort facts to sway the public toward their cause (A). They seek to influence the policies of government, while political parties attempt to control government (C). Interest groups vary in their degree of financial support (D).

5. **D.** In order for cases to be heard by the Supreme Court, the "rule of four" requires that at least four justices agree to place the case on the Court's docket. A writ of certiorari (A) is an order issued by the Supreme Court directing a lower court to send up a record of a case for review. A precedent (B) is an example set by a court decision for future court cases. An *amicus curiae* (C) is a "friend of the court" brief.

6. **A.** The electoral college vote may result in no candidate having a majority of votes and election of president going to the House of Representatives (B). Popular vote is closer to a direct democracy and electoral vote is closer to indirect democracy (C). Many critics of the electoral college vote point to it being outdate, unreliable, and allows for "faithless" electors (D).

7. **B.** In the impeachment process, the House checks the power of the executive branch by bringing charges of impeachment against the president. The chief justice of the Supreme Court sits as the presiding judge in the impeachment trial, thus checking the power of the legislative branch over the executive branch (D). A two-thirds vote of the Senate is required for conviction (A). Impeachment is the act of bringing charges against the president; it may or may not result in conviction and the subsequent removal of the president from office (C).

8. **D.** One method of ratification is by special conventions held in three-fourths of the states. These conventions are called by the states, not by Congress (A). Amendments may be proposed by a national convention (B) or by a two-thirds vote of both houses of Congress (C).

9. **A.** In Federalist #10, James Madison referred to factions, meaning political parties and interest groups.

10. **A.** The drawing of electoral districts within a state in order to favor one political party or candidate is known as gerrymandering. The other answer choices do not describe gerrymandering.

11. **C.** Voter turnout in presidential election increased between 2000 and 2016 (A). Voter turnout in midterm elections decreased between 1992 and 2008 (B). Voter turnout in midterm elections stayed relative static between 1972 and 1990 (D).

12. **B.** Fewer citizens vote in midterm elections (A, C). While more citizens vote in presidential elections, the United States does not have an election holiday (D).

13. **C.** State primaries and caucuses generally occur earliest in the presidential election contest. The next stage is usually the national party convention (A) and selection of the running mate. The next stage is the popular election (B) followed by the electoral college election (D).

14. **C.** Conference committees are created to iron out the differences in the House and Senate versions of a bill. Their goal is to create a compromise bill that, once passed by the House and Senate, can be sent to the president for signature or veto.

15. **D.** The establishment clause does not offer tax breaks for religious activities (A). Guarding against government interference in the practice of religion is the free exercise clause (B). *Wisconsin v. Yoder* was a free exercise case and *Engle v. Vitale* was an establishment case (C).

16. **C.** When the president vetoes a bill, it is sent back to Congress, where it may become law if it is overridden by a two-thirds vote of both houses.

17. **D.** The assignment of rules occurs in the Rules Committee in the House of Representatives, but no such committee exists in the Senate. Filibusters (B) may occur in the Senate but not in the House of Representatives. Floor debate (A) and referral to committee (C) occur in both the House of Representatives and the Senate.

18. **B.** District courts serve as the trial courts within the federal court system. The remaining answer choices do not refer to trial courts.

19. **C.** Congressional district maps are drawn by state legislatures, where they are often gerrymandered to favor the party candidates of the party that controls the state legislature.

20. **D.** Gerrymandering often leads to less competition and a protection of officeholders by creating "safe districts."

21. **A.** The Speaker of the House is the presiding officer of the House of Representatives. The Speaker does not share power with the president *pro tempore* of the Senate (B). The Speaker is elected by the members of the majority party in the House (C). The majority leader and the majority whip, not the president, assist the Speaker (D).

22. **D.** *Amicus curiae* briefs are filed by "friends of the court," interested parties who have no standing in the case but who wish to provide information and opinions to the court for consideration.

A *per curiam* decision (A) is one delivered by the court as a whole. A certificate (B) is a method of bringing a case before the Supreme Court. A writ of certiorari (C) is an order by a higher court directing a lower court to provide the record in a case for review.

23. **C.** Political socialization involves personal acquisition of differing beliefs and political ideology.

24. **D.** Since the decision of the Supreme Court in *Citizens United v. Federal Election Commission*, corporations have been able to increase their campaign contributions, creating a greater influence on elections.

25. **A.** In *Citizens United v. Federal Election Commission*, the Supreme Court ruled that the First Amendment protects corporations, labor unions, and associations funding of independent political broadcasts in candidate elections.

26. **D.** Reserved powers are those powers, such as the establishment of public school systems, that have been reserved to the states. The remaining answer choices are powers of the national government.

27. **C.** The Full Faith and Credit Clause is found in Article IV of the Constitution, which addresses the relationship among the states.

28. **B.** The use of the media by the president is an informal power, while serving as commander-in-chief is a formal power (A). Providing the State of the Union Address is an informal power, while the veto of legislation is a formal power (C). Signing statements is an informal power but negotiating treaties is a formal power (D).

29. **B.** Hawaii had the lowest voter turnout at 50% (B). There is no information about presidential versus midterm or state/local elections (A) or voter turnout increasing or decreasing from year to year (C). There is no information about state populations (D).

30. **C.** Increasing requirements to prevent voter fraud would decrease voter turnout (A). Eliminating the Voting Rights Act would decrease voter turnout (B). Allowing voters to only vote on election day—no early or absentee voting—would decrease voter turnout (D).

31. **D.** In *Brown v. Board of Education*, the Supreme Court determined that segregation in public schools was unconstitutional. Slavery was addressed in *Scott v. Sanford* (A). In *Barron v. Baltimore* the Court refused to apply the Bill of Rights to the states (B). Second Amendment rights were addressed in *McDonald v. Chicago* (C).

32. **D.** Social welfare spending increased because of the Great Depression (A) and decreased under Bill Clinton and Ronald Reagan (B, C).

33. **D.** Revenue sharing is an example of fiscal federalism, in which the federal government uses grants to influence the states. The Founding Fathers favored dual federalism, which views the national and state governments each supreme within their own sphere of influence (A). The interstate highway system is an example of cooperative federalism, which involves sharing between the two levels of government (B). Fiscal federalism involves some control over the states by the national government's granting or withholding money for programs (C).

34. **A.** The Fifth Amendment prevents the federal government from depriving any person of life, liberty, or property without due process of law. The Fourteenth Amendment extends this prohibition to the states. Only the Fifth Amendment deals with criminal prosecutions (C). The Tenth and Fourteenth Amendments deal with powers reserved to the states (B). The Fourteenth Amendment includes the "equal protection" clause (D).

35. **A.** Presidents tend to influence the Court by selecting judges from their own political party. Presidents often want to select a candidate who would tend to vote according to the president's ideological position (B). They often consider race (C) to provide balance on the court or to satisfy certain segments of society. Presidents may consider endorsements of a justice from members of the Supreme Court (D).

36. **C.** Treaties are defined under Article II of the Constitution (A) and executive agreements are not mentioned. A treaty is a formal agreement while an executive agreement is an informal agreement (B). The number of executive agreements has increased significantly in recent years (D).

37. **C.** The use of executive agreements rather than treaties allows the president to bypass the Senate (C). The Supreme Court was created under Article III of the Constitution (A). The Seventeenth Amendment provides for the direct election of Senators (B). Article II of the Constitution gives the president the power to make treaties" by and with the Advice and Consent of the Senate, ... provided two-thirds of the Senators present concur" (D).

38. **D.** New technology has allowed voters to use the Internet to learn of candidate qualifications rather than relying only on party-generated information. Split-ticket voting (splitting the vote among candidates from more than one party) can be accomplished regardless of technology (A). Today's voters often fail to see a difference between the major parties (B). Today there is greater diversity within the major parties (C).

39. **C.** Gerrymandering involves drawing irregular-shaped districts in order to include populations that favor one party or group over another. All congressional districts must include populations of nearly equal size (A). It is not intended to gain equal representation for all minority groups (B). Gerrymandered districts remain single-member districts (D).

40. **C.** John Marshall proposes that all of government is bound by the Constitution and that any law which violates the Constitution should be null and void,

41. **D.** The power of the court to determine the constitutionality of acts of Congress or the president is judicial review.

42. **D.** In *Lemon v. Kurtzman* (1971) the Supreme Court created a three-prong test to determine the constitutionality of legislation based on the First Amendment's Establishment Clause. State governments paying for textbooks and teacher salaries created an excessive entanglement between the church and state and was therefore unconstitutional. The Supreme Court has used the "wall of separation" principle to forbid prayer in public school (A). It has struck down laws that prohibit the teaching of evolution (B) and that require giving equal time to the teaching of creationism (C).

43. **A.** Interest groups have numerous strategies: influencing elections by encouraging their members to vote for certain candidates, lobbying, litigation, and going public. Interest groups do not create multimember districts (B), organize government (C), or hold primary elections (D).

44. **B.** The chief justice of the Supreme Court presides over cases of presidential impeachment (A). The vice-presidential nominee is often chosen to provide geographical or ideological balance to the ticket (B). Since the Kennedy assassination, more attention has been focused on the vice president (C). Although the vice president presides over the Senate, he may only vote to break a tie (D).

45. **C.** The House of Representatives has more complex rules, and the Senate simpler rules (A). Speech/debate is limited in the House of Representatives but unlimited in the Senate (B). Members of the House of Representatives have a narrower interest because they represent districts; members of the Senate have broader interests because they represent the entire state.

46. **B.** In *Gideon v. Wainwright* the Court ruled that, in state trials, those who cannot afford an attorney would have one provided by the state. Choice (A) refers to *Miranda v. Arizona*. Choice (C) refers to *Gregg v. Georgia*. Choice (D) pertains to *Mapp v. Ohio*.

47. **C.** Between 1996 and 2017, the United States has had a divided government 17 times. Divided government occurs when one or both houses of Congress and the presidency are controlled by different political parties.

48. **C.** Jimmy Carter did not have to deal with divided government (A). Donald Trump is the most recent president who did not have divided government when elected (B). Divided government can happen when either house or the presidency is controlled by a different political party.

49. **D.** Traditional democratic theory states that government depends on the consent of the governed, given directly or through representatives. Choice (A) describes Max Weber's bureaucratic theory. Choice (B) describes hyperpluralism. Choice (C) defines the pluralist theory.

50. **C.** Entitlements, including programs such as Medicare, Medicaid, and food stamps, are examples of nondiscretionary spending, or spending required by existing laws for current programs. Interest on the national debt is mandatory, or nondiscretionary, spending (D). Defense spending is considered nondiscretionary (A). In recent years, the percentage of nondiscretionary spending has increased, while the percentage of discretionary spending has also increased (B).

51. **B.** Winning elections to control government is the primary goal of political parties (A). There is no formal method for providing a link between political parties and interest groups (C). Formulating public policy is a function of the government (D).

52. **A.** Grodzins offers reasons why federalism was chosen as a way or organizing the government under the Constitution. He does not suggest a separation of functions, a dominant role for the national government, or federalism being easy to operate.

53. **B.** *McCulloch v. Maryland* dealt with the supremacy of the national government under federalism. *Marbury v. Madison* concerns judicial review (A). *Schenck v. United States* is a free speech case (C), and *McDonald v. Chicago* deals with the Second Amendment (D).

54. **B.** Political action committees give more campaign contributions to conservatives in 2010, 2012, and 2016 than to liberals (A, C). Political action committees gave more in contributions in 2016 than in 2012 (D).

55. **A.** Supreme Court decisions such as *Citizens United v. Federal Election Commission* have made it easier for PACs to raise and distribute money (B). PACs often provide campaign contributions to both party candidates in order to "hedge their bet." If either candidate wins, they might be able to gain access to that candidate (C). SuperPACs have aided candidates, but PACs still exist and contribute millions of campaign dollars per election.

Scoring the Free-Response Questions

1. **Scoring the Concept Application Question: Total Value—3 points**

   (A) **1 point:** Describe a political institution, process, or behavior that links to the scenario. (Must link content from the scenario and provide a description to receive credit.) The formal powers of the president in the scenario include:
   - Commander-in-chief—involves military
   - Appoint ministers—secretary of state
   - Negotiate treaties—though may not require formal treaty

   (B) **1 point:** Describe a political institution, process, or behavior that links to the scenario. (Must link content from the scenario and provide a description to receive credit.) The informal powers of the president in the scenario include:
   - Executive agreement—president negotiates agreement with North Korea
   - Crisis manager—starvation in North Korea, nuclear threat
   - Chief legislator—needs funding from Congress

   (C) **1 point:** Explain how the scenario relates to a political institution, behavior, or process (Must demonstrate how the use of the formal power describe in Part A can be affected by its interaction with Congress.)

   > If the president is acting as commander-in-chief and sends the military, Congress might invoke the War Powers Act, a law passed in 1973 that allows Congress to limit the president's use of military forces. The president would have to inform Congress within 48 hours if he sends armed forces anywhere, and Congress must give approval for them to stay there for more than 90 days. When the president appoints members of the cabinet, the Senate must approve those appointments. The president must also gain ratification for treaties from the Senate by a two-thirds vote.

2. **Scoring the Quantitative Analysis Question: Total Value—4 points**

   (A) **1 point:** Describe the data presented in the quantitative graphic. The most common requirement to vote is no document required.

   (B) **2 points:** Describe a pattern and draw a conclusion for that pattern. (Must describe a pattern for 1 point and draw a conclusion about the pattern for the second point.) Answers may vary. Example of similarity: Many states in the Northeast have no document required as identification to vote. One reason that these states might not require any form of voter ID is the cost to some voters of obtaining documentation, or voters not having time to go through the process of obtaining a state ID.

   (C) **1 point:** Explain how specific data in the quantitative graphic demonstrates why some states may choose to use a stricter requirement of voter identification to vote, and some states may choose a more lenient requirement of voter identification to vote.

   > Proponents of voter ID laws argue the laws are implemented to prevent voter fraud. The stricter laws enacted by some states were not written to fight voter fraud effectively. The courts have ruled that the forms of ID lawmakers designated as being acceptable weren't necessarily the most secure kinds. Adding this extra step—obtaining an acceptable form of identification—adds to the burden placed on voters, and many states saw this as a barrier to voter turnout, choosing not to adopt voter ID laws.

3. **Scoring the SCOTUS Comparison Question: Total Value—4 points**
   (A) **1 point:** Identify the constitutional issue that is common to both Supreme Court cases. The constitutional provision that is common to both *United States v. Eichman* and *Texas v. Johnson* is the protection of free speech (symbolic speech) under the First Amendment.

   (B) **2 points:** Provide factual information from the required Supreme Court case (1 point) and explain how the reasoning and decisions of the required Supreme Court case apply to scenarios involving free speech (1 point).

   In *Texas v. Johnson*, the Supreme Court determined that Johnson's burning of the flag was expressive conduct (symbolic speech) protected by the First Amendment. The Texas law Johnson violated was unconstitutional. In response to *Texas v. Johnson*, Congress passed the Flag Protection Act of 1989, which attempted to sidestep the *Johnson* ruling. The Supreme Court decided that the federal government, like the states, cannot prosecute a person for burning a United States flag, because to do so would be violate the First Amendment right of free speech.

   (C) **1 point:** Describe an interaction between the holding in the nonrequired Supreme Court case and a relevant political institution, behavior, or process.

   Though *Texas v. Johnson* and *United States v. Eichman* have been upheld in other Supreme Court cases, disrespect for the American flag remains unpopular in America. The House of Representatives has voted on a constitutional amendment known as the Flag Desecration Amendment, giving Congress the authority to prohibit desecration of the flag. Although the amendment has passed the House of Representatives on several occasions, it has never passed the Senate, and therefore has never been sent to the states for ratification. The decisions in *Texas v. Johnson* and *United States v. Eichman* have expanded free speech protections for Americans.

4. **Scoring the Argument Essay: Total Value: 6 points**
   - **1 point:** Articulate a defensible claim or thesis that responds to the question and establishes a line of reasoning.
   - **2 points:** Describe one piece of evidence from one of the listed foundational documents (1 point) that is accurately linked to the proper role of the Supreme Court and indicate how that evidence supports the argument (1 point). (Must show how evidence supports argument to earn second point.)
   - **1 point:** Use a second piece of specific and relevant evidence to support the argument. (Must indicate how evidence supports argument.)
   - **1 point:** Explain how or why the evidence supports the claim or thesis.
   - **1 point:** Respond to an opposing or alternate perspective using refutation, concession, or rebuttal.

Score Conversion Worksheet

Using this worksheet, you can get a rough approximation of what your score would be on the AP U.S. Government and Politics Exam. Use the answer key to check the multiple-choice questions and the scoring rubrics to award yourself points on the free-response questions. Then compute your raw score on the exam using the worksheet. Finally, refer to the table below to translate your raw score to an AP score of 1 to 5.

Section I: Multiple-Choice

Number of questions answered correctly (55 possible) _____ × 1.09 = _____

Section I: Free-Response

Question 1 (3 points possible): _____ × 5 = _____

Question 2 (4 points possible): _____ × 3.75 = _____

Question 3 (4 points possible): _____ × 3.75 = _____

Question 4 (6 points possible): _____ × 2.5 = _____

RAW SCORE: Add your points in the column above (120 possible): _____

Conversion Table

RAW SCORE	APPROXIMATE AP SCORE
Mid-80s to 120	5
Mid-70s to low-mid-80s	4
High 40s to mid-70s	3
High 20s to high 40s	2
0 to high 20s	1

Note: At press time, the College Board has not released any information on the computation and conversion of raw scores for the new AP exam to be administered in May 2019. However, the College Board goes to great lengths to make sure that the scores on the new test will mean the same thing as on the old test with the same percentages of students scoring each grade (1–5). This score conversion worksheet is based on the assumption that the ranges for each grade (1–5) on the old test will stay about the same on the new test.

AP U.S. Government and Politics
Practice Exam 2

SECTION I
ANSWER SHEET

1 Ⓐ Ⓑ Ⓒ Ⓓ	21 Ⓐ Ⓑ Ⓒ Ⓓ	41 Ⓐ Ⓑ Ⓒ Ⓓ
2 Ⓐ Ⓑ Ⓒ Ⓓ	22 Ⓐ Ⓑ Ⓒ Ⓓ	42 Ⓐ Ⓑ Ⓒ Ⓓ
3 Ⓐ Ⓑ Ⓒ Ⓓ	23 Ⓐ Ⓑ Ⓒ Ⓓ	43 Ⓐ Ⓑ Ⓒ Ⓓ
4 Ⓐ Ⓑ Ⓒ Ⓓ	24 Ⓐ Ⓑ Ⓒ Ⓓ	44 Ⓐ Ⓑ Ⓒ Ⓓ
5 Ⓐ Ⓑ Ⓒ Ⓓ	25 Ⓐ Ⓑ Ⓒ Ⓓ	45 Ⓐ Ⓑ Ⓒ Ⓓ
6 Ⓐ Ⓑ Ⓒ Ⓓ	26 Ⓐ Ⓑ Ⓒ Ⓓ	46 Ⓐ Ⓑ Ⓒ Ⓓ
7 Ⓐ Ⓑ Ⓒ Ⓓ	27 Ⓐ Ⓑ Ⓒ Ⓓ	47 Ⓐ Ⓑ Ⓒ Ⓓ
8 Ⓐ Ⓑ Ⓒ Ⓓ	28 Ⓐ Ⓑ Ⓒ Ⓓ	48 Ⓐ Ⓑ Ⓒ Ⓓ
9 Ⓐ Ⓑ Ⓒ Ⓓ	29 Ⓐ Ⓑ Ⓒ Ⓓ	49 Ⓐ Ⓑ Ⓒ Ⓓ
10 Ⓐ Ⓑ Ⓒ Ⓓ	30 Ⓐ Ⓑ Ⓒ Ⓓ	50 Ⓐ Ⓑ Ⓒ Ⓓ
11 Ⓐ Ⓑ Ⓒ Ⓓ	31 Ⓐ Ⓑ Ⓒ Ⓓ	51 Ⓐ Ⓑ Ⓒ Ⓓ
12 Ⓐ Ⓑ Ⓒ Ⓓ	32 Ⓐ Ⓑ Ⓒ Ⓓ	52 Ⓐ Ⓑ Ⓒ Ⓓ
13 Ⓐ Ⓑ Ⓒ Ⓓ	33 Ⓐ Ⓑ Ⓒ Ⓓ	53 Ⓐ Ⓑ Ⓒ Ⓓ
14 Ⓐ Ⓑ Ⓒ Ⓓ	34 Ⓐ Ⓑ Ⓒ Ⓓ	54 Ⓐ Ⓑ Ⓒ Ⓓ
15 Ⓐ Ⓑ Ⓒ Ⓓ	35 Ⓐ Ⓑ Ⓒ Ⓓ	55 Ⓐ Ⓑ Ⓒ Ⓓ
16 Ⓐ Ⓑ Ⓒ Ⓓ	36 Ⓐ Ⓑ Ⓒ Ⓓ	
17 Ⓐ Ⓑ Ⓒ Ⓓ	37 Ⓐ Ⓑ Ⓒ Ⓓ	
18 Ⓐ Ⓑ Ⓒ Ⓓ	38 Ⓐ Ⓑ Ⓒ Ⓓ	
19 Ⓐ Ⓑ Ⓒ Ⓓ	39 Ⓐ Ⓑ Ⓒ Ⓓ	
20 Ⓐ Ⓑ Ⓒ Ⓓ	40 Ⓐ Ⓑ Ⓒ Ⓓ	

AP U.S. Government and Politics
Practice Exam 2

Section I: Multiple-Choice Questions
Total Time—80 minutes
55 Questions

Directions: Each question or incomplete sentence below is followed by four suggested answers or completions. Select the one that is best, and then fill in the corresponding oval on the answer sheet.

Questions 1 and 2 refer to the graph below.

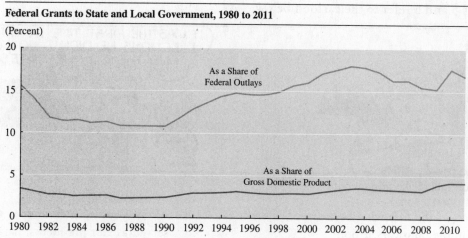

Source: Congressional Budget Office based on *Budget of the United States Government, Fiscal Year 2013: Historical Tables*, Table 12.1

1. Which of the following is an accurate statement about the information in the line graph?
   (A) Federal grants to state and local governments decreased between 1990 and 2000.
   (B) Federal grants to state and local governments slightly increased as a share of gross domestic product.
   (C) Federal grants to state and local governments slightly decreased as a share of gross domestic product.
   (D) Federal grants to state and local governments increased between 1980 and 1990.

2. Based on the information in the line graph, which of the following is the most likely implication of federal grant spending to state and local governments?
   (A) State and local governments can depend on a stable share of federal outlays to support necessary programs.
   (B) Grants supporting a wide range of state and local programs will continue to fluctuate as a share of federal outlays.
   (C) Gross domestic product is decreasing, which will affect how much state and local governments will receive in federal outlays.
   (D) State and local governments should expect increases in the amount of grant funding they receive in the future.

GO ON TO THE NEXT PAGE

3. In nearly every congressional election, the candidates talk about overhauling
   (A) the number of terms a member of Congress can stay in office
   (B) the franking privilege enjoyed by members of Congress
   (C) the cumbersome committee structure of both houses of Congress
   (D) the persistence of pork-barrel legislation

4. Which of the following is an accurate statement about the electoral college system?
   (A) Voters directly elect the president when they go to the polls in early November.
   (B) It is possible for a candidate to win the popular vote on the national level but still lose the presidential election.
   (C) The House of Representatives chooses the vice president.
   (D) Candidates campaign in many small states in the days leading up to a presidential election.

Questions 5 and 6 refer to the cartoon below.

Source: mooselakecartoons.com

5. Which of the following best describes the message in the political cartoon?
   (A) Sometimes the candidate you vote for is not the candidate that wins the election.
   (B) Not every election is important enough to cast a vote.
   (C) Voting is an important civic responsibility for citizens.
   (D) Voting is a privilege not exercised by all.

6. Which of the following is least likely to vote?
   (A) A wealthy, white businessman
   (B) A high-school dropout
   (C) A female professional
   (D) A labor union member

7. Impeachment proceedings were started against both Presidents Richard Nixon and Bill Clinton. Which statement best compares the two situations?
   (A) The House Judiciary Committee passed articles of impeachment against both presidents.
   (B) Both men were formally impeached by the House of Representatives.
   (C) Both men had a trial in the Senate; both were convicted.
   (D) The case of Richard Nixon was very similar to the case of Andrew Johnson; the case of Bill Clinton was not.

8. Many people, including a number who have served as vice presidents, have observed that the vice president of the United States has little real power. The powers of the vice president include which of the following?
   (A) Voting in the House of Representatives as a member
   (B) Presiding over presidential impeachment trials in the United States Senate
   (C) Serving as an advisor to the U.S. Supreme Court
   (D) Taking over for a disabled president under the terms of the Twenty-Fifth Amendment

9. Which of the following best describes a result of the Great (Connecticut) Compromise?
   (A) A bicameral legislature was created.
   (B) All states had equal representation in both legislative bodies.
   (C) A single executive was chosen who could only serve one term.
   (D) A national court structure was established.

GO ON TO THE NEXT PAGE

Questions 10 and 11 refer to the graph below.

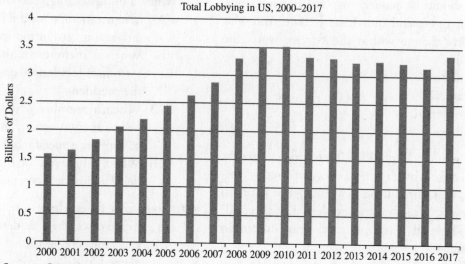

Total Lobbying in US, 2000–2017

Source: OpenSecrets.org

10. Which of the following statements is reflected in the data in the bar graph?
    (A) Lobbying in the United States was at its highest in 2017.
    (B) Lobbying in the United States was at its lowest in 2001.
    (C) Since 2000, the amount spent on lobbying in the United States has more than doubled.
    (D) Since 2000, the amount spent on lobbying in the United States has generally remained constant.

11. Which of the following might explain the reasons for the trend indicated in the bar graph?
    (A) Lobbying laws require lobbyists to register and that information must be publicly disclosed.
    (B) Elected officials who benefit from the work of lobbyists are encouraging the growth.
    (C) The total number of lobbyists is growing.
    (D) Lobbying laws are updated often to account for changes in the way lobbying is done.

12. Which of the following is an important significance of *McCulloch v. Maryland* (1819)?
    (A) Affirmed the supremacy of the federal government over the states
    (B) Placed limits on the powers of Congress
    (C) Established the doctrine of judicial review
    (D) Established the doctrine of dual federalism

13. Which of the following is a power reserved to state governments?
    (A) Regulation of interstate commerce
    (B) Negotiating treaties with foreign governments
    (C) Regulation of immigration
    (D) Regulation of the public schools

14. Which of the following is an accurate comparison of liberal and conservative views?

	LIBERAL	CONSERVATIVE
(A)	Less government involvement in the economy	More government involvement in the economy
(B)	Supports government enforcement of traditional values	Supports government enforcement of progressive values
(C)	Supports lower taxes and less regulation of businesses	Supports higher taxes and regulation of businesses
(D)	Government needs to protect civil liberties and individual human rights	Government has a responsibility to solve social problems

GO ON TO THE NEXT PAGE

15. A political candidate who states that the government should be actively involved in supporting human rights and individual welfare, and who supports change within the system, would be termed a
    (A) moderate
    (B) radical
    (C) conservative
    (D) liberal

16. During the 1936 presidential election campaign, a poll taken by *Literary Digest* incorrectly predicted that Alfred Landon would defeat Franklin Roosevelt. What was the problem with this poll?
    (A) The poll was conducted only in certain states.
    (B) The manner in which the question was worded favored Landon.
    (C) More men than women were asked the question.
    (D) Those who responded to the poll were not a true cross-section of the voting public.

17. The clear majority of cases appealed to the Supreme Court are never actually ruled on by the Court. Which of the following is a reason the Court may decide not to rule on a case?
    (A) The case has already been decided by the lower and appeals courts, so there is no need for the Supreme Court to act.
    (B) The case would require too much time for the Court.
    (C) The case has passed the "date of expiration" established by the Court.
    (D) The case does not pass the "rule of four."

18. Which of the following most accurately describes when a filibuster might occur?
    (A) When a member of the House of Representatives wants to introduce new legislation
    (B) When a member of the Senate wants to introduce legislation specifically desired by the president
    (C) When a member of the Senate wishes to persuade members of the opposition party to support a specific bill
    (D) When a member of the Senate wishes to delay action or a vote on a specific bill

19. To enforce federal laws or federal court decisions in extreme cases, the president can
    (A) call for congressional impeachment of elected officials from states that do not comply with federal law
    (B) order the U.S. military to see that federal law is enforced
    (C) appoint new governors in states that do not comply with federal law
    (D) disband the state legislatures in states that do not comply with federal law

20. Which of the following is an accurate comparison of political parties and interest groups?

	POLITICAL PARTIES	INTEREST GROUPS
(A)	More tightly organized and financed through dues-paying members	More loosely organized and financed through contributions and donations
(B)	Support candidates for elective office	Nominate candidates to run for elective office
(C)	Focus on a broad range of issues that appeal to a larger segment of the population	Narrow focus on a specific issue
(D)	Compete for influence over elected officials so they can influence public policy	Compete for control of the legislative branch by trying to win a majority of seats

GO ON TO THE NEXT PAGE

21. If a new census determines that a state's population has declined significantly from the last census, which of the following might be expected to happen as a result?
    (A) An increase in federal funding for that state
    (B) An increase in the overall "political pull" of that state
    (C) A possible decline in the number of representatives from that state in the House of Representatives
    (D) A greater chance that a candidate from that state would be chosen as a vice presidential candidate to "balance the ticket"

22. Which of the following best describes the pluralist theory of democratic government?
    (A) A small number of elites rule in their own self-interest.
    (B) There are many strong groups influencing government, and each pulls the government in numerous directions, creating gridlock.
    (C) Bureaucrats, who carry on the day-to-day workings of the government, control public policy.
    (D) Interest groups continually compete in the public arena; as a result, bargaining and compromise is a necessity.

23. The ideas of the Enlightenment had an impact on many of those who wrote the U.S. Constitution. Which political concept is generally associated with the Enlightenment?
    (A) The idea of a social contract between the government and the governed
    (B) The idea that the primary purpose of government is to govern the common people who need firm control
    (C) The idea that governments have natural rights which citizens do not have
    (D) The idea that citizens never have the right to rebel against the government

24. Which of the following best describes a disadvantage of federalism?
    (A) It encourages wide diversity in local government.
    (B) It may create a duplication of offices and functions.
    (C) It keeps government very close to the people.
    (D) States serve as training grounds to create eventual national leaders.

25. Which of the following best describes how the election of United States senators was changed by the Seventeenth Amendment in 1913?
    (A) Senators were elected by popular vote instead of by state legislatures.
    (B) Senatorial terms were lengthened to six years.
    (C) Starting in 1914, not all senators were elected at the same time.
    (D) The minimum age for senators was increased.

GO ON TO THE NEXT PAGE

Questions 26 and 27 refer to the infographic below.

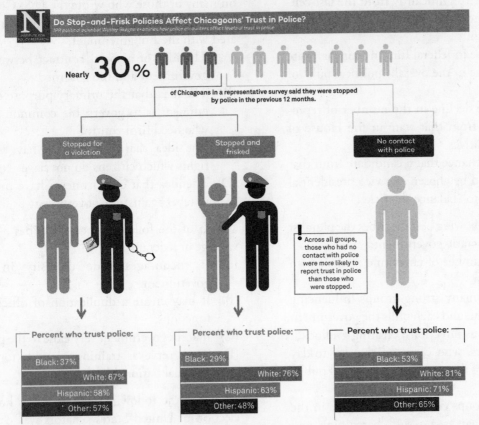

Source: Skogan, Wesley G., "*Stop-and-Frisk and Trust in Police in Chicago (WP-16-08)*." Used with permission.

26. Based on the infographic, which of the following claims would an opponent of stop and frisk most likely make?
   (A) The number of police encounters, or lack thereof, had no effect on trust in police.
   (B) Being stopped and frisked was "extremely common" among people living in Chicago.
   (C) Racial minorities were more likely to report an unpleasant encounter with police.
   (D) The frequency of police encounters was about the same across all demographic groups.

27. Based on the infographic, which Supreme Court case deals with the constitutional principles of stop and frisk?
   (A) *Marbury v. Madison* (1803)
   (B) *Terry v. Ohio* (1968)
   (C) *Miranda v. Arizona* (1966)
   (D) *Texas v. Johnson* (1989)

28. Which of the following is an accurate comparison of judicial activism and judicial restraint?

	JUDICIAL ACTIVISM	JUDICIAL RESTRAINT
(A)	Involves playing a role in formulating social policies on issues	Involves reviewing an existing law rather than modifying the existing law
(B)	Courts should follow original intent of the Founding Fathers	Courts should follow the "spirit" of the law
(C)	Proponents favor the status quo and a strict construction of the Constitution	Proponents favor change and a loose construction of the Constitution
(D)	Strict constructionism	Loose constructionism

GO ON TO THE NEXT PAGE

29. Some commentators predict a decline in the power of political parties in the United States. Which of the following might be a reason for this decline?
    (A) More and more Americans vote straight-ticket ballots.
    (B) The number of Americans who identify themselves as Democrats far outnumber those who consider themselves Republicans, thus creating an "unfair" political system.
    (C) Many Americans feel there is no real difference between the two political parties.
    (D) Many candidates are now more reliant on political parties.

30. Which of the following is necessary for a treaty to be ratified?
    (A) It must be passed by both houses of Congress by a majority vote.
    (B) It must be passed by both houses of Congress by a two-thirds majority vote.
    (C) It must be passed by the Senate by a majority vote.
    (D) It must be passed by the Senate by a two-thirds majority vote.

31. Which of the following is an accurate comparison of the pluralist and elite theories of democracy?

	PLURALIST THEORY	ELITE THEORY
(A)	Real power is held by a relatively small number of people	Real power is held by groups, each one advocating for its own chosen policies
(B)	Interest groups benefit democracy by bringing representation to all people	System of interlocking connections based on class or position that control the government
(C)	Corporate interests control government	No one group is able to dominate
(D)	A unified group of individuals possesses a dominant influence over the public policy process and its outcomes	Groups are so varied and strong that gridlock occurs

32. "Iron triangles" are alliances involving which of the following groups?
    (A) Congressional committees, interest groups, and bureaucratic agencies
    (B) Congressional subcommittees, interested members of the media, and political parties
    (C) Interest groups, members of the media, and bureaucratic agencies
    (D) Bureaucratic agencies, the White House Executive Office, and congressional committees

33. Which issue has recently been a "litmus test" for potential Supreme Court justices?
    (A) Gays in the military
    (B) Abortion
    (C) The power of the presidency
    (D) The right of an individual to own weapons

34. Which Supreme Court decision has had the greatest effect on public school education in the United States in the past 60 years?
    (A) *Shaw v. Reno* (1993)
    (B) *Tinker v. Des Moines Independent Community School District* (1969)
    (C) *Brown v. Board of Education* (1954)
    (D) *Gideon v. Wainwright* (1963)

GO ON TO THE NEXT PAGE

Questions 35 and 36 refer to the map below.

Estimated Medicaid Spending per Enrollee, by State, Federal Fiscal Year 2008

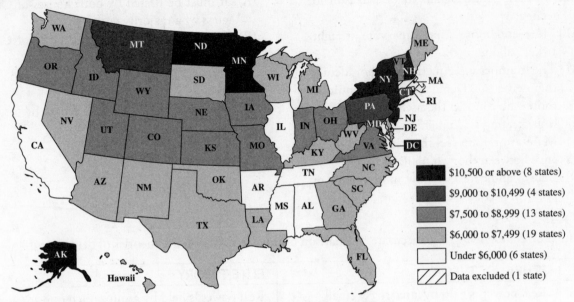

Source: U.S. Government, General Accounting Office (GAO-14-456)

35. Which of the following is the most common level of Medicaid spending per enrollee?
    (A) Under $6,000
    (B) $6,000 to $7,499
    (C) $7,500 to $8,999
    (D) $10,500 or above

36. Which of the following most accurately explains the variation in Medicaid spending per enrollee from state to state?
    (A) States participating in Medicaid must provide the same coverage of benefits.
    (B) States do not have discretion in setting eligibility levels.
    (C) Differences in the cost of obtaining health care in different states affect the amount state Medicaid programs have available to spend to purchase services.
    (D) States are free to pay physicians whatever is charged; some physicians charge more than others.

37. Recent Supreme Court rulings concerning religion have emphasized which of the following?
    (A) It is constitutional for a public school to have informal prayer periods in its daily schedule.
    (B) It is constitutional for a state to reimburse parochial schools for religious textbooks.
    (C) Public schools that teach evolution must also teach creationism.
    (D) School-sanctioned prayers in public schools during the school day are unconstitutional.

38. What pivotal 1963 Supreme Court case held that the state must provide the defendant with an attorney in state courts if he or she cannot afford one?
    (A) *Gideon v. Wainwright* (1963)
    (B) *Engel v. Vitale* (1962)
    (C) *United States v. Lopez* (1995)
    (D) *Roe v. Wade* (1973)

GO ON TO THE NEXT PAGE

39. Which of the following is an accurate comparison of the Articles of Confederation and United States Constitution?

	ARTICLES OF CONFEDERATION	UNITED STATES CONSTITUTION
(A)	Congress regulated interstate trade through the Commerce Clause	No provision to regulate interstate trade but can regulate intrastate trade
(B)	Both the central government and the states had the power to tax	Taxes are the expressed power of individual states
(C)	Sovereignty resides in the states	Sovereignty may be shared between the central government and the states
(D)	President elected by the people in a popular vote	President elected indirectly through an electoral college

40. Which of the following is a reason why some conservatives criticize recent federal legislation to improve student test scores (the No Child Left Behind Act)?
    (A) The Act contradicts previous federal legislation on education.
    (B) The Act is not fully supported by the Department of Education.
    (C) The Act is not fully supported by teacher unions.
    (D) They believe that the control of education should be left to the states.

41. Which of the following are the main authors of the initial budget proposal presented to Congress by the president?
    (A) Officials from the Department of the Treasury
    (B) Staff members of the congressional appropriations committees
    (C) Staff members from the Congressional Budget Office
    (D) Staff members from the Office of Management and Budget

42. Shays' Rebellion and other acts of violence in 1787–1788 demonstrated to many in the new nation that
    (A) the Articles of Confederation had to be revised to create a stronger national government
    (B) the economic well-being of the country was still tied to Great Britain
    (C) the nation had expanded too quickly
    (D) the government of Massachusetts was ineffective

43. What was the major reason that some states formerly had poll taxes and literacy requirements for voting?
    (A) To maintain Republican Party control
    (B) To prevent third parties from gaining influence
    (C) To prevent African Americans and other minorities from voting
    (D) To ensure that incumbents remained in power

44. When Congress passed the Brady Bill, which required a five-day waiting period before the purchase of a handgun, it was following which step of the policymaking process?
    (A) Agenda setting
    (B) Policy formulation
    (C) Policy evaluation
    (D) Policy adoption

45. In the 1989 *Texas v. Johnson* decision, the Supreme Court ruled that the burning of an American flag was constitutionally protected. According to the Court, this decision was based on which of the following reasons?
    (A) There was precedent in previous rulings.
    (B) Flag burning is a symbolic form of speech.
    (C) The flag burning had taken place on a military base.
    (D) Protestors had gotten a permit for the rally where the flag was burned.

GO ON TO THE NEXT PAGE

Questions 46 and 47 refer to the pie graph below.

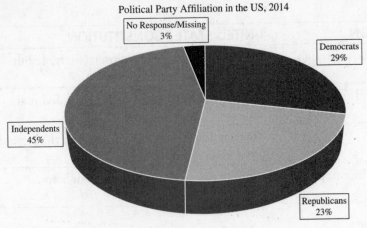

Political Party Affiliation in the US, 2014

Source: Gallup July 7–10, 2014

46. Which of the following accurately describes the information presented in the pie chart?
   (A) Independents are a larger percentage of the population than Democrats and Republicans combined.
   (B) Republicans are a larger percentage of the population than Democrats.
   (C) More than half of the population identifies as an Independent.
   (D) Democrats are a larger percentage of the population than Republicans.

47. Which of the following best explains the large size of those identifying as Independent in the United States?
   (A) Americans are becoming frustrated with the way the government is working and give low-favorable ratings to the two major parties.
   (B) Many Americans claim to be independent because they are undecided voters when election time nears.
   (C) Americans often choose to be Independent because they do not have the money to join the Democratic or Republican parties.
   (D) The Democratic and Republican parties are too radical for most voters.

Questions 48 and 49 refer to the passage below.

"Special-interest organizations are most easily formed when they deal with small numbers of individuals who are acutely aware of their exclusive interests. To describe the conditions of pressure-group organization in this way is, however, to say that it is primarily a business phenomenon. Aside from a few very large organizations (the churches, organized labor, farm organizations, and veterans' organizations) the residue is a small segment of the population. *Pressure politics is essentially of small groups.*"

—E. E. Schattschneider,
The Semisovereign People

48. Which statement is most consistent with the author's view in this passage?
   (A) Only small groups within large organizations create interest groups.
   (B) Only business interest groups can be successful in organizing.
   (C) Special interest groups tend to have an upper-class bias within the group.
   (D) Special interest groups represent all segments of the population.

49. Which theory of democracy would the author most likely support?
   (A) Traditional democratic theory
   (B) Pluralist theory
   (C) Elitist or class theory
   (D) Bureaucratic theory

GO ON TO THE NEXT PAGE

50. Which of the following most accurately describes the incumbency effect?
    (A) Members of the House of Representatives benefit more than members of the Senate.
    (B) Members of the Senate benefit more than members of the House of Representatives.
    (C) Members of the House of Representatives and Senate benefit equally.
    (D) Incumbency does not benefit either members of the House of Representatives or Senate.

51. What is a possible result of a "midterm" or "off-year" election?
    (A) The president may be forced to resign.
    (B) The political power of Congress increases.
    (C) The power base of Congress may change.
    (D) The Constitution may change.

52. After 1950, the success of the Civil Rights Movement was aided most by
    (A) African Americans lowering their expectations
    (B) the passage of the Fourteenth Amendment
    (C) a shift of the movement to the courts
    (D) African Americans winning election to public office

53. Which of the following occurs latest in the passage of a bill in Congress?
    (A) The conference committee
    (B) The referral to committee
    (C) The investigation and hearings
    (D) The debate on the floor
    (E) The amendment committee

Questions 54 and 55 refer to the passage below.

"It was desirable that the sense of the people should operate in the choice of the person to whom so important a trust was to be confided. This end will be answered by committing the right of making it, not to any preestablished body, but to men chosen by the people for the special purpose, and at the particular conjuncture.

"It was equally desirable, that the immediate election should be made by men most capable of analyzing the qualities adapted to the station, and acting under circumstances favorable to deliberation, and to a judicious combination of all the reasons and inducements which were proper to govern their choice.... A small number of persons, selected by their fellow-citizens from the general mass, will be most likely to possess the information and discernment requisite to such complicated investigations.

"It was also peculiarly desirable to afford as little opportunity as possible to tumult and disorder. The choice of SEVERAL, to form an intermediate body ... chosen in each State, are to assemble and vote in the State in which they are chosen, this detached and divided situation will expose them much less to heats and ferments, which might be communicated from them to the people, than if they were all to be convened at one time, in one place."

—Publius (Alexander Hamilton),
Federalist No. 68

54. Which statement is most consistent with the author's view in this passage?
    (A) The best method for electing the president and vice president is popular vote by the people.
    (B) The best method for electing the president and vice president would be an independent group representing each state, chosen by the people.
    (C) Political parties are more in tuned to presidential choice than the masses.
    (D) Elections for the president and vice president should be held at one time and in one place.

55. Why did the Founding Fathers create this method for electing the president and vice president?
    (A) It was a compromise between the North and South in order to get the Constitution approved.
    (B) They did not trust the people, Congress, or the state legislatures to elect the president.
    (C) It reinforced the power of the federal government over the states.
    (D) The citizens at that time did not want to elect the president or vice president and preferred this method.

STOP. END OF SECTION I

Section II: Free-Response Questions
Total Time—100 minutes

Directions: You have 100 minutes to answer all four of the following questions. Respond to all parts of all four questions. Before beginning to write, you should take a few minutes to plan and outline each answer. Spend approximately 20 minutes each on questions 1, 2, and 3 and 40 minutes on question 4. Illustrate your essay with substantive examples where appropriate.

1. The southern border that the United States shares with Mexico spans almost 2,000 miles. The Department of Homeland Security's Customs and Border Protection monitors the border. Walls, fences, sensors, and cameras already exist along a 670-mile portion of the border in an effort to decrease illegal immigration and drug trafficking.

   President Trump is expected to finally go to California ... in mid-March to see prototypes for a potential border wall and learn more about the construction.... Protests are likely amid debate over the president's support for new immigration limits. Eight border wall prototypes are on display.... The 30-foot-tall barriers use varying configurations of steel, concrete—even spikes—to create ramparts far more formidable than almost anything in place along the 2,000-mile border.

   —*Washington Post, February 26, 2018*

   After reading the scenario, respond to A, B, and C below:
   (A) Describe a power that Congress could use to address the issue of a border wall.
   (B) In the context of the scenario, explain how the use of congressional power described in Part A can be affected by interaction with the presidency.
   (C) In the context of the scenario, explain how the interaction between Congress and the presidency can be affected by linkage institutions.

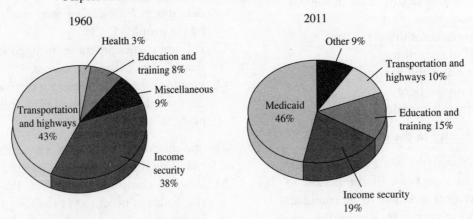

Purpose of Federal Grants to State and Local Governments

Source: Congressional Budget Office

2. Use the pie charts to answer the questions.
   (A) Identify the level of spending which increased the most between 1960 and 2011.
   (B) Describe a similarity or difference in the purpose of federal grants to state and local governments, as illustrated by the pie chart, and draw a conclusion about that similarity or difference.
   (C) Explain how the usage of federal grants to state and local governments as show in the pie charts demonstrates the principle of federalism.

GO ON TO THE NEXT PAGE

3. Smith Betts, "a farm hand, out of a job and on relief ... a man of little education," was indicted for robbery in Maryland. Betts was unable to afford a lawyer and requested one be appointed for him, but the judge in the case denied the request on the grounds that indigent defendants were offered counsel only in criminal prosecutions for rape and for murder. Betts pled not guilty and requested a trial without a jury. Betts cross examined prosecution witnesses, called witnesses on his behalf, and chose not to take the stand himself. Betts was found guilty and given a sentence of eight years.

In the subsequent case, *Betts v. Brady* (1942), the Supreme Court held in a 6-3 decision that no constitutional violation had occurred. The majority opinion states the right to counsel does not require states to provide counsel to any defendant. Justice Owen Roberts' opinion repeatedly makes the point that not all defendants in all cases will need the assistance of counsel in order to receive a fair trial with due process. He stated that the right to counsel only prevented the state from interfering in a defendant's request for representation rather than requiring a state to offer counsel.

(A) Identify the constitutional clause that is common to both *Betts v. Brady* (1942) and *Gideon v. Wainright* (1963).

(B) Based on the constitutional clause identified in Part A, explain why the facts of *Gideon v. Wainright* led to a different holding than the holding in *Betts v. Brady*.

(C) Describe a consequence of the ruling in *Betts v. Brady* on the court system.

4. Develop an argument that explains whether the United States Constitution or the Articles of Confederation created a more democratic government.

In your essay, you must:

- Articulate a defensible claim or thesis that responds to the prompt and establishes a line of reasoning.
- Support your claim or thesis with at least TWO pieces of accurate and relevant information:
  — At least ONE piece of evidence must be from one of the following foundational documents:
    — Articles of Confederation
    — Federalist No. 51
    — U.S. Constitution
  — Use a second piece of evidence from another foundational document from the list or from your study of the electoral process.
- Use reasoning to explain why your evidence supports your claim or thesis.
- Respond to an opposing or alternative perspective using refutation, concession, or rebuttal.

STOP. END OF SECTION II

Answer Key for Multiple-Choice Questions

1. B	16. D	31. B	46. D
2. B	17. D	32. A	47. A
3. D	18. D	33. B	48. C
4. B	19. B	34. C	49. B
5. C	20. C	35. B	50. A
6. B	21. B	36. C	51. C
7. A	22. D	37. D	52. C
8. D	23. A	38. A	53. A
9. A	24. B	39. C	54. B
10. C	25. A	40. D	55. B
11. C	26. C	41. D	
12. A	27. B	42. A	
13. D	28. A	43. C	
14. A	29. C	44. D	
15. D	30. D	45. B	

› Answers and Explanations for the Multiple-Choice Questions

1. **B.** Federal grants to state and local governments increased between 1990 and 2000 (A). Federal grants to state and local governments slightly increased as a share of gross domestic product (C). Federal grants to state and local governments decreased between 1980 and 1990 (D).

2. **B.** State and local governments depend on the federal government's budget for funding for grants. The amount of money spent on many grants is discretionary and can be changed from budget to budget as the needs of the government change (A, D). The graph does not show whether gross domestic product is increasing or decreasing (C).

3. **D.** Although term limits can sometimes be an issue (A), the one issue that is continually critiqued in congressional elections is pork barrel spending, by which members of Congress bring projects and programs back to their own districts, sometimes with the use of earmarks in appropriations bills. Predictably, many citizens oppose pork barrel spending in principle but are not upset when their own member of Congress brings projects "home." The president does have some influence over the annual congressional agenda, but that is not an issue in congressional elections. The franking privilege (B) (which is also not an election issue) allows members of Congress to send mail to constituents without paying postage; members of Congress are thus able to brag about all they have done, for free. The committee structure is not an issue (C).

4. **B.** Voters indirectly elect the president through the electoral college when they go to the polls in early November (A). The Senate chooses the vice president if no candidate gets a majority in the electoral college (C). Candidates generally campaign in the larger states and swing states with more electoral votes in the days leading up to a presidential election (D).

5. **C.** Voting is an important civic responsibility for citizens, and every election is important. Although the candidate you vote for does not always win the election (A) and voting is a privilege not exercised by all (D) might be true, these are not the point the author is making. Every election is important enough to cast a vote (C).

6. **B.** Least likely to vote would be the high-school dropout. The wealthy, white businessman (A), woman professional (C), and labor union member (D) are all more likely to vote.

7. **A.** The House Judiciary Committee passed articles of impeachment against both Presidents Clinton and Nixon. Richard Nixon resigned before the entire House of Representatives voted on these (A). Bill Clinton and Andrew Johnson were both impeached by the House of Representatives but acquitted by the Senate (C). The press sensationalized the impeachment hearings of Bill Clinton, particularly in its coverage of Clinton's affair with a White House intern. The press was very critical of Richard Nixon throughout his impeachment process.

8. **D.** The Twenty-Fifth Amendment provides that the vice president shall become president in the event of death, resignation, removal from office, or impairment that prevents the current president from fulfilling his or her duties. The vice president is not a member of the House of Representatives and therefore cannot vote (A). The chief justice of the Supreme Court presides over presidential impeachment trials in the United States Senate (B). The vice president is not an advisor to the Supreme Court (C).

9. **A.** While larger states wanted a legislature that would give them more representatives and the smaller states wanted a legislature in which all states would have equal representation, the Connecticut Compromise established two legislative bodies, the House of Representatives and the Senate.

10. **C.** Lobbying in the United States was at its highest in 2011 (A). Lobbying in the United States was at its lowest in 2000 (B). Since 2000 the amount spent on lobbying in the United States has generally increased (D).

11. **C.** The total number of lobbyists is growing. Registration of lobbyists (A) and lobbying laws (D) would discourage lobbying and lobbyists. Elected officials who benefit from the work of lobbyists are not encouraging the growth (B).

12. **A.** In *McCulloch v. Maryland* (1819), the Supreme Court affirmed the supremacy of the federal government over the states. It did not place limits on the powers of Congress (B), establish the doctrine of judicial review (*Marbury v. Madison*) (C), or establish the doctrine of dual federalism.

13. **D.** Regulation of public schools is a reserved power of the states. Regulation of interstate commerce (A), negotiating treaties with foreign governments (B), and regulation of immigration (C) are powers of the national government under the United States Constitution.

14. **A.** Liberals prefer more government involvement in the economy, while conservatives prefer less government involvement in the economy. Liberals support government enforcement of progressive values and conservatives support government enforcement of traditional values (B). Liberals support higher taxes and regulation of business and conservatives support lower taxes and less regulation of businesses (C). Liberals believe that government needs to protect civil liberties and individual human rights; conservatives believe that government has a responsibility to solve social problems (D).

15. **D.** Liberals would argue that changes in society should take place within the system; radicals would say that it may be necessary to go outside of the system to create real change (B). A moderate would be less likely to be an advocate of fundamental changes in government involvement (A). A conservative is unlikely to support greater government involvement in individual welfare (C).

16. **D.** Those polled were chosen from automobile registrations and telephone directories, so this was not a representative sample. Many supporters of Franklin Roosevelt did not have cars or telephones.

17. **D.** The "rule of four" refers to the requirement that four of the nine Supreme Court justices need to agree that a case should be heard by the Supreme Court; if at least four justices do not agree to hear the case, it is not considered by the Court. Even if a case has already been decided by the lower and appeals courts, the Supreme Court—the court of last resort—may agree to hear the case (A). The Supreme Court determines its own docket or calendar of cases; it does not choose cases based on how much time they might take to resolve (B). There is no formal "date of expiration" for Supreme Court cases (C).

18. **D.** A filibuster is used by a member or members of the Senate to delay action on a bill they oppose that is expected to be approved by the body as a whole.

19. **B.** As commander-in-chief, the president can use the military to enforce U.S. laws and maintain order. Presidents Eisenhower and Kennedy used the military to enforce federal court orders relating to civil rights in the South. The federal government, including the president, does not have the legal ability to directly intervene in the affairs of state government; thus, the federal government has no ability to call for the impeachment of state officials (A), appoint new governors (B), or disband state legislatures (C).

20. **C.** Political parties are more loosely organized and financed through contributions and donations (A), nominate candidates to run for elective office (B), and compete for control of the legislative branch by trying to win a majority of seats (D). Interest groups are more tightly organized and financed through dues-paying members (A), support candidates for elective office (B), and compete for influence over elected officials so they can influence public policy (D).

21. **B.** The selection of committee chairpersons in Congress is not related to the population of their states; chairpersons are still chosen largely by seniority, although other factors are beginning to play a part, too. A decline in population might cause a state to lose representatives in the House of Representatives (C); with fewer representatives, the "political pull" of the state can be expected to decline as well (D). Thus, a decline in population can be expected to lead to a decline in federal funding for that state (A).

22. **D.** The pluralist theory holds that vigorous competition among interest groups to achieve their goals necessitates a government of compromise and a continual reevaluation of priorities. Response (A) represents the elite theory of government, and choice (B) is representative of the theory of hyperpluralism. Response (C) reflects the bureaucratic theory of government.

23. **A.** Enlightenment thinkers wrote about the natural rights of persons (citizens) and believed the power of government should be limited (C); the idea that people "need firm control" is inconsistent with most Enlightenment thought (B). The idea of the "social contract" was emphasized by Rousseau, the concept of branches of government was discussed by Montesquieu, and the belief that citizens have the right to rebel against a government that doesn't protect their rights was espoused by John Locke (D).

24. **B.** The possibility that federalism may create a duplication of offices and function is a disadvantage of the system. All the other responses are advantages of the federalist system.

25. **A.** Goals of many supporters of the Progressive movement included six-year terms for senators (B), staggered elections (C), and that the age requirement to be a senator increased (D), but these were not changed by the Seventeenth Amendment. The Seventeenth Amendment did change how senators were elected to allow election by popular vote instead of by state legislatures.

26. **C.** Racial minorities were more likely to report an unpleasant encounter with police. The number of police encounters, or lack thereof, did influence trust in police (A). Being stopped and frisked occurred among 30% of people living in Chicago (B). The frequency of police encounters varied widely across demographic groups (D).

27. **B.** In *Terry v. Ohio* the Supreme Court held that the police may search criminal suspects for safety purposes without a warrant. *Marbury v. Madison* established judicial review (A). *Miranda v. Arizona* required that suspects in police custody have certain rights, and that they must be informed of those rights (right to remain silent, right to an attorney) (C). *Texas v. Johnson* established flag burning as a protected, free speech right under the First Amendment (D).

28. **A.** Judicial activism involves playing a role in formulating social policies on issues; judicial restraint involves reviewing an existing law rather than modifying the existing law. Supporters of judicial activism believe that the courts should follow the "spirit" of the law (B), favor change and a loose construction of the Constitution (C), and are generally loose constructionists (D). Supporters of judicial restraint believe that the courts should follow the original intent of the Founding Fathers (B), favor the status quo and the strict construction of the Constitution (C), and are generally strict constructionists.

29. **C.** More Americans are voting split-ticket ballots (A). More Americans have registered as Democrats than Republicans, but few are calling this "unfair" (B). Many candidates are now less reliant on political parties (D).

30. **D.** After a president (or his or her representatives) has negotiated a treaty, it must be ratified by the Senate before it takes effect (A, B). Ratification requires that the Senate approve the treaty by a two-thirds majority (C). The most famous example of a treaty not ratified by the Senate was the treaty negotiated by Woodrow Wilson ending World War I.

31. **B.** The pluralist theory occurs when interest groups benefit democracy by bringing representation to all people; the elite theory occurs when a system of interlocking connections based on class or position control the government. In the pluralist theory real power is held by groups, each one advocating for its own chosen policies (A), no one group can dominate (C), and groups are so varied and strong that gridlock occurs (D). In the elite theory, real power is held by a relatively small number of people (A), corporate interests control government (C), and a unified group of individuals possesses a dominant influence over the public policy process and its outcomes (D)

32. **A.** Iron triangles are formed between interest groups and members of the executive and legislative branches of government. Because of common goals, all elements of the iron triangle may work together to help each other achieve

their goals. For example, a staffer from the executive branch may seek out members of the environmental lobby for ideas when crafting environmental legislation to send on to Congress; those same lobbyists might work with members of Congress to fine-tune the details of the legislation and to gain congressional support for it; congressional and executive branch staffers might work together on compromise legislation that could be supported by both branches.

33. **B.** For many vocal interest groups in U.S. politics in the 1990s and early 21st century, the debate over Supreme Court nominees was dominated by the single issue of abortion, thus the position many people (including many senators) took to support or oppose a Supreme Court nominee depended on their perception of whether the candidate would support or overturn *Roe v. Wade*. In chemistry, a litmus test is a simple test used to determine whether a solution is acidic. The term was applied to politics to refer to the simple test (in this case, whether the nominee supports *Roe v. Wade*) that many used to determine if a nominee should become a Supreme Court justice.

34. **C.** *Brown v. Board of Education* was the 1954 Supreme Court decision stating that "separate but equal" school facilities are unconstitutional. Enforcement of this ruling played an important and controversial role in education through the 1960s, the 1970s, and beyond. *Shaw v Reno* (1993) held that majority-minority districts, created under the Voting Rights Act of 1965, may be constitutionally challenged by voters if race is the only factor used in creating the district (A). *Tinker v. Des Moines* (1969) held that public school students have the right to wear black armbands in school to protest the Vietnam War (B). *Gideon v. Wainwright* (1963) guaranteed the right to an attorney for the poor or indigent in state felony cases (D).

35. **B.** The most common level of Medicaid spending per enrollee is $6,000 to $7,499 with 19 states. Response A spending was in 6 states. Response C spending occurred in 13 states. Response D spending occurred in 8 states.

36. **C.** Differences in the cost of obtaining health care in different states affects the amount state Medicaid programs have available to spend to purchase services. States participating in Medicaid do not have to provide the same coverage of benefits (A). States have discretion in setting eligibility levels (B). States largely determine provider payments within limited federal requirements (D)

37. **D.** The Court has been consistent in ruling that both formal or informal school prayer is unconstitutional in public schools (A). The Court has ruled that states are allowed expenditure of public/state funds to purchase and supply nonsectarian (nonreligious) textbooks to parochial school students (B). There is no requirement that public schools teaching evolution must also teach creationism (C).

38. **A.** *Gideon v. Wainwright* (1963), which overturned a previous ruling, held that the state must provide an attorney for a defendant who cannot afford one. *Engel v. Vitale* (1962) held that school sponsorship of religious activities violates the free exercise clause of the First Amendment (B). *United States v. Lopez* (1995) held that Congress could not use the commerce clause to make possession of a gun in a school zone a federal crime (C). *Roe v. Wade* (1973) extended the right of privacy to a woman's decision to have an abortion (D).

39. **C.** Under the Articles of Confederation, sovereignty resided in the states; under the Constitution, sovereignty is shared between the central government and the states. The Articles of Confederation have no provision for the regulation of interstate trade, but under the Constitution, Congress may regulate interstate trade (A). Under the Articles of Confederation, taxes were the expressed power of the states; under the Constitution, Congress and the states share the power to tax (B). Under the Articles of Confederation there was no president, while under the Constitution the president is elected indirectly through the electoral college (D).

40. **D.** Many conservatives believe that the federal government has taken too much power away from state and local officials. They maintain that education should not be controlled by the federal government. Others have criticized the legislation, saying it doesn't go far enough to impose federal control over education. This position is associated with liberals, not conservatives.

41. D. Using the president's priorities and guidelines, the Office of Management and Budget authors the initial budget proposal that the president presents to Congress. This budget is then vigorously scrutinized by members of Congress and the Congressional Budget Office (C). The Department of the Treasury (A) and the National Economic Council play no direct role in the creation of the annual budget (B).

42. A. Shays' Rebellion and other acts of unrest convinced many that a new national government had to be created, with many more powers than were given to the government under the Articles of Confederation. The powers given to the national government as outlined in the U.S. Constitution were much greater.

43. C. Literacy tests and poll taxes were used for decades in the South to prevent African Americans from registering to vote.

44. D. Congress was involved in the policy adoption step, in which government adopts a plan of action, including the passage of legislation, to solve a problem. Agenda setting (A) is the recognition of an issue as a problem that must be addressed. Policy formulation (B) involves finding ways to solve the problem. Policy evaluation (C) is the analysis of policy and its impact upon the problem.

45. B. The ruling in *Texas v. Johnson* shows the importance the Supreme Court places on the concept of free expression as a First Amendment right.

46. D. Democrats (29%) are a larger percentage of the population than Republicans (23%). Independents (45%) are a larger percentage of the population than Democrats and Republicans combined (52%) (A). Republicans (23%) are a smaller percentage of the population than Democrats (29%) (B). Less than half of the population identifies as Independent (45%) (C).

47. A. Americans are becoming frustrated with the way the government is working, and low favorable ratings of the two major parties ensue. There is no correlation between claiming to be Independent and being undecided (B). Joining a political party does not cost money (C). The Democratic and Republican parties are perceived as becoming more moderate to attract more voters (D).

48. C. Special interest groups tend to have an upper-class bias within the group. Any size group can create an interest group (A). Any interest group can be successful in organizing (B). Special interest groups do not represent all segments of the population (D).

49. B. Pluralist theory suggests that interest groups compete in the political arena, with each promoting its policy preferences through organized efforts. Traditional democratic theory suggests that government depends on the consent of the governed, which may be given directly or through representatives (A). Elitist theory suggests that a small number of powerful elites, such as corporate leaders or top military officers, form an upper class that rules in its own self-interest (C). Bureaucratic theory suggests that a hierarchical structure and standardized procedures allow bureaucrats, who carry out the day-to-day workings of government, to control the government.

50. A. Because the terms of the members of the House of Representatives last only two years, the incumbency effect benefits members of the House of Representatives more than it benefits members of the Senate.

51. C. Frequently, during off-year elections, the party of the president may lose seats in Congress, changing the base of power. Off-year elections do not force the president to resign (A), nor does the political power of Congress increase (B). The Constitution changes only by amendment (D).

52. C. The success of the Civil Rights Movement after 1950 was aided by the movement's shift to the courts. The Fourteenth Amendment, ratified in 1868, defined citizenship and the rights of citizens (B). The number of African Americans in public office did not increase significantly until the 1970s (D).

53. A. The conference committee occurs latest in this list of steps in the passage of a bill through Congress. Conference committees are organized when the House and the Senate pass a bill in different forms. The steps in the passage of a bill are B, C, D, and A.

54. B. The best method for electing the president and vice president would be an independent group (electoral college) representing each state, chosen by the people. The Founding Fathers were fearful of electing the president and vice president by a popular vote of the people (A). Political parties were not provided for in the Constitution (C). The passage suggests that elections for president and vice president should not be held at one time and in one place, but rather in the individual states (D).

55. **B.** The Founding Fathers create this method for electing the president and vice president because they did not trust the people, Congress, or the state legislatures to elect the resident. It was a compromise between the large and small states (A) to get the Constitution approved. It reinforced federalism and gave the states a role in choosing the president (C). The Founding Fathers were fearful that citizens at that time were uninformed or not educated enough to elect the president or vice president and preferred this indirect method. (D).

Scoring the Free-Response Questions

1. Scoring the Concept Application Question: Total Value—3 points

(A) **1 point:** Describe a political institution, process, or behavior that links to the scenario. (Must link content from the scenario and provide a description to receive credit.) The powers Congress could use to address the issue (border wall) in the scenario include:

- Appropriations—Congress could pass or refuse to pass appropriations to pay for the wall
- Tax—Congress could raise taxes to gain revenue to pay for the wall
- Ratify treaties—Congress might ratify or refuse to ratify a treaty between the United States and Mexico concerning the border wall
- Pass legislation—Congress might pass legislation making the border wall unnecessary
- Override veto—Congress might override a presidential veto of legislation concerning the border wall

(B) **1 point:** Describe a political institution, process, or behavior that links to the scenario. (Must link content from the scenario and provide a description to receive credit.) Congress' powers might be affected by the president in the scenario by:

- Treaty—the president negotiates a treaty with Mexico concerning the border wall, and the Senate must ratify the treaty for it to become effective
- Executive agreement—the president negotiates agreement with Mexico to bypass Congress
- Veto power—the president might veto congressional legislation

(C) **1 point:** Explain how the scenario relates to a political institution, behavior, or process. (Must demonstrate how the use of the formal power describe in Part A can be affected by its interaction with linkage institutions.)

The news media acts as a watchdog over the government and reports to the people what the government is doing. If the media reports about the border wall in a negative manner, the public becomes informed and may speak out about their concerns. Interest groups may lobby Congress or the executive branch concerning issues about the border wall. Political parties may make the issue a part of their platform for future elections, and candidates representing the parties may campaign either supporting or opposing the building of the border wall, which will affect the results of the elections.

2. Scoring the Quantitative Analysis Question: Total Value—4 points

(A) **1 point:** Describe the data presented in the quantitative graphic.
The level of spending which increased the most between 1960 and 2011 was for Medicaid.

(B) **2 points:** Describe a pattern and draw a conclusion for that pattern. (Must describe a pattern for 1 point and draw a conclusion about the pattern for the second point.)

Answers may vary. Example of differences: large decreases in money spent on transportation and highways (33%), education and training (7%), income security was cut in half (19%), and health was changed to Medicaid with a substantial increase (43%). The conclusion might be that there was a refocus of needs in the purpose of federal grants and that government supported health care through Medicaid was important enough to be increased substantially.

(C) **1 point:** Explain how specific data in the quantitative graphic demonstrates the principle of federalism.

> Federalism is demonstrated in the pie charts through the government's grants of money to the states and local governments to help them deal with issues that they might not have sufficient funding to afford. The national government relies on the states to administer some federal policies, a practice called fiscal federalism. Grants-in-aid refers to the federal government giving money to the states for a purpose. These grants may be block grants (money given for a fairly broad purpose with few strings attached) or categorical grants (money given for a specific purpose that comes with restrictions concerning how the money should be spent).

3. **Scoring the SCOTUS Comparison Question: Total Value—4 points**

(A) **1 point:** Identify the constitutional issue that is common to both Supreme Court cases. The constitutional provision that is common to both *Betts v. Brady* and *Gideon v. Wainright* is the Sixth Amendment's right to counsel.

(B) **2 points:** Provide factual information from the required Supreme Court case (1 point) and explain how the reasoning and decisions of the required Supreme Court case apply to scenarios involving the Sixth Amendment (1 point).

> Clarence Earl Gideon was an uneducated, poor drifter who spent time in and out of prison for nonviolent crimes. He was charged with breaking and entering a pool hall, a felony under Florida law. During his trial, he asked the judge to appoint counsel for him because he could not afford an attorney. The judge denied Gideon's request because Florida law only permitted appointment of counsel for poor defendants charged with capital offenses. Gibeon then represented himself at his trial and was found guilty and sentenced to five years in prison. Gideon challenged his conviction and sentence claiming the judge's refusal to appoint counsel violated his constitutional rights. The Supreme Court held that the Sixth Amendment's guarantee of counsel is a fundamental right essential to a fair trial and, therefore, applies to the states through the Due Process Clause of the Fourteenth Amendment, overturning *Betts v. Brady*.

(C) **1 point:** Describe an interaction between the holding in the nonrequired Supreme Court case and a relevant political institution, behavior, or process.

> In *Betts v. Brady*, the Court ruled that the Sixth Amendment does not require states to provide counsel to all criminal defendants at trial. With this decision, state governments were free to continue as they had previously, denying the right to counsel in certain types of cases. This ruling was overturned by the court's ruling in *Gideon v. Wainwright*.

4. **Scoring the Argument Essay: Total Value: 6 points**

- **1 point:** Articulate a defensible claim or thesis that responds to the question and establishes a line of reasoning.
- **2 points:** Describe one piece of evidence from one of the listed foundational documents (1 point) that is accurately linked to the Articles of Confederation or Constitution being more democratic, and indicate how that evidence supports the argument (1 point). (Must show how evidence supports argument to earn second point.)
- **1 point:** Use a second piece of specific and relevant evidence to support the argument. (Must indicate how evidence supports argument.)
- **1 point:** Explain how or why the evidence supports the claim or thesis.
- **1 point:** Respond to an opposing or alternate perspective using refutation, concession, or rebuttal.

Score Conversion Worksheet

Using this worksheet, you can get a rough approximation of what your score would be on the AP U.S. Government and Politics Exam. Use the answer key to check the multiple-choice questions and the scoring rubrics to award yourself points on the free-response questions. Then compute your raw score on the exam using the worksheet. Finally, refer to the table below to translate your raw score to an AP score of 1 to 5.

Section I: Multiple Choice

Number of questions answered correctly (55 possible) _____ × 1.09 = _____

Section I: Free-Response

Question 1 (3 points possible): _____ × 5 = _____

Question 2 (4 points possible): _____ × 3.75 = _____

Question 3 (4 points possible): _____ × 3.75 = _____

Question 4 (6 points possible): _____ × 2.5= _____

RAW SCORE: Add your points in the column above (120 possible): _____

Conversion Table

RAW SCORE	APPROXIMATE AP SCORE
Mid-80s to 120	5
Mid-70s to low-mid-80s	4
High 40s to mid-70s	3
High 20s to high 40s	2
0 to high 20s	1

Note: At press time, the College Board has not released any information on the computation and conversion of raw scores for the new AP exam to be administered in May 2019. However, the College Board goes to great lengths to make sure that the scores on the new test will mean the same thing as on the old test with the same percentages of students scoring each grade (1–5). This score conversion worksheet is based on the assumption that the ranges for each grade (1–5) on the old test will stay about the same on the new test.

AP U.S. Government and Politics
Practice Exam 3

SECTION I
ANSWER SHEET

1 (A) (B) (C) (D)
2 (A) (B) (C) (D)
3 (A) (B) (C) (D)
4 (A) (B) (C) (D)
5 (A) (B) (C) (D)
6 (A) (B) (C) (D)
7 (A) (B) (C) (D)
8 (A) (B) (C) (D)
9 (A) (B) (C) (D)
10 (A) (B) (C) (D)
11 (A) (B) (C) (D)
12 (A) (B) (C) (D)
13 (A) (B) (C) (D)
14 (A) (B) (C) (D)
15 (A) (B) (C) (D)
16 (A) (B) (C) (D)
17 (A) (B) (C) (D)
18 (A) (B) (C) (D)
19 (A) (B) (C) (D)
20 (A) (B) (C) (D)

21 (A) (B) (C) (D)
22 (A) (B) (C) (D)
23 (A) (B) (C) (D)
24 (A) (B) (C) (D)
25 (A) (B) (C) (D)
26 (A) (B) (C) (D)
27 (A) (B) (C) (D)
28 (A) (B) (C) (D)
29 (A) (B) (C) (D)
30 (A) (B) (C) (D)
31 (A) (B) (C) (D)
32 (A) (B) (C) (D)
33 (A) (B) (C) (D)
34 (A) (B) (C) (D)
35 (A) (B) (C) (D)
36 (A) (B) (C) (D)
37 (A) (B) (C) (D)
38 (A) (B) (C) (D)
39 (A) (B) (C) (D)
40 (A) (B) (C) (D)

41 (A) (B) (C) (D)
42 (A) (B) (C) (D)
43 (A) (B) (C) (D)
44 (A) (B) (C) (D)
45 (A) (B) (C) (D)
46 (A) (B) (C) (D)
47 (A) (B) (C) (D)
48 (A) (B) (C) (D)
49 (A) (B) (C) (D)
50 (A) (B) (C) (D)
51 (A) (B) (C) (D)
52 (A) (B) (C) (D)
53 (A) (B) (C) (D)
54 (A) (B) (C) (D)
55 (A) (B) (C) (D)

AP U.S. Government and Politics
Practice Exam 3

Section I: Multiple-Choice Questions
Total Time—80 minutes
55 Questions

Directions: Each question or incomplete sentence below is followed by four suggested answers or completions. Select the one that is best, and then fill in the corresponding oval on the answer sheet.

1. The state of Texas is considering a proposed constitutional referendum to allow casino gambling which would create a state gambling commission and allow 21 casinos statewide. Which of the following is the best description of voter input on a constitutional amendment?
   (A) Participatory democracy
   (B) Pluralist democracy
   (C) Elite democracy
   (D) Hyper-pluralist democracy

2. Which of the following is an example of the system of checks and balances under the U.S. Constitution?
   (A) The president nominates federal judges and the House of Representatives confirms the appointments.
   (B) Congress can override Supreme Court decisions by majority vote of both houses of Congress.
   (C) The Senate can impeach federal officers, including the president, and the House of Representatives holds impeachment trials.
   (D) Congress can pass legislation over a presidential veto by a two-thirds vote of both houses of Congress.

3. Which of the following methods of financial aid from the national government to the states provide the broadest discretion in how the state spends the grant money?
   (A) Categorial grants
   (B) Project grants
   (C) Block grants
   (D) Formula grants

4. Which of the following accurately describes an exit poll?
   (A) A poll of voters taken immediately after they have voted and are leaving the polling place
   (B) An unofficial vote taken to acquire information on the general trend of opinion on a particular issue
   (C) A poll in which responses are obtained over several consecutive periods of time
   (D) A poll that serves as a standard by which other polls may later be measured

5. Which of the following is an accurate comparison of open and closed primaries?

	OPEN PRIMARY	CLOSED PRIMARY
(A)	Allows independent voters to participate in the election process	Strengthens party unity
(B)	Prevents "raiding" of the other party's primary	Only registered members of a particular political party can vote in the primary.
(C)	The voter does not have to be a member of a political party in order to vote in the primary.	Allows for "raiding" of the other party's primary
(D)	Voters must be a member of a particular political party in order to vote in the primary.	Voters do not have to be associated with a political party in order to vote in the primary.

GO ON TO THE NEXT PAGE

Questions 6 and 7 refer to the passage below.

". . . voters are not fools . . . individual voters act in odd ways . . . yet . . . the electorate behaves about as rationally and responsibly as we should expect, given the clarity of the alternatives presented . . . and the character of the information available to it . . . an electorate moved by concern about central and relevant questions of public policy, of governmental performance, and of executive personality."
— *The Responsible Electorate*, V.O. Key, Jr.

6. Which of the following statements is most consistent with the author's argument in this passage?
   (A) Voters do not take economic matters into account when making electoral choices.
   (B) Most elections are decided on a single issue.
   (C) Election returns do not establish why voters voted the way they did, only that the winner attracted a majority of votes.
   (D) Voters are most influenced by political party in making electoral decisions.

7. Based on the information in the passage, which of the following is the most likely suggestion of why voters' behaviors are important?
   (A) The theories show voters are rarely concerned about public policy and governmental performance.
   (B) The theories show that candidates and their advisers hope to understand why voters vote a certain way.
   (C) The theories show that economic interests are most important in political campaigns.
   (D) The theories show that most elections depend on a single issue.

8. The National Education Association's political action committee wants to donate funds to maximize its political influence in the next election. Which of the following would best accomplish this goal?
   (A) An incumbent from the House of Representatives
   (B) A presidential candidate
   (C) A member of the minority party
   (D) A challenger to a "safe-seat" representative

Questions 9 and 10 refer to the map below.

Capital Punishment in the United States, 2018

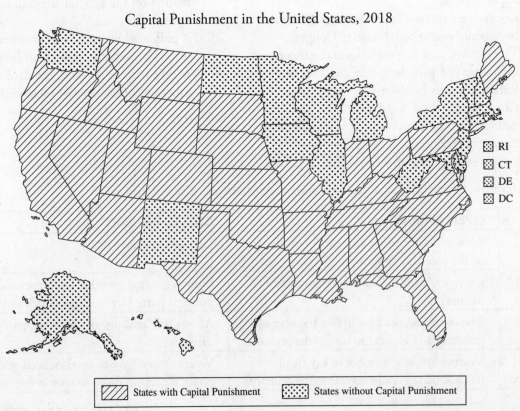

RI
CT
DE
DC

///// States with Capital Punishment   ::::: States without Capital Punishment

GO ON TO THE NEXT PAGE

9. Based on the map, which of the following is an accurate statement about capital punishment in the United States?
   (A) Capital punishment occurs most often in the southern and southwestern United States.
   (B) Capital punishment occurs most often in the northeastern and southeastern United States.
   (C) Capital punishment occurs most often in the northeastern and midwestern United States.
   (D) Capital punishment occurs least often in the midwestern and western United States.

10. Which of the following is best illustrated by the map on capital punishment in the United States?
    (A) Natural rights
    (B) Federalism
    (C) Popular sovereignty
    (D) Democracy

11. Which of the following best identifies the components of an iron triangle?
    (A) Congressional committees, regulatory commissions, and government corporations
    (B) Bureaucratic agencies, congressional committees, and interest groups
    (C) Interest groups, political parties, and political action committees
    (D) The legislative, executive, and judicial branches of government

12. Which of the following is an accurate comparison of the equal protection and due process clauses of the Fourteenth Amendment?

	EQUAL PROTECTION CLAUSE	DUE PROCESS CLAUSE
(A)	Helped bring about desegregation, integration, and affirmative action	Government must respect all the legal rights that are owed to a person according to the law.
(B)	Found in both the Fifth and Fourteenth Amendments	Core of the Civil Rights Movement
(C)	Implemented to ensure the fair treatment of all citizens of the United States	*Brown v. Board of Education* (1954)
(D)	*Gideon v. Wainwright* (1963)	Used to fulfill the belief that "all men are created equal" written in the Declaration of Independence

13. Ronald Reagan was elected president in 1980 and reelected in 1984. After serving two terms, many Republicans wanted Reagan to run for a third term of office. Which of the following was necessary before Reagan could run for a third term?
    (A) Repeal of the Twenty-Second Amendment
    (B) Repeal of the Twenty-Fifth Amendment
    (C) Special permission to run from Congress
    (D) Special permission to run from Congress and the Supreme Court

14. Which of the following accurately describes a major argument of Federalist #78?
    (A) Hamilton argued for a single executive under the Constitution.
    (B) Madison addressed the question of factions and how best to deal with them.
    (C) Madison addressed the issue of checks and balances and advocated a separation of powers within the national government.
    (D) Hamilton defended the importance of an independent judiciary and judicial review.

GO ON TO THE NEXT PAGE

15. Which of the following is most likely to support increased taxes on the rich?
    (A) Republican
    (B) Democrat
    (C) Libertarian
    (D) Conservative

16. On which constitutional principle did the Supreme Court base its ruling in *Citizens United v. Federal Elections Commission* (2010)?
    (A) Freedom of the press
    (B) Freedom of speech
    (C) Right to trial by jury
    (D) Right to an attorney

Questions 17 and 18 refer to the infographic below.

Amending the Constitution

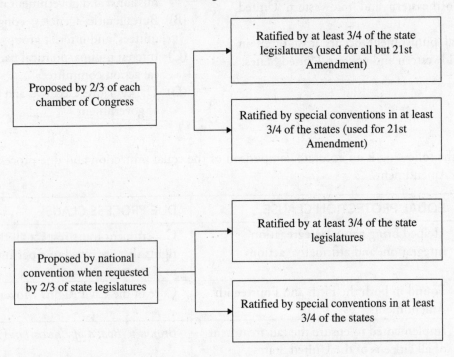

17. Based on the infographic, which of the following correctly illustrates the proposal and ratification process?
    (A) There are two methods which can be used to amend the Constitution.
    (B) Most amendments were ratified in special conventions in the states.
    (C) A national convention to amend the Constitution has been requested by the states only once.
    (D) Amendments are more often proposed by Congress and ratified by the state legislatures.

18. Based on the infographic, which of the following is best illustrated by the amendment process?
    (A) Popular sovereignty
    (B) Federalism
    (C) Natural rights
    (D) Republicanism

19. Which of the following Supreme Court cases is associated with the principle of judicial review?
    (A) *Marbury v. Madison* (1803)
    (B) *McCulloch v. Maryland* (1819)
    (C) *Brown v. Board of Education* (1954)
    (D) *New York Times Co. v. United States* (1971)

20. On which constitutional principle did the Supreme Court base its ruling in *Gideon v. Wainwright* (1961)?
    (A) Freedom of the press
    (B) Freedom of speech
    (C) Right to trial by jury
    (D) Right to an attorney

GO ON TO THE NEXT PAGE

21. In the election of 1980, Ronald Reagan defeated President Jimmy Carter in a landslide election. Many of the voters who cast ballots for Ronald Reagan did so in response to a worsening economy and the Iranian hostage crisis. Which of the following best explains this type of voting behavior?
    (A) Rational-choice voting
    (B) Prospective voting
    (C) Retrospective voting
    (D) Party-line voting

22. Which of the following is an accurate comparison of the Democratic and Republican parties?

	DEMOCRATIC PARTY	REPUBLICAN PARTY
(A)	The Affordable Care Act (Obamacare) provides guaranteed health care as a fundamental right for every American.	Supports guaranteeing lesbian, gay, bisexual, and transgender rights
(B)	Supports federal licensing of gun owners and national gun registration as a violation of the Second Amendment and an invasion of privacy	Supports gun control legislation including the registration of all guns; mandatory child safety locks; as well as requiring a photo license I.D., a background check, and a gun safety test in order to buy a new handgun
(C)	Normally aligns more closely with liberal ideology	Normally aligns more closely with conservative ideology
(D)	Every woman should have access to quality reproductive health care services, including safe and legal abortion.	Supports the belief in same-sex marriage and believes that Congress should have the ability to define marriage

23. Which of the following best illustrates major differences between the House of Representatives and the Senate?
    (A) The House of Representatives can filibuster a bill; the Senate requires limited debate on all bills.
    (B) Judicial confirmations take place in the House of Representatives; treaty ratification occurs in the Senate.
    (C) The House of Representatives brings charges of impeachment; the Senate passes amendments to the Constitution
    (D) Revenue bills must begin in the House of Representatives; impeachment trials take place in the Senate.

24. Which of the following is most likely to be a "swing" state in the next election?

	1980	1984	1988	1992	1996	2000	2004	2008	2012	2016
(A)	R	R	D	R	D	R	R	D	D	R
(B)	R	R	R	D	D	R	R	R	R	R
(C)	R	R	R	R	R	R	R	R	R	R
(D)	D	D	D	D	D	D	D	D	D	D

GO ON TO THE NEXT PAGE

Questions 25 and 26 refer to the passage below.

Adults Living in a Gun-owning Household

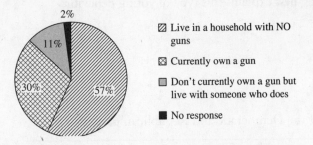

☑ Live in a household with NO guns

☒ Currently own a gun

▨ Don't currently own a gun but live with someone who does

■ No response

Source: Pew Research Center "Key Takeaways on Americans' Views of Guns and Gun Ownership" June 27, 2017 http://www.pewresearch.org/fact-tank/2017/06/22/key-takeaways-on-americans-views-of-guns-and-gun-ownership/

25. Which of the following accurately describes the information presented in the pie chart?
    (A) Three-fourths of adults in the United States do not own a gun.
    (B) More than 50% of adults live in a household with a gun.
    (C) Legislation restricting gun ownership has prevented most adults from owning a gun.
    (D) The total percentage of adults who live in a household with a gun is 41%.

26. Which of the following Supreme Court cases is relevant to the subject of the pie chart?
    (A) *United States v. Lopez* (1995)
    (B) *Gideon v. Wainwright* (1963)
    (C) *McDonald v. Chicago* (2010)
    (D) *Shaw v. Reno* (1993)

27. Which of the following most accurately reflects congressional control over the bureaucracy?
    (A) Congress appoints the heads of bureaucratic agencies and can remove them.
    (B) Congress can require agency heads to routinely appear before congressional committees.
    (C) Congress can issue fines to the bureaucracy for not following congressional directives.
    (D) Congress can submit *amicus curiae* briefs to the agency.

28. Which of the following most accurately describes the use of random sampling?
    (A) Asking every student in your high school to fill out a survey
    (B) Asking people on the internet to answer a public opinion poll
    (C) Developing a systematic process that gives all people an equal chance to be surveyed
    (D) Developing a poll that only asks yes and no questions

29. Which of the following is an accurate description of political parties today?
    (A) The role of political parties has been weakened due to candidate-centered campaigns.
    (B) The role of political parties has been strengthened by the winner-take-all system.
    (C) The role of political parties has been weakened by the introduction of third-party and independent candidates.
    (D) The role of political parties has been strengthened by the use of social media for campaign communication and fundraising.

Questions 30 and 31 refer to the passage below.

"... experience under the Articles led the Founding Fathers to favor more centralization of executive authority ... leadership was necessary to overcome the tendency toward inertia ... It enabled the American republic to meet the great crises of its history ... set up a permanent tension between the Presidency and the other branches of government ... presidential primacy, so indispensable to the political order, has turned into presidential supremacy ... become an imperial Presidency ... shift in the political balance between Congress and the Presidency ... increasing presidential domination of the legislative process or in the increasing delegation of power by Congress to presidents ... shift in the constitutional balance ... appropriation by the Presidency ... of powers reserved by the Constitution ... to Congress."

— *The Imperial Presidency*, Arthur Schlesinger

GO ON TO THE NEXT PAGE

30. Which of the following statements is most consistent with the author's argument in this passage?
    (A) The imperial presidency allowed Congress to become the most powerful branch of government, with the president approving almost all legislation Congress passed.
    (B) The checks and balances in the Constitution encourage an imperial presidency to exist.
    (C) The imperial presidency has allowed the president and Congress to work together without conflict.
    (D) Supporters of the imperial presidency argue that the president often needs to act more swiftly than would be possible if he or she had to wait for congressional approval.

31. Which of the following governmental policies would most likely occur under an imperial presidency?
    (A) An increase in the amount of congressional oversight of the executive branch
    (B) Passage of "New Deal" programs to combat the economy of the Great Depression
    (C) Declining executive discretion over the use of federal funds, which are increasingly committed to mandatory programs
    (D) A decrease in the size and authority of the executive branch

32. Which of the following is an accurate comparison of dual and cooperative federalism?

	DUAL FEDERALISM	COOPERATIVE FEDERALISM
(A)	Responsibilities of federal and state governments overlap, making no clear distinction between the two.	Best illustrated by federal grant-in-aid programs that encourage state governments to implement programs funded by Congress
(B)	Limits the power of the national government and gives states the ability to make their own decisions	Layer-cake federalism
(C)	Marble-cake federalism	Promotes competition between the national government and the states
(D)	State and federal governments remain supreme within their own spheres.	State and federal governments interact willingly and collectively to solve common problems.

GO ON TO THE NEXT PAGE

Questions 33 and 34 refer to the cartoon below.

Source: "Mike Keefe, InToon.com" Used with permission.

33. Which of the following best describes the message in the political cartoon?
    (A) Television provides the government with the most accurate information through the news.
    (B) As a part of the executive branch, the media serves as a linkage institution between government and the people.
    (C) The media's role in the political system is minor.
    (D) The media has a significant influence on society even though it is not a branch of government.

34. Which of the following Supreme Court cases is most relevant to the topic of the cartoon?
    (A) *New York Times Co. v. United States* (1971)
    (B) *McDonald v. Chicago* (2010)
    (C) *Baker v. Carr* (1961)
    (D) *Shaw v. Reno* (1993)

35. Which of the following most accurately describes the president's cabinet?
    (A) Its members must have experience serving in government.
    (B) All members have the same amount of influence on the president's agenda.
    (C) Its members cannot be fired by the president once they take office.
    (D) Its members serve at the will of the president and have differing levels of influence on the president.

GO ON TO THE NEXT PAGE

36. Which of the following is an accurate comparison of the Declaration of Independence and the Constitution?

	DECLARATION OF INDEPENDENCE	CONSTITUTION
(A)	Contains seven articles	Lists the grievances against the king
(B)	Is a formal statement by the people asserting their right to choose their own government	Replaced the Articles of Confederation as a framework for government
(C)	Included a Bill of Rights containing individual freedoms	Includes three separate branches of government
(D)	Is based on Enlightenment ideas of John Locke	Is based on the social contract theory of government

37. The practice of two members of the House of Representatives promising to vote for each other's legislation is
(A) Incumbency
(B) Casework
(C) Logrolling
(D) Pork barrel legislation

Questions 38–40 refer to the graph below.

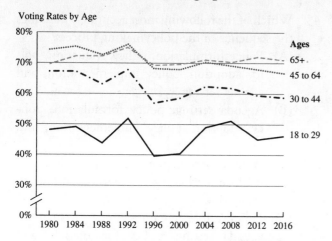

Voting Rates by Age

Source: U.S. Census Bureau https://www.census.gov/library/visualizations/2017/comm/voting-rates-age.html

38. Which of the following best describes a trend in the line graph above?
(A) Voting rates have increased for those age 65 and older since 1992.
(B) Voting rates have decreased for those age 18 to 29 since 2000.
(C) Voting rates have increased for those age 45 to 60 since 2004.
(D) Voting rates have decreased for those age 30 to 44 since 1980.

39. Which of the following accurately describes the information presented in the line graph?
(A) Voting rates in 2016 were highest for those age 45 to 64.
(B) Voting rates in 2016 were lowest for those age 18 to 29.
(C) Those age 65 and older have always had the highest voting rates.
(D) Voting rates for all age groups decreased in 2016.

40. Which of the following is an accurate conclusion based on a comparison of the trends in the line graph above and your knowledge of voter behavior?
(A) Younger voters are more likely to vote than older voters.
(B) Older voters are less likely to vote than younger voters.
(C) Younger voters are less likely to vote than older voters.
(D) Voting rates have increased in recent years for all voters.

41. Nominations to the Supreme Court must be approved in the Senate by a
(A) Simple majority
(B) Two-thirds majority
(C) Three-fourths majority
(D) Three-fifths majority

GO ON TO THE NEXT PAGE

42. Which of the following is an accurate statement about the Articles of Confederation?
    (A) The Articles of Confederation gave states with larger populations more representation in Congress than states with smaller populations.
    (B) The Articles of Confederation created a weak central government with most powers reserved to the states.
    (C) The Articles of Confederation provided for a strong military which was able to address the issue of Shays' Rebellion.
    (D) The Articles of Confederation provided for strong legislative, executive, and judicial branches of government.

43. Which of the following best illustrates how the ideologies of the two major parties shapes public policy?
    (A) The Democratic Party platform generally aligns more closely to conservative ideology.
    (B) The Republican party Platform generally aligns more closely to libertarian ideology.
    (C) The Democratic party platform generally aligns more closely to liberal ideology.
    (D) The Republican party platform generally aligns more closely to liberal ideology.

44. In 2020, a census of the population will be taken and based on that census, the House of Representatives will be reapportioned. Which of the following most accurately explains why the House of Representatives will need to be reapportioned?
    (A) Because the House of Representatives is based on population, when there are population changes across the country, the number of seats in the House of Representatives must be adjusted among the states to reflect those changes.
    (B) The House of Representatives needs to be enlarged to reflect population growth in the country.
    (C) Congressional districts must be redrawn to reflect changes in the state's population.
    (D) Because the House of Representatives is based on equality, population changes across the country have no effect on how seats in the House of Representatives are divided among the states.

45. Which of the following most accurately describes the sequence in the policymaking process?
    (A) Policy formulation, policy evaluation, policy adoption, policy implementation, and agenda setting
    (B) Agenda setting, policy formulation, policy adoption, policy implementation, and policy evaluation
    (C) Policy adoption, policy implementation, policy formulation, agenda setting, and policy evaluation
    (D) Policy implementation, policy evaluation, agenda setting, policy formulation, and policy adoption

GO ON TO THE NEXT PAGE

Questions 46–48 refer to the graph below.

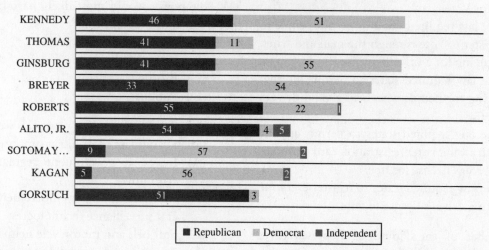

POLITICAL PARTY VOTE FOR SUPREME
COURT CONFIRMATION

Source: U.S. Senate https://www.senate.gov/pagelayout/reference/nominations/Nominations.htm

46. Which of the following statements is reflected in the data in the graph?
    (A) Justice Kagan had the highest number of votes for confirmation.
    (B) Justice Thomas had the lowest number of votes for confirmation.
    (C) Justice Ginsburg had the highest number of Republican votes for confirmation.
    (D) Justice Kagan had the lowest number of Democratic votes for confirmation.

47. Which of the following is an accurate statement concerning the Supreme Court confirmation process?
    (A) The president nominates, and the House of Representative confirms appointments.
    (B) The House of Representatives nominates, and the Senate confirms appointments.
    (C) The Senate nominates, and the House of Representatives confirms appointments.
    (D) The president nominates, and the Senate confirms appointments.

48. If a member of the president's cabinet disagrees with the president, which of the following is most likely to occur?
    (A) The president must have the approval of both houses of Congress to dismiss the official from his or her cabinet position and his administration.
    (B) The president may dismiss the official from his or her cabinet position and his administration.
    (C) The president cannot proceed without the full approval of the cabinet.
    (D) The president must have the approval of the Supreme Court to dismiss the official from his or her cabinet position and his administration.

49. Which of the following is the single largest influence on a person's political socialization?
    (A) The geographic region of the country where the person lives
    (B) The religious beliefs of the person
    (C) The political beliefs and party affiliation of the person's family
    (D) The schools and the educational background of the person

GO ON TO THE NEXT PAGE

50. In 1993 the National Voter Registration Act (Motor Voter Law) was passed by Congress. Which of the following most accurately describes the Motor Voter Law?
    (A) The law required states to permit people to register to vote through the mail and when applying for a driver's license.
    (B) The law required states to permit internet voting for people who held a valid driver's license.
    (C) The law required states to permit anyone with a valid voter registration card to obtain a driver's license for free.
    (D) The law required states to register everyone with a driver's license to vote.

51. A member of the House of Representatives has introduced a bill to reform Social Security. Once the bill has cleared its assigned committee, which of the following must occur before the bill is debated on the floor of the House of Representatives?
    (A) The bill must be forwarded to the Senate.
    (B) The bill must be amended.
    (C) The bill must pass the House Rules Committee.
    (D) The bill must be signed by the Speaker of the House.

52. Which of the following amendments is correctly paired with a Supreme Court case involving that amendment?
    (A) First Amendment – *Roe v. Wade* (1973)
    (B) Second Amendment – *Tinker v. Des Moines Independent Community School District* (1969)
    (C) Sixth Amendment – *Shaw v. Reno* (1993)
    (D) Fourteenth Amendment – *Brown v. Board of Education* (1954)

53. The belief that the "necessary and proper" clause and the "supreme law of the land" clause would make the central government an uncontrollable power would most likely have been held by which of the following?
    (A) Alexander Hamilton
    (B) James Madison
    (C) Brutus
    (D) Publius

54. Which of the following proposals would a Libertarian candidate most likely support?
    (A) Increased government regulation of the economy
    (B) Restrictions on law enforcement use of general surveillance technologies
    (C) Seat belt and motorcycle helmet laws
    (D) An increase in mandatory taxes

55. Which of the following is a characteristic of a valid, scientific public opinion poll?
    (A) Random, representative sample of respondents
    (B) Small sample size and high margin of error
    (C) Telephone or internet responses included
    (D) Variations in question wording

STOP. END OF SECTION I

Section II: Free-Response Questions
Total Time—100 minutes

Directions: You have 100 minutes to answer all four of the following questions. Respond to all parts of all four questions. Before beginning to write, you should take a few minutes to plan and outline each answer. Spend approximately 20 minutes each on questions 1, 2, and 3 and 40 minutes on question 4. Illustrate your essay with substantive examples where appropriate.

1. President Trump on Monday nominated Judge Brett M. Kavanaugh ... to fill Justice Anthony M. Kennedy's seat on the Supreme Court, setting up an epic confirmation battle and potentially cementing the court's rightward tilt for a generation ... Justice Kennedy, who is retiring, held the swing vote in many closely divided cases on issues like abortion, affirmative action, gay rights and the death penalty. Replacing him with a committed conservative, who could potentially serve for decades, will fundamentally alter the balance of the court and put dozens of precedents at risk ... In his remarks, Judge Kavanaugh, who once clerked for Justice Kennedy, said he would "keep an open mind in every case." But he declared that judges "must interpret the law, not make the law."

—*New York Times*, July 9, 2018

After reading the scenario, respond to A, B, and C below:
(A) Describe the role of the Senate in the process of filling a vacancy in the Supreme Court.
(B) In the context of the scenario, explain how the role of the Senate described in Part A can be affected by its interaction with the executive branch.
(C) In the context of the scenario, explain how the confirmation process can be impacted by linkage institutions.

2017 Poverty Rate in the United States

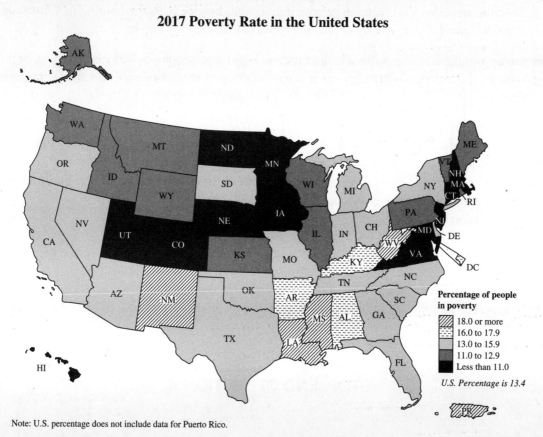

Percentage of people in poverty

- 18.0 or more
- 16.0 to 17.9
- 13.0 to 15.9
- 11.0 to 12.9
- Less than 11.0

U.S. Percentage is 13.4

Note: U.S. percentage does not include data for Puerto Rico.

Source: U.S. Census Bureau https://www.census.gov/library/visualizations/2018/comm/acs-poverty-map.html

GO ON TO THE NEXT PAGE

2. Use the information from the map above to answer the questions.
   (A) Identify the most common poverty level of states in the Southeast.
   (B) Describe a similarity or difference in poverty levels by state or region, as illustrated in the map, and draw a conclusion about that similarity or difference.
   (C) Explain how the poverty level as shown in the map demonstrates the principle of federalism.

3. The Church of Lukumi Babalu Aye practiced Santeria, a religion based on African, Caribbean, and Roman Catholic practices. Santeria engaged in animal sacrifice to "keep the spirits alive" as a form of worship. After the church announced plans to establish a church in Hialeah, Florida, the city council held an emergency public meeting and unanimously passed several laws prohibiting the ritual sacrifice of animals. Violations were punishable by fines, imprisonment, or both.

   In *Church of the Lukumi Babalu Aye v. City of Hialeah,* (1993), the Supreme Court unanimously held that laws targeting specific religions violate the First Amendment: "... a law that burdens religious practice need not be justified by a compelling governmental interest if it is neutral and of general applicability. However, where such a law is not neutral or not of general application, it must undergo the most rigorous of scrutiny: It must be justified by a compelling governmental interest and must be narrowly tailored to advance that interest. Neutrality and general applicability are interrelated, and failure to satisfy one requirement is a likely indication that the other has not been satisfied." The city ordinances that had been passed to prevent animal sacrifices in connection with Santeria rituals were therefore held unconstitutional by the Supreme Court.

   (A) Identify the constitutional clause that is common to both *Church of the Lukumi Babalu Aye, Inc. v. City of Hialeah* (1993) and *Wisconsin v. Yoder* (1972).
   (B) Based on the constitutional clause identified in part A, explain why the facts of *Wisconsin v. Yoder* led to a different holding than the holding in *Church of the Lukumi Babalu Aye, Inc. v. City of Hialeah.*
   (C) Describe an action that members of the public who disagree with the holding in *Church of the Lukumi Babalu Aye, Inc. v. City of Hialeah* could take to limit its impact.

4. Develop an argument that explains which of the models of representation—trustee, delegate, or politico—best achieves the founders' intent for American democracy in terms of ensuring a stable government run by the people.

   In your essay, you must:
   - Articulate a defensible claim or thesis that responds to the prompt and establishes a line of reasoning.
   - Support your claim with at least TWO pieces of accurate and relevant information:
     - At least ONE piece of evidence must be from one of the following foundational documents:
       — Declaration of Independence
       — Federalist #10
       — U.S. Constitution
     - Use a second piece of evidence from another foundational document from the list or from your study of the electoral process.
   - Use reasoning to explain why your evidence supports your claim/thesis.
   - Respond to an opposing or alternative perspective using refutation, concession, or rebuttal.

STOP. END OF SECTION II

Answer Key for Multiple-Choice Questions

1. A	16. B	31. B	46. B
2. D	17. D	32. D	47. D
3. C	18. B	33. D	48. B
4. A	19. A	34. A	49. C
5. A	20. D	35. D	50. A
6. C	21. C	36. B	51. C
7. B	22. C	37. C	52. D
8. A	23. D	38. D	53. C
9. A	24. A	39. B	54. B
10. B	25. D	40. C	55. A
11. B	26. C	41. A	
12. A	27. B	42. B	
13. A	28. C	43. C	
14. D	29. A	44. A	
15. B	30. D	45. B	

› Answers and Explanations for the Multiple-Choice Questions

1. **A.** Participatory democracy is the concept of traditional democratic theory which includes direct and representative democracy. Pluralist democracy occurs when interest groups compete in the political arena, with each promoting its own policy preference (B). Elite democracy occurs when a small number of powerful elites such as corporate leaders rule in their own self-interest (C). Hyper-pluralist theory suggests that many groups are pulling government in different directions at the same time, causing gridlock and ineffectiveness (D).

2. **D.** Congress can override a presidential veto by a two-thirds vote of both houses. The Senate confirms federal judge appointments (A), Congress cannot override Supreme Court decisions (B), and the House of Representatives brings charges of impeachment, whereas the Senate holds impeachment trials (C).

3. **C.** Block grants can be used for a variety of purposes within a broad category with few strings attached. Categorical grants have a specific purpose and may have strings attached (A), project grants are a form of categorical grant awarded based on a competitive application (B), and formula grants are a form of categorical grant awarded based on an established formula (D).

4. **A.** An exit poll is a poll of voters taken immediately after they have voted and are leaving the polling place. A straw poll is an unofficial vote taken to acquire information on the general trend of opinion on an issue (B). A poll in which responses are obtained over several consecutive periods of time is a tracking poll (C). A benchmark is a poll that serves as a standard by which other polls may later be measured (D).

5. **A.** Open primaries allow independent voters to participate, and closed primaries help strengthen party unity. Closed primaries prevent party raiding (B), open primaries allow for party raiding (C), and in an open primary, voters do not have to be associated with a political party, but in a closed primary, voters must be a member of a political party to vote (D).

6. **C.** Voters often take economic matters into account in elections (A). Most elections are decided based on a variety of issues (B). Voters are influenced by many factors, including personal background of the candidate, campaign issues, voter image or perception of the candidate, propaganda, and political party (D).

7. **B.** If candidates and campaigns can understand why voters vote a certain way, they can manage their campaigns to attract those voters to their candidate. Studies have shown that voters are concerned about public policy and governmental performance (A), as well as many other issues (D). Economic interest may be one of many issues in a campaign (C).

8. **A.** Political action committees often donate to incumbents because they may already have a relationship with the incumbent and the high rate of reelection of incumbents in the House of Representatives (D). A presidential candidate (B) and member of the minority party (C) would have less influence in the House of Representatives. The challenger to a "safe-seat" representative most likely would not win election and therefore have no power.

9. **A.** The map shows that capital punishment is most common in the southern and southwestern United States.

10. **B.** The map best illustrates federalism since each state can decide for itself if it wants to use capital punishment. Natural rights are the basic rights that are guaranteed to all people (A). Popular sovereignty occurs when people are the source of governmental authority (C). Democracy is a system of government with the people ruling directly or through representative government (D).

11. **B.** Iron triangles are composed of bureaucratic agencies, congressional committees, and interest

groups. Regulatory commissions and government corporations are not part of iron triangles (A). Political parties and political action committees are not part of iron triangles (C). The three branches of government are not part of iron triangles (D).

12. **A.** The core of the Civil Rights Movement was the equal protection clause (B). The equal protection clause was used as a basis for *Brown v. Board of Education* and helped bring about desegregation in public schools (C). *Gideon v. Wainwright* was decided based on the due process clause (D).

13. **A.** The Twenty-Second Amendment limits the president to two elected terms of office. The Constitution would have to be amended with a repeal of the Twenty-Second Amendment to allow a president to run for a third term. The Twenty-Fifth Amendment deals with presidential succession and disability (B). Neither Congress nor the Supreme Court can give permission for a president to run for a third term (C and D).

14. **D.** In Federalist #78, Alexander Hamilton defended the importance of an independent judiciary and judicial review. Hamilton argued for a single executive under the Constitution in Federalist #70 (A). Madison addressed the question of factions and how best to deal with them in Federalist #10 (B). Madison addressed the issue of checks and balances and advocated a separation of powers within the national government in Federalist #51 (C).

15. **B.** Democrats are most likely to support increased taxes on the rich. Republicans, libertarians, and conservatives would most likely support tax decreases (A, C, and D).

16. **B.** *Citizens United v. Federal Elections Commission* involved dealing with regulation of political campaign spending by organizations as a form of free speech.

17. **D.** There are four methods of amending the Constitution (A). Most amendments were ratified by state legislatures (B). A national convention to amend the Constitution has never been used (C).

18. **B.** The amendment process is an example of federalism because both the national government (proposal stage) and the states (ratification stage) are needed to amend the constitution. Popular sovereignty occurs when people are the source of governmental authority (A). Natural rights are the basic rights that are guaranteed to all people (C). Republicanism is a state in which supreme power is held by the people and their elected representatives (D).

19. **A.** *Marbury v. Madison* is the Supreme Court case that established the principle of judicial review in 1803. *McCulloch v. Maryland* established that the necessary and proper clause of the U.S. Constitution gives the federal U.S. government certain implied powers that are not explicitly enumerated in the Constitution and the supremacy of the Constitution under Article VI. (B) *Brown v. Board of Education* declared state laws establishing separate public schools for black and white students to be unconstitutional (C). *New York Times Co. v. United States* reaffirmed freedom of the press and the unconstitutionality of prior restraint in the publishing of the Pentagon Papers (D).

20. **D.** In *Gideon v. Wainwright,* the Supreme Court unanimously ruled that states are required under the Sixth Amendment to the U.S. Constitution to provide an attorney to defendants in criminal cases who are unable to afford their own attorneys.

21. **C.** Retrospective voting is voting to decide whether the party or candidate in power should be a re-elected based on the recent past. Rational-choice voting is based on what is perceived to be in the U.S. citizen's individual interest (A). Prospective voting is based on predictions of how a party or candidate will perform in the future (B). Party-line voting is supporting a party by voting for candidates from one political party for all public offices across the ballot (D).

22. **C.** The Democratic party supports guarantees for lesbian, gay, bisexual, and transgender rights (A); supports gun control legislation, including the registration of all guns, mandatory child safety locks, requiring a photo license I.D., a background check, and a gun safety test to buy

a new handgun (B); and supports the belief in same-sex marriage (D).

23. **D.** The Senate can filibuster a bill, whereas the House of Representatives requires limited debate on all bills (A). Judicial confirmations and treaty ratification take place in the Senate (B). Amendments require proposal by two-thirds of both houses of Congress and ratification by three-fourths of either the state legislatures or state conventions (C).

24. **A.** A swing state refers to any state that could reasonably be won by either the Democratic or Republican presidential candidate; therefore, these states are usually targeted by both major-party campaigns, especially in competitive elections.

25. **D.** The total percentage of adults who live in a household with a gun is 41% (30% + 11%). Sixty-eight % (11% + 57%) of adults in the United States do not own a gun (A). Forty-one % (30 % + 11%) of adults live in a household with a gun (B). The graph does not illustrate if legislation restricting gun ownership has prevented most adults from owning a gun (C).

26. **C.** The subject of the pie chart is adults living in a gun-owning household, which relates to the Second Amendment and *McDonald v. Chicago*. The Court held that the right of an individual to "keep and bear arms" is protected under the Second and Fourteenth Amendments. *United States v. Lopez* dealt with the issue of federalism and the powers of Congress under the commerce clause (A). *Gideon v. Wainwright* held that states are required under the Sixth Amendment to the U.S. Constitution to provide an attorney to defendants in criminal cases who are unable to afford their own attorneys (B). *Shaw v. Reno* held that redistricting based on race must be held to a standard of strict scrutiny under the equal protection clause and that those doing the redistricting must ensure compliance with the Voting Rights Act of 1965 (D).

27. **B.** The heads of bureaucratic agencies are either appointed by the president with Senate confirmation or hired under the merit system (A). Congress determines the funding of bureaucratic agencies but cannot fine the bureaucracy (C). *Amicus curiae* briefs are presented to the courts by interested groups or individuals who are not party to the case but who support or reject arguments of the case (D).

28. **C.** Random sampling is a systematic process that gives all people an equal chance to be surveyed. Asking every student in your high school to fill out a survey (A), asking people on the internet to answer a public opinion poll (B), or developing a poll that only asks yes and no questions (D) would not meet the criteria for random sampling.

29. **A.** The role of political parties has been decreased by the winner-take-all system (B). The introduction of third-party and independent candidates has been shown to have little effect on the major parties (C). The role of political parties has been lessened by the use of social media for campaign communication and fundraising because social media allows the candidates to bypass the political party and reach out directly to the people (D).

30. **D.** In an imperial presidency, Congress defers many of its powers to the president (A). The checks and balances in the Constitution should prevent an imperial presidency (B). An imperial presidency might create conflict between the president and Congress (C).

31. **B.** An imperial presidency would likely lead to a decrease in the amount of congressional oversight of the executive branch (A), increasing executive discretion over the use of federal funds (C), and an increase in the size and authority of the executive branch (D).

32. **D.** Responsibilities of federal and state governments overlap, making no clear distinction between the two in cooperative federalism (A). Dual federalism is sometimes referred to as "layer-cake" federalism because of the separation between the two levels of government (B). Dual federalism promotes competition between the national government and the states, while cooperative federalism is sometimes referred to a "marble-cake" federalism because of the interaction and cooperation between the two levels of government (C).

33. **D.** Although the media is not a branch of government, they are sometimes referred to as the "fourth estate," a force or institution whose influence is not officially recognized. The government receives much of its information through official government channels and all forms of media (A). Although the media serves as a linkage institution between government and the people, they are not a part of government (B). Today, the media serves a major role in the political system (C).

34. **A.** The subject of the cartoon was the three branches of government and included the media as one of the three branches. The power and role of the media was questioned in *New York Times Co. v. United States*, where the Court ruled on freedom of the press and prior restraint under the First Amendment. In *McDonald v. Chicago*, the Court held that the right of an individual to "keep and bear arms" is protected under the Second and Fourteenth Amendments (B). *Baker v. Carr* established the right of federal courts to review redistricting issues, which had previously been termed "political questions" outside the courts' jurisdiction and determined that congressional districts within a state must be equal in population (C). *Shaw v. Reno* held that redistricting based on race must be held to a standard of strict scrutiny under the equal protection clause and that those doing the redistricting must ensure compliance with the Voting Rights Act of 1965 (D).

35. **D.** The members of the cabinet serve at the will of the president and have differing levels of influence on the president. There are no formal qualifications for cabinet members (A). Different presidents have given differing amounts of influence to members of their cabinet (B). The president can ask for the resignation of cabinet members, especially if those members do not support the president's agenda (C).

36. **B.** The Declaration of Independence lists the grievances against the king, and the Constitution contains seven articles (A). The Constitution includes a Bill of Rights containing individual freedoms (C). The Declaration of Independence was based on the social contract theory of government (D).

37. **C.** Logrolling is the practice of two members of the House of Representatives promising to vote for each other's legislation. Incumbency is the holding of an office (A). Casework is the assistance given to constituents by congressional members or their staff either answering questions or helping them with problems (B). Pork barrel legislation is legislation that brings benefits to constituents through sometimes unnecessary or unwise projects within a state or district, to enhance the member's chances of getting reelected (D).

38. **D.** Voting rates have decreased for those age 30 to 44 since 1980. Voting rates have decreased for those age 65 and older since 1992 (A). Voting rates have increased for those age 18 to 29 since 2000 (B). Voting rates have decreased for those age 45 to 60 since 2004 (C).

39. **B.** Voting rates in 2016 were lowest for those age 18 to 29. Voting rates in 2016 were highest for those age 65 and older (A). Those age 45 to 64 have had the highest voting rates in the year shown (C). Voting rates increased in 2016 for those 18 to 29 (D).

40. **C.** Younger voters are less likely to vote than older voters (A and B). Voting rates have increased in recent years only for those 18 to 29 (D).

41. **A.** Nominations to the Supreme Court must be approved by a simple majority vote, or one-half plus one.

42. **B.** The Articles of Confederation gave each state equal representation in Congress (A). The Articles of Confederation only allowed the national government to request troops from the states, giving the country either a weak military or no military (C). The Articles of Confederation provided for only a weak legislative branch of government (D).

43. **C.** The Democratic Party platform generally aligns more closely to liberal ideology (A). The Republican Party platform generally aligns more closely to conservative ideology (B and D).

44. **A.** The House of Representatives is set by the Reapportionment Act of 1929 at 435 and cannot be enlarged unless Congress passes new

legislation to change the law (B). The redrawing of congressional districts to reflect changes in the state's population is called redistricting and is done after reapportionment occurs (C). The House of Representatives is based on population, and population changes across the country will affect how seats in the House of Representatives are divided among the states (D).

45. B. The policymaking process involves agenda setting, policy formulation, policy adoption, policy implementation, and policy evaluation.

46. B. Justice Kagan had the highest number of votes for confirmation (A). Justice Roberts had the highest number of Republican votes for confirmation (C). Justice Gorsuch had the lowest number of Democratic votes for confirmation (D).

47. D. The president nominates and the Senate confirms appointments.

48. B. The president may dismiss the official from his or her cabinet position in his administration without the approval of either house of Congress (A), the cabinet (C), or the Supreme Court (D).

49. C. The single largest influence on a person's political socialization is their family's political affiliation. Although the geographic region of the country where the person lives (A), religious beliefs of the person (B), and schools and the educational background of the person (D) do influence socialization, they are not more influential than family.

50. A. States are not required to permit internet voting (B). States are not required to permit anyone with a valid voter registration card to obtain a driver's license for free (C). States are not required to register everyone with a driver's license to vote (D).

51. C. All bills in the House of Representatives must pass the House Rules Committee, which determines under what rules, such as for how long, and under what conditions the full body will debate bills, before they can be debated on the House floor. Bills do not have to be sent to the Senate (A), be amended (B), or be signed by the Speaker of the House (D) prior to debate.

52. D. *Roe v. Wade* was decided based on the right to privacy under the due process clause of the Fourteenth Amendment (A). *Tinker v. Des Moines Independent Community School District* was decided on freedom of speech under the First Amendment (B). *Shaw v. Reno* was decided based on the equal protection clause of the Fourteenth Amendment (C).

53. C. The *Federalist Papers*, written in support of the U.S. Constitution, which includes the necessary and proper clause and the supremacy clause, were written by Alexander Hamilton (A), James Madison (B) under the pseudonym of Publius (D). Brutus, thought to be Robert Yates, was an Anti-Federalist writing to oppose the U.S. Constitution's ratification by the states.

54. B. The Libertarian Party is a political party in the United States that promotes civil liberties, noninterventionism, laissez-faire capitalism, and decreasing the size and scope of government. Libertarians would oppose increased government regulation of the economy (A), seat belt and motorcycle helmet laws (C), and increases in taxes (D).

55. A. A valid, scientific public opinion poll should have a random, representative sample of respondents. The sample size should be adequate to ensure randomness, and the margin of error should be small (B). Internet responses should not be included, as they are seldom random or representative (C). Question wording should not be ambiguous or biased and should be the same for all respondents (D).

Scoring the Free-Response Questions

1. **Scoring the Concept Application Question: Total Value—3 points**
   (A) **1 point:** Describe a political institution, process, or behavior that links to the scenario. The role of the Senate in the process of filling a vacancy in the Supreme Court includes the following:
   - When a vacancy on the Supreme Court occurs, the president nominates a replacement to fill that vacancy, usually someone who supports the president's agenda.
   - The nomination is sent to the Senate Judiciary Committee for consideration.
   - The Senate Judiciary Committee holds a hearing on the nominee, relying on information collected by the FBI and other sources. During the hearings, witnesses, both supporting and opposing the nomination, present their views. Senators question the nominee on his or her qualifications, judgment, and philosophy.
   - The Judiciary Committee then votes on the nominations and sends a recommendation to the full Senate regarding whether the nominee should be confirmed or rejected, or if no recommendation will be given.
   - The full Senate debates the nomination, with Senate rules allowing unlimited debate unless cloture is invoked.
   - The full Senate votes on the nomination, with a simple majority of Senators present and voting required to confirm the nominee. In cases of a tie, the President of the Senate (Vice President) casts the deciding vote.

   (B) **1 point:** Explain how the response in part (A) affects or is affected by a political process, government entity, or citizen behavior as related to the scenario. (Must link content from the scenario and provide a description to receive credit.)

   The role of the Senate can be affected by the Senate's interaction with the executive branch because the Senate relies on the executive branch agencies, such as the FBI, to provide information concerning the nominee prior to the Senate Judiciary hearings. Members of the Senate could also be informally lobbied by the president or his staff to support a nominee.

   (C) **1 point:** In the context of the scenario, explain how the confirmation process can be impacted by linkage institution.

   Interest groups often weigh in on Supreme Court nominees by sending information to the Senate Judiciary Committee. One example would be the American Bar Association, which rates nominees based on professional competence and previous rulings. These ratings can have an impact on how members of the committee question or vote on the nominee.

2. **Scoring the Quantitative Analysis Question: Total Value—4 points**
   (A) **1 point:** Describe the data presented in the quantitative graphic.
   The most common poverty level by states in the Southeast is 13 to 15.9%.
   (B) **2 points:** Describe a similarity or difference and draw a conclusion about that similarity or difference. (Must describe a similarity or difference for 1 point and draw a conclusion about the similarity or difference for the second point.)

   Answers may vary. Example: The poverty rate in New Mexico is higher than the poverty rate in Alaska. The poverty rate in Alaska is lower because Alaska has higher taxes and spends more on social welfare programs.

(C) **1 point:** Explain how specific data in the quantitative graphic demonstrates the principle of federalism.

The data in the graphic demonstrates federalism because it shows that the states have the authority to spend on anti-poverty programs as they see fit and that the federal government has no say in how or how much the states spend to address the poverty issue.

3. **Scoring the SCOTUS Comparison Question: Total Value—4 points**
    (A) **1 point:** Identify the constitutional clause that is common to both Supreme Court cases.
    The constitutional provision that is common to both *Church of the Lukumi Babalu Aye, Inc. v. City of Hialeah* (1993) and *Wisconsin v. Yoder* (1972) is the free exercise clause of the First Amendment.
    (B) **2 points:** Provide factual information from the required Supreme Court case (1 point) and explain how the reasoning and decisions of the required Supreme Court case apply to scenarios involving freedom of religion (1 point).

    In *Wisconsin v. Yoder*, the Supreme Court ruled that Amish children could not be required to attend school under compulsory education laws beyond the 8th grade. The fundamental right to freedom of religion was determined to outweigh the state's interest in educating the children. In *Church of the Lukumi Babalu Aye, Inc. v. City of Hialeah*, the Court held that because the law targeted a specific religious practice, the state must provide a compelling interest for the law, which it did not.
    (C) **1 point:** Describe an interaction between the holding in the nonrequired Supreme Court case and a relevant political institution, behavior, or process.

    Members of the public who disagree with the holding in *Church of the Lukumi Babalu Aye, Inc. v. City of Hialeah* could form a social movement or interest group to lobby public officials for legislation to address a compelling government interest such as sanitation or health issues.

4. **Scoring the Argument Essay: Total Value: 6 points**
    - **1 point:** Articulate a defensible claim or thesis that responds to the question and establishes a line of reasoning.
    - **2 points:** Describe one piece of evidence from one of the listed foundational documents (1 point) that is accurately linked to one of the models of representation, and indicate how that evidence supports the argument (1 point). (Must show how evidence supports the argument to earn the second point.)
    - **1 point:** Use a second piece of specific and relevant evidence to support the argument. (Must indicate how evidence supports the argument.)
    - **1 point:** Explain how or why the evidence supports the claim or thesis.
    - **1 point:** Respond to an opposing or alternate perspective using refutation, concession, or rebuttal.

Score Conversion Worksheet

Using this worksheet, you can get a rough approximation of what your score would be on the AP U.S. Government and Politics Exam. Use the answer key to check the multiple-choice questions and the scoring rubrics to award yourself points on the free-response questions. Then compute your raw score on the exam using the worksheet below. Finally, refer to the table below to translate your raw score to an AP score of 1 to 5.

Section I: Multiple-Choice

Number of questions answered correctly (55 possible) _____ × 1.09 = _____

Section I: Free-Response

Question 1 (3 points possible): _____ × 5 = _____

Question 2 (4 points possible): _____ × 3.75 = _____

Question 3 (4 points possible): _____ × 3.75 = _____

Question 4 (6 points possible): _____ × 2.5 = _____

RAW SCORE: Add your points in the column above (120 possible): _____

Conversion Table

RAW SCORE	APPROXIMATE AP SCORE
Mid-80s to 120	5
Mid-70s to low-mid-80s	4
High-40s to mid-70s	3
High-20s to high-40s	2
0 to high-20s	1

Note: At press time, the College Board has not released any information on the computation and conversion of raw scores for the new AP exam to be administered in May 2019. However, the College Board goes to great lengths to make sure that the scores on the new test will mean the same thing as on the old test with the same percentages of students scoring each grade (1–5). This score conversion worksheet is based on the assumption that the ranges for each grade (1–5) on the old test will stay about the same on the new test.

AP U.S. Government and Politics
Practice Exam 4

SECTION I
ANSWER SHEET

1 (A) (B) (C) (D)	21 (A) (B) (C) (D)	41 (A) (B) (C) (D)
2 (A) (B) (C) (D)	22 (A) (B) (C) (D)	42 (A) (B) (C) (D)
3 (A) (B) (C) (D)	23 (A) (B) (C) (D)	43 (A) (B) (C) (D)
4 (A) (B) (C) (D)	24 (A) (B) (C) (D)	44 (A) (B) (C) (D)
5 (A) (B) (C) (D)	25 (A) (B) (C) (D)	45 (A) (B) (C) (D)
6 (A) (B) (C) (D)	26 (A) (B) (C) (D)	46 (A) (B) (C) (D)
7 (A) (B) (C) (D)	27 (A) (B) (C) (D)	47 (A) (B) (C) (D)
8 (A) (B) (C) (D)	28 (A) (B) (C) (D)	48 (A) (B) (C) (D)
9 (A) (B) (C) (D)	29 (A) (B) (C) (D)	49 (A) (B) (C) (D)
10 (A) (B) (C) (D)	30 (A) (B) (C) (D)	50 (A) (B) (C) (D)
11 (A) (B) (C) (D)	31 (A) (B) (C) (D)	51 (A) (B) (C) (D)
12 (A) (B) (C) (D)	32 (A) (B) (C) (D)	52 (A) (B) (C) (D)
13 (A) (B) (C) (D)	33 (A) (B) (C) (D)	53 (A) (B) (C) (D)
14 (A) (B) (C) (D)	34 (A) (B) (C) (D)	54 (A) (B) (C) (D)
15 (A) (B) (C) (D)	35 (A) (B) (C) (D)	55 (A) (B) (C) (D)
16 (A) (B) (C) (D)	36 (A) (B) (C) (D)	
17 (A) (B) (C) (D)	37 (A) (B) (C) (D)	
18 (A) (B) (C) (D)	38 (A) (B) (C) (D)	
19 (A) (B) (C) (D)	39 (A) (B) (C) (D)	
20 (A) (B) (C) (D)	40 (A) (B) (C) (D)	

AP U.S. Government and Politics Practice Exam 4

Section I: Multiple-Choice Questions
Total Time—80 minutes
55 Questions

Directions: Each question or incomplete sentence below is followed by four suggested answers or completions. Select the one that is best, and then fill in the corresponding oval on the answer sheet.

Questions 1 and 2 refer to the info graphic below.

MIRANDA WARNING

1. YOU HAVE THE RIGHT TO REMAIN SILENT.

2. ANYTHING YOU SAY CAN AND WILL BE USED AGAINST YOU IN A COURT OF LAW.

3. YOU HAVE THE RIGHT TO TALK TO A LAWYER AND HAVE HIM PRESENT WITH YOU WHILE YOU ARE BEING QUESTIONED.

4. IF YOU CANNOT AFFORD TO HIRE A LAWYER, ONE WILL BE APPOINTED TO REPRESENT YOU BEFORE ANY QUESTIONING IF YOU WISH.

5. YOU CAN DECIDE AT ANY TIME TO EXERCISE THESE RIGHTS AND NOT ANSWER ANY QUESTIONS OR MAKE ANY STATEMENTS.

WAIVER

DO YOU UNDERSTAND EACH OF THESE RIGHTS I HAVE EXPLAINED TO YOU?
HAVING THESE RIGHTS IN MIND, DO YOU WISH TO TALK TO US NOW?

1. Based on the infographic, which of the following constitutional amendments is being addressed?
   (A) The First Amendment
   (B) The Second Amendment
   (C) The Fifth Amendment
   (D) The Sixth Amendment

2. Which of the following Supreme Court decisions is most closely related to the infographic?
   (A) *Schenck v. U.S.* (1919)
   (B) *McDonald v. Chicago* (2010)
   (C) *U.S. v. Lopez* (1995)
   (D) *Gideon v. Wainwright* (1963)

3. Which of the following created the reserved powers of the states?
   (A) Necessary and Proper Clause
   (B) Tenth Amendment
   (C) Fourteenth Amendment
   (D) Establishment Clause

4. Which of the following is an accurate comparison of congressional and presidential powers?

	CONGRESSIONAL POWERS	PRESIDENTIAL POWERS
(A)	Regulate commerce	Declare war
(B)	Receive ambassadors	Borrow money for the United States
(C)	Raise and collect taxes	Negotiate treaties
(D)	Grant reprieves and pardons	Set up courts

GO ON TO THE NEXT PAGE

5. A Democratic candidate for president would be most likely to support which of the following proposals?
   (A) Nationalized health care
   (B) Strengthening the military and defense programs
   (C) Traditional marriage and family based on one man and one woman
   (D) Decreasing environmental regulation

6. Which of the following best describes Madison's argument in Federalist #10?
   (A) Factions are necessary to encourage a democratic form of government.
   (B) Factions should be encouraged because they would help control the minority.
   (C) Factions are unavoidable, but a republican form of government can control them.
   (D) Factions would allow the national government too much power, so they should be controlled.

7. Which of the following most accurately describes the Great (Connecticut) Compromise?
   (A) It provided that the president would be chosen by an electoral college, rather than by the people.
   (B) It provides that slaves would count as three-fifths of a person for the purposes of taxation and representation.
   (C) It provided for a bicameral Congress, with the lower house based on state population and the upper house based on equality of the states.
   (D) It provided that Congress could not end the slave trade for 20 years and no taxes on exports could be collected.

8. Which of the following best describes a possible consequence of divided government?
   (A) Legislation can be passed much more easily; therefore, legislative productivity increases.
   (B) Gridlock may occur as both parties see a chance to enact their preferences.
   (C) The House of Representatives and the Senate are required to form issue networks and iron triangles to pass legislation.
   (D) Congress must reduce the size of its staff in order to meet the federal budget.

9. Which of the following informal powers might a president use to accomplish his goals?
   (A) Suggesting pork barrel legislation
   (B) Issuing executive orders
   (C) Passing a constitutional amendment
   (D) Gerrymandering congressional districts

10. Which of the following actions by public school districts would most likely be protected under the Equal Protection Clause of the Fourteenth Amendment?
    (A) The creation of separate school facilities for whites and blacks
    (B) The integration of school facilities for whites and blacks
    (C) The use of a quota system to assign students to schools based on racial balances
    (D) Separate assignments for students based on race

11. If the presidential election is thrown into the House of Representatives,
    (A) members of the House vote as state delegations, with each state receiving one vote.
    (B) members of the House vote as individuals, with the winner receiving a majority of votes.
    (C) members of the House vote as individuals, with the winner receiving two-thirds of votes.
    (D) members of the House vote as individuals, with the winner receiving 270 or more votes.

GO ON TO THE NEXT PAGE

Questions 12 and 13 refer to the pie chart below.

Source of Funds to 2010 Congressional Candidates

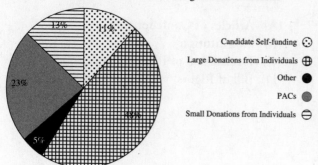

Candidate Self-funding ⊙
Large Donations from Individuals ⊕
Other ●
PACs ◐
Small Donations from Individuals ⊖

https://www.opensecrets.org/resources/dollarocracy/04.php

12. Which of the following accurately describes the information presented in the pie chart?
    (A) The largest category of campaign funding is from political action committees (PACs).
    (B) The smallest category of campaign funding is from individual small donations.
    (C) The largest category of campaign funding is from individual large donations.
    (D) The smallest category of campaign funding is from political action committees (PACs).

13. Which of the following Supreme Court decisions is most relevant to the topic of the pie chart?
    (A) *Baker v. Carr* (1962)
    (B) *United States v. Lopez* (1995)
    (C) *Shaw v. Reno* (1993)
    (D) *Citizens United v. Federal Elections Commission* (2010)

14. Which of the following most accurately illustrates an advantage of federalism?
    (A) Federalism provides a system to avoid concentration of political power.
    (B) Federalism provides for a complex set of governments to deal with.
    (C) Federalism provides the states with finances to fund programs.
    (D) Federalism provides conflicts of authority, so all opinions may be heard.

15. Which of the following argues for a strong executive leader, as provided for by the Constitution, rather than the weak executive council under the Articles of Confederation?
    (A) Brutus #1
    (B) James Madison in Federalist #10
    (C) James Madison in Federalist #51
    (D) Alexander Hamilton in Federalist #70

Questions 16 and 17 refer to the cartoon below.

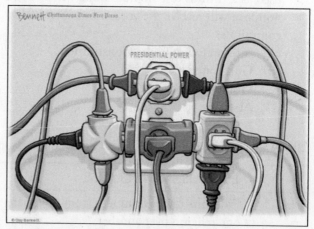

16. Which of the following best describes the message of the political cartoon?
    (A) The growth of the president's power is necessary because presidents should be strong and powerful.
    (B) The increasing use of administrative power is testing the boundaries of executive authority and should be a cause for concern.
    (C) The power of the presidency, moreover, was never intended to be minimal.
    (D) The system of checks and balances works to keep any one branch of government from becoming too powerful.

GO ON TO THE NEXT PAGE

17. Which of the following has been used by Congress to limit the powers of the president?
    (A) Patriot Act
    (B) Gerrymandering
    (C) War Powers Resolution
    (D) Bipartisan Campaign Reform Act

18. The Senate Judiciary Committee is considering a potential nominee for the Supreme Court. Which of the following issues has recently been used as a "litmus test" to determine whether the nominee will receive the vote of members of the committee?
    (A) Interpretation of the Constitution
    (B) Gun control
    (C) Homosexuals in the military
    (D) Abortion

19. Which of the following documents is based on the principles of natural rights and social contract?
    (A) Articles of Confederation
    (B) Constitution
    (C) Declaration of Independence
    (D) Bill of Rights

20. Which of the following is an accurate comparison of the Establishment and Free Exercise Clauses?

	ESTABLISHMENT CLAUSE	FREE EXERCISE CLAUSE
(A)	Prohibits the government from preferring one religion over another	*Engel v. Vitale* (1962)
(B)	Government may not pressure people to participate in a religious practice (e.g., prayer), and it may not discriminate between religious groups.	Congress may target a specific religious activity if they believe that activity is wrong.
(C)	Prohibits the government from creating an official national religion for the country	Guarantees a person the right to practice a religion without limitations, unless the government can show a compelling state interest exists.
(D)	*Wisconsin v. Yoder* (1972)	Measured by the "Lemon Test"

21. Which of the following scenarios most accurately illustrates the process of political socialization?
    (A) With the introduction of new media sources, such as the internet, individuals watch more news.
    (B) A student takes a government class in high school and develops opinions about politics.
    (C) The president delivers his State of the Union address to Congress.
    (D) Congress becomes increasingly partisan when voting on domestic issues.

22. James Smith has been convicted of capital murder and been sentenced to death by lethal injection. Which of the following most accurately reflects the status of capital punishment under the Eighth Amendment's prohibition of cruel and unusual punishment?
    (A) The Supreme Court has not ruled on the status of capital punishment.
    (B) The Supreme Court has held that capital punishment is unconstitutional under all circumstances since it violates the Eighth Amendment.
    (C) The Supreme Court has held that capital punishment is constitutional under certain circumstances.
    (D) The Supreme Court has held that capital punishment can only be used for conviction of federal crimes.

GO ON TO THE NEXT PAGE

23. An interest group donating money to the political campaign of a member of Congress is an example of
    (A) participatory democracy.
    (B) pluralist democracy.
    (C) elite democracy.
    (D) hyper-pluralist democracy.

24. Which of the following scenarios would most likely be considered a violation of the exclusionary rule?
    (A) Prohibiting immigrants with infectious diseases from entering the United States
    (B) Allowing state governments to exclude people based on race from public accommodations
    (C) Requiring all state public facilities be accessible to persons with disabilities
    (D) Allowing illegally obtained evidence to be used against a person at trial

Questions 25 and 26 refer to the map below.

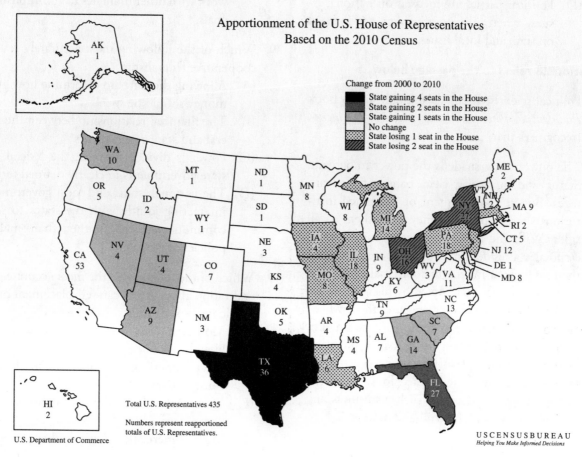

Apportionment of the U.S. House of Representatives Based on the 2010 Census

Change from 2000 to 2010
- State gaining 4 seats in the House
- State gaining 2 seats in the House
- State gaining 1 seats in the House
- No change
- State losing 1 seat in the House
- State losing 2 seat in the House

Total U.S. Representatives 435

Numbers represent reapportioned totals of U.S. Representatives.

U.S. Department of Commerce

USCENSUSBUREAU
Helping You Make Informed Decisions

Source: U.S. Census Bureau: https://www.census.gov/library/visualizations/2017/comm/voting-rates-age.html

25. Which of the following is the most common change in apportionment based on the 2010 census?
    (A) States gaining two seats in the House
    (B) States gaining one seat in the House
    (C) States losing one seat in the House
    (D) States with no change

26. Which of the following is an accurate statement about the information in the map?
    (A) Most of the states that gained seats were in the southern and western United States.
    (B) Most of the states that lost seats were in the southern and western United States.
    (C) Several states gained more than two seats.
    (D) Most of the states that gained seats were in the northern and midwestern United States.

GO ON TO THE NEXT PAGE

27. Which of the following most accurately describes the fundamental difference between political parties and interest groups?
    (A) Political parties represent a broad range of issues, whereas interest groups represent a narrower range of issues.
    (B) Political parties work to influence government, whereas interest groups want to control government through the winning of elections.
    (C) Political parties can raise funds and campaign for or against candidates, whereas interest groups may not support or oppose a candidate in any way.
    (D) Political parties are focused on national issues, whereas interest groups are focused on state and local issues.

Question 28 refers to the passage below.

Political scientist Richard Neustadt, in his book *Presidential Power and the Modern Presidents*, [recognizes that] ...

The power to persuade is the power to bargain. Status and authority yield bargaining advantages. But in a government of "separated institutions sharing powers," they yield them to all sides. With the array of vantage points at his disposal, a President may be far more persuasive than his logic or his charm could make him. But outcomes are not guaranteed by his advantages. There remain the counter pressures those whom he would influence can bring to bear on him from vantage points at their disposal. Command has limited utility; persuasion becomes give-and-take. It is well that the White House holds the vantage points it does. In such a business any President may need them all-and more ...

28. Which of the following statements best summarizes the author's argument?
    (A) Presidential power does not come from the office but rather from the president's ability to bargain and persuade others to do what he wants them to do.
    (B) The president's powers come from the fact that he is leader of the executive branch.
    (C) The founding fathers intended the president to have vast, unchecked powers to accomplish his job.
    (D) The government is composed of shared powers, and the president must learn to work with other branches to accomplish his goals.

29. Which of the following most accurately reflects cooperative federalism?
    (A) Allowing the states to determine how grant money should be spent
    (B) The financial relationship between the federal and state governments
    (C) Power is divided between the federal and state governments in clearly defined terms.
    (D) The national, state, and local governments interacting jointly with the states to solve common problems, rather than making policies separately

30. Which of the following is the most accurate generalization about American self-placement on an ideological spectrum?
    (A) Most Americans identify themselves as liberals.
    (B) Most Americans identify themselves as conservatives.
    (C) Most Americans identify themselves as libertarians.
    (D) Most Americans identify themselves as moderates.

31. Which of the following is an accurate comparison of the House of Representatives and the Senate?

	HOUSE OF REPRESENTATIVES	SENATE
(A)	Has fewer rules of debate set by the Rules Committee	Has more rules for debate set by the Rules Committee
(B)	Must initiate all revenue bills	Ratifies treaties
(C)	Confirms judicial appointments	More influential in foreign affairs
(D)	Holds trials of impeachment	Brings charges of impeachment

GO ON TO THE NEXT PAGE

32. The Supreme Court has agreed to review a case from the lower courts. The next step in the process would be for the Supreme Court to issue a(n)
    (A) *amicus curiae* brief
    (B) writ of *habeas corpus*
    (C) rule of four opinion
    (D) writ of *certiorari*

33. Which of the following government officials would most likely be influenced by a public opinion poll?
    (A) A president who just won reelection to a second term
    (B) A member of a federal agency overseeing regulations for a law passed by Congress
    (C) A member of the Supreme Court deciding an important case
    (D) A member of the House of Representatives running for reelection

Questions 34 and 35 refer to the chart below.

American Support of Affirmative Action on College Campuses

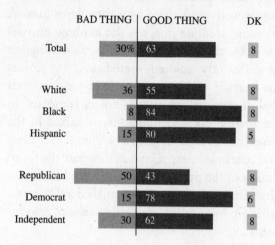

Source: "Public Strongly Backs Affirmative Action Programs on Campus." Pew Research Center, Washington, D.C. April 22, 2014 http://www.pewresearch.org/fact-tank/2014/04/22/public-strongly-backs-affirmative-action-programs-on-campus/

34. Which of the following statements is reflected in the data in the chart?
    (A) Blacks are more supportive of affirmative action than Hispanics.
    (B) Republicans are more supportive of affirmative action than Democrats.
    (C) Whites are more supportive of affirmative action than Independents.
    (D) Independents are less supportive of affirmative action than Republicans.

35. Which of the following is an accurate conclusion based on a comparison of data in the chart between race and political party identification?
    (A) Affirmative action programs help non-minorities more than minorities.
    (B) Affirmative action programs help minorities more than non-minorities.
    (C) Affirmative action programs should be abolished.
    (D) Affirmative action programs are supported by both major political parties.

36. Which of the following is an accurate comparison of the caucus and a primary system?

	CAUCUS	PRIMARY
(A)	Used in New Hampshire	Used in Iowa
(B)	Considered more democratic	Considered less democratic
(C)	Participants tend to be more informed and more interactive.	Favors candidates who have a dedicated and organized following
(D)	Face-to-face meeting of party members who openly decide which candidate to support	Voters go to the polls and cast secret ballots for the candidate of their choosing.

GO ON TO THE NEXT PAGE

Questions 37 and 38 refer to the passage below.

The American form of government is often, but erroneously symbolized by a three-layer cake. A far more accurate image is the rainbow or marble cake, characterized by inseparable mingling of differently colored ingredients, the colors up hearing and vertical and diagonal strands and unexpected whirls. As colors are mixed in the marble cake, so functions are mixed in the American Federal System ... A long, extensive, and continuous experience is therefore the foundation of the present system of shared functions characteristic of the American Federal System, what we have called the marble cake of government.

— *The Federal System,* Morton Grodzins

37. Which of the following statements best summarizes the author's argument?
   (A) Federalism in the United States involves a sharing of functions between the state and national governments.
   (B) Federalism no longer exists in the United States.
   (C) A pluralist system between political parties and interest groups allows the state and national government to work together when necessary.
   (D) Federalism in the United States is so complex that no one really understands it.

38. Which of the following most accurately reflects the author's description of a "marble cake"?
   (A) Dual federalism
   (B) Cooperative federalism
   (C) Pluralism
   (D) Traditional federalist theory

39. Which of the following best illustrates the 1960 presidential debates between Richard Nixon and John F. Kennedy?
   (A) The importance of experience in presidential politics
   (B) The visual power of television in American politics
   (C) The role of radio broadcasting in the United States
   (D) The importance of issues in presidential debates

40. Which of the following is most important in the success of a public opinion poll?
   (A) Those chosen to participate must be representative of the general population and chosen at random.
   (B) The respondent should have no prior knowledge of the issues addressed in the poll.
   (C) The poll should have a sampling error of zero.
   (D) Questions asked in the poll should be lengthy and detailed about the issues addressed in the poll.

41. Which of the following is an accurate description of block and categorical grants?

	BLOCK GRANTS	**CATEGORICAL GRANTS**
(A)	Can be used for a variety of purposes within a broad category	Have a specific purpose defined by law
(B)	Requirements imposed by the national government on the states	National and state governments work together to solve problems
(C)	State and national governments remain supreme within their own sphere of influence.	May require matching funds
(D)	Include project and formula grants	No strings attached in the form of aid to state and local governments

GO ON TO THE NEXT PAGE

42. Which of the following most accurately describes the 1962 Supreme Court decision regarding redistricting in *Baker v. Carr?*
    (A) Congressional districts within a state must be equal in population.
    (B) Congressional districts within a state must be equal in geographic size.
    (C) Redistricting can be accomplished within a state however the state sees fit.
    (D) A census is required every ten years so that states may gerrymander their districts.

Questions 43 and 44 refer to the line graph below.

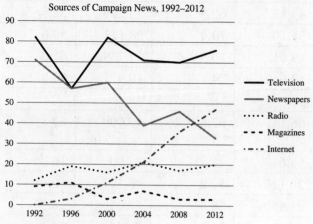

Sources of Campaign News, 1992–2012

Source: Pew Research Center

43. Which of the following best describes a trend in the line graph above?
    (A) The use of television as a source for campaign news is increasing.
    (B) The use of magazines as a source for campaign news is increasing.
    (C) The use of the internet as a source for campaign news is decreasing.
    (D) The use of newspapers as a source for campaign news is decreasing.

44. Which of the following is an accurate conclusion based on a comparison of the trends in the line graph above and your knowledge of the media.
    (A) Television and newspapers continue to be the major source of campaign news.
    (B) The internet is the fastest growing source of campaign news.
    (C) Television and radio are no longer important sources of campaign news.
    (D) Newspapers and the radio are the least favorite source of campaign news.

45. Members of the House of Representatives who run for reelection win over 90% of the time. Which of the following best explains why reelection is so high for members of the House of Representatives?
    (A) The reelection effect
    (B) The unified government effect
    (C) The incumbency effect
    (D) The gerrymandering effect

46. Many people, including numerous vice presidents, have observed that the vice president has very little power within the national government. Which of the following is a constitutional power of the vice president?
    (A) Helping to "balance the ticket" in a presidential election
    (B) Advising the president on matters of domestic and foreign policy
    (C) Taking over for a disabled president if necessary
    (D) Presiding over an impeachment trial of the president

GO ON TO THE NEXT PAGE

Questions 47 and 48 refer to the table below.

Reported Voting and Registration, by Sex and Age: November 2014

ALL RACES	TOTAL POPULATION	TOTAL CITIZEN POPULATION	REPORTED REGISTERED		REPORTED VOTED	
			NUMBER	PERCENT	NUMBER	PERCENT
Both sexes						
Total 18 years and over	239,874	219,941	142,166	64.6	92,251	41.9
18 to 24 years	29,658	27,539	11,610	42.2	4,721	17.1
25 to 44 years	81,886	71,395	43,187	60.5	23,209	32.5
45 to 64 years	82,772	76,882	54,107	70.4	38,111	49.6
65 to 74 years	26,609	25,717	19,612	76.3	15,739	61.2
75 years and over	18,949	18,408	13,649	74.1	10,471	56.9
Male						
Total 18 years and over	115,637	105,299	66,147	62.8	43,009	40.8
18 to 24 years	14,903	13,652	5,661	41.5	2,190	16.0
25 to 44 years	40,336	34,822	20,126	57.8	10,597	30.4
45 to 64 years	40,137	37,203	25,459	68.4	18,055	48.5
65 to 74 years	12,441	12,030	9,129	75.9	7,494	62.3
75 years and over	7,820	7,592	5,772	76.0	4,673	61.5
Female						
Total 18 years and over	124,237	114,642	76,019	66.3	49,243	43.0
18 to 24 years	14,756	13,887	5,949	42.8	2,532	18.2
25 to 44 years	41,550	36,573	23,061	63.1	12,612	34.5
45 to 64 years	42,634	39,678	28,649	72.2	20,056	50.5
65 to 74 years	14,168	13,687	10,483	76.6	8,244	60.2
75 years and over	11,129	10,816	7,877	72.8	5,799	53.6

Source: U.S. Census Bureau, Current Population Survey, November 2014.

47. Which of the following statements is reflected in the data in the table?
    (A) Citizens 18 to 24 years old have the highest percentage of registrations to vote.
    (B) Males 65 to 74 years old have the highest percentage of reported voters.
    (C) Females 45 to 64 years old have the lowest percentage of reported voters.
    (D) Citizens 75 years and older have the highest percentage of registrations to vote.

48. Based on the data in the table, which of the following is an accurate conclusion on registration and voting in the United States?
    (A) Females are more likely to vote than males.
    (B) Males are more likely to vote than females.
    (C) Older females are more likely to vote than older males.
    (D) Younger males are more likely to vote than older males.

GO ON TO THE NEXT PAGE

49. Which of the following statements relates to the Supreme Court decision in *United States v. Lopez* (1995)?
   (A) The "necessary and proper" clause allows Congress to establish gun-free school zones.
   (B) The possession of a gun in a school zone is not an economic activity that Congress has authority to limit under the commerce clause.
   (C) The Second Amendment protects individual's rights to own and carry guns, including in school zones.
   (D) Controlling guns in school zones falls under Congress's authority to regulate interstate trade under the commerce clause.

50. Which of the following is the primary duty of the federal bureaucracy?
   (A) To implement and administer federal laws and programs
   (B) To create iron triangles to help the government run more efficiently
   (C) To oversee and regulate the executive branch
   (D) To provide contacts for citizens to communicate their ideas and needs to government

51. Based on his arguments in Federalist #51, James Madison would agree with which of the following statements?
   (A) Life tenure of federal judges allows for an independent judiciary.
   (B) A single executive is "far more safe" than an executive council.
   (C) The power of the president to veto legislation should act as a check on the legislature.
   (D) The effects of factions could best be controlled in a large society under a representative form of government.

52. Members of Congress pass legislation prohibiting the drilling for oil in the Alaskan National Wildlife Refuge, and the president signs the bill into law. Which of the following would most likely carry out that legislation?
   (A) The Environmental Committees of the House of Representatives and Senate
   (B) An agency within the executive branch, such as the Environmental Protection Agency
   (C) The Executive Office of the President's Environmental Committee
   (D) The White House Office

53. Which of the following best illustrates the failure of the Articles of Confederation and the necessity for creating a new government under the Constitution?
   (A) The Confederation government's inability in addressing Shays' Rebellion
   (B) The attack on Washington by British forces
   (C) States refusing to send delegates to the Confederation Congress
   (D) The inability of the Congress to choose a president for the executive branch

54. A member of the House of Representative is voting on a bill to increase spending for the interstate highway system across the United States. The member decides to vote based on a poll taken in her home district. Which of the following best describes the member's beliefs about constituent accountability?
   (A) Trustee
   (B) Politico
   (C) Delegate
   (D) Partisan

55. Which of the following most accurately explains why *McCulloch v. Maryland* (1819) was a landmark case involving federalism?
   (A) As a result of this case, the Supreme Court became a co-equal power in the national government.
   (B) The Supreme Court created a representative democracy for the United States.
   (C) The Supreme Court upheld the "separate but equal" clause of the Constitution.
   (D) The Supreme Court upheld the supremacy clause of the Constitution.

STOP. END OF SECTION I

Section II: Free-Response Questions
Total Time—100 minutes

Directions: You have 100 minutes to answer all four of the following questions. Respond to all parts of all four questions. Before beginning to write, you should take a few minutes to plan and outline each answer. Spend approximately 20 minutes each on questions 1, 2, and 3 and 40 minutes on question 4. Illustrate your essay with substantive examples where appropriate.

1. After reading the scenario, respond to A, B, and C below.

> Career officials flee posts ... while hundreds of key posts remain vacant ... angry citizens disrupt their representatives' town hall meetings, screaming, "Do your job!" At each level of American politics, partisan gridlock has ground government to a halt and prompted widespread charges of waste, fraud and corruption. A century ago, the solution to such problems—and the path to efficient, effective governance—seemed clear: Remove power from partisan politicians, confer authority on appointed experts and insulate those experts from political influence so they could better serve the public interest. But for the past half-century, American politicians moved in the opposite direction, undermining the idea of government as a profession requiring training, experience and commitment to public service ... the federal bureaucracy has been shrinking for nearly half a century ... [P]erhaps Americans should reconsider the possibilities of government by professional experts ... [M]any lasting achievements of American public life—from environmental protection and food safety to space exploration and economic stability—resulted from a willingness to confer authority on public-spirited professionals and to insulate them from the demands of partisan competition. In this rancorous era, Americans might well reconsider the advantages of bureaucracy.

> *Washington Post, August 9, 2017*

(A) Describe the primary role of the bureaucracy in the policymaking process.

(B) In the context of the scenario, explain how the role of the bureaucracy described in Part A can be affected by its interaction with the presidency.

(C) In the context of the scenario, explain how the bureaucracy can be affected by linkage institutions.

Electoral College Gains and Losses Following 2010 Census

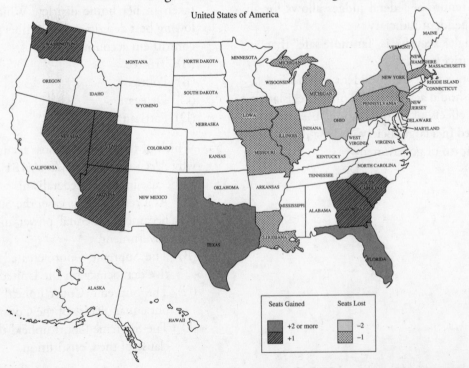

GO ON TO THE NEXT PAGE

2. Use the map to answer the questions.
   (A) Identify the two states with the largest number of gains in the electoral college following the 2010 census.
   (B) Describe a trend in location of the states with gains in the electoral college following the 2010 census.
   (C) Explain how the impact of gains or losses in the electoral college following the 2010 census might affect the electoral process.

3. Hoping to reduce violent crime, the District of Columbia city council passed the Firearms Control Regulation Act in 1995, making it illegal to carry an unregistered firearm and prohibiting the registration of handguns. The chief of police was permitted to issue one-year licenses for handguns. Dick Heller, a District of Columbia special policeman, was authorized to carry a handgun while at work, so he applied to register a handgun he wished to keep at home. The District of Columbia refused Heller's application.

   In *District of Columbia v. Heller* (2008), the Supreme Court held in a 5–4 decision that individuals have a right "to possess a firearm unconnected with service in a militia, and to use that arm for traditionally lawful purposes, such as self-defense within the home." The Court also held that the "... right is not unlimited. It is not a right to keep and carry a weapon whatsoever in any manner whatsoever and for whatever purpose ... prohibitions have been upheld ..."
   (A) Identify the constitutional amendment that is common to both *District of Columbia v. Heller* (2008) and *McDonald v. Chicago* (2010).
   (B) Based on the constitutional amendment identified in part A, explain why the facts of *District of Columbia v. Heller* led to a similar holding as the holding in *McDonald v. Chicago*.
   (C) Describe an action that members of the public who disagree with the holding in *District of Columbia v. Heller* could take to limit its impact.

4. Develop an argument that explains which theory on the role of the judicial system—judicial activism or judicial restraint—best achieves the founders' intent for American democracy in terms of ensuring a stable government run by the people.

   In your essay, you must:
   - Articulate a defensible claim or thesis that responds to the prompt and establishes a line of reasoning
   - Support your claim with at least TWO pieces of accurate and relevant information:
     - At least ONE piece of evidence must be from one of the following foundational documents:
       — Federalist #51
       — Federalist #78
       — U.S. Constitution
     - Use a second piece of evidence from another foundational document from the list or from your study of the electoral process.
   - Use reasoning to explain why your evidence supports your claim/thesis.
   - Respond to an opposing or alternative perspective using refutation, concession, or rebuttal.

STOP. END OF SECTION II

Answer Key for Multiple-Choice Questions

1. C	16. B	31. B	46. C
2. D	17. C	32. D	47. B
3. B	18. D	33. D	48. A
4. C	19. C	34. A	49. B
5. A	20. C	35. B	50. A
6. C	21. B	36. D	51. C
7. C	22. C	37. A	52. B
8. B	23. B	38. B	53. A
9. B	24. D	39. B	54. B
10. B	25. D	40. A	55. D
11. A	26. A	41. A	
12. C	27. A	42. A	
13. D	28. A	43. D	
14. A	29. D	44. B	
15. D	30. D	45. C	

› Answers and Explanations for the Multiple-Choice Questions

1. **C.** The Miranda warnings are required police warnings of the right to silence given to criminal suspects who are in the custody of police before they can ask questions regarding what took place during a crime. They were established as a result of *Miranda v. Arizona* (1963) to protect Fifth Amendment rights. The First Amendment addresses the issue of freedom of religion, speech, press, petition, and assembly (A). The Second Amendment protects the right to bear arms (B). The Sixth Amendment provides protections of a trial by jury and the right to an attorney (D).

2. **D.** *Schenck v. U.S* provided that freedom of speech protections under the First Amendment could be restricted if the words spoken or printed represented to society a "clear and present danger" (A). *McDonald v. Chicago* found that the right of an individual to "keep and bear arms" is protected under the Second Amendment and the due process clause of the Fourteenth Amendment (B). *U.S. v. Lopez* limited Congress's power under the commerce clause of the Constitution (C).

3. **B.** The Tenth Amendment states, "The powers not delegated to the United States by the Constitution, nor prohibited by it to the states, are reserved to the states respectively, or to the people." The necessary and proper clause in Article I, Section 8 of the Constitution expands the powers of Congress to "make all laws necessary" for executing its other powers (A). The Fourteenth Amendment provides for citizenship, equal protection of the laws, and due process (C). The establishment clause of the First Amendment protects against the national government establishing a national church (D).

4. **C.** The power to declare war is a congressional power (A). The power to receive ambassadors is a presidential power, and the power to borrow money is a congressional power (B). The power to grant reprieves and pardons is a presidential power, and the power to establish courts is a congressional power (D).

5. **A.** A Republican candidate would most likely support strengthening the military and defense programs (B), traditional marriage and family based on one man and one woman (C), and decreasing environmental regulation (D).

6. **C.** In Federalist #10, Madison argued that factions are unavoidable, but a republican form of government can control them. Madison suggests how to guard against factions who might have interests that contradict the rights of others or the rights of the community. He stated that a strong republic would be able to guard against factions better than smaller individual states.

7. **C.** The Great Compromise provided for a bicameral Congress with the lower house based on state population and the upper house based on equality of the states as a solution to the differences between the Virginia and New Jersey plans presented at the constitutional convention. Separate compromises provided that the president would be chosen by an electoral college, rather than by the people (A), that slaves (Three-fifths compromise) would count as three-fifths of a person for the purposes of taxation and representation (B), and that Congress (Commerce and Slave Trade compromise) could not end the slave trade for 20 years and could not impose taxes on exports (D).

8. **B.** Divided government may cause gridlock, making it harder to pass legislation and slowing the legislative process (A). Issue networks and iron triangles are not required in the House of Representative or Senate; however, they may include congressional committees, executive agencies, and interest groups (C). Divided government does not force Congress to reduce the size of its staff (D).

9. **B.** Pork barrel legislation is generally used by members of Congress to bring projects to their home state of district in the hopes of getting reelected (A). The president plays no formal role in the passage of a constitutional amendment (C) or gerrymandering of congressional districts (D).

10. **B.** Separate school facilities for whites and blacks was declared unconstitutional under the equal protection clause of the Fourteenth Amendment in *Brown v. Board of Education* (A). The use of a quota system to assign students to schools based on racial balances (C) and separate assignments for students based on race (D) are also unconstitutional.

11. **A.** If no candidate for president receives 270 or more electoral votes, then the House of Representatives chooses the president from among the top three candidates. Each state delegation receives 1 vote, with a majority of 26 or more votes needed to win.

12. **C.** The largest category of campaign funding (48%) is from individual large donations. Political action committees only contribute 23% (A and D). Individual small donations are 13%, which is not the smallest category (B).

13. **D.** The pie chart addresses the issue of campaign funding, which was an issue in *Citizens United v. Federal Elections Commission. Baker v. Carr* established the right of federal courts to review redistricting issues, which had previously been termed "political questions" outside the courts' jurisdiction (A). *United States v. Lopez* dealt with the issue of federalism and the powers of Congress under the commerce clause (B). *Shaw v. Reno* held that redistricting based on race must be held to a standard of strict scrutiny under the equal protection clause and that those doing the redistricting must ensure compliance with the Voting Rights Act of 1965 (C).

14. **A.** One advantage of federalism is that it provides a system to avoid concentration of political power. Federalism providing for a complex set of governments to deal with (B) and creating conflicts of authority (D) are disadvantages. Federalism does not provide the states with finances to fund programs unless the federal government provides funding through a form of grant-in-aid (C).

15. **D.** Brutus #1 is an Anti-Federalist article discussing objections to the ratification of the Constitution (A). In Federalist #10, Madison discusses the need to guard against factions (B), and in Federalist #51, Madison discusses the importance of separation of powers and checks and balances (C).

16. **B.** The author is portraying the increasing use of administrative power is testing the boundaries of executive authority and should be a cause for concern by utilizing an unsafe, overloaded electrical plug. There is no indication that the growth of presidential power is necessary (A), it was never intended to be minimal (C), or that there is a system of checks and balances (D).

17. **C.** Congress passed the War Powers Resolution during the Vietnam War in 1973 to check the president's power to commit the United States to an armed conflict without the consent of Congress. The Patriot Act is an antiterrorism law enacted by Congress in response to the terrorist attacks that took place on September 11, 2001 (A). Gerrymandering occurs at the state level when in the process of redistricting, state legislatures draw congressional districts to the advantage of one political party or group over another (B). The Bipartisan Campaign Reform Act was passed in 2002 to further regulate the financing of political campaigns (D).

18. **D.** The Senate Judiciary Committee often asks questions about a potential nominee's views on abortion since it is such a controversial issue with clear divisions between liberal and conservative ideologies.

19. **C.** In the Declaration of Independence, Thomas Jefferson discusses natural rights such as "life, liberty and the pursuit of happiness" and the concept of social contract being an agreement between the government and the governed. The Articles of Confederation was a plan for government (a constitution) that was in effect from 1781 to 1789, outlining the structure of government (A). The Constitution replaced the Articles of Confederation in 1789 as the constitution for the U.S. government (B). The Bill of Rights was added to the Constitution in 1791 to provide individual rights to the people (D).

20. **C.** In *Engel v. Vitale,* the Court ruled it unconstitutional for state officials to compose an official school prayer based on the establishment clause (A). Congress may not target specific religious activity unless they can prove a "compelling interest." (B) In *Wisconsin v. Yoder,* the Supreme Court ruled that Amish children could not be

required to attend school under compulsory education laws beyond the 8th grade based on the free exercise clause. The Lemon Test is based on the establishment clause (D).

21. **B.** Political socialization is a lifelong process by which people form their ideas about politics and acquire political values. Family, the educational system, our peer groups and affiliations, and the mass media all play a role. A student taking a government class in high school and developing opinions about politics is the best illustration of political socialization.

22. **C.** The Supreme Court has ruled numerous times on the status of capital punishment (A). The Supreme Court has held that capital punishment is constitutional under certain circumstances (B). The Supreme Court has held that capital punishment can only be used for conviction of both federal and state crimes (D).

23. **B.** Pluralist democracy occurs when interest groups compete in the political arena, which might include an interest group donating money to the political campaign of a member of Congress. Participatory democracy emphasizes wide-ranging participation in the political process (A). Elite democracy occurs when a small number of powerful elites such as corporate leaders rule in their own self-interest (C). Hyper-pluralist theory suggests that many groups are pulling government in different directions at the same time, causing gridlock and ineffectiveness (D).

24. **D.** The exclusionary rule prohibits evidence acquired as a result of an illegal search or seizure from being used as evidence in a trial. The exclusionary rule does not prohibit immigrants with infectious diseases from entering the United States (A), allow state governments to exclude people based on race from public accommodations (B), or require all state public facilities be accessible to persons with disabilities (C).

25. **D.** States with no change is the most common change in apportionment based on the 2010 census. While some states gained or lost representatives because of population shifts, many states saw no change in the total number of representatives apportioned.

26. **A.** Most of the states that lost seats were in the northeastern United States (B). Only Texas gained more than two seats (C). Most of the states that gained seats were in the southern and western United States (D).

27. **A.** Political parties represent a broad range of issues, whereas interest groups represent a narrower range of issues. Political parties work to control government through the winning of elections, whereas interest groups want to influence government (B). Political parties can raise funds and campaign for or against candidates; interest groups may form political action committees to support or oppose a candidate (C). Both political parties and interest groups may focus on national issues or state and local issues (D).

28. **A.** Richard Neustadt, in his book *Presidential Power and the Modern Presidents,* argued that presidential power comes from the president's power to persuade, not because he is the leader of the executive branch (B). The founding fathers wanted to make sure that no one person or part of government became too powerful, therefore including separation of powers and checks and balances as part of our governmental system (C). Although it is true that the government is composed of shared powers and the president must work with the other branches to accomplish his goals, it is not the author's argument (D).

29. **D.** Cooperative federalism involves cooperation among federal, state, and local governments to solve common problems. Revenue sharing allowed states wide discretion in determining how grant money should be spent (A). Fiscal federalism describes the financial relationship between the federal and state governments (B). Dual federalism involves federal and state governments each having defined responsibilities within their own sphere of influence (C).

30. **D.** Most Americans today identify themselves as moderate on a political spectrum.

31. **B.** The House of Representatives has more rules for debate set by the Rules Committee; the Senate has fewer rules for debate because they have no Rules Committee (A). The Senate confirms judicial appointments (C). The Senate holds trials of

impeachment; the House of Representatives brings charges of impeachment (D).

32. **D.** *Amicus curiae* briefs are presented to the courts by interested groups or individuals who are not party to the case but who support or reject arguments of the case (A). A writ of *habeas corpus* requires a judge to evaluate whether there is sufficient cause to keep a person in jail (B). The rule of four is a requirement that a case can only be heard by the Supreme Court if four justices vote to hear the case (C).

33. **D.** A member of the House of Representatives running for reelection would most likely be influenced by a public opinion poll. A president who just won reelection to a second term cannot run again (A), and members of the Supreme Court are appointed for life terms to keep them independent of political pressures (C). A member of a federal agency overseeing regulations for a law passed by Congress is not elected, and therefore does not have to bend to public opinion (B).

34. **A.** Blacks (84%) are more supportive of affirmative action than Hispanics (80%). Republicans (43%) are less supportive of affirmative action than Democrats (78%) (B). Whites (55%) are less supportive of affirmative action than Independents (62%) (C). Independents (62%) are more supportive of affirmative action than Republicans (43%) (D).

35. **B.** Affirmative action programs were designed to correct the effects of past discrimination and therefore help minorities more than non-minorities.

36. **D.** The primary is used in New Hampshire, while the caucus is used in Iowa (A). The primary is considered more democratic since all eligible voters can participate, while the caucus is considered less democratic because they do not use secret ballot and may exclude certain segments of voters who cannot take off work to attend (B). The caucus favors candidates who are dedicated, organized, and willing to participate (C).

37. **A.** Federalism in the United States involves a sharing of functions between the state and national governments, much like a marble cake (cooperative federalism). Federalism continues

to exist in the United States (B). A pluralist system refers to interest groups competing in the political arena (C). Although federalism can be complex, it is the division of power between the states and the federal government (D).

38. **B.** Dual federalism is sometimes referred to as "layer-cake" federalism because of the separation between the two levels of government (A). A pluralist system refers to interest groups competing in the political arena and is not a form of federalism (C). Traditional federalist theory would be a description of dual federalism, since it existed from the early years of our country until the 1930s (D).

39. **B.** The 1960 presidential debates were the first televised debates, illustrating the visual power of the television in American politics. Many who saw the debate declared that Kennedy had won, while those who only heard the debate thought Nixon had done better.

40. **A.** Public opinion polls must be based on random, representative sampling of the general population to be successful. Respondents may have prior knowledge of the issues (B). While sampling error should be as low as possible, a zero-sampling error would be impossible (C). Question wording should be unbiased and not lead the respondents to any one answer (D).

41. **A.** Requirements imposed by the national government on the states are mandates; national and state governments working together to solve problems is cooperative federalism (B). State and national governments remaining supreme within their own sphere of influence is dual federalism (C). Project and formula grants are forms of categorical grants; revenue sharing is aid to states and local governments with no strings attached (D).

42. **A.** *Baker v. Carr* established the right of federal courts to review redistricting issues, which had previously been termed "political questions" outside the courts' jurisdiction and determined that congressional districts within a state must be equal in population, not geographic size (B). Redistricting within a state must follow certain guidelines including compactness and contiguity (C). Gerrymandering is unconstitutional; states

are prohibited from engaging in drawing districts in order to help one party or group over another (D).

43. **D.** Television as a source for campaign news is decreasing (A). Magazines as a source for campaign news is decreasing (B). The internet as a source for campaign news is increasing (C).

44. **B.** The internet is the fastest growing source of campaign news. Television and the internet are the largest sources of campaign news (A). Television is still an important source of campaign news (C). Magazines and the radio are the least favorite source of campaign news (D).

45. **C.** Reelection is so high for members of the House of Representatives because of the incumbency effect. Name recognition, casework, credit claiming, media access, ease of fundraising, experience running a campaign, proven record, and redistricting can all aid incumbents in their reelection bid.

46. **C.** Helping to "balance the ticket" in a presidential election (A) and advising the president on matters of domestic and foreign policy (B) are not constitutional powers. The Chief Justice of the Supreme Court presides over an impeachment trial of the president (D).

47. **B.** Citizens 65 to 74 years old have the highest percentage (76.3%) of registrations to vote (A). Males 18 to 27 years old have the lowest percentage (16%) of reported voters (C). Citizens 65 to 74 years have the highest percentage (76.3%) of registrations to vote (D).

48. **A.** Data from the table shows that females are more likely to vote than males (B). Older males are more likely to vote than older females (C). Older males are more likely to vote than younger males (D).

49. **B.** In *United States v. Lopez* (1995), the Supreme Court held that the Congress's passage of the Gun-Free School Zones Act of 1990, which banned possession of handguns near schools, was unconstitutional because it did not have a substantial impact on interstate commerce. The necessary and proper clause relates to *McCulloch v. Maryland* (1819), allowing Congress to have

expanded powers to create a national bank as a necessary and proper extension of their powers to tax and coin money (A). Although the Second Amendment does protect an individual's right to own and carry guns, states have the right to limit or exclude certain areas, such as school zones (C). Controlling guns in school zones does not fall under Congress's authority to regulate interstate trade under the commerce clause (D).

50. **A.** The primary duty of the federal bureaucracy is to implement and administer federal laws and programs. The federal bureaucracy does not create iron triangles, but agencies of the bureaucracy may participate in an iron triangle (B). The federal bureaucracy is part of the executive branch with the president as its leader (C). The federal bureaucracy is not responsible for providing contacts for citizens to communicate their ideas and needs to government (D).

51. **C.** In Federalist #51, Madison discusses separation of powers and checks and balances to prevent any one part of government from becoming too powerful, therefore, the power of the president to veto legislation is a check of the executive branch on the legislative branch. In Federalist #78, Hamilton argues for life tenure of federal judges to allow for an independent judiciary (A). In Federalist #70, Hamilton explains that a single executive is "far more safe" than an executive council (B). In Federalist #10, Madison discusses how the effects of factions could best be controlled in a large society under a representative form of government (D).

52. **B.** Committees in the House of Representatives and Senate review and pass legislation but do not enforce that legislation (A). Neither the Executive Office of the President's Environmental Committee nor the White House Office enforces legislation (C and D).

53. **A.** Under the Articles of Confederation, the Congress could only request troops from the states. Because the states refuse to send troops, there was no military force to address the issue of Shays' Rebellion. After the Revolutionary War was won by the colonists, the British did not attack Washington (B). State did send delegates to the Confederation Congress (C). There was

no executive branch under the Articles of Confederation (D).

54. **C.** When a member of the House of Representatives decides to vote based on constituent desires, that member is acting as a delegate. A member acting as a trustee would make political decisions based on the greater, common good, not necessarily what their constituents want (A). A politico is a combination of the delegate and trustee, often acting on their own until the constituents voice opposition (B). A partisan member would vote along with his or her political party (D).

55. **D.** *McCulloch v. Maryland* established that the "necessary and proper" clause of the U.S. Constitution gives the federal U.S. government certain implied powers that are not explicitly enumerated in the Constitution and the supremacy of the Constitution under Article VI. The Supreme Court becoming a co-equal power in the national government does not reflect federalism (A). The Constitution created a representative democracy for the United States (B). The Supreme Court upheld the "separate but equal" clause of the Constitution in *Brown v. Board of Education* (C).

Scoring the Free-Response Questions

1. **Scoring the Concept Application Question: Total Value—3 points**

   (A) **1 point:** Describe a political institution, process, or behavior that links to the scenario.

   The primary role of the bureaucracy in the policymaking process is the implementation of policy by experts shielded from political influence so they could better serve the public interest.

   (B) **1 point:** Explain how the response in part (A) affects or is affected by a political process, government entity, or citizen behavior as related to the scenario. (Must link content from the scenario and provide a description to receive credit.)

   The president is head of the executive branch and therefore the head of the bureaucracy. The president can appoint and remove agency heads and other top bureaucrats, reorganize the bureaucracy (with congressional approval), propose changes to the agency's annual budget, ignore legislative initiatives originating within the bureaucracy, initiate or adjust policies that may alter the bureaucracy's activities, and issue executive orders and signing statements.

   (C) **1 point:** In the context of the scenario, explain how the bureaucracy can be affected by linkage institutions.

   The bureaucracy can be affected by interest groups (and congressional committees) as they work together in "iron triangles" to create a relationship that results in the mutual benefit of all three of them. Interest groups try to influence how the bureaucracy might implement policies. They also work together to make policies and pass laws.

2. **Scoring the Quantitative Analysis Question: Total Value—4 points**

   (A) **1 point:** Describe the data presented in the quantitative graphic.

   The two states with the largest number of gains in the electoral college following the 2010 census are Florida and Texas.

   (B) **2 points:** Describe a similarity or difference and draw a conclusion about that similarity or difference. (Must describe a similarity or difference for 1 point and draw a conclusion about the similarity or difference for the second point.)

   Answers may vary. Example: One similarity is that most of the states that lost seats in the electoral college were from the northeastern and midwestern United States. The loss of population from these states (people moving from the northeast or Midwest) to other states might account for the changes.

   (C) **1 point:** Explain how specific data in the quantitative graphic demonstrates the principle of federalism.

   Gains in the electoral college will give some states more influence over presidential elections. In order to win the presidency, a candidate must win 270 or more electoral votes. As population changes, states may gain (if population increases) or lose (if population decreases) seats in the electoral college. State may be more important in the electoral process because of an increase in electoral votes in the next presidential election.

3. **Scoring the SCOTUS Comparison Question: Total Value—4 points**

(A) **1 point:** Identify the constitutional clause that is common to both Supreme Court cases.

The constitutional provision that is common to both to both *District of Columbia v. Heller* (2008) and *McDonald v. Chicago* (2010) is the Second Amendment.

(B) **2 points:** Provide factual information from the required Supreme Court case (1 point) and explain how the reasoning and decisions of the required Supreme Court case apply to scenarios involving the second amendment (1 point).

The Supreme Court ruled in *District of Columbia v. Heller* that the Second Amendment protected an individual right to keep weapons at home for self-defense. The Heller case was regarded as a forerunner to the McDonald case. In *McDonald v. Chicago,* the Supreme Court incorporated the Second Amendment right to own guns for self-defense to state and local governments.

(C) **1 point:** Describe an interaction between the holding in the nonrequired Supreme Court case and a relevant political institution, behavior, or process.

Members of the public who disagree with the holding in *District of Columbia v. Heller* could form a social movement or interest group to lobby Congress for a proposal to amend the Constitution or repeal the Second Amendment to ban private ownership of guns.

4. **Scoring the Argument Essay: Total Value: 6 points**

- **1 point:** Articulate a defensible claim or thesis that responds to the question and establishes a line of reasoning.
- **2 points:** Describe one piece of evidence from one of the listed foundational documents (1 point) that is accurately linked to judicial activism or judicial restraint, and indicate how that evidence supports the argument (1 point). (Must show how evidence supports the argument to earn the second point.)
- **1 point:** Use a second piece of specific and relevant evidence to support the argument. (Must indicate how evidence supports the argument.)
- **1 point:** Explain how or why the evidence supports the claim or thesis.
- **1 point:** Respond to an opposing or alternate perspective using refutation, concession, or rebuttal.

Score Conversion Worksheet

Using this worksheet, you can get a rough approximation of what your score would be on the AP U.S. Government and Politics Exam. Use the answer key to check the multiple-choice questions and the scoring rubrics to award yourself points on the free-response questions. Then compute your raw score on the exam using the worksheet below. Finally, refer to the table below to translate your raw score to an AP score of 1 to 5.

Section I: Multiple-Choice

Number of questions answered correctly (55 possible) _____ × 1.09 = _____

Section I: Free-Response

Question 1 (3 points possible): _____ × 5 = _____

Question 2 (4 points possible): _____ × 3.75 = _____

Question 3 (4 points possible): _____ × 3.75 = _____

Question 4 (6 points possible): _____ × 2.5 = _____

RAW SCORE: Add your points in the column above (120 possible): _____

Conversion Table

RAW SCORE	APPROXIMATE AP SCORE
Mid-80s to 120	5
Mid-70s to low-mid-80s	4
High 40s to mid-70s	3
High 20s to high 40s	2
0 to high 20s	1

Note: At press time, the College Board has not released any information on the computation and conversion of raw scores for the new AP exam to be administered in May 2019. However, the College Board goes to great lengths to make sure that the scores on the new test will mean the same thing as on the old test with the same percentages of students scoring each grade (1–5). This score conversion worksheet is based on the assumption that the ranges for each grade (1–5) on the old test will stay about the same on the new test.

5 Minutes to a 5

180 Activities and Questions in

5 Minutes a Day

INTRODUCTION

Welcome to *5 Minutes to a 5: 180 Questions and Activities!* This bonus section is another tool for you to use as you work toward your goal of achieving a 5 on the AP exam in May. It includes 180 AP questions and activities that cover the most essential course materials and are meant to be completed in conjunction with the *5 Steps* book.

One of the secrets to excelling in your AP class is spending a bit of time *each day* studying the subject(s). The questions and activities offered here are designed to be done one per day, and each should take 5 minutes or so to complete. (There may be exceptions. Depending on the exam, some exercises may take a little longer and some a little less.) You will encounter stimulating questions to make you think about a topic in a big way, some very subject-specific activities which cover the main book's chapters; some science subjects will offer at-home labs; and some humanities subjects will offer ample chunks of text to be read on one day, with questions and activities for follow-up on the following day(s). There will also be suggestions for relevant videos for you to watch and/or websites to visit. Most questions and activities are linked to the specific chapters of your book, so you are constantly fortifying your knowledge.

Remember—approaching this section for 5 minutes a day is much more effective than binging on a week's worth in one sitting! So, if you practice all the extra exercises in this section and reinforce the main content of this book—we are certain you will build the skills and confidence needed to succeed on your exam. Good luck!

—Editors of McGraw-Hill Education

Check off each activity as it is completed.

1. ❏	46. ❏	91. ❏	136. ❏
2. ❏	47. ❏	92. ❏	137. ❏
3. ❏	48. ❏	93. ❏	138. ❏
4. ❏	49. ❏	94. ❏	139. ❏
5. ❏	50. ❏	95. ❏	140. ❏
6. ❏	51. ❏	96. ❏	141. ❏
7. ❏	52. ❏	97. ❏	142. ❏
8. ❏	53. ❏	98. ❏	143. ❏
9. ❏	54. ❏	99. ❏	144. ❏
10. ❏	55. ❏	100. ❏	145. ❏
11. ❏	56. ❏	101. ❏	146. ❏
12. ❏	57. ❏	102. ❏	147. ❏
13. ❏	58. ❏	103. ❏	148. ❏
14. ❏	59. ❏	104. ❏	149. ❏
15. ❏	60. ❏	105. ❏	150. ❏
16. ❏	61. ❏	106. ❏	151. ❏
17. ❏	62. ❏	107. ❏	152. ❏
18. ❏	63. ❏	108. ❏	153. ❏
19. ❏	64. ❏	109. ❏	154. ❏
20. ❏	65. ❏	110. ❏	155. ❏
21. ❏	66. ❏	111. ❏	156. ❏
22. ❏	67. ❏	112. ❏	157. ❏
23. ❏	68. ❏	113. ❏	158. ❏
24. ❏	69. ❏	114. ❏	159. ❏
25. ❏	70. ❏	115. ❏	160. ❏
26. ❏	71. ❏	116. ❏	161. ❏
27. ❏	72. ❏	117. ❏	162. ❏
28. ❏	73. ❏	118. ❏	163. ❏
29. ❏	74. ❏	119. ❏	164. ❏
30. ❏	75. ❏	120. ❏	165. ❏
31. ❏	76. ❏	121. ❏	166. ❏
32. ❏	77. ❏	122. ❏	167. ❏
33. ❏	78. ❏	123. ❏	168. ❏
34. ❏	79. ❏	124. ❏	169. ❏
35. ❏	80. ❏	125. ❏	170. ❏
36. ❏	81. ❏	126. ❏	171. ❏
37. ❏	82. ❏	127. ❏	172. ❏
38. ❏	83. ❏	128. ❏	173. ❏
39. ❏	84. ❏	129. ❏	174. ❏
40. ❏	85. ❏	130. ❏	175. ❏
41. ❏	86. ❏	131. ❏	176. ❏
42. ❏	87. ❏	132. ❏	177. ❏
43. ❏	88. ❏	133. ❏	178. ❏
44. ❏	89. ❏	134. ❏	179. ❏
45. ❏	90. ❏	135. ❏	180. ❏

TASK VERBS

- Identify: Provide a specific answer that does not require causal explanation.

- Define: Provide a specific meaning for a word or concept.

- Describe/Discuss: Show understanding of a particular concept or political phenomenon; give examples that illustrate it.

- Explain: Demonstrate understanding of how or why a relationship exists by clearly articulating the logical connection or causal pattern between or among various political phenomena (using phrases such as "because . . . ," "therefore . . . ," or "causing . . .").

- Compare: Provide an explicit statement that connects two or more concepts; include the similarities/differences between them.

Day 1

Define *government*.

_____

_____

_____

_____

Define *public policy*.

_____

_____

_____

_____

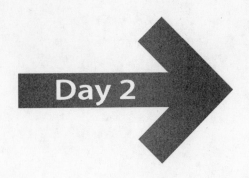

Define *politics*.

_____

_____

_____

_____

Explain how government and politics are related.

_____

_____

_____

_____

Day 3

Watch the video "An Introduction to Government and Politics" at www.youtube.com/ watch?v=AnHW_t8Qwwc. This video is a basic introduction to the AP Government and Politics curriculum. It provides an overview of the six major content areas, including vocabulary terms relevant to the course.

Describe democracy as a form of government.

_____

_____

_____

_____

Describe direct democracy.

_____

_____

_____

_____

Describe representative democracy.

_____

_____

_____

_____

_____

Day 5

Theories of democratic government are theories about who has power and influence over public policy and decision making at various levels of government. Modern theories include traditional democratic theory, pluralist theory, and elite theory.

Complete the chart:

Theory	Description/Basis of Power	Characteristics
Traditional Democracy		
Pluralism		
Elite/Class Theory		

Day 6

Other modern theories of democratic government include the bureaucratic theory and hyperpluralism.

Complete the chart:

Theory	Description/Basis of Power	Characteristics
Bureaucratic Theory		
Hyperpluralism		

Identify John Locke.

_____

_____

_____

_____

Define *social contract*.

_____

_____

_____

_____

Identify the basic tenets of John Locke's theory, and explain why they are important to government in the United States.

_____

_____

_____

_____

Complete the time line with the following by placing the event in the box next to the correct date:

Articles of Confederation go into effect   Declaration of Independence
Articles of Confederation written   First Congress meets
Bill of Rights   Ratification of Constitution by nine states
Constitutional Convention   Shays' Rebellion
(May–September)

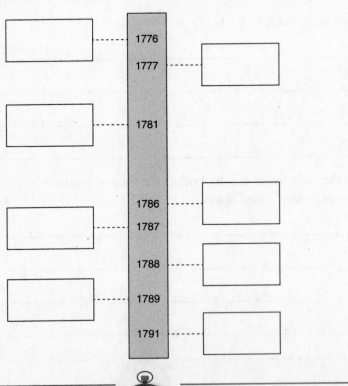

Day 9

Watch the video "The Passing of the Declaration of Independence—John Adams—HBO" at www.youtube.com/watch?v=uNOTozVp_i4. This video shows a re-creation of the key historical event of a roll call vote that would determine whether the states would accept Richard Henry Lee's resolution on declaring independence. One negative vote would cause the resolution to fail.

Day 10

Watch the video "A Reading of the Declaration of Independence (Mirror)" at www
.youtube.com/watch?v=DSKOx8DKPIg. Morgan Freeman narrates this short documentary in which celebrities read the U.S. Declaration of Independence.

Complete the following chart describing the features of government under the Articles of Confederation.

Type of governmental system	
Number of legislative houses	
Method of representation	
Executive branch	
Judicial branch	
Passage of legislation	
Amendment of articles	

5 Minutes to a 5

‹ 337

Identify at least five major weaknesses of the Articles of Confederation.

1. _____

2. _____

3. _____

4. _____

5. _____

Day 13

When and where did the Constitutional Convention meet?

_____

_____

_____

_____

Describe the purpose of the Constitutional Convention.

_____

_____

_____

_____

Describe a federal system.

_____

_____

_____

_____

Explain why the delegates at the Constitutional Convention chose a federal system.

_____

_____

_____

_____

Complete the following chart to compare the Virginia Plan and the New Jersey Plan.

	Virginia Plan	New Jersey Plan
Type of legislature		
Election of legislature		
Basis of representation		
Executive branch		
Judicial branch		

Day 16

Describe each of the following compromises that resulted from the Constitutional Convention.

Compromise	Description
Great (Connecticut) Compromise	
Three-Fifths Compromise	
Commerce and Slave Trade Compromise	

5 Minutes to a 5

Place each of the following descriptions into the correct column:

- Stressed the weaknesses of the Articles of Confederation
- Opposed the Constitution
- Wanted a Bill of Rights to protect citizens from the government
- Promoted checks and balances to protect against abuses by government
- Led by James Madison, Alexander Hamilton, and John Jay
- Favored the Constitution
- Wanted strong state governments; feared a strong national government
- Saw the Constitution as a bill of rights that placed limitations on the government and reserved powers for the states
- Led by Patrick Henry, Richard Henry Lee, George Mason, and Samuel Adams
- Provided for the protection of property rights

Federalists	Anti-Federalists
•	•
•	•
•	•
•	•
•	
•	

Day 18

Describe the Federalist Papers.

_____

_____

_____

_____

Identify the authors of the Federalist Papers.

_____

_____

_____

_____

Match each of the basic principles within the Constitution to its correct description.

_____ Checks and balances

_____ Federalism

_____ Limited government

_____ Popular sovereignty

_____ Separation of powers

A. The belief that government is not all-powerful; government has only those powers given to it.

B. The people are the source of the government's authority.

C. Power is separated among three branches of government; each has its own powers and duties and is independent of and equal to the other branches.

D. Each branch is subject to restraints by the other two branches.

E. Powers are divided between the national government and the states.

5 Minutes to a 5

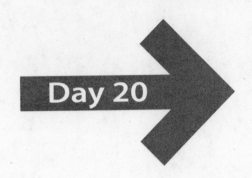

Match each of the following basic principles of the Constitution with the correct scenario.

_____ **1.** Checks and balances   _____ **4.** Limited government

_____ **2.** Federalism   _____ **5.** Popular sovereignty

_____ **3.** Judicial review   _____ **6.** Separation of powers

A. Article V of the Constitution gives the responsibility for amending the Constitution to Congress and the states. Neither Congress nor the states can amend the Constitution alone.

B. No amendment may be passed that causes a state to lose its equal representation in the Senate without its consent.

C. The Supreme Court has not yet ruled whether a state law requiring handgun registration is constitutional.

D. If Congress does not agree with a ruling of the Supreme Court, it can introduce an amendment to the Constitution that would nullify the ruling.

E. The Constitution allows voters to choose members of the House of Representatives every two years and members of the Senate every six years.

F. Of the three branches of government, only the legislative branch has the power to declare war.

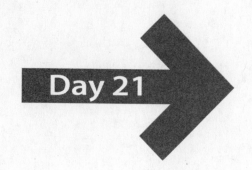
Watch the video "Federalist #51 Explained: American Government Review" at www
.youtube.com/watch?v=5FQ_Y2FUa6Q. Then read the full text or a short summary
of Federalist #51 at http://billofrightsinstitute.org/founding-documents/primary-
source-documents/the-federalist-papers/federalist-papers-no-51.

Answer the following questions:

- What did Madison mean by "the partition of power among several departments"?

- What arguments did Madison use to defend a governmental system based on checks
  and balances?

- What concerns did Madison express about the relative power of the legislative
  branch in relation to the executive branch?

Place each of the following checks in the correct square based on what branch of government holds that power.

- May veto acts of Congress
- May rule legislative acts unconstitutional
- Appoints federal judges
- Creates lower federal courts
- May refuse to enforce court decisions
- May propose constitutional amendments that overrule court decisions
- Appropriates funds
- Has a chief justice who presides over any impeachment trial of the president
- May rule executive actions unconstitutional
- May override the president's veto by a two-thirds vote of both houses

Legislative Branch over Executive Branch	**Executive Branch over Legislative Branch**	**Judicial Branch over Legislative Branch**
• •	•	• •

Legislative Branch over Judicial Branch	**Executive Branch over Judicial Branch**	**Judicial Branch over Executive Branch**
• •	• •	•

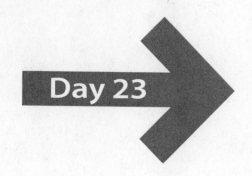

What are formal amendments? Describe their effect on the Constitution.

_____

_____

_____

_____

Identify two formal methods by which amendments may be proposed to the Constitution.

_____

_____

_____

_____

Identify two formal methods by which amendments may be ratified.

_____

_____

_____

_____

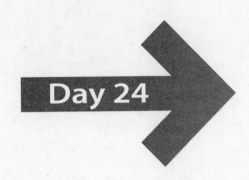

List and describe the informal methods by which the Constitution may be changed.

1. _____

_____

2. _____

_____

3. _____

_____

Explain why informal methods are used more often than the formal method.

_____

_____

_____

_____

Watch the video "Marbury v. Madison" at www.youtube.com/watch?v=hjVAGF-N8oQ. This video is an animated case brief of *Marbury v. Madison*, explaining the facts of the case and the decision that established the concept of judicial review.

Discuss Chief Justice Marshall's conclusions in the case of *Marbury v. Madison*.

_____

_____

_____

_____

Define *judicial review*.

_____

_____

_____

_____

_____

From the descriptions below, indicate the correct number of the amendment from the Bill of Rights.

_____ Protects against self-incrimination; guarantees due process, eminent domain, and grand jury indictment for capital crimes

_____ Ensures against excessive bail or fines and against cruel and unusual punishment

_____ Ensures the right to keep and bear arms

_____ Guarantees freedom of religion, speech, press, assembly, and petition

_____ Guarantees the rights to a speedy, public trial and an impartial jury; to confront witnesses; and to have an attorney

_____ Preserves the right to a jury trial in civil cases

_____ Regulates search, seizure, and warrants

_____ Reserves the powers of the states and the people

_____ Sets conditions for quartering troops in private homes

_____ Addresses the unenumerated rights of the people

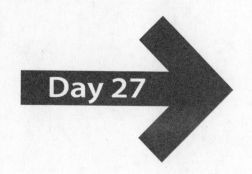

From the descriptions below, indicate the correct number of the amendment from the Constitution.

_____ Abolishes poll taxes

_____ Abolishes slavery

_____ Addresses congressional pay

_____ Addresses presidential succession, disability, and vice presidential vacancies

_____ Allows for voting rights in the District of Columbia in presidential elections

_____ Authorizes income tax

_____ Establishes direct election of senators by popular vote

_____ Establishes women's suffrage

_____ Gives eighteen-year-olds the right to vote

_____ Guarantees the right to vote regardless of race, color, or previous condition of servitude

_____ Guarantees the rights of citizenship, due process, and equal protection

_____ Limits presidential terms of office

_____ Prohibits intoxicating liquors

_____ Provides for the election of the president and vice president by separate ballot in the Electoral College

_____ Repeals Prohibition

_____ Sets terms and sessions of the executive and legislative branches ("lame duck")

_____ Restricts lawsuits against states

5 Minutes to a 5

Define *federalism*.

_____

_____

_____

_____

Explain why the Founding Fathers chose federalism for our national government.

_____

_____

_____

_____

Explain how federalism works in the United States.

_____

_____

_____

_____

Place each of the following powers of government in the correct category.

- Administer elections
- Borrow money
- Coin and print money
- Conduct foreign relations
- Declare war
- Enact and enforce laws
- Establish courts
- Establish federal courts below the Supreme Court

- Establish local governments
- Establish public school systems
- Levy taxes
- Make all laws "necessary and proper"
- Protect the public's health, welfare, and morals
- Provide an army and a navy
- Regulate foreign and interstate commerce
- Regulate intrastate commerce
- Spend for the general welfare

National Powers	Concurrent Powers	State Powers
•	•	•
•	•	•
•	•	•
•	•	•
•	•	•
•	•	•
•	•	•

Day 30

Classify each of the following descriptions of federalism as an advantage or a disadvantage of federalism.

- Accommodated already existing state governments
- Avoids concentration of political power
- Is complex, including many governments
- Has the possibility of conflicts of authority
- Duplicates offices and functions
- Is ideally suited to a large geographic area because it encourages diversity in local government
- Has the inflexibility inherent in a written constitution
- Keeps government close to the people
- Allows states to serve as training grounds for national leaders

Advantages of Federalism	Disadvantages of Federalism
•	•
•	•
•	•
•	•
•	

Match each of the following terms with the correct definition.

_____ Concurrent powers

_____ Delegated powers

_____ Implied powers

_____ Inherent powers

_____ Prohibited powers

_____ Reserved powers

A. Expressed, or enumerated, powers given specifically to the national government (Articles I–V)

B. Although not expressed, powers that may reasonably be inferred from the Constitution (Article I, Section 8, Clause 18—the necessary and proper clause, or elastic clause)

C. Powers that exist for the national government because the government is sovereign

D. Powers that belong to both the national and the state governments

E. Powers belonging specifically to the states because they were neither delegated to the national government nor denied to the states (Article IV; Amendment 10)

F. Powers that are denied to the national government, state governments, or both (Article I, Sections 9 and 10; Amendments to the Bill of Rights)

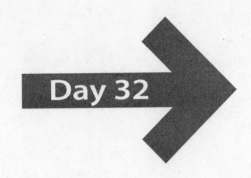

Explain how each of the following constitutional provisions supports the principle of federalism.

Tenth Amendment—reserved powers to the states and the people

_____

_____

_____

_____

Article V—amending the Constitution

_____

_____

_____

_____

5 Minutes to a 5

Day 33

Explain how each of the following constitutional provisions supports the principle of federalism.

Article VI—the supremacy clause

_____

_____

_____

_____

Article VII—ratification of the Constitution

_____

_____

_____

_____

Day 34

Match each of the following terms with the correct definition.

_____ Extradition

_____ Full faith and credit clause

_____ Interstate compacts

_____ Privileges and immunities clause

A. States are required to recognize the laws and legal documents of other states, such as birth certificates, marriage licenses, driver's licenses, and wills.

B. States are prohibited from unreasonably discriminating against residents of other states. Nonresidents may travel through other states; buy, sell, and hold property; and enter into contracts (does not extend to political rights such as the right to vote or run for political office, or to the right to practice certain regulated professions such as teaching).

C. States may return fugitives to another state from which they have fled to avoid criminal prosecution at the request of the governor of the other state.

D. States may make agreements, sometimes requiring congressional approval, to work together to solve regional problems. Some examples are "hot-pursuit agreements," parole and probation agreements, the Port Authority of New York and New Jersey, and regulating the common use of shared natural resources.

Place each of the following descriptions of federalism into the correct column.

- Marble cake federalism
- Began in the 1930s
- Nixon, Reagan, and Bush
- Earliest interpretation of federalism
- Expanded during the Great Society programs of President Johnson
- Devolution
- Layer cake federalism
- National and state governments sharing the making and implementation of policies
- Each level of government being separate from the other levels
- Transfer of more responsibility to the states on how grant money would be spent

Dual Federalism	Cooperative Federalism	New Federalism
•	•	•
•	•	•
•	•	•

Define *devolution*.

_____

_____

_____

_____

Explain how devolution increases the power of the states relative to the national government.

_____

_____

_____

_____

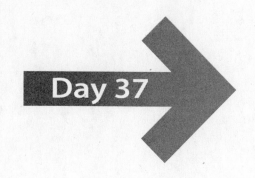

Match each of the following terms with the correct definition.

_____ Block grants   _____ Grant-in-aid programs

_____ Categorical grants   _____ Mandates

_____ Fiscal federalism   _____ Revenue sharing

A. Money and resources provided by the federal government to the state and local governments to be used for specific projects or programs

B. Grants that have a specific purpose defined by law, such as sewage treatment facilities or school lunch programs; may even require "matching funds" from the state or local governments

C. General grants that can be used for a variety of purposes within a broad category, such as education, health care, or public services; fewer strings attached so state and local governments have greater freedom in how the money is spent

D. The federal government's patterns of taxation, spending, and providing grants to influence state and local governments

E. Proposed under the Johnson administration and popular under the Nixon administration, a "no strings attached" form of aid to state and local governments; could be used for virtually any project; eliminated during the Reagan administration

F. Requirements imposed by the federal government requiring that state and local governments meet those requirements (For example, the Americans with Disabilities Act [1990] requires that all public buildings be accessible to persons with disabilities.)

Explain how each of the following have been used over time to expand federal power.

Necessary and proper clause (elastic clause)

_____

_____

_____

Commerce clause

_____

_____

_____

_____

Explain how each of the following have been used to increase the power of the federal government over the states.

Mandates

_____

_____

_____

_____

Categorical grants

_____

_____

_____

_____

Explain how each of the following have been used to increase the power of the states relative to the federal government.

Block grants

_____

_____

_____

_____

Tenth Amendment

_____

_____

_____

_____

Day 41

Define *political culture*.

_____

_____

_____

_____

Explain how political culture differs from political ideology.

_____

_____

_____

_____

Match each of the following American democratic values with the correct definition.

_____ Compromise

_____ Equality

_____ Individual freedoms

_____ Limited government

_____ Majority rule/minority rights

_____ Private property

A. Public policy is determined by a majority of citizens, but the majority may not rightfully use its power to deprive minority groups of their rights.

B. The equality of every individual is protected before the law and in the political process.

C. Ownership of property is protected by law and supported by the capitalist system.

D. Civil liberties are guaranteed, and there are protections from infringements on them.

E. Different interests and opinions may be combined to form public policy that best benefits society.

F. The powers of government are restricted in a democracy by the will of the people and the law.

Day 43

Define *political socialization.*

_____

_____

_____

Identify and discuss the major influences that contribute to political socialization.

_____

_____

_____

_____

Define *public opinion*.

_____

_____

_____

Explain how public opinion is measured.

_____

_____

_____

_____

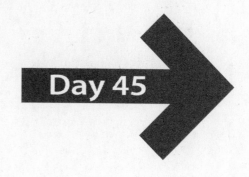

Identify at least three characteristics of a valid, scientific public opinion poll.

1. _____

2. _____

3. _____

Explain why these characteristics are necessary.

_____

_____

_____

_____

Day 46

Define *ideology*.

_____

_____

_____

_____

Define *political ideology*.

_____

_____

_____

_____

Day 47

Participate in the Youth Leadership Initiative's Political Ideology Survey. Take the online survey at www.youthleadership.net/econgress/political_ideology_survey?_yli_session=4e3e8eeed513c5bce37026e1965e7b5b to help you determine your political party preference.

Postsurvey questions for thought:

• What was the final result of your survey?

• Did you place on the political spectrum where you thought you would?

• What description did the survey give your placement?

Day 48

Match each of the following with the correct definition.

_____ Conservative

_____ Liberal

_____ Moderate

_____ Radical

_____ Reactionary

A. Favors rapid, fundamental change in existing social, economic, or political order; may be willing to resort to extreme means, even violence or revolution to accomplish such change (extreme change to create an entirely new social system)

B. Supports active government in promoting individual welfare and supporting civil rights; accepts peaceful political and social change within the existing political system

C. Has a political ideology that falls between liberal and conservative and may include some elements of both; usually thought of as tolerant of others' political opinions and not likely to hold extreme views on issues

D. Promotes a limited governmental role in helping individuals economically; supports traditional values and lifestyles; favors a more active role for government in promoting national security; and approaches change cautiously

E. Advocates a return to a previous state of affairs, often a social order or government that existed earlier in history; may be willing to go to extremes to achieve these goals

Day 49

Define *political party.*

_____

_____

_____

_____

Identify the components of a political party.

1. _____

2. _____

3. _____

Explain how political parties serve in each of the following roles.

Party in the electorate (PIE)

_____

_____

_____

_____

Party in government (PIG)

_____

_____

_____

_____

Party in organization (PO)

_____

_____

_____

_____

5 Minutes to a 5

Day 51

Identify and describe the main functions of political parties.

1. _____

   _____

2. _____

   _____

3. _____

   _____

4. _____

   _____

Day 52

Read Federalist #10 (James Madison) at http://teachingamericanhistory.org/library/document/federalist-no-10. Then watch the following two videos on the subject:

1. "Explaining Federalist Paper #10: US Government Review" at www.youtube.com/watch?v=GNN95-ICOMI. This video is a short summary of the meaning behind Federalist Paper #10, written by James Madison.

2. "AP United States Government Project: The Federalist Papers #10" at www.youtube.com/watch?v=Uu3POpPbZcw. This presentation analyzes the essay written by James Madison regarding factions and considering the arguments made by Madison for the ratification of the Constitution.

Answer the following questions:

• What is a faction?

• How did Madison view the existence of a faction in America?

• What factors were most likely the source of any faction that arose, according to Madison?

• What form of government did Madison want to create?

• How can we cure the "mischief of faction"?

Define *one-party system.*

_____

_____

_____

_____

Define *two-party system.*

_____

_____

_____

_____

Define *multiparty system.*

_____

_____

_____

_____

_____

Day 54

Explain why the United States has a two-party tradition.

1. _____

_____

2. _____

_____

3. _____

_____

Define *divided government*.

_____

_____

_____

_____

Define *gridlock*.

_____

_____

_____

_____

Explain why divided government often leads to gridlock.

_____

_____

_____

_____

_____

Define *electoral dealignment.*

_____

_____

_____

_____

Define *electoral realignment.*

_____

_____

_____

_____

Day 57

List and describe the four major types of minor political parties.

1. _____

   _____

2. _____

   _____

3. _____

   _____

4. _____

   _____

Explain how each of the following is a barrier to minor party success.

Single-member districts

_____

_____

_____

_____

Winner-take-all system

_____

_____

_____

_____

Identify factors that have led to the decline in political parties in recent years.

1. _____

_____

2. _____

_____

3. _____

_____

4. _____

_____

5. _____

_____

6. _____

_____

5 Minutes to a 5

Day 60

Define *political participation.*

_____

_____

_____

Identify the most common form of political participation.

_____

_____

_____

_____

Other than voting, what are other forms of political participation?

_____

_____

_____

_____

Define *suffrage*.

_____

_____

_____

Identify who makes up the electorate.

_____

_____

_____

_____

Day 63

List and describe the constitutional amendments that have increased suffrage in the United States.

1. _____

_____

2. _____

_____

3. _____

_____

4. _____

_____

5. _____

_____

Day 64

Match each of the following terms with the correct definition.

_____ Direct primary

_____ Initiative

_____ Recall

_____ Referendum

A. Allows a special election initiated by petition so citizens can remove an official from office before a term expires

B. Allows citizens to vote directly on issues called propositions (proposed laws or constitutional amendments)

C. Allows voters to petition to propose issues to be decided by qualified voters

D. Allows citizens to nominate candidates

Identify three reasons for low voter turnout in the United States.

1. _____

   _____

2. _____

   _____

3. _____

   _____

Match each of the following terms with the correct definition.

_____ Primary

_____ General election

_____ Special election

A. Elections that are held whenever an issue must be decided by voters

B. Nominating elections in which voters choose the candidates who will represent the party

C. Elections in which voters choose from among all the candidates representing all the parties

Match each of the following terms with the correct definition.

_____ Closed primary

_____ Open primary

_____ Blanket primary

_____ Runoff election

A. Voters may vote for candidates of either party, choosing a Republican for one office and a Democrat for another office.

B. Only voters who are registered in the party may vote to choose the candidate.

C. When no candidate receives a majority of the votes, the top two candidates face off against each other.

D. Voters may vote to choose the candidates of either party, whether they belong to that party or not; voters make the decision of which party to support.

Place each of the following steps in the presidential election process in the correct order by placing 1 in front of the step that occurs first, 2 in front of the next step, and so on.

_____ Announcement

_____ Campaigning/general election

_____ Electoral College vote

_____ Exploration

_____ Nominating convention

_____ Primary/caucus

_____ Inauguration

Define *presidential preference primary.*

_____

_____

_____

_____

Define *caucus.*

_____

_____

_____

_____

Define *frontloading*.

_____

_____

_____

_____

Explain how frontloading affects candidates.

_____

_____

_____

_____

5 Minutes to a 5

Day 71

Explain Super Tuesday.

_____

_____

_____

_____

Explain why Super Tuesday is important to candidates.

_____

_____

_____

_____

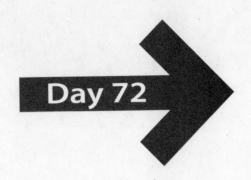

Day 72

Go to www.270towin.com/maps/2016-election-battleground-states and look at the interactive map of the United States. Click on the interactive map to predict who will win the presidential election.

Define *battleground state/swing state.*

_____

_____

_____

_____

Discuss how candidates approach their campaigns in battleground/swing states.

_____

_____

_____

_____

Define the *coattail effect*.

_____

_____

_____

_____

Describe the Electoral College.

_____

_____

_____

_____

Identify how many total electors make up the Electoral College.

_____

_____

_____

_____

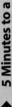

Explain why the Founding Fathers provided for the Electoral College to elect the president.

1. _____

_____

2. _____

_____

3. _____

_____

4. _____

_____

Identify how many electoral votes each state receives.

_____

_____

_____

_____

5 Minutes to a 5

Discuss when and where the Electoral College meets.

_____

_____

_____

_____

Discuss how many electoral votes are necessary for a candidate to win the election.

_____

_____

_____

_____

Explain what happens if no candidate for president receives a majority of electoral votes.

_____

_____

_____

_____

Explain what happens if no candidate for vice president receives a majority of electoral votes.

_____

_____

_____

_____

5 Minutes to a 5

Match each of the following terms with the correct definition.

_____ Critical elections

_____ Dealigning elections

_____ Deviating elections

_____ Maintaining elections

_____ Realigning elections

A. Elections that occur when the traditional major party maintains power based on the loyalty of voters

B. Elections in which the minority party is able to win with the support of majority party members, independents, and new voters (The long-term party preferences of voters does not change.)

C. Elections that demonstrate sharp changes in existing patterns of party loyalty due to changing social and economic conditions

D. Elections in which the minority party wins by building a new coalition of voters that continues over successive elections

E. Elections in which party loyalty becomes less important to voters (Many voters may see themselves as independents or engage in split-ticket voting.)

Match each of the following Supreme Court rulings with the correct description.

_____ *Buckley v. Valeo* (1976)

_____ *Citizens United v. FEC* (2010)

_____ *McCutcheon v. FEC* (2014)

A. The government cannot prevent citizens from giving campaign contributions to as many different candidates and political parties as they want. This ruling struck down the aggregate (total) limits placed on campaign contributions.

B. The Supreme Court struck down spending limits established under the Federal Election Campaign Act (FECA) amendments of 1974 as unconstitutional restrictions of the First Amendment's freedom of expression. The Court ruled that there could be no restrictions on contributions from individuals and groups, as long as they were independent of any official election campaigns. The ruling led to the rise of political action committees (PACs).

C. The Supreme Court ruled that limiting the ability of businesses, unions, and other groups to fund their own efforts to elect or defeat candidates for office is unconstitutional. Political spending is a form of protected speech under the First Amendment.

Discuss the provisions of the Federal Election Campaign Act (FECA).

_____

_____

_____

Discuss what amendments were added to the FECA in 1974.

_____

_____

_____

_____

Define *soft money*.

_____

_____

_____

_____

Discuss what reforms were implemented as a result of the Bipartisan Campaign Reform Act (BCRA) in 2002.

_____

_____

_____

_____

5 Minutes to a 5

Define *527*s.

_____

_____

_____

_____

Watch the 527 ads at www.livingroomcandidate.org/news/perma/new-527-ads-are
-released-one-anti-obama-one-anti-mccain.

Define *interest groups.*

_____

_____

_____

_____

Explain how interest groups are different from political parties.

_____

_____

_____

_____

Identify the four major functions of interest groups.

1. _____

_____

2. _____

_____

3. _____

_____

4. _____

_____

Describe each of the following strategies used by interest groups.

Influencing elections

_____

_____

_____

_____

Lobbying

_____

_____

_____

_____

Describe each of the following strategies used by interest groups.

Litigation

_____

_____

_____

_____

Going public

_____

_____

_____

_____

Define *political action committee (PAC)*.

_____

_____

_____

_____

Explain how political action committees are regulated.

_____

_____

_____

_____

_____

Explain how interest groups are regulated.

_____

_____

_____

_____

Define *mass media*.

_____

_____

_____

Describe what makes the mass media different from other linkage institutions.

_____

_____

_____

_____

Watch the video "Media Institution: Crash Course Government and Politics #44" at www.youtube.com/watch?v=6F0g4N415uw. This video discusses types of media; roles of the media, especially in politics; strengths and weaknesses of the media; how the media affects voters; and the importance of the media as a linkage institution.

Identify the five major forms of mass media.

1. _____

2. _____

3. _____

4. _____

5. _____

Place a check next to the roles of the mass media.

_____ Agenda setting

_____ Holding elections

_____ Nominating candidates

_____ Acting as an organization tool for the government

_____ Providing a link between citizens and government

_____ Shaping public opinion

_____ Informing the public

_____ Serving as a watchdog that investigates/examines government

Define *news*.

_____

_____

_____

_____

Identify the "gatekeepers."

_____

_____

_____

_____

Explain how gatekeepers affect what is news.

_____

_____

_____

_____

Define *news leaks*.

_____

_____

_____

_____

Explain why the executive branch would use leaks.

_____

_____

_____

_____

Describe how the media covers the actions of the president.

_____

_____

_____

Describe how the media covers the actions of Congress.

_____

_____

_____

_____

Define *pack journalism*.

_____

_____

_____

Define *horse race journalism*.

_____

_____

_____

_____

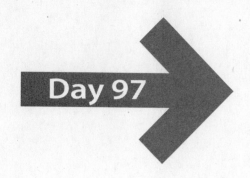

Discuss the influence of the media on each of the following:

Public agenda

_____

_____

_____

_____

Electoral politics

_____

_____

_____

_____

Discuss the influence of the media on each of the following.

Executive branch

_____

_____

_____

_____

Legislative branch

_____

_____

_____

_____

Judicial branch

_____

_____

_____

_____

5 Minutes to a 5

Identify the portion of the U.S. Constitution that created the legislative branch.

_____

_____

_____

_____

Define *bicameral legislature.*

_____

_____

_____

_____

Explain why the Founding Fathers created a bicameral legislature.

_____

_____

_____

_____

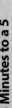

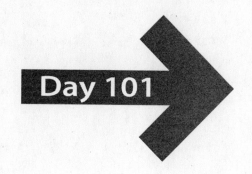

Complete the following chart about the House of Representatives and the Senate.

	House of Representatives	Senate
Membership/size		
Term of office		
Qualifications		
Method of election		

Match each of the following terms with the correct definition.

_____ Apportionment

_____ Reapportionment

_____ Congressional redistricting

_____ Gerrymandering

A. The drawing of congressional districts to favor one political party or group over another

B. Distribution among the states based on the population of each of the states

C. The drawing, by state legislature, of congressional districts for those states with more than one representative

D. The redistribution of congressional seats after the census determines changes in population distribution among the states

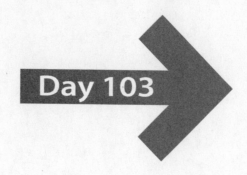
Explain how congressional reapportionment can benefit or hurt states.

_____

_____

_____

_____

Participate in the Redistricting Game at http://redistrictinggame.org.

The Redistricting Game allows participants to view a short informational video about redistricting and then try to redistrict an imaginary state. The game offers several types of redistricting and levels of difficulty. Explain how congressional reapportionment can benefit or hurt states.

According to the original Constitution, how were members of the Senate chosen?

_____

_____

_____

_____

Discuss how members of the Senate are chosen today.

_____

_____

_____

_____

Day 106

Define *incumbency effect.*

_____

_____

_____

Identify which house of Congress experiences a stronger incumbency effect.

_____

_____

_____

_____

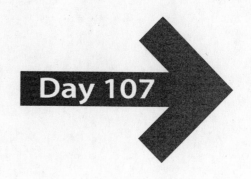

Describe how each of the following adds to the incumbency effect for members of Congress.

Name recognition

_____
_____
_____
_____

Credit claiming

_____
_____
_____
_____

Casework for constituents

_____
_____
_____
_____

More visible/franking privilege

_____
_____
_____
_____

Describe how each of the following adds to the incumbency effect for members of Congress.

Media exposure

_____

_____

_____

Fund-raising activities

_____

_____

_____

Experience in campaigning

_____

_____

_____

Voting record

_____

_____

_____

_____

5 Minutes to a 5

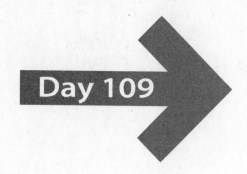

Identify the presiding officer of the House of Representatives.

_____

_____

_____

_____

Explain how the presiding officer of the House of Representatives is chosen.

_____

_____

_____

_____

_____

Describe the role of each of the following in Congress.

Majority leader

_____

_____

_____

_____

Minority leader

_____

_____

_____

_____

Majority whip/minority whip

_____

_____

_____

_____

Identify who serves as presiding officer of the Senate.

_____

_____

_____

_____

Discuss the limitations placed on the presiding officer of the Senate.

_____

_____

_____

_____

Identify the role of the president pro tempore of the Senate.

_____

_____

_____

Explain how the president pro tempore of the Senate is chosen.

_____

_____

_____

_____

Describe the role of committees/subcommittees in Congress.

_____

_____

_____

_____

Describe the role of the committee chairperson.

_____

_____

_____

_____

Match each of the following types of committees to the correct description.

_____ Conference

_____ Joint

_____ Select

_____ Standing

A. A permanent committee that deals with specific policy matters

B. A temporary committee of members from both houses of Congress, created to resolve the differences in House and Senate versions of a bill

C. A committee of members from both houses of Congress that often performs routine duties

D. A temporary committee appointed for a specific purpose, such as investigating a particular issue

Describe the role of each of the following committees in the House of Representatives.

House Rules Committee

_____

_____

_____

_____

House Ways and Means Committee

_____

_____

_____

_____

House Appropriations Committee

_____

_____

_____

_____

Describe the role of each of the following committees in the Senate.

Senate Foreign Relations Committee

_____

_____

_____

_____

Senate Judiciary Committee

_____

_____

_____

_____

Senate Appropriations Committee

_____

_____

_____

_____

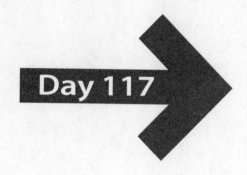

Discuss the role of a legislative caucus.

_____

_____

_____

_____

Day 118

Describe each of the following models of congressional representation.

Delegate

_____

_____

_____

_____

Trustee

_____

_____

_____

_____

Discuss each of the following.

Expressed powers of Congress

_____

_____

_____

_____

Implied powers of Congress

_____

_____

_____

_____

_____

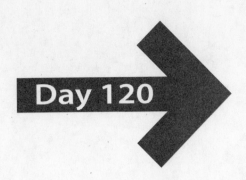
Describe the role of Congress in the impeachment process.

_____

_____

_____

_____

5 Minutes to a 5

Day 121

Describe the investigative/oversight powers of Congress.

_____

_____

_____

_____

Watch the following two videos:

"Schoolhouse Rock—How a Bill Becomes a Law" at www.youtube.com/watch?v=Otbml6WIQPo

"How a Bill Really Becomes a Law: What Schoolhouse Rock Missed" at www.youtube.com/watch?v=QH0Hl31vdF4

Define *bill*.

_____

_____

_____

_____

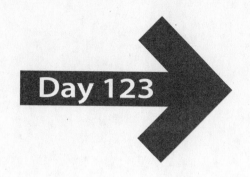

Day 123

Place each of the following steps in the correct order to show the process of how a bill becomes a law when introduced in the House of Representatives.

_____ Assigned to committee

_____ Introduced

_____ Committee approves or rejects bill

_____ Conference committee

_____ Floor debate

_____ Floor vote

_____ Presidential action

_____ Returned to committee

_____ Returned to House for floor vote

_____ Rules committee

_____ Sent to Senate

_____ Sent to subcommittee for further study

Match each of the following legislative tactics to the correct definition.

_____ Amendments

_____ Cloture

_____ Filibuster

_____ Pork barrel legislation

_____ Riders

A. Unlimited debate in an attempt to stall action on a bill; occurs in the Senate only

B. An attempt to provide funds and projects for a member's home district or state

C. Additions or changes to legislation that deal specifically with the legislation

D. Additions to legislation that usually have no connection to the legislation but that would not pass on their own merit

E. A method by which the Senate can limit debate and end a filibuster

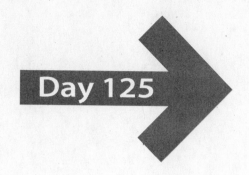

Identify each of the individuals and groups that may influence how members of Congress vote.

1. _____

2. _____

3. _____

4. _____

5. _____

Read the short article about party polarization "Mischiefs of Faction: Reflections on Parties and Their Place in Politics" at www.mischiefsoffaction.com/2012/10/partisan-polarization-in-congress.html.

Define *party polarization*.

_____

_____

_____

_____

Explain how party polarization affects public policymaking.

_____

_____

_____

_____

Identify the portion of the Constitution that created the executive branch.

_____

_____

_____

_____

Describe the executive branch.

_____

_____

_____

_____

How long is the president's term of office?

_____

_____

_____

Describe the provisions of the Twenty-second Amendment.

_____

_____

_____

_____

Explain why the Twenty-fifth Amendment was added to the Constitution.

_____

_____

_____

_____

Discuss the major provisions of the Twenty-fifth Amendment concerning presidential disability.

_____

_____

_____

_____

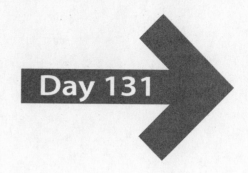
Identify and describe the constitutional duties of the vice president.

_____

_____

_____

_____

Identify and discuss the factors that influence the selection of the vice president.

_____

_____

_____

_____

Match each of the following presidential powers with the correct category.

- Accords diplomatic recognition to foreign governments
- Appoints members of the federal judiciary
- Appoints and removes officials
- Appoints party members to government positions (patronage)
- Chooses the vice presidential nominee
- Enforces laws, treaties, and court decisions
- Grants reprieves, pardons, and amnesty
- Has final decision-making authority in matters of national and foreign defense
- Issues annual budget and economic reports
- Meets with foreign leaders in international conferences
- Presides over the executive branch
- Proposes legislation and uses influence to get it passed
- Provides for domestic order
- Receives foreign dignitaries
- Serves as commander-in-chief of the armed forces
- Signs or vetoes bills
- Strengthens the party by helping members get elected ("coattails")

Executive Powers	Legislative Powers	Judicial Powers
•	•	•
•	•	•
•	•	•
Diplomatic Powers	**Military Powers**	**Party Powers**
•	•	•
•	•	•
•	•	•

To avoid the possibility of abuses by the executive, the Founding Fathers provided checks on that executive's powers. Explain how each of the following limits the power of the president.

Approval power over appointments

_____

_____

_____

_____

Power of the purse

_____

_____

_____

_____

Power of impeachment

_____

_____

_____

_____

Power to override presidential vetoes

_____

_____

_____

_____

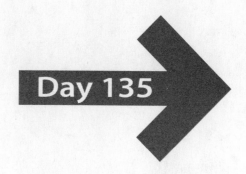

Discuss the provisions of the War Powers Act.

_____

_____

_____

_____

Define *legislative veto*.

_____

_____

_____

_____

Define *bureaucracy*.

_____

_____

_____

_____

Identify the three basic principles of a bureaucracy.

1. _____

2. _____

3. _____

Day 138

Visit the American Presidency Project website at www.presidency.ucsb.edu/data/orders.php. It contains a chart of the number of executive orders issued by presidents from George Washington to Barack Obama.

Define *executive orders*.

_____

_____

_____

_____

Explain how executive orders increase the power of the president.

_____

_____

_____

_____

Compare the characteristics of treaties and executive agreements.

Treaty	Executive Agreement
•	•
•	•

Explain how each of the following can limit presidential powers.

Congress

_____

_____

_____

_____

Courts

_____

_____

_____

_____

Match each of the following entities to the correct description.

_____ Cabinet departments

_____ Government corporations

_____ Independent executive agencies

_____ Independent regulatory agencies

A. Fifteen executive departments created to advise the president and operate a specific policy area of governmental activity

B. Similar to departments but without cabinet status

C. Independent from the executive; created to regulate or police

D. Created by Congress to carry out business-like activities; generally recompensed for services

Day 142

Describe the role of each of the following.

Executive Office of the President (EOP)

_____

_____

_____

_____

White House Office

_____

_____

_____

National Security Council

_____

_____

_____

Office of Management and Budget (OMB)

_____

_____

_____

_____

5 Minutes to a 5

Define *iron triangles*.

_____

_____

_____

_____

Define *issue networks*.

_____

_____

_____

_____

Identify executive influences on the bureaucracy.

_____

_____

_____

_____

Identify congressional influences on the bureaucracy.

_____

_____

_____

_____

Match each of the following interactions of an iron triangle with the correct number from the figure.

_____ Congress provides positive legislation, access to the legislative arena, and information.

_____ Congressional committee members provide budgetary support, information, access to the legislative process, and positive legislation.

_____ Interest groups provide information, electoral support, and campaign contributions.

_____ The bureaucracy provides positive legislative enforcement and information.

_____ The bureaucracy provides positive legislative enforcement, information, research, and access to the legislative process.

_____ Interest groups provide information, research, enforcement, and budgetary support through testimony.

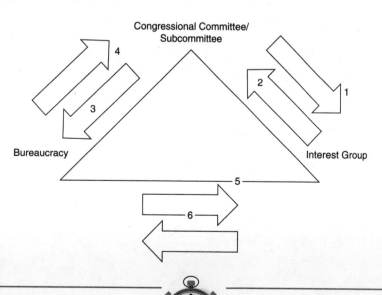

Watch the video "Federalist #78 Explained: Government Review" at www.youtube .com/watch?v=L5gAVO6op8A. The video gives an overview of Federalist #78 and Alexander Hamilton's defense of the judiciary.

Answer the following questions:

- According to Alexander Hamilton, why is the judicial branch the least dangerous of the three branches?

- Why did Hamilton believe that the judiciary must declare any legislative act that is contrary to the Constitution "void"?

- What did Hamilton hope judges would do when interpreting the Constitution?

Day 147

Match each of the following terms to the correct definition.

_____ Appellate jurisdiction

_____ Concurrent jurisdiction

_____ Original jurisdiction

A. Lower courts that have the authority to hear cases for the first time

B. Courts that hear reviews or appeals of decisions from the lower courts

C. Allows certain types of cases to be tried in either the federal or the state courts

Identify the primary function of each of the following national courts.

Supreme Court

_____

_____

_____

_____

Courts of Appeals

_____

_____

_____

_____

District Courts

_____

_____

_____

_____

_____

5 Minutes to a 5

Day 149

Describe three political factors that affect the president's decisions when appointing members of the federal judiciary.

1. _____

_____

2. _____

_____

3. _____

_____

Identify two legislative powers that serve as a check on court decisions.

_____

_____

_____

_____

Identify two executive powers that serve as a check on court decisions.

_____

_____

_____

_____

Describe the role that each of the following plays in the process of a case coming to the Supreme Court.

Writ of certiorari

_____

_____

_____

_____

Rule of four

_____

_____

_____

_____

Match each of the following terms to the correct definition.

_____ Majority opinion

_____ Concurring opinion

_____ Dissenting opinion

A. A majority of justices who agree on the decision and its reasons

B. A justice who agrees with the majority opinion but not with the reasoning behind the decision

C. A justice or justices who disagree with the majority opinion

Day 153

Define *judicial activism.*

_____

_____

_____

_____

Define *judicial restraint.*

_____

_____

_____

_____

Define *civil liberties*.

_____

_____

_____

Define *civil rights*.

_____

_____

_____

Day 155

Describe each of the following fundamental freedoms guaranteed by the Constitution.

Writ of habeas corpus

_____

_____

_____

Bills of attainder

_____

_____

_____

Ex post facto laws

_____

_____

_____

_____

Discuss each of the following clauses of the Fourteenth Amendment.

Due process clause

_____

_____

_____

Equal protection clause

_____

_____

_____

Citizenship clause

_____

_____

_____

_____

Define *selective incorporation*.

_____

_____

_____

Explain how selective incorporation protects the rights of citizens.

_____

_____

_____

_____

Describe each of the following clauses of the First Amendment.

Establishment clause

_____

_____

_____

Free exercise clause

_____

_____

_____

Match each of the following freedom of religion cases with the correct decision.

_____ *Engel v. Vitale* (1962)

_____ *Lemon v. Kurtzman* (1971)

_____ *Reynolds v. United States* (1879)

_____ *Wisconsin v. Yoder* (1972)

_____ *Employment Division of Oregon v. Smith* (1990)

A. The Court upheld the federal law that prohibited polygamy, even though a Mormon from Utah claimed that the law limited his religious freedom.

B. The Court ruled that states could not require Amish parents to send their children to public school beyond the eighth grade because it would violate long-held religious beliefs.

C. The Court ruled that a state could deny unemployment benefits to workers fired for using drugs (peyote) as part of a religious ceremony.

D. The Court ruled that school-sanctioned prayer in public schools is unconstitutional.

E. The Court struck down a law reimbursing parochial schools for textbooks and teacher salaries and established a test to determine whether a law violates the First Amendment's freedom of religion article.

Identify the purpose of the Lemon Test.

_____

_____

_____

Describe the three provisions of the Lemon Test.

_____

_____

_____

5 Minutes to a 5

Define *pure speech*.

_____

_____

_____

Define *speech plus*.

_____

_____

_____

Define *symbolic speech*.

_____

_____

_____

Match each of the following First Amendment cases with the correct decision.

_____ *Engel v. Vitale* (1962)

_____ *Tinker v. Des Moines* (1969)

_____ *Wisconsin v. Yoder* (1972)

_____ *Schenck v. United States* (1919)

_____ *New York Times v. United States* (1971)

A. The Court ruled that wearing black armbands in protest of the Vietnam War was symbolic speech and protected by the First Amendment.

B. The Court ruled school sponsorship of religious activities violates the establishment clause.

C. The Court ruled compelling Amish students to attend school past the eighth grade violates the free exercise clause of the First Amendment.

D. The Court ruled speech creating a "clear and present danger" is not protected by the First Amendment.

E. The Court reaffirmed its position on prior restraint, refusing to stop the publication of the Pentagon Papers.

Define *eminent domain*.

_____

_____

_____

Explain how the Supreme Court interpreted the right to privacy in each of the following cases.

Griswold v. Connecticut (1965)

_____

_____

_____

Roe v. Wade (1973)

_____

_____

_____

Identify the provisions of the Fourth Amendment.

_____

_____

_____

Define *exclusionary rule*.

_____

_____

_____

Define *inevitable discovery*.

_____

_____

_____

_____

Define *good faith exception*.

_____

_____

_____

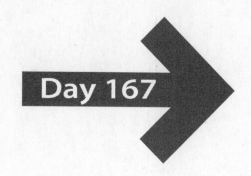

Match each of the following cases to the correct decision.

_____ *Gideon v. Wainwright* (1963)

_____ *Roe v. Wade* (1973)

_____ *Miranda v. Arizona* (1966)

A. The Court ruled that suspects in police custody have certain rights (such as the right to remain silent or the right to an attorney) and that they must be informed of those rights.

B. The Court ruled that in state trials, those who cannot afford an attorney will have one provided by the state, overturning *Betts v. Brady*.

C. The Court extended the right of privacy to a woman's decision to have an abortion.

5 Minutes to a 5

Read the comparison of *Plessy v. Ferguson* and *Brown v. Board of Education*, with short quotes from the rulings, on the PBS website "The Supreme Court" at www.pbs.org/wnet/supremecourt/rights/change1.html.

Discuss the decision of the Supreme Court in each of the following cases.

Plessy v. Ferguson (1896)

_____

_____

_____

Brown v. Board of Education (1954)

_____

_____

_____

Explain how each of the following expanded the electorate.

Twenty-fourth Amendment

_____

_____

_____

Voting Rights Act of 1965

_____

_____

_____

Define *affirmative action*.

_____

_____

_____

Describe the significance of *Regents of the University of California v. Bakke* (1978).

_____

_____

_____

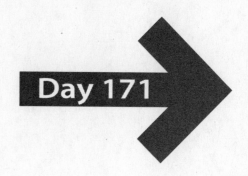
Day 171

Define *public policy.*

_____

_____

_____

Define *political agenda.*

_____

_____

_____

_____

Number each of the following policymaking steps in the correct order.

_____ Agenda setting

_____ Policy adoption

_____ Policy evaluation

_____ Policy formulation

_____ Policy implementation

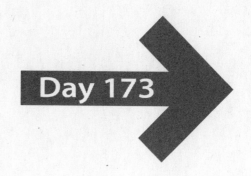

Match each of the following policymaking steps with the correct description.

_____ Agenda setting

_____ Policy formulation

_____ Policy adoption

_____ Policy implementation

_____ Policy evaluation

A. Recognizing an issue as a problem that must be addressed as a part of the political agenda. Problems are often brought to the political agenda by citizens, interest groups, the media, or governmental entities.

B. Finding ways to solve a problem by exploring alternative plans of action and developing proposals for solutions.

C. Adopting a plan of action to solve a problem. This may require the passage of legislation.

D. Executing the plan of action. This is performed by the appropriate agency or agencies.

E. Analyzing the policy and its impact on the problem. This includes judging the policy's effectiveness and making adjustments if necessary.

Identify the major provisions of each of the following public policy acts of Congress.

Civil Rights Act of 1964

_____

_____

_____

Americans with Disabilities Act (1990)

_____

_____

_____

Social Security Act (1935)

_____

_____

_____

_____

Define *fiscal policy*.

_____

_____

_____

Explain the difference between discretionary and nondiscretionary spending.

_____

_____

_____

5 Minutes to a 5

See information on the president's budget for fiscal year 2017 at www.whitehouse.gov/omb/budget.

Define *federal budget*.

_____

_____

_____

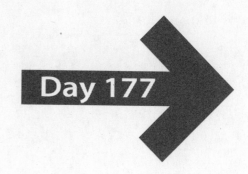

Day 177

Discuss the role of the executive branch in the federal budget process.

_____

_____

_____

Discuss the role of Congress in the federal budget process.

_____

_____

_____

Describe the role of the president in the development of foreign policy.

_____

_____

_____

Describe the role of Congress in the development of foreign policy.

_____

_____

_____

Answers

Day 1

Government comprises the formal and informal institutions, people, and processes used to create and conduct public policy.

Public policy is the exercise of governmental powers in creating those things necessary to maintain legitimate authority and control over society.

Day 2

According to Harold Laswell, politics is "who gets what, when, and how." Politics involves the individuals and groups (who) who use various tactics (how) over time (when) to achieve their goals (what).

Government involves the official rules of society (such as the U.S. Constitution and the Bill of Rights), while politics is how society uses those rules to accomplish goals (how the game is played). An example of government would be the constitutional provision for the president to veto legislation; politics would be the president threatening to use the veto to influence Congress.

Day 3

Watch the video "An Introduction to Government and Politics" at www.youtube.com /watch?v=AnHW_t8Qwwc. This video is a basic introduction to the AP Government and Politics curriculum. It provides an overview of the six major content areas, including vocabulary terms relevant to the course.

Day 4

Democracy is a Greek term that means "rule by the people." In a democracy, power is granted through the consent of the people. U.S. president Abraham Lincoln defined democracy as "government of the people, by the people, for the people." A democracy may be either direct or representative.

A direct democracy, or pure democracy, allows citizens to meet and make decisions about public policy issues, usually through direct voting on those issues.

A representative democracy, or indirect democracy, allows citizens to choose officials (representatives) who make decisions about public policy. The United States practices representative democracy, with the citizens electing members of Congress, state legislatures, and so on to make public policy decisions for them.

Day 5

Theory	Description/Basis of Power	Characteristics
Traditional Democracy	A majority of people determine policy on a particular issue. The civil rights/liberties of numerical minorities are protected as well.	No one group constitutes a majority on all issues. Compromise is necessary to get enough agreement to achieve a majority.
Pluralism	Certain interest groups have power on certain topics. Not all people in society are represented by interest groups, and not all groups are equally powerful. (*Robert Dahl*)	No one group dominates on every issue, but these groups compete. The groups with more money and contacts have more power.
Elite/Class Theory	One core elite—typically of the wealthiest people—influences government. The core may change from time to time. (*C. Wright Mills*)	There is a powerful elite (corporate leaders, top military officers, and government officials) upper class, and government is a tool of this class. All politicians serve as pawns for the interests of the elite.

Day 6

Theory	Description/Basis of Power	Characteristics
Bureaucratic Theory	Bureaucrats who carry out the day-to-day workings of government hold real power over decision making and implementation of public policy. (*Max Weber*)	Bureaucracies have a hierarchical structure, impersonality, standardized procedures, and specialized division of labor.
Hyperpluralism	Many groups are strong and have influence over government at the same time.	Government is often pulled in numerous directions at the same time, causing gridlock and ineffectiveness.

Day 7

John Locke was an Enlightenment philosopher and writer who supported the social contract theory.

A social contract is a voluntary agreement between government and the governed. In *Two Treatises on Civil Government* (1689), Locke stated the following:

- People are born with natural rights (life, liberty, and property), and no government may take these rights away.

- Governments are created to support and protect these rights.

- If government fails to support and protect these rights, the people may choose to change their government (right to revolt).

Locke's theory of social contract was the basis for much of Thomas Jefferson's ideas in the Declaration of Independence (1776).

Day 8

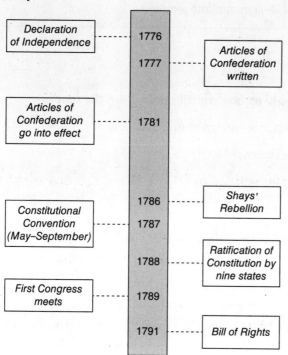

Day 9

Watch the video "The Passing of the Declaration of Independence—John Adams— HBO" at www.youtube.com/watch?v=uNOTozVp_i4. This video shows a re-creation of the key historical event of a roll call vote that would determine whether the states would accept Richard Henry Lee's resolution on declaring independence. One negative vote would cause the resolution to fail.

Day 10

Watch the video "A Reading of the Declaration of Independence (Mirror)" at www .youtube.com/watch?v=DSKOx8DKPIg. Morgan Freeman narrates this short documentary in which celebrities read the U.S. Declaration of Independence.

Day 11

Type of Governmental System	Confederation
Number of legislative houses	One (unicameral)
Method of representation	One vote for each, regardless of population or size
Executive branch	No national executive
Judicial branch	No national judiciary
Passage of legislation	Nine of thirteen states required to pass legislation
Amendment of Articles	Unanimous vote required

Day 12

Any of the following are correct.

1. Congress could not tax; it could only request contributions from the states.

2. Congress could not regulate interstate or foreign commerce.

3. Congress had no power to enforce its laws.

4. The government had no executive branch.

5. The government had no national judiciary.

6. Approval of nine of the thirteen states was needed to pass legislation.

7. Unanimous consent was required to amend the Articles of Confederation.

Day 13

The Constitutional Convention, sometimes called the Philadelphia Convention, met in Philadelphia, Pennsylvania. It began in May 1787 and continued until September of that same year.

The original purpose of the Constitutional Convention was to revise the Articles of Confederation. After Shays' Rebellion had occurred, many people began to realize that the government created under the Articles of Confederation was too weak to deal with the nation's problems. Economic chaos and violence led the states to call for a convention of delegates from all states to strengthen the government. Very early during the convention, however, the delegates decided that they would write a new constitution instead of revising the Articles.

Day 14

In a federal system, power is divided between the states and the national government. Certain powers are given to the national government and other powers are left to the states.

The delegates chose a federal system because it would create a stronger national government than had existed under the Articles of Confederation but not as strong as had existed under King George III. It seemed a reasonable compromise to strengthen the powers of the national government while still maintaining the powers of the states.

Day 15

	Virginia Plan	New Jersey Plan
Type of legislature	Bicameral	Unicameral; one vote for each state
Election of legislature	Lower house by the people; upper house by the lower house	Chosen by state legislatures
Basis of representation	Population and/or monetary contributions to the national government by individual states	Equal representation among states
Executive branch	Single executive chosen by the legislative branch	Plural executive chosen by the legislative branch
Judicial branch	Judges chosen by the legislative branch	Judges appointed for life by the executive branch

Day 16

Compromise	Description
Great (Connecticut) Compromise	• Settled disputes between the states over the structure of the legislative branch • Created a bicameral Congress • Based representation in the lower house on the population of the state • Provided for equal representation of the states in the upper house
Three-Fifths Compromise	• Determined that each state would count three-fifths of its slave population for purposes of determining both representation in Congress and taxation
Commerce and Slave Trade Compromise	• Resolved differences between northern and southern states over the issues of slavery and the taxation of exports • Prohibited Congress from taxing exports from the states and from banning the slave trade for a period of twenty years

Day 17

Federalists	Anti-Federalists
• Stressed the weaknesses of the Articles of Confederation • Promoted checks and balances to protect against abuses • Led by James Madison, Alexander Hamilton, and John Jay • Favored the Constitution • Saw the Constitution as a bill of rights that placed limitations on the government and reserved powers for the states • Provided for the protection of property rights	• Opposed the Constitution • Wanted a Bill of Rights to protect citizens from the government • Wanted strong state governments; feared a strong national government • Led by Patrick Henry, Richard Henry Lee, George Mason, and Samuel Adams

Day 18

The Federalist Papers were a series of eighty-five essays published in the New York newspapers under the name "Publius." They defended the new government created under the Constitution in an attempt to convince delegates and the people of New York to support the ratification of the Constitution; in other words, the essays defined the reasons for ratifying the Constitution.

The authors of the Federalist Papers included Alexander Hamilton, James Madison, and John Jay. Hamilton wrote fifty-two essays, while Madison and Jay wrote twenty-eight and five, respectively.

Day 19

  D   Checks and balances
  E   Federalism
  A   Limited government
  B   Popular sovereignty
  C   Separation of powers

Day 20

  D   1. Checks and balances
  A   2. Federalism
  C   3. Judicial review
  B   4. Limited government
  E   5. Popular sovereignty
  F   6. Separation of powers

Day 21

Watch the video "Federalist #51 Explained: American Government Review" at www.youtube.com/watch?v=5FQ_Y2FUa6Q. Then read the full text or a short summary of Federalist #51 at http://billofrightsinstitute.org/founding-documents/primary-source-documents/the-federalist-papers/federalist-papers-no-51.

Madison defined the relationship among the three branches of government as independent; however, the government should have a system of checks and balances so no one branch could become too powerful.

- People needed a government to keep them under control.

- Government had the potential to be corrupt and therefore had to be checked.

- Minority groups needed protection from a tyranny of the majority.

- Levels of government such as national, state, and local served to protect against too much power at any one level.

Madison feared that the legislative branch might become too powerful; therefore, power should be divided to protect the people from a possible tyranny of the legislature.

Day 22

Legislative Branch over Executive Branch	**Executive Branch over Legislative Branch**	**Judicial Branch over Legislative Branch**
• Appropriates funds • May override the president's veto by a two-thirds of both houses	• May veto acts of Congress	• May rule legislative acts unconstitutional • Has a chief justice who presides over any impeachment trial of the president

Legislative Branch over Judicial Branch	**Executive Branch over Judicial Branch**	**Judicial Branch over Executive Branch**
• Creates lower federal courts • May propose constitutional amendments that overrule court decisions	• Appoints federal judges • May refuse to enforce court decisions	• May rule executive actions unconstitutional

Day 23

Formal amendments are written changes to the Constitution. They add to, change the wording of, or delete language from the Constitution. Only twenty-seven formal amendments have been added to the Constitution since its adoption. The process is found in Article V of the Constitution.

Formal amendments to the Constitution may be proposed by

- a two-thirds vote of each house of Congress or

- a national convention called by Congress at the request of two-thirds of the state legislatures.

Formal amendments to the Constitution may be ratified by

- three-fourths of the state legislatures or

- special conventions in three-fourths of the states.

Day 24

1. Legislative actions: Congress has used the "elastic clause," or the necessary and proper clause (Article I, Section 8, Clause 18), to pass legislation beyond what is specifically provided for in the Constitution.

2. Executive actions: The manner in which presidents have used their powers have often expanded presidential authority. One example might be the use of executive agreements instead of treaties to bypass the Senate.

3. Judicial interpretation/judicial review: Although not mentioned in the Constitution, judicial review has allowed those who serve as justices and the time in which they serve to influence how the Constitution has been interpreted.

The informal amendment processes are used more often because the formal amendment process is much more difficult. The formal process requires both the national level of government (Congress) and the states to participate. The formal process takes more time.

Day 25

Marshall's conclusions focused on three points:

1. Marbury had been lawfully appointed and confirmed as justice of the peace and therefore had a right to his commission.

2. Marbury was entitled to redress under the law for deprivation of that right.

3. The Court refused to issue the writ of mandamus, holding that the section of the Judiciary Act of 1789, which authorized that power to the Court, was unconstitutional. It violated Article III of the Constitution, which specifically outlines the Supreme Court's original jurisdiction (right to hear a case). The Judiciary Act of 1789 had sought to expand the Supreme Court's original jurisdiction beyond that granted by the Constitution.

In the case of *Marbury v. Madison* (1803), the Supreme Court recognized its power of judicial review: the Court's authority to review laws and legislative acts to determine whether they violate the Constitution.

Day 26

    5   Protects against self-incrimination; guarantees due process, eminent domain, and grand jury indictment for capital crimes

    8   Ensures against excessive bails or fines and against cruel and unusual punishment

    2   Ensures the right to keep and bear arms

    1   Guarantees freedom of religion, speech, press, assembly, and petition

    6   Guarantees the rights to a speedy, public trial and an impartial jury; to confront witnesses; and to have an attorney

7	Preserves the right to a jury trial in civil cases
4	Regulates search, seizure, and warrants
10	Reserves powers of the states and the people
3	Sets conditions for quartering troops in private homes
9	Addresses the unenumerated rights of the people

Day 27

24	Abolishes poll taxes
13	Abolishes slavery
27	Addresses congressional pay
25	Addresses presidential succession, disability, and vice presidential vacancies
23	Allows for voting rights in the District of Columbia in presidential elections
16	Authorizes income tax
17	Establishes direct election of senators by popular vote
19	Establishes women's suffrage
26	Gives eighteen-year-olds the right to vote
15	Guarantees the right to vote regardless of race, color, or previous condition of servitude
14	Guarantees the rights of citizenship, due process, and equal protection
22	Limits presidential terms of office
18	Prohibits intoxicating liquors
12	Provides for election of the president and vice president by separate ballot in the Electoral College
21	Repeals Prohibition
20	Sets terms and sessions of the executive and legislative branches ("lame duck")
11	Restricts lawsuits against states

Day 28

Federalism is a political system in which the powers of government are divided between a national government and regional (state) governments.

Federalism arose from the desire of the Founding Fathers to create a stronger national government while preserving the existing states and state governments. It also helps to prevent tyranny of the national government and keeps government closer to the people (local control). Many believe federalism was necessary to get the states to agree to the Constitution.

Each level of government has certain authority over the same territory and people. The U.S. Constitution outlines each level of government's authority, powers, and prohibitions.

Day 29

National Powers	Concurrent Powers	State Powers
• Coin and print money • Conduct foreign relations • Declare war • Establish federal courts below the Supreme Court • Make all laws "necessary and proper" • Provide an army and a navy • Regulate foreign and interstate commerce	• Borrow money • Enact and enforce laws • Establish courts • Levy taxes • Spend for the general welfare	• Administer elections • Establish local governments • Establish public school systems • Protect the public's health, welfare, and morals • Regulate intrastate commerce

Day 30

Advantages of Federalism	Disadvantages of Federalism
• Accommodates already existing state governments • Avoids concentration of political power • Is ideally suited to a large geographic area because it encourages diversity in local government • Keeps government close to the people • Allows states to serve as training grounds for national leaders	• Is complex, including many governments • Has the possibility of conflicts of authority • Duplicates offices and functions • Has the inflexibility inherent in a written constitution

Day 31

D	Concurrent powers
A	Delegated powers
B	Implied powers
C	Inherent powers
F	Prohibited powers
E	Reserved powers

Day 32

The Tenth Amendment specifically reserves powers to the states and the people as long as that power has not been already delegated to the national government: "The powers not delegated to the United States by the Constitution, nor prohibited by it to the States, are reserved to the States respectively, or to the people."

Formal amendments to the Constitution require action by both the federal government (proposing amendments or calling for a national convention to propose amendments) and the states (ratifying amendments through existing state legislatures or special conventions).

Day 33

The supremacy clause is used to resolve conflicts between national and state laws. Because two levels of government are operating over the same territory and people at the same time, conflicts may arise. The supremacy clause establishes that "the Constitution, its laws and treaties" are "the supreme law of the land." The Supreme Court upheld this supremacy in *McCulloch v. Maryland* (1819).

Ratification of the Constitution required action by both the federal government (proposing amendments or calling for a national convention to propose amendments) and the states (ratifying amendments through existing state legislatures or special conventions).

Day 34

C	Extradition
A	Full faith and credit clause
D	Interstate compacts
B	Privileges and immunities clause

Day 35

Dual Federalism	Cooperative Federalism	New Federalism
• Marble cake federalism • Earliest interpretation of federalism • Each level of government being separate from the other levels	• Began in the 1930s • Expanded during the Great Society programs of President Johnson • Layer cake federalism • National and state governments sharing the making and implementation of policies	• Nixon, Reagan, and Bush • Devolution • Transfer of more responsibility to the states on how grant money would be spent

Day 36

Devolution is an effort to shift responsibility of domestic programs (welfare, health care, and job training) to the states in order to decrease the size and activities of the federal government (first-order devolution). Some states have attempted to shift responsibilities on further to local governments (second-order devolution).

By shifting the responsibility of domestic programs to the states, the federal government is giving the states some responsibility and discretion in how that program is administered. This increases the power of the states relative to the national government.

Day 37

__C__	Block grants
__B__	Categorical grants
__D__	Fiscal federalism
__A__	Grant-in-aid programs
__F__	Mandates
__E__	Revenue sharing

Day 38

The Supreme Court ruled in *McCulloch v. Maryland* (1819), that although no provision of the Constitution grants the federal government the expressed power to create a national bank, the authority to do so can be implied by the necessary and proper clause (Article I, Section 8, Clause 18). This ruling established the implied powers of the national government and national supremacy, the basis used to strengthen the power of the national government.

At issue in *Gibbons v. Ogden* (1824) was the definition of commerce and whether the national government had exclusive power to regulate interstate commerce. The Marshall court defined commerce in a broad manner and determined that the power to regulate interstate commerce belongs exclusively to the national government. Today, the national government uses the commerce clause to justify the regulation of numerous areas of economic activity.

Day 39

The federal government directs/orders/requires the states to implement policies (such as the Americans with Disabilities Act), thus reducing state discretion and increasing federal power over the states.

Categorical grants are designed for a specific purpose and often come with stipulations on how the money can be spent. States that take categorical grants must follow these stipulations, limiting the states' powers to regulate their own affairs and increasing the national government's power over the states.

Day 40

Block grants are general grants that can be used for a variety of purposes within a broad category (education, health care, transportation). These grants have few strings attached, which gives the states more discretion/freedom in how the money is spent, thereby increasing the power of the states relative to the federal government.

The Tenth Amendment reserves powers not granted to the federal government to the states and the people. This increases the power of the states relative to the federal government by allowing the states to use the Tenth Amendment to justify state actions.

Day 41

A political culture is a set of basic values and beliefs about a country or government that is shared by most citizens. These fundamental values are often translated to government through voting patterns. American political culture is founded on the concepts of social contract, natural rights, and free markets.

Political culture and political ideology are two different ideas. Political culture is more of a general concept, focusing on shared values, attitudes, and ideas that many people have about the government of a country. Political ideology is much more specific and may lead to disagreements between people and political parties. The Democratic Party has a political ideology that is very different than that of the Republican Party. Each party has different beliefs about the role of government in society. Because these political ideologies are very different, they clearly mark the differences between the political parties.

Day 42

E	Compromise
B	Equality
D	Individual freedoms
F	Limited government
A	Majority rule/minority rights
C	Private property

Day 43

Political socialization is a complex process by which citizens acquire a sense of political identity. This process begins in early childhood and continues throughout a person's life. It allows citizens to become aware of politics, learn political facts, and form political values and beliefs.

Political socialization may be influenced by any of the following:

- Family, which often helps shape political party identification

- School, which teaches patriotism, basic governmental functions and structure; encourages political participation

- Group affiliations, which provide common bonds between people with similar likes

- Demographic factors, including occupation, race, gender, age, religion, region of the country, income, education, ethnicity

- Media, which informs the public about issues and helps set the public agenda

- Opinion leaders, who may be respected individuals and leaders

- Events, including both positive or negative events that may instill attitudes about government or government leaders

Day 44

Public opinion is a collection of the shared attitudes of many different people in matters relating to politics, public issues, or the making of public policy. It is shaped by people's political culture and political socialization.

The measurement of public opinion is a complex process, often conveying unreliable results. Elections, interest groups, the media, and personal contacts may signal public opinion on certain issues; however, the most reliable measure of public opinion is the public opinion poll. Businesses, governments, political candidates, and interest groups all use polls.

Day 45

- Randomized and representative sampling: Those chosen to participate in the poll must be a representative sample of the general population and chosen at random.

- Question wording: Directions for the poll should be clear; questions should be written in a way that is unbiased and unambiguous; questions should not lead a respondent to a particular answer.

- Large sample size/low margin of error: There is an inverse relationship between sample size and margin of error.

    Sampling errors can lead to misinformation.

Day 46

An ideology is a consistent set of beliefs that affects our outlook on the world. Ideologies can vary greatly in the following ways:

- Complexity—Some ideologies are very simple, and others are very detailed.

- Consistency—Ideologies may remain the same over a period of time or shift significantly.

- Flexibility—Some ideologies allow for individual interpretation, while others are strict in their interpretation.

    A political ideology is a set of beliefs about politics and public policy that creates a structure for looking at government and public policy. Political ideologies can change over time but generally determine how people view the government and its proper role.

Day 47

Participate in the Youth Leadership Initiative's Political Ideology Survey. Take the online survey at www.youthleadership.net/econgress/political_ideology_survey?_yli_session=4e3e8eeed513c5bce37026e1965e7b5b to help you determine your political party preference.

    Postsurvey questions for thought:

- What was the final result of your survey?

- Did you place on the political spectrum where you thought you would?

- What description did the survey give your placement?

Day 48

D	Conservative
B	Liberal
C	Moderate
A	Radical
E	Reactionary

Day 49

A political party is a voluntary association of people who seek to control government through common principles based on peaceful and legal actions, such as winning elections. Political parties serve as one of the linkage institutions that bring people and the government together.

1. Party in the electorate (PIE)

2. Party in government (PIG)

3. Party in organization (PO)

Day 50

The PIE are all the people who perceive themselves as party members. Many voters have a party identification that guides and influences their votes. There are no dues or membership cards; one only needs to claim to be a member.

The PIG consists of appointed and elected officials who call themselves members of the party (such as the president and Congress). These leaders do not always agree on policy, but they are the main spokespersons of the party.

The PO has a national office, a full-time staff, rules and bylaws, and budgets. American parties are loosely organized at the national, state, and local levels. The party organization works to strengthen the party, raise money, organize the conventions, and pursue electoral victories for candidates representing the party.

Day 51

1. Recruit candidates: Political parties find candidates interested in running for political office.

2. Nominate and support candidates for office: Political parties help raise money and run candidates' campaigns through the party organization; they narrow the field from many to one who will represent the party, simplifying voters' choices.

3. Educate the electorate: Political parties inform and energize their members. They send out brochures, run media campaigns, knock on doors, and call voters on the phone.

4. Organize the government: Political parties bring order to government. The organization of Congress and state legislature is based on political party controls (majority party v. minority party), and political appointments are often made based on party lines.

Day 52

- A faction is a number of citizens, whether a majority or minority, who are united by some interest, passion, or impulse.

- Madison feared faction but thought its effects could be managed by the existence of many competing factions.

- Madison saw wealth and property differences as the most likely source of faction.

- Madison wanted to create a republic.

- We can destroy liberty or make everyone the same. Madison believed that destroying liberty was worse than the existence of factions, and making everyone the same was impractical.

Day 53

In a one-party system, only one party exists or has a chance of winning elections. Generally, party leaders dominate and must approve the candidates for political office. Membership in the party may be limited so that only a small portion of the population may participate.

Although there may be several political parties, in a two-party system, only two major parties compete for power and dominate elections. Minor, or third parties, have little or no impact on most elections, especially at the national level.

In a multiparty system, several major and a number of minor parties compete in elections, and any of the parties stands a good chance of winning. The multiparty system often forces the sharing of political power (coalitions) between parties if no one party receives a clear majority of the vote.

Day 54

1. Historical roots: Our British heritage is based on a two-party tradition.

2. Electoral system: Single-member districts mean that only one representative is chosen from each district (one winner per office).

3. Election laws: Laws vary from state to state, which makes it difficult for minor parties to get on the ballot in many states.

Day 55

Divided government occurs when one party controls the executive branch, and the other party controls one or both houses of Congress.

Gridlock is when opposing parties and interests often block each other's proposals, creating a political stalemate or inaction between the executive and legislative branches of government.

When opposing parties control the institutional levers of power in the American system of separated powers, gridlock will naturally follow as both parties see a chance to enact their preferences and, hence, press their advantage.

Day 56

Dealignment occurs when a significant number of voters choose to no longer support a particular political party.

Realignment occurs when voting patterns shift to form new coalitions of party support.

Day 57

1. Ideological: parties based on a particular set of social, political, or economic beliefs (such as communist, socialist, libertarian)

2. Splinter/personality/factional: parties that have split away from one of the major parties; usually formed around a strong personality who does not win the party nomination; may disappear when that leader steps aside (for example, Theodore Roosevelt's "Bull Moose" Progressive Party)

3. Single issue: parties that concentrate on a single public policy matter (such as right to life)

4. Protest: parties usually rooted in periods of economic discontent; may be sectional in nature (for example, the Populist Party)

Day 58

A single-member district is a district that has a single representative rather than multiple ones (one member is elected to serve the district). This discourages the creation of minor parties because single-member districts favor two-party systems—the major, established parties are able to overwhelm minor ones. A minor party would negatively affect a major party since it would take votes away from the major party, despite the fact that the minor one has no chance of winning (as with the Bull Moose Party and Republicans, and the Green Party and Democrats).

Under the winner-take-all system, the candidate who wins the popular vote in a state wins all of the electoral votes for that state. While minor party candidates may receive popular votes, if they do not win the popular vote for that state, the minor party receives no electoral votes. If minor party candidates do not win electoral votes, it becomes more difficult to raise funds for the next election.

Day 59

1. Third-party challenges: In recent elections, third-party challengers have taken votes from the major candidates, lessening those candidates' ability to win a majority of the vote.

2. Loss of support by party loyalists: The number of independent voters has increased.

3. Increase in split-ticket voting: Many voters no longer vote a straight ticket (for all candidates of one political party); rather, they split their vote among candidates from more than one party.

4. Lack of perceived differences between the parties: Voters often believe there are no major differences in the parties or their candidates.

5. Party reforms: Changes within the parties themselves to create greater diversity and openness have allowed for greater conflict within some parties.

6. Methods of campaigning: New technologies have allowed candidates to become more independent of parties and more directly involved with the voters.

Day 60

Political participation is all the actions people use in seeking to influence or support government and politics.

The most common form of political participation is voting.

Day 61

Other than voting, forms of political participation may include the following:

- Discussing politics
- Attending political meetings
- Forming/joining interest groups or political action committees (PACs)
- Contacting public officials
- Campaigning for a candidate or political party
- Contributing money to a candidate or political party
- Running for office
- Protesting government decisions

Day 62

Suffrage is the right to vote. It is a political right that belongs to all those who meet certain requirements set by law.

Article I of the Constitution requires each state to allow those qualified to vote for their state legislature to qualify to vote for members of the House of Representatives: "Electors in each State shall have the Qualifications requisite for Electors of the most numerous Branch of the State Legislature."

Over the years, amendments and legislation have furthered defined who may vote:

- Fifteenth Amendment gave freed male slaves the right to vote.
- Nineteenth Amendment gave women the right to vote.
- Twenty-fourth Amendment abolished the poll tax as a requirement to vote.
- Twenty-sixth Amendment lowered the voting age to eighteen.
- Voting Rights Acts outlawed discriminatory practices in registration and voting.

Today, in *most* states, the electorate is made up of all those who are qualified to vote by meeting the following requirements:

- Citizens of the United States (required in all fifty states)
- Eighteen years of age or older (Twenty-sixth Amendment)
- Residents of the state
- Registered to vote in that state

Day 63

1. Fifteenth Amendment: suffrage for African-American males

2. Nineteenth Amendment: women's suffrage

3. Twenty-third Amendment: suffrage for residents of Washington, D.C.

4. Twenty-fourth Amendment: elimination of the poll tax

5. Twenty-sixth Amendment: suffrage for citizens who are eighteen and older

Day 64

  D   Direct primary
  C   Initiative
  A   Recall
  B   Referendum

Day 65

Any of the following are correct:

1. Apathy: Voters may have a lack of interest in politics or believe that voting is not important.

2. Lack of political efficacy: Many people do not believe their vote out of millions of votes will make a difference.

3. Registration process: The differences in the registration process from state to state may create an institutional barrier. The National Voter Registration Act of 1995 (Motor Voter Law) was designed to make voter registration easier by allowing people to register at driver's license bureaus and some public offices.

4. Mobility of the electorate: Moving around leads voters to feel a lack of social belonging.

5. Expansion of the electorate: Constitutional changes have led to an increase in the number of potential voters (Twenty-sixth Amendment), but many of those now-eligible voters do not vote.

6. Failure of political parties to mobilize voters: Voters experience negative campaigning, numerous and frequent elections, and a lack of party identification.

7. No perceived differences between the candidates or parties: Both parties and their candidates are seen as virtually the same by voters.

8. Mistrust of government: Voters may believe that all candidates are untrustworthy or unresponsive, due in part to the Watergate and Iran-Contra scandals.

Day 66

__B__	Primary
__C__	General election
__A__	Special election

Day 67

__B__	Closed primary
__D__	Open primary
__A__	Blanket primary
__C__	Runoff election

Day 68

__2__	Announcement
__5__	Campaigning/general election
__6__	Electoral College vote
__1__	Exploration
__4__	Nominating convention
__3__	Primary/caucus
__7__	Inauguration

Day 69

A presidential preference primary is used by many states to determine whom each state's delegates to the national party convention will support. Voters vote in a primary (nominating) election, and party delegates to the conventions support the winner of the state primary. New Hampshire is famous for being the first state to hold its primary during the election cycle.

A caucus is used in some states to allow party members to meet on a designated day to nominate party candidates. Caucuses are open to all party members. Iowa still uses caucuses to nominate candidates.

Day 70

Frontloading is the tendency for states to move up their presidential primary or caucus to gain national attention and have more of an impact on the presidential election process.

Frontloading can give an advantage to the front-runner because he or she gains an early momentum and is able to raise more funds; it can cause other candidates to drop out of the race sooner.

Day 71

Super Tuesday is the date, usually in March, when a large number of states hold presidential primaries.

Candidates who win a majority of the Super Tuesday primaries receive a large number of national convention delegates toward winning their party's nomination.

Day 72

Battleground or swing states are those states that are closely contested in a presidential election.

Candidates will often spend more time and money in those states. Whereas other states have a voting history that is more predictable, in battleground/swing states, either of the major candidates have a reasonable chance of winning the popular vote and therefore that state's electoral vote.

Day 73

The coattail effect is the tendency for a popular political party leader to attract votes for other candidates of the same party in an election. This effect often occurs when the popularity of a presidential candidate allows lesser-known or weaker candidates from the presidential candidate's party to win by riding the coattails of the nominee.

Day 74

The Electoral College is a group of people representing all fifty states, who formally cast votes for the election of the president and vice president. Members of the Electoral College meet in mid-December in their respective state capitals to cast ballots for the president and vice president.

There are a total of 535 electors.

Day 75

The Founding Fathers provided for the Electoral College to elect the president for the following reasons:

1. They provided it as a compromise between the large and small states.

2. They thought it best if educated individuals made the final decision about who would serve as president.

3. It reinforced federalism, allowing the states to be part of the decision-making process.

4. They did not trust a direct election of the president by the people, Congress, or state legislatures.

Day 76

Each state receives a number of electors equal to the number of congressional districts plus senatorial seats it has in Congress. For example, if a state has six congressional districts and two senatorial seats, that state has eight electors.

Article II, Section I of the U.S. Constitution states that "Each State shall appoint, in such Manner as the Legislature thereof may direct, a Number of Electors, equal to the whole Number of Senators and Representatives to which the State may be entitled in the Congress: but no Senator or Representative, or Person holding an Office of Trust or Profit under the United States, shall be appointed an Elector."

The Twenty-third Amendment to the U.S. Constitution also provides that the "District constituting the seat of Government of the United States shall appoint in such manner as the Congress may direct: A number of electors of President and Vice President equal to the whole number of Senators and Representatives in Congress to which the District would be entitled if it were a State, but in no event more than the least populous State."

Day 77

After the general election, the electors meet in their respective state capitals on the first Monday after the second Wednesday in December.

The candidate who receives a majority (270) of electoral votes is declared the winner.

Day 78

If no candidate for president receives a majority of electoral votes, the House of Representatives chooses the president from the top three candidates.

If no candidate for vice president receives a majority of electoral votes, the Senate chooses the vice president from the top two candidates.

Day 79

C	Critical elections
E	Dealigning elections
B	Deviating elections
A	Maintaining elections
D	Realigning elections

Day 80

B	*Buckley v. Valeo* (1976)
C	*Citizens United v. FEC* (2010)
A	*McCutcheon v. FEC* (2014)

Day 81

The Federal Election Campaign Act (FECA) was passed in 1971, restricting the amount of campaign funds that can be spent on advertising, requiring disclosure of campaign contributions and expenditures, and limiting the amounts candidates and their families can donate to their own campaigns. It also allowed taxpayers to designate a donation on their tax return to the major political party candidates, beginning in the 1976 presidential election.

In 1974, after the Watergate scandal, Congress amended the Federal Election Campaign Act to establish a Federal Election Commission (FEC) to enforce the Act and established public financing for presidential candidates in primaries and the general election. The measure also restricted contributions by prohibiting foreign contributions, limiting individual contributions, and restricting the formation of PACs and their contributions.

Day 82

Soft money is donations to political parties that could be used for general purposes. Originally, the money was supposed to be used for voter registration drives, national party conventions, and issue ads. Political parties were allowed to raise unlimited amounts of money because it was not to be used for campaigning. However, soft money has generally been spent in ways that ultimately help individual candidates.

In 2002, Congress passed the Bipartisan Campaign Reform Act (BCRA), sometimes referred to as McCain-Feingold, banning the use of soft money in federal campaigns and increasing the 1974 limits on individual and group contributions to candidates.

Day 83

A 527 political organization is a largely unregulated interest group that focuses on a single policy and attempts to influence elections. Such organizations can raise unlimited funds from individuals, corporations, or labor unions, but they must register with the Internal Revenue Service and disclose their contributions and expenditures.

Because they may not campaign for specific candidates or coordinate with any candidate's campaign, many 527s are used to raise money to spend on the advocacy of issues and voter mobilization.

Watch the 527 ads at www.livingroomcandidate.org/news/perma/new-527-ads-are -released-one-anti-obama-one-anti-mccain.

Day 84

Interest groups are organizations of people with shared ideas and attitudes who attempt to influence public policy.

Interest groups are different from a political party in that they have no legal status in the election process. They do not nominate candidates for public office; however, they may actively support candidates who are sympathetic to their cause. While political parties are interested in controlling government, interest groups are concerned with influencing the policies of government, usually focusing on issues that directly affect their membership.

Day 85

1. Raise awareness and stimulate interest in public affairs by educating their members and the public

2. Represent their membership, serving as a link between members and government

3. Provide information to government, especially data and testimony useful in making public policy

4. Provide channels for political participation that enable citizens to work together to achieve a common goal

Day 86

Influencing elections encourages members to vote for candidates who support their views. This influences party platforms and the nomination of candidates, campaigning, and the contribution of money to parties and candidates through political action committees (PACs).

Lobbying is the process of attempting to influence policymakers, often by supplying data to government officials and their staffs to convince these policymakers that their case is more deserving than another's.

Day 87

Litigation is the process of bringing lawsuits. Interest groups often take an issue to court if they are unsuccessful in gaining the support of Congress; this strategy was used successfully by the National Association for the Advancement of Colored People (NAACP) to argue against segregation during the 1950s.

Going public involves appealing to the public for support by bringing attention to an issue or using public relations to gain support for the image of the interest group itself.

Day 88

A political action committee (PAC) is organized for the purpose of raising and spending money to elect and defeat candidates. Most PACs represent business, labor, or interest groups. The campaign finance reforms of the 1970s prohibited corporations and labor unions from making direct contributions to candidates running for federal office. Political action committees were formed as political arms of interest groups.

PACs can give $5,000 to a candidate committee per election (primary, general, or special). They can also give up to $15,000 annually to any national party committee and $5,000 annually to any other PAC. Political action committees may receive up to $5,000 from any one individual, PAC, or party committee per calendar year.

Federal law regulates PACs. The committees must register with the federal government, raise money from multiple contributors, donate to several candidates, and follow strict accounting rules.

Day 89

The first major attempt to regulate lobbying came in 1946 with the passage of the Federal Regulation of Lobbying Act, which required lobbyists to register with the clerk of the House of Representatives and the secretary of the Senate if their principal purpose was to influence legislation. This law was directed only at those who tried to influence members of Congress.

In 1995, Congress passed the Lobbying Disclosure Act, creating much stricter regulations by requiring registration if lobbying was directed at members of Congress, congressional staff, or policymakers within the executive branch. It also required the disclosure of more information concerning the activities and clients of lobbyists.

Day 90

Mass media refers to all forms of communication that transmit information to the general public.

Although the mass media are not the only means of communication between citizens and government (political parties, interest groups, and voting are other means), they are the only linkage mechanism that specializes in communication.

Day 91

1. Newspapers

2. Magazines

3. Radio

4. Television

5. Internet

Day 92

√	Agenda setting
	Holding elections
	Nominating candidates
	Acting as an organization tool for the government
√	Providing a link between citizens and government
√	Shaping public opinion
√	Informing the public
√	Serving as a watchdog that investigates/examines government

Day 93

News is any important event that has happened within the past twenty-four hours. The media decides what is news by deciding what to report.

Gatekeepers are usually media executives, news editors, and prominent reporters who decide what news to present and how it will be presented.

News is generally directed through gatekeepers—media executives, news editors, and prominent reporters—who decide which events to present and how to present them. Time limitations and the potential impact of the story are major factors in selecting what is news. The criteria by which news is judged are:

- Is it new?

- Is it unusual?

- Is it interesting?

- Is it significant?

- Is it about people?

Day 94

News leaks consist of information released by officials who are guaranteed anonymity. Leaks can be intentional or unintentional.

Leaks may be intentional to interfere with the opposition or to "float" an idea and measure public reaction (trial balloon).

Day 95

The major news organizations maintain journalists in major cities and government centers to report political events firsthand. Washington, D.C., has the largest press corps of any city in the United States, with one-third of the press assigned to cover the White House. News events may be staged as media events. The White House allows special access to the president, with the press receiving information through the Office of the Press Secretary.

Fewer reporters regularly cover Congress, which does not maintain as tight a control over news stories as the White House does. Most of the coverage of Congress concerns the House of Representatives, the Senate, or Congress as an organization, rather than individual members. News about Congress may cover confirmation hearings, oversight investigations, or scandals among members.

Day 96

Pack journalism is journalism whereby reporters adopt the viewpoints of other journalists with whom they spend time and exchange information. Pack journalism often leads to uniformity of news coverage.

Horse race journalism in elections resembles coverage of horse races because of the focus on which candidates are winning and which candidates are losing, or which candidate is ahead and which candidate is behind, instead of on the issues of the campaign.

Day 97

The media can influence the public agenda in each of the following ways:

- The media helps determine what issues people will think about and discuss.

- The media focuses people's attention toward or away from issues.

- Government leaders pay close attention to the media.

The media can influence campaigns and elections in each of the following ways:

- Candidates are less reliant on political parties because they can reach the voters directly.

- A candidate's image in the media can influence voters.

- The media can use sound bites to portray the candidates to the voters.

Day 98

The president and the media can have a mutually beneficial relationship. The president provides news for the media; the media provide a forum for the president. Nevertheless, the media often report negatively on presidential actions, resulting in a strain on the relationship.

Most of the coverage of Congress is on individual lawmakers (especially congressional leaders) and is reported to newspapers in the lawmakers' home states.

The public relies on the mass media to learn about Supreme Court and federal court decisions. The courts receive much less coverage than the president or Congress do.

Day 99

Article I of the Constitution outlines the legislative branch:

- Section 1: The Congress
- Section 2: The House of Representatives
- Section 3: The Senate
- Section 4: Elections and Meetings of Congress
- Section 5: Rules of Procedure for Congress
- Section 6: Privileges and Restrictions of Members of Congress
- Section 7: How Laws Are Made
- Section 8: Powers Granted to Congress
- Section 9: Powers Denied to Congress
- Section 10: Powers Denied to the States

A bicameral legislature is a legislature consisting of two houses or chambers. In the United States, those chambers are the House of Representatives and the Senate.

Day 100

The current structure of Congress was the result of the Connecticut (Great) Compromise, reached at the Constitutional Convention. The Founding Fathers based their compromise in part on the belief that each house would serve as a check on the power of the other. The House of Representatives was to be based on the population in the states and representative of the people, with its members chosen by popular vote. The Senate was to represent the states, with each state having the same number of senators, who were chosen by the state legislatures.

Day 101

	House of Representatives	Senate
Membership/size	435 members (apportioned by population)	100 members (two from each state)
Term of office	Two years (entire House elected every two years)	Six years (staggered terms with one-third of the Senate elected every two years)
Qualifications	At least twenty-five years of age Citizen for seven years Must live in the state where the district is located	At least thirty years of age Citizen for nine years Must live in the state
Method of election	By districts within the state	By the state at large

Day 102

__B__ Apportionment
__D__ Reapportionment
__C__ Congressional redistricting
__A__ Gerrymandering

Day 103

Reapportionment can increase or decrease the number of seats a state has in the House of Representatives. If a state's representation in the House of Representatives increases, that state has a larger influence in Congress; if a state's representation in the House of Representatives decreases, that state has a smaller influence in Congress. Reapportionment also affects the number of electors given to each state in the Electoral College and can therefore increase or decrease that state's electoral vote in a presidential election.

Day 104

Participate in the Redistricting Game at http://redistrictinggame.org.

The Redistricting Game allows participants to view a short informational video about redistricting and then try to redistrict an imaginary state. The game offers several types of redistricting and levels of difficulty.

Day 105

Members of the Senate were originally chosen by the state legislatures in each state.

Since 1913, the Seventeenth Amendment allows for the direct election of senators by the people of the state.

Day 106

The incumbency effect is the tendency of those already holding office to win reelection.

The incumbency effect tends to be stronger for members of the House of Representatives and weaker for the Senate.

Day 107

Voters are more likely to recognize the officeholder and vote for him or her rather than the challenger. Name recognition is considered a major obstacle for challengers.

The officeholder may have brought government projects and money (such as pork barrel spending) into the state or district. Projects may help create jobs or enrich the lives of constituents.

Incumbents are given the staff and resources to provide services to constituents, like helping them solve problems involving the government or the bureaucracy.

Incumbents can often use the perks of the office to communicate with constituents, such as sending official mail to constituents using the incumbent's signature as postage.

Day 108

Incumbents are more likely than a challenger to gain free publicity from the media during a campaign. Members of the U.S. House and Senate have easy and ready access to the news media, make regular appearances on television and radio programs, and are frequently mentioned in newspaper articles and editorials.

Incumbents are often able to raise large amounts of campaign contributions.

Incumbents have already experienced the campaign process, having run at least one successful election campaign. This provides invaluable experience with creating and managing a campaign organization, often with an effective volunteer organization and financial support already in place for the next campaign.

Voters can evaluate incumbents based on their voting records. Voters can see where the incumbent stands on issues.

Day 109

The Speaker of the House is the presiding officer and most powerful member of the House of Representatives. Major duties include assigning bills to committee, controlling floor debate, and appointing party members to committees.

The Speaker of the House is elected by members of his or her political party within the House. Article I, Section II of the U.S. Constitution states, "The House of Representatives shall choose their Speaker and other Officers." Although the Constitution does not require the Speaker to be a member of the House, all Speakers have been members.

When a Congress convenes for the first time, each major party nominates a candidate for Speaker. Members customarily elect the Speaker by roll-call vote. A member usually votes for the candidate from his or her own party but can vote for anyone, whether that person has been nominated or not.

To be elected, a candidate must receive a majority of the votes cast. If no candidate receives a majority of votes, the roll call is repeated until a majority is reached and the Speaker is elected.

Day 110

The majority leader and minority leader—also called party floor leaders—are selected by the party conference and the party caucus.

The majority leader in the House of Representatives works closely with the Speaker of the House to advance the goals of the majority party. This might include helping plan the legislative agenda for the House and directing floor debate. The majority leader in the Senate is the most influential member of the Senate and serves as the majority party spokesperson.

The minority leaders in both the House and Senate lead and serve as spokespersons for the minority party. Minority leaders direct the party's legislative strategies and operations, organizing opposition to the majority party.

Whips help the floor leaders by directing party members in voting, informing members of impending votes, keeping track of vote counts, and pressuring members to vote with the party.

Day 111

The presiding officer of the Senate is called the president of the Senate. The U.S. vice president, although not a Senate member, is the presiding officer of the Senate, according to the Constitution.

While serving as president of the Senate, the vice president may not debate and only votes to break a tie.

Day 112

The president pro tempore ("president for a time") is a constitutionally recognized officer of the Senate who presides over the chamber in the absence of the vice president.

The president pro tempore is elected by the Senate and is customarily the senator of the majority party with the longest record of continuous service.

Day 113

Most of the work of Congress is accomplished through committees and subcommittees. Each committee/subcommittee's membership is proportioned to reflect each party's membership in that house of Congress. Members try to serve on committees/subcommittees where they can influence public policy relating to their district or state or influence important national public policy.

Committees/subcommittees permit Congress to divide the work between members, allowing for more in-depth review of proposed legislation. They hold hearings and hear testimony, oversee the executive branch, identify issues appropriate for legislative review, and may even propose legislation. Committee/subcommittee members often play a key role in floor debate about the bills they have promoted.

Committee chairpersons are members of the majority party in each house chosen by party caucus. They set agendas, assign members to subcommittees, and decide whether the committee will hold public hearings and which witnesses to call. They manage floor debate of a bill when it is presented to the full House or Senate.

Day 114

B	Conference committee
C	Joint committee
D	Select committee
A	Standing committee

Day 115

The House Rules Committee, formally called the Committee on Rules, is composed of members from the House of Representatives. It acts as a gatekeeper and reviews all the bills to decide if, and in what order, the bills will be presented to the House for consideration. The House Rules Committee has the power to control the date and extent of debate of a proposed bill and the degree to which it may be amended. (For more information, go to https://rules.house.gov.)

The House Ways and Means Committee is the oldest committee of Congress. It is the primary tax-writing committee in the House of Representatives. It derives most of its jurisdiction from Article I, Section VII of the U.S. Constitution, which declares, "All Bills for raising Revenue shall originate in the House of Representatives." (For more information, go to http://waysandmeans.house.gov.)

The House Appropriations Committee is responsible for passing appropriations bills that regulate expenditures by the government, making it one of the most powerful committees in the House. Originally, this task was part of the House Ways and Means Committee, but due to the growth of government, Congress created two other committees to divide the workload. Today, Ways and Means controls taxes, the Committee on Banking and Commerce regulates banking, and the Appropriations Committee controls government spending. (For more information, go to http://appropriations.house.gov.)

Day 116

The Senate Foreign Relations Committee is responsible for most foreign-policy legislation and debate in the Senate. The committee oversees the funding of foreign aid programs, weapons sales, and training for allies; is responsible for holding confirmation hearings for high-level Department of State positions; debates treaties and legislation; and holds jurisdiction over all diplomatic nominations. For more information, go to www.foreign.senate.gov.

The Senate Judiciary Committee plays an important role in the consideration of the president's nominations to all federal courts, including the Supreme Court. This committee also hears nominations to the Department of Justice, Department of Homeland Security, and Department of Commerce. The Senate Judiciary Committee provides oversight of the Department of Justice and its agencies, including the Federal Bureau of Investigation and the Department of Homeland Security. For more information, go to www.judiciary.senate.gov.

The Senate Appropriations Committee is the largest committee in the U.S. Senate. It is charged with writing the legislation that allocates federal funds to the numerous government agencies, departments, and organizations on an annual basis. For more information, go to www.appropriations.senate.gov.

Day 117

A legislative caucus is an informal group formed by members of the legislative branch (Congress) who share a common purpose and advocate to promote their common goals and interests.

You can view a list of just some of the House congressional caucuses at https://cha.house.gov/sites/republicans.cha.house.gov/files/documents/114CMOList%289.7.16%29_0.pdf.

Day 118

In the delegate model of representation, decisions made by the elected official represent his or her constituents' views (officials do what voters tell them to do). This behavior is often based on the goal of being reelected.

In the trustee model of representation, decisions made by the elected official reflect his or her own personal views on the public good. While representatives may consider the views of their constituents, they do not act on the basis of those views.

Some textbooks also discuss a politico model of representation, in which elected officials may use both the delegate and trustee models, depending on the issues.

Day 119

The expressed powers of Congress are powers granted specifically to Congress, mostly found in Article I, Section 8 of the Constitution. These include the power to declare war, levy taxes, raise an army and maintain the navy, and regulate commerce.

The elastic clause of the Constitution grants Congress the power to pass laws "necessary and proper" for the exercise of its expressed powers. This power is found in Article I, Section 8, Clause 18. The necessary and proper clause grants Congress powers not explicitly stated in the Constitution but assumed to exist because they are necessary to implement the expressed powers granted in Article I.

Day 120

The Constitution gives the House of Representatives the power to impeach the president and other government officials. Impeachment means that a charge of wrongdoing or misconduct is filed. To impeach an official, a majority of the members of the House of Representatives must vote for the charges of impeachment.

Once the charges have been filed and voted on by the House, the Senate has the power to try impeachment cases. The Senate serves as a court, with conviction requiring a vote of two-thirds of the Senate. Removal of the official from office occurs only if the official is found guilty of the charges.

Two presidents have been impeached: Andrew Johnson and Bill Clinton. Both were found not guilty of the impeachment charges. Richard Nixon resigned from office rather than face impeachment charges in the Watergate scandal.

Day 121

Congress may use its oversight powers to investigate matters within the range of its legislative authority. This often involves the review of policies and programs of the executive branch. Congressional oversight of the presidency or the bureaucracy can limit the powers of the president and, therefore, the executive branch.

Methods of oversight might include the following:

- Control over budget

- Hearings and committee investigations

- Power to organize and reorganize agencies

- Setting agency guidelines

- Reauthorization and jurisdiction of agencies

- Program evaluation

Day 122

A bill is a proposed law.

Day 123

2	Assigned to committee
1	Introduced
5	Committee approves or rejects bill
10	Conference committee
7	Floor debate
8	Floor vote
12	Presidential action
4	Returned to committee
11	Returned to House for floor vote
6	Rules committee
9	Sent to Senate
3	Sent to subcommittee for further study

Day 124

C	Amendments
E	Cloture
A	Filibuster
B	Pork barrel legislation
D	Riders

Day 125

1. Constituents

2. Other lawmakers and staff

3. Political party

4. President

5. Lobbyists and interest groups

Day 126

Party polarization refers to an increase in the division along party lines on given issues or policy, or when a person is more likely to be strictly defined by his or her identification with a particular political party or ideology.

Party polarization can lead to gridlock, allowing for the passage of less legislation, more filibusters in the Senate, or fewer confirmations of appointments. Polarization along party lines can result in a lack of compromise among legislative members as each remains adamant about their stance on an issue.

Day 127

Article II of the Constitution provided for the creation of an executive branch.

The executive branch is composed of a single executive (president) with powers limited by the checks and balances held by the legislative and judicial branches. The president is elected indirectly through the Electoral College.

Day 128

Presidents are elected for a four-year term.

The addition of the Twenty-second Amendment came about as a result of the multiple elections of Franklin D. Roosevelt. The amendment limits the president to no more than two elected terms or only one elected term if the president serves more than two years of someone else's term.

Day 129

The original Constitution does not state that the vice president shall actually become president; that tradition began with the death of W. H. Harrison. After the assassination of John F. Kennedy, the Twenty-fifth Amendment was added to the Constitution, stating that the vice president becomes president if the office of president becomes vacant.

That amendment also provides for the new president to nominate a new vice president, with the approval of a majority of both houses of Congress. The first use of the Twenty-fifth Amendment occurred when Spiro Agnew resigned the vice presidency and was replaced by Gerald Ford in 1973. The following year, it was used again when President Richard Nixon resigned, and Vice President Gerald Ford became president. Ford nominated, and Congress confirmed, Nelson Rockefeller as his new vice president.

Day 130

If the president is unable to perform the duties of his or her office, the vice president may become "acting president" under one of the following conditions:

- The president informs Congress of the inability to perform his or her duties.

- The vice president and a majority of the cabinet inform Congress, in writing, that the president is disabled and unable to perform those duties.

The president may resume the duties of office upon informing Congress that no disability exists. If the vice president and a majority of the cabinet disagree, Congress has twenty-one days to decide the issue of presidential disability by a two-thirds vote of both houses.

Day 131

According to the Constitution, the vice president has two duties:

- To preside over the Senate and cast tie-breaking votes if necessary

- To help determine presidential disability under the Twenty-fifth Amendment and take over the presidency if necessary

The vice president also holds the title of president of the Senate. Since the vice president is not a member of the Senate, he or she cannot debate and can only vote in the case of a tie.

The vice president is also first in the line of succession to the presidency. If a question of disability arises regarding the president, the vice president and a majority of the cabinet must agree that the president can no longer fulfil his or her duties. The vice president could then become "acting president."

Day 132

Because the vice president may become president, the formal qualifications for vice president are the same as those for president. The selection of the nominee for vice president occurs at the national convention when the presidential nominee selects a running mate. Often the choice of nominee is influenced by the party's desire to balance the ticket; that is, to improve a candidate's chances of winning the election by choosing someone from a different faction of the party or from a different geographic section of the country.

Day 133

Executive Powers	Legislative Powers	Judicial Powers
• Appoints and removes officials • Enforces laws, treaties, and court decisions • Presides over the executive branch	• Issues annual budget and economic reports • Proposes legislation and uses influence to get it passed • Signs or vetoes bills	• Appoints members of the federal judiciary • Grants reprieves, pardons, and amnesty
Diplomatic Powers	**Military Powers**	**Party Powers**
• Accords diplomatic recognition to foreign governments • Meets with foreign leaders in international conferences • Receives foreign dignitaries	• Has final decision-making authority in matters of national and foreign defense • Provides for domestic order • Serves as commander-in-chief of the armed forces	• Appoints party members to government positions (patronage) • Chooses the vice presidential nominee • Strengthens the party by helping members get elected ("coattails")

Day 134

The Senate is given the power to confirm or reject presidential appointments. This gives it power over whom the president nominates and who is eventually confirmed.

While the president creates a federal budget, it must be approved by Congress, which can enact taxes and allocate funds to federal agencies and departments. Congress can therefore limit the president's ability to spend money by not allocating money to a specific purpose.

The House of Representatives has the power to impeach (bring charges of wrongdoing) the president, and the Senate has the requirement to serve as a jury in the trial of an impeached president. This gives Congress power over the president in that he or she can be removed from office if found guilty.

Answers

Congress has the power to override presidential vetoes by a two-thirds vote of both houses. This limits the president's power because Congress can pass legislation without the president's approval.

Day 135

Provisions of the War Powers Act include the following:

- Within forty-eight hours, the president must notify Congress of committing armed forces to military action, detailing the circumstances and scope of his or her actions.

- Commitment of troops must end after sixty days, allowing for a thirty-day withdrawal period, unless Congress agrees to a longer period or declares war.

- Congress may end the combat commitment at any time by passing a concurrent resolution.

The War Powers Act was passed by two-thirds of Congress, overriding a presidential veto by Richard Nixon.

Day 136

A legislative veto allows Congress to reject the actions of the president or executive agency by a vote of one or both houses without the consent of the president. The legislative veto was declared unconstitutional by the Supreme Court in 1983.

Day 137

A bureaucracy is a systematic way of organizing a large, complex administrative structure. The bureaucracy is responsible for carrying out the day-to-day tasks of the organization.

The three basic principles of a bureaucracy are as follows:

- Hierarchical authority—similar to a pyramid, with those at the top having authority over those below

- Job specialization—with each worker having defined duties and responsibilities, and a division of labor among workers

- Formal rules—with established regulations and procedures that must be followed

Day 138

Executive orders are commands given by the president to an agency to carry out policies or existing laws.

Executive orders seek to change policy or clarify the law in some way that also has the effect of law. It is as powerful or as significant as legislation that Congress passes and the president signs.

Day 139

Treaty	Executive Agreement
• Requires the consent of the Senate (two-thirds vote) to become effective • Binding on future administrations	• Does not require Senate approval to become effective • Not binding on future administrations and may even be reversed

An online article published by the *Wall Street Journal*, "Treaties vs. Executive Agreements: When Does Congress Get a Vote?" indicated that a 2009 University of Michigan study found 52.9 percent of international agreements were executive agreements from 1839 until 1889, but from 1939 until 1989, the ratio had risen to 94.3 percent.

Day 140

Congress has several checks that can be used to limit the powers of the president:

• Approval power over appointments

• Legislation that limits presidential powers

• Power of impeachment

• Override of presidential veto by a two-thirds vote of both houses

• Authorization of executive agency budgets (power of the purse)

The courts, especially the Supreme Court, can use their powers of judicial review and declare actions of the president or executive branch to be unconstitutional. Justices also are appointed for life tenure, giving them independence from both the executive and legislative branches.

Day 141

___A___ Cabinet departments
___D___ Government corporations
___B___ Independent executive agencies
___C___ Independent regulatory agencies

Day 142

The Executive Office of the President includes the advisors closest to the president. Established in 1939, every president has reorganized the EOP according to his style of leadership. Within the executive office are several separate agencies. The EOP is headed by the White House chief of staff.

The White House Office includes the personal and political staff members who help with the day-to-day management of the executive branch. This includes the chief of staff, counsel to the president, and press secretary.

The National Security Council was established by the National Security Act of 1947 to advise the president on matters of domestic and foreign national security.

The council is composed of senior national security advisors and cabinet officials. The council also serves to coordinate policies among the various government agencies.

The Office of Management and Budget is the largest part of the Executive Office of the President, helping the president and the executive branch to prepare the annual federal budget. The OMB also has oversight of executive branch agencies and departments.

Day 143

Iron triangles are alliances that develop between bureaucratic agencies, interest groups, and congressional committees or subcommittees. These alliances may work to help each other to achieve common goals, with Congress and the president often deferring to their influence.

Issue networks are groups of individuals in Washington—located within interest groups, congressional staff, think tanks, universities, and the media—who regularly discuss and advocate public policies. Unlike iron triangles, issue networks continually form and disband according to the policy issues. Issue networks are often composed of individuals who have policy expertise and are drawn to issues because of intellectual and emotional commitments.

Day 144

The president can do the following:

- Appoint the right people to head an agency

- Issue executive orders

- Alter an agency's budget

- Reorganize an agency

Congress can do the following:

- Influence the appointment of agency leadership

- Alter an agency's budget

- Conduct oversight hearings

- Rewrite legislation or make legislation more detailed

Day 145

  __1__ Congress provides positive legislation, access to the legislative arena, and information.

  __3__ Congressional committee members provide budgetary support, information, access to the legislative process, and positive legislation.

  __2__ Interest groups provide information, electoral support, and campaign contributions.

  __4__ The bureaucracy provides positive legislative enforcement and information.

  __6__ The bureaucracy provides positive legislative enforcement, information, research, and access to the legislative process.

  __5__ Interest groups provide information, research, enforcement, and budgetary support through testimony.

Day 146

Watch the video "Federalist #78 Explained: Government Review" at www.youtube .com/watch?v=L5gAVO6op8A. The video gives an overview of Federalist #78 and Alexander Hamilton's defense of the judiciary.

- The judicial branch lacks influence over the power of the purse (money) and the power of the sword (military).

- Hamilton believed that the judiciary was the protector of the people's rights as embodied in the Constitution.

- Hamilton hoped that the judges would realize the meaning of the Constitution and treat it as the superior law of the land.

Day 147

__B__ Appellate jurisdiction
__C__ Concurrent jurisdiction
__A__ Original jurisdiction

Day 148

The Supreme Court was created under the Constitution to serve as the highest court in the federal judicial system. It is the final authority in dealing with all questions arising from the Constitution, federal laws, and treaties.

Congress created the Courts of Appeals to help lessen the workload of the Supreme Court. The Courts of Appeals decide appeals from U.S. district courts and review decisions of federal administrative agencies.

District courts serve as trial courts at the federal level. They decide civil and criminal cases arising under the Constitution and federal laws or treaties.

Day 149

When making appointments to the federal judiciary, presidents often consider the following:

- Party affiliation—choosing judges from their own political party

- Judicial philosophy—appointing judges who share their political ideology

- Race, gender, religion, and region—considering these criteria to help bring balance to the court or satisfy certain segments of society

- Judicial experience—previous judicial experience as judges in district courts, courts of appeals, and state courts

- "Litmus test"—a test of ideological purity toward a liberal or conservative stand on certain issues such as abortion

- Acceptability—noncontroversial and therefore acceptable to members of the Senate Judiciary Committee and the Senate, as well as other groups such as the American Bar Association, interest groups, and even other justices that may have an opinion on acceptability

Day 150

Legislative powers that can serve as a check on court decisions include:

- Amending the Constitution to override court decisions can change the meaning of the Constitution.

- Impeachment and removal of judges can change the makeup of the courts.

- Confirmation or rejection of court nominees by the Senate can affect the makeup of the court.

- New legislation can address issues found deficient in court decisions.

- Creating or changing the jurisdiction of lower courts.

- Altering the size of the Supreme Court.

Executive powers that can serve as a check on court decisions include:

- The President can choose how the executive branch enforces court decisions or may encourage a lack of enforcement of the court decision.

- Power of appointment allows the president to nominate judges to the federal courts.

- Pardons and amnesty allow the president to lessen the impact of a crime or offense.

Day 151

A writ of certiorari is an order by the Court (when petitioned) that directs a lower court to send up the records of a case for review; it usually requires the need to interpret law or decide a constitutional question.

Cases that are accepted for review must pass the rule of four—four of the nine justices must agree to hear the case.

Thousands of cases are appealed to the Supreme Court every year; only a few hundred are actually heard. Most of the cases are denied because the justices either agree with the lower court's decision or believe the cases do not involve a significant point of law.

Day 152

_B_	Concurring opinion
_C_	Dissenting opinion
_A_	Majority opinion

Day 153

Judicial activism holds that the Supreme Court should play an active role in determining national policies. The philosophy advocates applying the Constitution to social and political questions, especially where constitutional rights have been violated or unacceptable conditions exist.

The philosophy of judicial restraint holds that the court should avoid taking the initiative on social and political questions, operating strictly within the limits of the Constitution and upholding acts of Congress unless the acts clearly violate specific provisions of the Constitution. Judicial restraint involves only a limited use of judicial powers and advocates the belief that the Court should be relatively passive, allowing the executive and legislative branches to lead the way in policymaking.

Day 154

Civil liberties are those rights that belong to everyone; they are protections against government and are guaranteed by the Constitution, legislation, and judicial decisions.

Civil rights are the positive acts of government designed to prevent discrimination and provide equality before the law.

Day 155

A writ of habeas corpus is a court order requiring that someone in custody be brought before the court and informed of the charges against them. Not only is this right protected by the U.S. Constitution (Article I, Sections 8 and 9), but many states also provide for this protection in their state constitutions.

A bill of attainder is a legislative act that attempts to punish an individual or a group without the benefit of a trial. This would deny an accused person the benefit of trial by jury. Both the national government and the state governments are prohibited from issuing a bill of attainder (Article I, Sections 8 and 9).

An ex post facto law makes illegal an act that was legal when it was committed. Ex post facto laws would make conduct that was not criminal when it was performed now a criminal act. These laws have also been used to change the rules of evidence to make conviction easier. Both the national government and the state governments are prohibited from issuing an ex post facto law (Article I, Sections 8 and 9).

Day 156

The due process clause of the Fourteenth Amendment forbids government (states) from taking life, liberty, or property without due process, which includes both procedural due process (notice and the right to be heard) and substantive due process (fair and reasonable laws). Due process is also guaranteed by the Fifth Amendment.

The equal protection clause provides that government (states) must apply the law equally and cannot give preference to one person or class of people over another. This prohibits the government from discriminating. Equal protection is used to protect certain classes of people (based on race, natural origin, gender, age, and so on) from discrimination by government.

The citizenship clause provides that any person born or naturalized in the United States, and subject to its jurisdictions, is a citizen of the United States and the state in which he or she lives. This clause defines who is considered a citizen of the United States.

Day 157

Selective incorporation is a judicial doctrine whereby most, but not all, of the protections found in the Bill of Rights are made applicable to the states via the due process clause of the Fourteenth Amendment. At the present time, the Third and Seventh Amendments and the grand jury requirement of the Fifth Amendment have not been applied specifically to the states.

Because the Bill of Rights was designed to restrict federal powers, it originally only applied to the federal government. In *Barron v. Baltimore* (1833), the Supreme Court ruled that the Bill of Rights applied only to the federal government and not to state governments.

That meant that states could—and did—pass laws that violated protections such as freedom of speech and freedom of the press. States could establish religions, arrest and interrogate criminal suspects, and conduct trials in whatever manner they chose. Federal courts had no authority to intervene.

The Fourteenth Amendment, ratified in 1868, prohibits states from denying anyone life, liberty, or property without due process of law. This protects the rights of citizens by guaranteeing that neither the national nor the state governments can infringe on basic rights.

Day 158

Congress cannot establish any religion as the national religion, favor one religion over another, or tax American citizens to support any one religion. This means that Americans do not have an official, government-recognized, national religion. This clause is often referred to as creating a "wall of separation between church and state," as Thomas Jefferson described it.

The free exercise clause guarantees the right to practice any religion or no religion at all. In its interpretations of the free exercise clause, the Supreme Court has made distinctions between belief and practice. The Court has ruled that while religious belief is absolute, the practice of those beliefs may be restricted, especially if those practices conflict with criminal laws. Free exercise is not absolute. Religious freedom to practice cannot be used to justify illegal behaviors.

Day 159

D	*Engel v. Vitale* (1962)
E	*Lemon v. Kurtzman* (1971)
A	*Reynolds v. the United States* (1879)
B	*Wisconsin v. Yoder* (1972)
C	*Employment Division of Oregon v. Smith* (1990)

Day 160

In *Lemon v. Kurtzman*, the Supreme Court established a standard by which to measure the constitutionality of state laws in regard to freedom of religion. This three-part standard is referred to as the Lemon Test. Legislation must pass all three parts to be constitutional.

To pass the Lemon Test a state must prove the following:

1. The law must have a primarily secular (not religious) purpose

2. The law's principal effect must neither aid nor inhibit religion

3. The law must not create excessive entanglement between government and religion

Day 161

Pure speech is the most common form of speech. It includes verbal speech and is given the most protection by the courts.

Speech plus includes the combined use of verbal and symbolic speech, such as a rally and then picketing. Speech plus may be limited.

Symbolic speech involves using actions and symbols to convey an idea rather than words (such as burning a draft card or flag, wearing an armband in protest). Symbolic speech may be subject to government restrictions if it endangers public safety.

Day 162

B	*Engel v. Vitale* (1962)
A	*Tinker v. Des Moines* (1969)
C	*Wisconsin v. Yoder* (1972)
D	*Schenck v. United States* (1919)
E	*New York Times v. United States* (1971)

Day 163

Eminent domain allows government to take property for public use but also requires that government provide just compensation for that property, a requirement provided for in the Fifth Amendment to the Constitution. The government takes private property through condemnation proceedings. Throughout these proceedings, the property owner has the right of due process.

Day 164

The Supreme Court first recognized that certain amendments of the Bill of Rights create a "zone of privacy" in *Griswold v. Connecticut*, a 1965 ruling that upheld marital privacy and struck down bans on contraception. The Court ruled that the First, Third, Fourth, Ninth, and Fourteenth Amendments created "zones of privacy" and enhanced the concept of enumerated rights.

Roe v. Wade firmly established the right to privacy as fundamental and required that any governmental infringement of that right be justified by a compelling state interest. The outcome was a continuation of the recognition of a constitutional right of privacy and involved the right of a woman to determine whether or not to terminate a pregnancy.

Several amendments to the U.S. Constitution have been used in varying degrees of success in determining a right to privacy of one's person:

- The First Amendment protects the privacy of beliefs.
- The Third Amendment protects the privacy of the home against the use of it for housing soldiers.
- The Fourth Amendment protects against unreasonable searches.
- The Fifth Amendment protects against self-incrimination, which in turn protects the privacy of personal information.
- The Ninth Amendment says that the "enumeration in the Constitution of certain rights shall not be construed to deny or disparage other rights retained by the people." This has been interpreted as justification for broadly reading the Bill of Rights to protect privacy in ways not specifically provided for in the first eight amendments.

Day 165

The Fourth Amendment provides the following:

- Protections against unreasonable searches and seizures

- A requirement for a warrant to make an arrest or a search

- A requirement for probable cause, supported by witnesses, to obtain a warrant

The amendment states, "The right of the people to be secure in their persons, houses, papers, and effects, against unreasonable searches and seizures, shall not be violated, and no Warrants shall issue, but upon probable cause, supported by Oath or affirmation, and particularly describing the place to be searched, and the persons or things to be seized."

Day 166

The exclusionary rule provides that evidence obtained illegally under the protections of the Fourth Amendment cannot be used at trial. If the evidence was obtained through an unreasonable search and seizure, the use of that evidence is prohibited.

The inevitable discovery rule provides that evidence obtained by illegal means may be admissible in certain cases. If the prosecution proves that evidence would have been obtained legally at some point, then the evidence obtained by illegal means becomes admissible. This is an exception to the exclusionary rule.

The good faith exception doctrine is an exception to the exclusionary rule and provides that illegally gathered evidence can be admitted at trial if police officers have reason to believe their actions are legal.

Day 167

B	*Gideon v. Wainwright* (1963)
C	*Roe v. Wade* (1971)
A	*Miranda v. Arizona* (1966)

Day 168

In *Plessy v. Ferguson*, the Supreme Court upheld Jim Crow laws by allowing separate facilities for the different races if those facilities were equal. This created the separate but equal doctrine: that separate facilities for blacks and whites satisfied the Fourteenth Amendment so long as they were equal.

In *Brown v. Board of Education*, the Supreme Court overturned the *Plessy* decision, ruling that separate but equal is unconstitutional. The Court ruled unanimously that "separate but equal" public schools for blacks and whites were unconstitutional. This case served as a stimulus for the modern civil rights movement.

In *Brown v. Board of Education II* (1955), the Supreme Court ordered the desegregation of schools "with all deliberate speed."

Day 169

The Twenty-fourth Amendment (1964) outlawed poll taxes in federal elections. This allowed more people to vote, increasing the electorate.

The Voting Rights Act of 1965 allowed federal registrars to register voters and outlawed literacy and other discriminatory tests in voter registration. This allowed more people to register to vote, increasing the electorate.

Day 170

Affirmative action is a policy designed to correct the effects of past discrimination. Most issues of affirmative action are race- or gender-based.

In 1978, the Supreme Court ruled in *Regents of the University of California v. Bakke* that the affirmative action quotas used by the University of California in its admissions policies were unconstitutional, and that Allan Bakke had been denied equal protection because the university used race as the sole criterion for admissions. The Court ruled that affirmative action programs may be constitutional if race is considered as one of many admission factors and used to remedy past findings of discrimination and to promote diversity.

Day 171

Public policy is composed of the choices that government makes in response to a political issue. It is how government deals with some problem or matter of concern (what government does).

The political agenda is the set of issues that are the subject of decision making and debate within a given political system at any one time. These are the issues that merit action, as determined by the public or those in power.

Day 172

- __1__ Agenda setting
- __3__ Policy adoption
- __5__ Policy evaluation
- __2__ Policy formulation
- __4__ Policy implementation

Day 173

- __A__ Agenda setting
- __B__ Policy formulation
- __C__ Policy adoption
- __D__ Policy implementation
- __E__ Policy evaluation

Day 174

The Civil Rights Act of 1964 prohibited discrimination in employment and in places of public accommodation, outlawed bias in federally funded programs, and created the Equal Employment Opportunity Commission (EEOC).

The Americans with Disabilities Act forbid employers and owners of public accommodations from discriminating against people with disabilities (making all facilities wheelchair-accessible, and so on). The Act created the telecommunications relay service, which allows hearing- and speech-impaired people access to telephone communications.

As a result of the Great Depression, the Social Security Act was passed to provide for a permanent old-age pension system. This system was later extended to include dependents, the disabled, and other groups.

Day 175

Fiscal policy is the process by which a government adjusts its spending levels (expenditures) and tax (revenue) rates to influence a nation's economy. Fiscal policy involves the changes government makes in expenditures and/or taxes to achieve economic goals of full employment, price stability, and economic growth.

Discretionary spending consists of government expenditures that are set on a yearly basis. This is the money that members of Congress can adjust or change, depending on the government's priorities at that time. Health care and defense spending are examples.

Nondiscretionary spending, or mandatory spending, is spending that is automatically obligated due to previously enacted legislation. Social Security and interest on the national debt are examples.

Day 176

The federal budget is an itemized plan for the annual public expenditures of the United States. It is the government's estimate of spending and revenue for each fiscal year. The revenue for most governments comes from taxes.

Day 177

Each federal agency submits a detailed estimate of its needs for the coming fiscal year to the Office of Management and Budget (OMB). The OMB holds meetings at which representatives from the various agencies may explain their proposal and try to convince the OMB that their needs are justified. The OMB works with the president's staff to combine all requests into a single budget package, which the president submits to Congress in January or February.

Congress sends appropriations bills to the president for approval. If no budget is approved, Congress must pass temporary emergency funding, or the government will shut down.

Day 178

The president submits a budget proposal to Congress. Congress debates and often modifies the president's proposal. The Congressional Budget Office (CBO) provides Congress with economic data.

Congressional committees hold hearings, analyze the budget proposals, and by September, offer budget resolutions to their respective houses (which must be passed by September 15). The Appropriations Committee for each house submits bills to authorize spending.

Day 179

The president is often considered the leader in the development of foreign policy. Presidential authority for foreign policy originates from the constitutional powers, historical precedent, and institutional advantages of the executive.

Article II gives the president the authority as commander-in-chief of the armed forces. The president, with the consent of the Senate, has the power to appoint ambassadors, ministers, consuls, and cabinet leaders of agencies related to foreign policy (including secretary of state and secretary of defense). The president negotiates treaties and executive agreements and can issue foreign policy statements that can set the tone for foreign policy. The president receives ambassadors for foreign countries.

Day 180

Article I gives Congress the authority to declare war and raise and support an army and navy (armed forces). Congress may pass legislation relating to foreign policy.

The Senate confirms presidential appointments to foreign policy positions (Department of State, Department of Defense, ambassadors, and so on) and may ratify or reject treaties.

Congress may affect the development and implementation of foreign policy through the power of the purse. It appropriates funding and controls the budgets of agencies and departments related to foreign policy issues.

Congress plays a role in America's foreign policy through its power to set and regulate foreign commerce and immigration. It sets quotas on immigration, chooses which countries will benefit for most-favored-nation status in trade agreements, and votes on foreign aid.

Appendixes

Websites Related to the Advanced Placement Exam
Glossary of Terms

WEBSITES RELATED TO THE ADVANCED PLACEMENT EXAM

There are thousands of sites on the web that may be related in some way to the study of government and politics. This is not a comprehensive list of all of these websites. It is a list that is most relevant to your preparation and review for the AP U.S. Government and Politics exam. It is up to you to log on to a site of interest to you and see for yourself what it offers and whether it will benefit you.

Since you are preparing for an Advanced Placement exam, go to the source as your first choice.

The College Board—http://www.collegeboard.com/ap/students/index.html

Here you will find:

- Welcome page with student and parent information about AP
- FAQs about AP, with frequently asked questions and answers
- Benefits of AP for students, parents, and schools
- Exam information, including a calendar of exams, fees, and exam day details
- AP prep, with College Board resources, study skills, and test-taking tips
- Subjects page, where you can view sample multiple-choice questions for each AP subject, sample free-response questions (with rubrics and student samples) for the past three years, the course description, and links to related sites

Other Government and Politics sites:

- The White House—http://www.whitehouse.gov
- The House of Representatives—http://www.house.gov
- The Senate—http://www.senate.gov
- The U.S. Supreme Court—http://www.supremecourtus.gov
- Oyez Project—http://www.oyez.org

Each of these websites will lead you to many others. There are just too many to list here; in fact, there are hundreds of thousands of sites listed on the web.

I suggest you use your favorite search engine (I like http://www.google.com) and type in ADVANCED PLACEMENT GOVERNMENT AND POLITICS. From that point you can surf the Internet for sites that suit your particular needs or interests. You will have to take the time to explore the sites and evaluate their usefulness. Some AP teachers have created great sites with links to other sites that you may find of value.

GLOSSARY OF TERMS

Affirmative action—A policy designed to correct the effects of past discrimination; requirement by law that positive steps be taken to increase the number of minorities in businesses, schools, colleges, and labor.

Agenda setting—The process of forming the list of matters that policymakers intend to address.

Amendment—A revision or change to a bill, law, or constitution.

Amicus curiae **brief**—Friend of the court; interested groups may be invited to file legal briefs supporting or rejecting arguments of the case.

Anti-Federalists—Opposed the adoption of the U.S. Constitution because it gave too much power to the national government at the expense of the state governments and lacked a bill of rights.

Appellate jurisdiction—Gives the court authority to hear cases on appeal from the lower courts.

Apportionment—Distribution of representatives among the states based on the population of each state.

Appropriations—Money granted by Congress or a state legislature for a specific purpose.

Article III—Establishes the Supreme Court and gives Congress the power to establish the lower (inferior) courts, provides that judicial compensation cannot be lowered during tenure, provides jurisdiction of the courts, and addresses treason and its punishment.

Articles of Confederation—The first national constitution of the United States, which created a government lasting from 1781 to 1789; replaced by the current Constitution.

At-large—All the voters of a state or county elect their representative.

Baker v. Carr **(1961)**—The Supreme Court ruled that reapportionment challenges are not political questions if brought under the Equal Protection Clause of the Fourteenth Amendment.

Benchmark—Initial poll on a candidate and issues on which campaign strategy is based and against which later polls are compared.

Bicameral—A legislature divided into two chambers; Congress has the Senate and the House of Representatives.

Bill of Rights—The first 10 amendments to the Constitution, guaranteeing certain rights and liberties to the people.

Bill—A law proposed by the legislature.

Bills of attainder—Finding a person guilty of a crime without a trial; prohibited under the Constitution.

Bipartisan Campaign Reform Act (BCRA)—banned the use of soft money in federal campaigns, placed limits on issue advertising, and increased the 1974 limits on individual and group contributions to candidates; also called McCain-Feingold.

Blanket primary—Voters may vote for candidates of either party.

Block grant—Money given to states for general programs within a broad category.

Brief orders—The returning of a case to a lower court because a similar case was recently decided.

Brief—Legal document submitted to the court setting forth the facts of a case and supporting a position.

Brown v. Board of Education **(1954)**—Supreme Court decision that overturned *Plessy v. Ferguson*, ended legal segregation, stating that school segregation is unconstitutional.

Brutus No. 1—Written by Anti-Federalist Robert Yates to convince the people of New York to not ratify the Constitution, suggesting that republics had to be small and homogeneous—not large and diverse—to be successful and arguing that a Bill of Rights was a critical part in the protection of the people's liberties.

Bureaucracy—A systematic way of organizing a complex, large, administrative structure with responsibility for carrying out the day-to-day tasks of the organization, departments, and agencies of the government.

Bureaucratic theory—The hierarchical structure and standardized procedures of government allow bureaucrats to hold the real power over public policy; proposed by Max Weber.

Cabinet—Government departments headed by presidential appointees to help establish public policy and operate a specific policy area of governmental activity.

Candidate-centered campaigns—Election campaigns and other political processes in which candidates, not political parties, have most of the initiative and influence.

Casework—Assistance given to constituents by congressional members, answering questions or doing favors.

Categorical grants—Federal grants for specific purposes defined by law.

Caucus—Locally held meeting in a state to select delegates who, in turn, will nominate candidates to political offices.

Certificate—A lower court asks the Supreme Court about a rule of law or procedure.

Checks and balances—Each branch of government is subject to restraints by the other two branches.

***Citizens United v. Federal Election Commission* (2010)**—Supreme Court ruled that limiting the ability of businesses, unions, and other groups to fund their own efforts to elect or defeat candidates for office is unconstitutional.

Civil liberties—Constitutional freedoms guaranteed to all citizens.

Civil Rights Act of 1964—Prohibited discrimination in employment and in places of public accommodation, outlawed bias in federally funded programs, and created the Equal Employment Opportunity Commission (EEOC).

Civil rights—Positive acts of government designed to prevent discrimination and provide equality before the law.

Civil Service—A system of hiring and promotion based on the merit principle and the desire to create nonpartisan government service.

Closed primary—Only registered party members may vote.

Cloture—Prevents filibustering and ends debate in the Senate by a three-fifths vote of the Senate.

Coattail effect—Weaker or lesser-known candidates from the president's party profit from the president's popularity by winning votes.

Commerce and Slave Trade Compromise—Resolved differences between northern and southern states; Congress could not tax exports nor ban the slave trade for 20 years.

Commerce Clause—Gives the national government the power to regulate trade with foreign nations, between the states (interstate commerce) and with the Indian tribes; often used by the courts to expand the powers of Congress.

Committee of the Whole—A congressional committee that includes all members of the House of Representatives, and which meets in the House Chamber for the consideration of measures under relaxed procedural rules.

Comparable worth—Women should be paid salaries equal to men for equivalent job responsibilities and skills.

Concurrent jurisdiction—The authority to hear cases is shared by federal and state courts.

Concurrent powers—Powers shared by the federal and state governments.

Concurring opinion—Justice or justices who agree with the majority's opinion but not with the reason behind the decision.

Conference committee—A temporary committee to work out a compromise version of a bill that has passed the House of Representatives and Senate in different forms.

Congressional districting—State legislatures draw congressional districts for states with more than one representative.

Conservative—A person whose political views favor more local, limited government, less government regulation, and conformity to social norms and values; tough on criminals.

Constituency service—Casework; assistance to constituents by congressional members.

Constituent—All residents of the state for senators, all residents of a district for House members.

Constitution—The document setting forth the laws and principles of the government; a plan of government.

Constitutional courts—Federal courts created by Congress under Article III of the Constitution, including the district courts, Courts of Appeals, and specialized courts such as the U.S. Court of International Trade.

Constitutional law—Laws relating to the interpretation of the Constitution.

Cooperative federalism—Cooperation among federal, state, and local governments; "marble-cake" federalism.

Courts of Appeals—Federal courts that review decisions of federal district courts, regulatory commissions, and other federal courts.

Critical election—Sharp changes in existing patterns of party loyalty due to changing social and economic conditions.

Dealigning election—Party loyalty becomes less important to voters, and they vote for the other party candidate or independents.

Dealignment—When a significant number of voters choose to no longer support a political party.

Declaration of Independence—Drafted in 1776 by Thomas Jefferson, declared America's separation from Great Britain.

Deficit—Government spending exceeds revenue.

Delegate—members of Congress who vote based on the wishes of their constituents, regardless of their own opinions.

Delegated powers—Powers specifically granted to the national government by the Constitution.

Democracy—A system whereby the people rule either directly or by elected representation.

Department of Education—Administers federal aid programs to public and private schools and engages in educational research.

Department of Homeland Security—Prevents terrorist attacks within the United States and helps recovery from attacks that do occur; includes Coast Guard, Secret Service, Border Patrol, Immigration and Visa Services, and Federal Emergency Management Agency (FEMA).

Department of Transportation—Promotes mass transit programs and programs for highways, railroads, and air traffic; enforces maritime law.

Department of Veterans' Affairs—Promotes the welfare of veterans of the armed forces and administers laws that provide benefits for former members of the armed services and their dependents.

Deviating election—Minority party is able to win the support of majority party members, independents, and new voters.

Devolution—An effort to shift responsibility of domestic programs (welfare, health care, and job training) to the states in order to decrease the size and activities of the federal government (first-order devolution); some states have attempted to shift responsibilities further to local governments (second-order devolution).

Direct democracy—Citizens meet and make decisions about public policy issues.

Direct primary—Party members vote to nominate their candidate for the general election.

Discharge petition—A method of bringing a bill out of committee and to the floor for consideration without a report from the committee; necessary when a committee chair refuses to place the bill on the committee's agenda.

Discretionary spending—Spending set by the government through appropriations bills, including operating expenses and salaries of government employees.

Discrimination—Unfair treatment of a person based on race or group membership.

Dissenting opinion—Justice or justices who disagree with the majority opinion.

District courts—Lowest level of federal courts, where federal cases begin, and trials are held.

Divided government—One party controls the executive, and the other party controls one or both houses of Congress.

Double jeopardy—Being tried twice for the same offense.

Dual federalism—Federal and state governments each have defined responsibilities within their own sphere of influence; "layer-cake" federalism.

Due Process Clause—Guarantee under the Fifth and Fourteenth Amendments that all levels of government must operate within the law and provide fair procedures of law.

Eighth Amendment—Ensures no excessive bails or fines, nor cruel and unusual punishment.

Elastic Clause—The Necessary and Proper Clause, Article I, Section 8, Clause 18, that allows Congress to pass laws to carry out its powers.

Electoral college—Representatives from each state who formally cast ballots for the president and vice president.

Electorate—People qualified to vote.

Elite theory—A small group of people, identified by wealth or political power, who rule in their self-interest.

Eminent domain—Allows the government to take property for public use but also requires the government to provide just compensation for that property.

***Engle v. Vitale* (1962)**—The Supreme Court ruled school-sanctioned prayer in public schools is unconstitutional.

Entitlement program—Payments are made to people meeting eligibility requirements, such as through Social Security.

Entrance/exit polls—Polls conducted as voters enter or leave selected polling places on election day.

Enumerated (expressed) powers—Powers given specifically to the national government; for Congress those powers are listed in Article I, Section 8, including coining money, taxing, and declaring war.

Environmental impact statement—Required studies and reports of likely environmental impacts, filed with the Environmental Protection Agency prior to the beginning of a project.

Equal Protection Clause—Constitutional guarantee that everyone be treated equally.

Equality of opportunity—All people should have the same opportunities to compete and achieve.

Establishment Clause—Prohibits the establishment of a national religion.

Ex post facto law—Laws applied to acts committed before passage of the laws are unconstitutional.

Exclusionary rule—Rule that evidence acquired as a result of an illegal act by police cannot be used against the person from whom it was seized.

Executive agreement—Agreement with another head of state not requiring approval from the Senate.

Executive orders—Orders issued by the president that carry the force of law.

Executive privilege—The right of the president to withhold information from Congress or refuse to testify; limited by the Supreme Court in *U.S. v. Nixon.*

Extradition—States may return fugitives to a state from which they have fled to avoid criminal prosecution at the request of the state's governor.

Federal budget—Amount of money the federal government expects to receive and authorizes government to spend for a fiscal (12-month period) year.

Federal Election Commission—created under the Federal Election Campaign Act of 1974 to administer and enforce campaign finance laws.

Federal system—Power is divided between the states and the federal government.

Federalism—A division of governmental powers between the national government and the states.

Federalist No. 10—Madison suggests that the union under the new constitution is a safeguard against factions, defined factions, and argued to either eliminate factions by removing their causes, or limit their impact by controlling their effects.

Federalist No. 51—Madison argues that the government under the new Constitution will not become too powerful because the separation of powers will keep each branch in check.

Federalist No. 70—Hamilton argues the need for a strong executive leader.

Federalist No. 78—Hamilton addresses the scope of power of the judicial branch—the judicial branch is created to protect the Constitution and maintain separation of powers and checks and balances; he proclaims that the judicial branch is the weakest of the three branches and that judges shall have life tenure; and he hints at the power of judicial review.

Federalist Papers—Written by Hamilton, Jay, and Madison to support ratification of the U.S. Constitution.

Federalists—Supported a strong central government and expanded legislative powers.

Fifteenth Amendment—Guarantees citizens' right to vote regardless of race, color, or previous condition of servitude.

Fifth Amendment—addresses protections against self-incrimination, guarantees of due process, eminent domain, and grand jury indictment for capital crimes.

Filibuster—A lengthy speech designed to delay the vote on a bill; used only in the Senate.

First Amendment—Guarantees freedom of religion, speech, press, assembly, and petition.

Fiscal federalism—National government's use of fiscal policy to influence states through the granting or withholding of appropriations.

Fiscal policy—The policies of taxation and spending that comprise the nation's economic policy.

Fiscal year—A 12-month period, October through September, for planning the federal budget.

Floor leaders—Direct party strategy and decisions in the House of Representatives and Senate.

Fourteenth Amendment—Guarantees rights of citizenship, due process, and equal protection.

Fourth Amendment—Protections from unlawful search and seizure.

Franking privilege—Privilege that allows members of Congress to mail letters and other materials to constituents postage-free.

Free enterprise—Private businesses operate in competition and free of government control; capitalism.

Free Exercise Clause—Congress may not make laws restricting or prohibiting a person's religious practices.

Freedom of expression—Freedom of speech or right to petition the government for redress as a First Amendment right.

Front-loading—Choosing an early date to hold the primary election.

Full Faith and Credit Clause—States are required to recognize the laws and legal documents of other states.

Gatekeepers—Media executives, news editors, and prominent reporters who decide what news to present and how it will be presented.

General election—Voters choose officeholders from among all the candidates nominated by political parties or running as independents.

Gerrymandering—Drawing of congressional districts to favor one political party or group over another.

Get-out-the-vote—A campaign near the end of an election to get voters out to the polls.

Gideon v. Wainwright (1963)—Court ruled that in state trials, those who cannot afford an attorney will have one provided by the state, overturning *Betts v. Brady*.

Government—The formal and informal institutions, people, and processes used to create and conduct public policy.

Grand Committee—A committee formed at the Constitutional Convention, composed of one member from each state, who helped create the Great Compromise to settle the dispute between the large and small states over representation in the houses of congress.

Grants-in-aid—Programs, money, and resources provided by the federal government to state and local governments to be used for specific projects and programs.

Grassroots—Average voter at the local level.

Great (Connecticut) Compromise—Settled disputes between the states over the structure of the legislative branch.

Gridlock—When opposing parties and interests block each other's proposals, creating a political stalemate or inaction between the executive and legislative branches of government.

Hatch Act—Prohibits government employees from engaging in political activities while on duty or running for office or seeking political funding while off duty; if in sensitive positions, they may not be involved with political activities on or off duty.

Hold—Informal practice by which a senator informs his or her floor leader that he or she does not wish a particular bill or other measure to reach the floor for consideration.

Hyperpluralism—Democracy seen as a system of many groups pulling government in many directions at the same time, causing gridlock and ineffectiveness.

Ideology—A consistent set of beliefs by groups or individuals.

Impeachment—Bringing charges of wrongdoing against a government official by the House of Representatives.

Implied powers—Not expressed but may be considered using the Necessary and Proper (Elastic) Clause.

Impoundment—Refusal of the president to spend money Congress has appropriated.

Incorporation—Application of portions of the Bill of Rights to the states under the Fourteenth Amendment.

Incorporation doctrine—The Supreme Court ruling that most guarantees in the Bill of Rights are applicable to the states through the Fourteenth Amendment.

Incrementalism—Small changes in policy over long periods of time; usually in reference to budget-making—that the best indicator of this year's budget is last year's budget plus a small increase.

Incumbency effect—Tendency of those already holding office to win reelection due to advantages of currently holding that office.

Incumbent—The person currently holding office.

Individualism—Individuals possess the freedom to make choices as they wish.

Inherent powers—Powers that exist for the national government because it is sovereign.

Initiative—Allows voters to petition to propose legislation and then submit it for a vote by qualified voters.

Interest group—A group of private citizens whose goal is to influence and shape public policy.

Interstate compacts—Agreements between states to work together on common issues.

Iron triangle—Alliances that develop between bureaucratic agencies, interest groups, and congressional committees or subcommittees.

Issue network—Individuals in Washington—located within interest groups, congressional staff, think tanks, universities, and the media—who regularly discuss and advocate public policies.

Joint committee—Committee made up of members of both houses of Congress.

Judicial activism—Holds that the Court should play an active role in determining national policies.

Judicial restraint—Holds that the Court should avoid taking the initiative on social and political questions, operating strictly within the limits of the Constitution.

Judicial review—Authority given the courts to review constitutionality of acts by the executive, states, or the legislature; established in *Marbury v. Madison.*

Jurisdiction—The authority of the courts to hear and decide issues in certain cases.

Legislative (congressional) caucus—An association of congressional members who advocate a political ideology, regional, ethnic, or economic interest.

Legislative courts—Courts created by Congress for a specialized purpose with a narrow range of authority.

Legislative veto—To reject the actions of the president or executive agency by a vote of one or both houses of Congress without the consent of the president; ruled unconstitutional by the Supreme Court in *Immigration and Naturalization Service v. Chadha.*

Lemon Test—Standard set by the Supreme Court in *Lemon v. Kurtzman* to measure the constitutionality of state laws regarding freedom of religion.

Letter from a Birmingham Jail—Response from Dr. Martin Luther King, Jr. to a newspaper letter criticizing civil rights demonstrations where he argues that he and his fellow demonstrators have a duty to fight for justice.

Liberal—A person whose views favor more government involvement in business, social welfare, minority rights, and increased government spending.

Limited government—Basic principle of U.S. government that each person has rights that government cannot take away.

Line item veto—The president can reject a part of a bill while approving the rest; declared unconstitutional by the Supreme Court.

Lobbying Attempting to influence policymakers through a variety of methods.

Lobbyist—Uses political persuasion to influence legislation and benefit his or her organization.

Logrolling—The exchange of political favors for support of a bill.

Loose constructionist—The belief that judges should have freedom in interpreting the Constitution.

Maintaining elections—Traditional majority power maintains power based on voters' party loyalty.

Majority leader—The elected leader of the party with the most seats in the House of Representatives or Senate.

Majority opinion—A statement that presents the views of the majority of Supreme Court justices regarding a case and the reasons for that decision.

Majority-minority district—a district in which a racial minority group or groups comprise a majority of the district's total population.

Mandates—Requirements imposed by the national government on state and local governments to comply with federal rules and regulations.

Mandatory spending—Required government spending by permanent laws.

Marbury v. Madison (1830)—Established the principle of judicial review.

Mark-up—Rewrite a bill into its final form after hearings have been held on it.

Mass media—All forms of communication that reach a large portion of the population.

McCulloch v. Maryland (1819)—Supreme Court decision upholding the supremacy of the national government over the states.

McDonald v. Chicago (2010)—The Supreme Court struck down a handgun ban at the state level, using judicial precedents under the Fourteenth Amendment's Due Process Clause, strengthening citizens' rights to keep and bear arms for self-defense in your own home.

Media event—A speech or photo opportunity staged to give a politician's view on an issue.

Merit system—A system of public employment in which selection and promotion depend on demonstrated performance rather than political patronage. Office of Personnel Management (OPM) administers civil service laws, rules, and regulations.

Miranda v. Arizona—Requires that anyone arrested for a crime be advised of the right to counsel and the right to remain silent.

Mid-term elections—Congressional elections that take place in years when no presidential election is occurring.

Moderate—Person whose views are between conservative and liberal and may include some of both ideologies.

Monetary policy—Economic policy in which the money supply is controlled through the Federal Reserve.

Motor Voter Law—Allows citizens to register to vote at welfare and motor vehicle offices.

National chairperson—Appointed by a committee as head of the party.

National debt—Amount of money owed by the government.

Natural rights—Basic rights that are guaranteed to all persons; basic rights that a government cannot deny.

Necessary and Proper Clause—Gives Congress the powers to pass all laws necessary to carry out their constitutional duties, found in Article I, Section 8, Clause 18; also called the "Elastic Clause."

New Deal coalition—Alliance of southern conservatives, religious, and ethnic minorities who supported the Democratic Party for 40 years.

New Jersey Plan—Proposal for a single-chamber congress in which each state had one vote; favored by the smaller states who preferred equal representation among the states.

New York Times Co. v. United States (1971)—The Supreme Court reaffirmed its position of prior restraint, refusing to stop the publication of the Pentagon Papers, and strengthening freedom of the press, even in times of national security.

Nineteenth Amendment—Establishes women's right to vote.

Ninth Amendment—Unenumerated rights of the people.

North American Free Trade Agreement (NAFTA)—Created to allow the free movement of goods between Canada, Mexico, and the United States by lessening and eliminating tariffs.

Off-year election—An election taking place in a year when no presidential elections are occurring; midterm election.

Open primary—Voters may choose the candidates of either party, whether they belong to the party or not.

Opinion leaders—Those individuals held in great respect because of their position, expertise, or personality, who may informally and unintentionally influence others.

Opinion poll—An assessment of public opinion by the questioning of a representative sample of the population.

Original jurisdiction—Court hears and decides a case for the first time.

Oversight—Congress monitors policies of the executive branch.

Pardon—A convicted person is exempt from the penalties of a crime.

Participatory democratic theory—Government depends upon the consent of the governed; often referred to as traditional democratic government because it emphasizes citizen participation.

Party in government—All of the appointed and elected officials at the national, state, and local levels who represent the party as members; office holders.

Party in organization—All of the people at the various levels of the party organization who work to maintain the strength of the party between elections, help raise money, and organize the conventions and party functions.

Party in the electorate—All of the people who associate themselves with one of the political parties.

Party-line voting—Voting for candidates based upon the party to which they belong, usually voting a straight ticket.

Plessy v. Ferguson—The Supreme Court case that upheld separate-but-equal segregation in 1896.

Pluralist theory—Interest groups compete in the political arena with each promoting its own policy preferences through organized efforts.

Pocket veto—The president lets ta bill die by neither signing nor vetoing it at the end of a legislative session.

Policy adoption—The approval of a policy by legislation.

Policy evaluation—Determines if a policy is achieving its goals.

Policy formulation—The crafting of a policy to resolve public problems.

Policy implementation—Carrying out a policy through government agencies and courts.

Political action committee (PAC)—Extension of an interest group that contributes money to political campaigns.

Political agenda—Issues that merit action, as determined by the public or those in power.

Political culture—A set of basic values and beliefs about one's country or government that is shared by most citizens and that influences political opinions and behaviors.

Political efficacy—Belief that a person can influence politics and public policymaking.

Political ideology—A consistent set of beliefs about politics and public policy that sets the framework for evaluating government and public policy.

Political party—Voluntary association of people who seek to control the government through common principles; based on peaceful and legal actions such as the winning of elections.

Political polarization—Increasing ideological differences between the parties which creates a distance where members of political parties vote along party lines and become less likely to cross party lines to vote with the other party, leading to gridlock.

Political socialization—Complex process by which people get their sense of political identity, beliefs, and values.

Politico—Members of Congress vote based on party loyalty.

Politics—Method of maintaining, managing, and gaining control of government.

Popular sovereignty—Basic principle of U.S. government which holds that the people are the source of all governmental power.

Pork barrel legislation—Legislation giving benefits to constituents through sometimes unnecessary or unwise projects within a state or district, to enhance a member's chance of reelection.

Precedents—Standards or guides based on prior decisions that serve as a rule for settling similar disputes.

President *pro tempore*—Serves as president of the Senate in the absence of the vice president; chosen by the majority party.

Presidential preference primaries—Voters select delegates to the presidential nominating convention.

Primary election—Nominating election held to choose party candidates who will run in the general election.

Prior restraint—Censorship of information before it is published or broadcast.

Privileges and Immunities Clause—States are prohibited from unreasonably discriminating against residents of other states.

Procedural due process—Method of government action, or how the law is carried out according to established rules and procedures.

Prospective voting—Voting based on how the voter believes the candidate will perform in office.

Public opinion—A collection of shared attitudes of citizens about government, politics, and the making of public policy.

Public policy—The exercise of government power in doing those things necessary to maintain legitimate authority and control over society.

Pure speech—Verbal communication of ideas and opinions.

Radical—Ideological view that favors rapid fundamental change in the existing social, economic, or political order.

Ratification—Method of enacting a constitution or amendment into law.

Rational-choice voting—Voting based on what voters perceive to be in their own best interest.

Reactionary—Ideological view that favors a return to a previous state of affairs.

Realigning elections—When a minority party wins by building a new coalition of voters that continues over successive elections.

Realignment—A shift of voting patterns to form new coalitions of party support.

Reapportionment—Redistribution of the congressional seats among the states after the census determines changes in population distribution.

Recall—Special election initiated by petition to allow citizens to remove an official from office before his or her term expires.

Referendum—Procedure whereby the state submits legislation to its voters for approval, allowing citizens to vote directly on issues.

Representative democracy—Citizens choose officials (representatives) who make decisions about public policy.

Republicanism—A system in which the people give authority to government and exercise their power by delegating it to representatives chosen by them through the election process.

Reserved powers—Powers belonging specifically to the states and the people because they were not delegated to the national government nor denied to the states.

Retrospective voting—Voting based on past performance of the candidate.

Revenue sharing—Giving money back to state and local governments with no strings attached.

Rider—An addition or amendment added to a bill that often has no relation to the bill but that may not pass on its own merits.

***Roe v. Wade* (1973)**—Supreme Court decision that reaffirmed the recognition of a constitutional right of privacy for a woman to determine whether to terminate a pregnancy, while recognizing that the state may have a compelling interest in maternal life and health.

Rule of four—Requirement that a case can only be heard by the Supreme Court if four justices vote to hear the case.

Rule of law—All people and institutions are subject to and accountable to law that is fairly applied and enforced.

Rules Committee—Determines the rules of debate for bills in the House of Representatives.

Runoff primary—When no candidate receives a majority of votes, an election held between the two candidates who received the most votes in the primary.

Sampling errors—Percentage of possible errors in the polling process.

Sampling—Using a representative cross-section of the general population chosen at random in the polling process.

Schenck v. United States (1919)—Supreme Court decision that speech was not protected during wartime because it would create a clear and present danger, establishing a standard for measuring what would and would not be protected speech.

Second Amendment—ensures the right to keep and bear arms.

Select committee—Committee selected for a specific purpose.

Self-incrimination—Accusing oneself or giving evidence that may prove oneself guilty.

Senatorial courtesy—The practice of allowing senators from the president's party who represent the state where a judicial district is located to approve or disapprove potential nominees for the lower federal courts.

Seniority system—System in which the chairmanship of a committee is given to the member with the longest continuous service.

Separation of powers—Practice by which power is separated among three branches of government; each branch has its own powers and duties and is independent of and equal to the other branches.

Seventeenth Amendment—established direct election of senators by popular vote.

Seventh Amendment—preserves the right to a jury trial in civil cases.

Shaw v. Reno (1993)—The Supreme Court ruled that legislative redistricting must be mindful of race and in compliance with the Voting Rights Act of 1965 and its amendments.

Shay's Rebellion—Uprising led by Daniel Shays in an effort to prevent courts from foreclosing on the farms of those who could not pay the taxes; caused many to criticize the Articles of Confederation and admit the weak central government was not working.

Signing statements—Written comments issued by a president at the time legislation is signed, making comments about the bill signed or indicating the president's attitude towards the bill and how they intend to ignore it or to implement it.

Single-member districts—Only one representative is chosen from each district.

Sixth Amendment—guarantees rights to a speedy, public trial and an impartial jury; to confront witnesses; and to have an attorney.

Social contract—A voluntary agreement between the government and the governed.

Social insurance programs—Programs to help the elderly, ill, and unemployed if the claimant has paid into them.

Social welfare program—Government program to enhance quality of life.

Soft money—Cash contributed to a political party or political action committee with no limits attached to the amount that can be received; *Citizens United v. Federal Election Commission* held that soft money constitutes a form of free speech protected by the First Amendment.

Soft money—Money distributed from a national political party organization that was not regulated by law; restricted by the Bipartisan Campaign Finance Reform Act of 2002.

Soundbite—A brief statement on TV or radio.

Speaker of the House—Leading officer in the House of Representatives, chosen by the majority party.

Speech plus—Verbal and symbolic speech used together.

Split-ticket voting—Voting for candidates from more than one party in the same election.

Standing committee—Permanent committee.

Stare decisis— Doctrine or policy of following rules or principles laid down in previous judicial decisions (precedents).

Straight-ticket voting—Voting for candidates all of the same party.

Straw poll—Early form of polling that asks the same question of a large number of people.

Strict constructionist—The view that justices should base decisions on a narrow interpretation of the Constitution.

Substantive due process—The policies of government or the subject matter of the laws determining what the law is about and whether the law is fair or if it violates constitutional protections.

Suffrage—The right to vote.

Super Tuesday—Day when most southern states hold presidential primaries.

Superdelegates—Party officials in the Democratic Party who attend the national convention without having to run in primaries or caucuses.

Supremacy Clause—National law supersedes all other laws passed by states; found in Article VI of the Constitution.

Supreme Court—The highest court in the federal government; final interpreter of the U.S. Constitution.

Symbolic speech—Using actions and symbols rather than words to convey an idea.

Tenth Amendment—Reserves powers of the states and the people.

Third Amendment—Sets conditions for quartering of troops in private homes.

Thirteenth Amendment—Abolishes slavery.

Three-Fifths Compromise—Agreement that each slave counted as three-fifths of a person in determining representation in the House of Representatives and for taxation.

Time, place, and manner restrictions—Limits that the government can impose on the occasion, location, and type of individual expression in some circumstances.

Tinker v. Des Moines Independent Community School District (1969)—Supreme Court ruled that wearing black armbands in protest of the Vietnam War was symbolic speech, protected by the First Amendment.

Title IX of the Education Amendments Act of 1972—Federal law that prohibits sex-based discrimination in any education program or activity that is federally funded.

Tracking polls—Continuous surveys that enable a campaign or news organization to chart a candidate's daily rise or fall in support.

Traditional democratic theory—Government depends upon the consent of the governed.

Trial balloon—Tests the public reaction to policy or appointments by releasing information to the media and gauging public reaction.

Trustee—After listening to constituents, elected representatives vote based on their own opinions.

Twelfth Amendment—Provides for election of president and vice president by separate ballot in electoral college.

Twentieth Amendment—Sets terms and sessions of executive and legislative branches; "lame duck."

Twenty-Fifth Amendment—Addresses presidential succession, disability, and vice-presidential vacancies.

Twenty-Fourth Amendment—Abolishes poll taxes as a requirement for voting.

Twenty-Second Amendment—Placed limits of two terms for presidential terms of office.

Twenty-Sixth Amendment—Lowered the voting age in federal elections to 18.

Twenty-Third Amendment—Allows for voting rights in District of Columbia in presidential elections.

Two-party system—Several political parties exist, but only two major political parties compete for power and dominate elections.

Unfunded mandates—Requires states to enforce legislation without the funding necessary.

United States v. Lopez—Supreme Court found that the 1990 Gun Free School Zones Act did violate the Constitution, claiming Congress was overreaching its powers granted under the Commerce Clause.

Veto—The constitutional power of the president to send a bill back to congress with reasons for rejecting it; a two-thirds vote in each house of Congress is needed to override a veto.

Virginia Plan—Madison's plan for a bicameral legislature, with the executive and judiciary chosen by the legislature.

Voting Rights Act of 1965—Allowed federal registrars to register voters and outlawed literacy tests and other discriminatory tests in voter registration.

War Powers Act—Limits the ability of the president to commit troops to combat.

War Powers Act—Passed by Congress in 1973 in reaction to American fighting in Southeast Asia; requires presidents to consult with Congress whenever possible prior to using military force and to withdraw forces after 60 days unless Congress declares war or grants extensions.

Watergate—Break-in at the Democratic National Committee headquarters at the Watergate building in 1972 that resulted in a cover-up and the subsequent resignation of President Nixon.

White House Office—Personal and political staff members who help with the day-to-day management of the executive branch; includes the chief of staff, counsel to the president, and press secretary.

Wisconsin v. Yoder (1972)—The Supreme Court ruled that Wisconsin could not require Amish parents to send their children to public school beyond the eighth grade because it would violate long-held religious beliefs.

Writ of certiorari—Order by the court directing a lower court to send up the records of a case for review.

Writ of habeas corpus—Requires a judge to evaluate whether there is sufficient cause to keep a person in jail.

NOTES